Contents

THE CHINESE OTHER
1850-1925

An Anthology of Plays

Dave Williams

Copyright © 1997 by
University Press of America,® Inc.
4720 Boston Way
Lanham, Maryland 20706

12 Hid's Copse Rd.
Cummor Hill, Oxford OX2 9JJ

Library of Congress Cataloging-in-Publication Data

The Chinese other, 1850-1925 : an anthology of plays / (edited by)
Dave Williams.
p.   cm.
Contents: Ah Sin / Bret Harte and Mark Twain--The Chinese must go /
Henry Grimm--A Bunch of buttercups / Emma E. Brewster--Patsy
O'Wang / T. S. Denison--The first born / Frank Powers--The queen of
Chinatown / Joseph Jarrow--K'ung Fu Tze / Paul Carus--The
Honorable Mrs. Ling's conversation / Jean H. Brown--The wedded
husband / Shen Hung--Chinese love / Clare Kummer.
1. Chinese Americans--Drama. 2. American drama--19th century. 3.
American drama--20th century. I. Williams, Dave.
PS627.C54C47   1997 812'.408035203951073--dc21   97-6725 CIP

ISBN 0-7618-0756-X (cloth: alk. ppr.)
ISBN 0-7618-0757-8 (pbk: alk. ppr.)

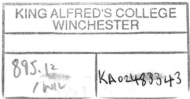
⊖™ The paper used in this publication meets the minimum
requirements of American National Standard for information
Sciences—Permanence of Paper for Printed Library Materials,
ANSI Z39.48—1984

Preface

Since the voyages of Columbus, the history of the New World and of the United States in particular has been in large measure the history of encounters -- or collisions -- between different racial groups. To begin with, Europeans and Native Americans vied for control of the land and its resources. Shortly thereafter, Europeans imported slaves from Africa, which created another complex and significant interracial relationship. Until the mid-1800s, however, the descendants of these Europeans, who now could justifiably be termed "Euroamericans," lacked any compelling reason to deal with the inhabitants of Asia, including China. Because the vast majority of Euroamericans remained physically and psychologically isolated from China and the Chinese, some vague, inherited preconceptions comprised the entire stock of Euroamerican imagery of the land and its people. Euroamerican society, its dramatists included, ignored China and the Chinese as a matter of course.

This situation changed, historically speaking, overnight. Beginning in 1850, thousands of Chinese came to California in search of quick wealth. Euroamericans suddenly found themselves in the actual physical presence of people who differed from them in almost every particular. More and more Chinese came; later, more and more of these arrivals decided to settle permanently on the West Coast rather than return to China. Euroamericans responded with strong emotion, and in some cases, with violence. The Euroamerican response, predominantly negative after a brief period of amiable curiosity, culminated in the 1882 Federal law drastically limiting Chinese immigration. They thus became the first people to be barred from America on the basis of race alone. A small but significant minority of Euroamericans did praise the Chinese and attempted to uphold their rights, but anti-Chinese hysteria carried the day. For the remainder of the nineteenth century and a good portion of the twentieth, the Chinese remained concentrated, semi-voluntarily, in urban "Chinatowns." Although in Euroamerica, the Chinese were not of it. In fundamental outline, this situation remained unchanged until the social upheavals of the 1970s.

One function of the stage is to serve as a site for any society to examine its significant issues and questions; this was even more true before film and television became the cutting-edge media they are today. As the Chinese moved in the Euroamerican perception from distant outlanders to resented laborers, and then to encysted exotics, it is therefore not surprising that Euroamerican playwrights reflected this evolution in their works. These plays therefore include some overt anti-Chinese racism, but that is far from the only attitude; in fact, there is an unexpected variety and complexity in dramatic portrayals of the Chinese by Euroamericans. Limitations of space prevent a complete presentation of every surviving early American play containing a Chinese character, but the present collection has aimed to showcase the greatest possible variety.

Although the plays collected in this volume are not of the highest literary quality and are almost totally unworthy to be staged today, the same could be said of nearly all American drama from colonial times to the early twentieth century. They do, however, have enormous interest as sociological and historical documents. Clearly and directly, they demonstrate the variety of Euroamerican reactions to people whose culture, language, and religion seemed bizarre and incomprehensible, and whose very humanity was consequently suspect. Moreover, the plays touch upon matters which remain pressing concerns today, and will likely never disappear completely. Although the specific matter addressed by these plays, the so-called "Chinese question," has vanished, the problem posed by the Other -- or, more properly, the problem members of one culture have in fitting the Other into their own conceptions of humanity -- remains. Finally, the plays as a whole are far from dreary, and there are moments of entertainment which will lighten the reading of even the most diligent scholar. I hope the reader finds this collection valuable, and enjoys it as much as I have enjoyed assembling and presenting it.

Dave Williams
Taichung, Taiwan ROC

Acknowledgements

The word "anthology" comes from Greek roots meaning "a gathering of flowers." Such words suggest blithe enjoyment, perhaps an activity undertaken merely to make a journey more enjoyable. In the case of this book, the image is completely apt; I originally collected these scripts with no intention whatsoever of publishing a collection, but rather as primary source material for my dissertation. After that project was finished, however, presenting the scripts as an anthology seemed to be the next logical step. I am now pleased to thank those people who have helped in making this collection a reality:

J. Ellen Gainor, who, in an offhand comment which she may not even remember, first gave me the idea for the project;

The Interlibrary Loan staff of Olin Library at Cornell University, who have done yeoman service in ably, cheerfully, and promptly furnishing me with some (well, *many*) rather obscure texts;

The Bancroft Library at the University of California at Berkeley, which not only provided many unique source and background materials, but also a wonderful research environment;

The various people, noted in some introductions to the individual plays, who have granted permission for publication;

My editors at University Press of America, Michelle R. Harris and Helen Hudson, who have guided a neophyte compiler through many difficulties; and

My parents, L. Pearce and Sylvia Williams, whose belief in me and my work has never wavered.

Finally, I especially appreciate and thank my wife, Xiaoxia Williams. Throughout the difficult times, she has cheerfully, freely, and lovingly provided every manner of emotional and logistical support. My public thanks are wholly inadequate to repay my debt to her.

If I have omitted some blooms which should have been included, included some which should have been omitted, or damaged any in any way, I naturally accept full and sole responsibility.

Introduction

It is a truism but still a truth that one can gain a deeper appreciation of the drama from any historical period by understanding the period itself. The American drama of the late nineteenth and early twentieth centuries is no exception. In the case of the plays presented here, a certain amount of historical and cultural background is of paramount importance, as the plays concerned with the Chinese were emphatically not art for art's sake. Rather, they were intertwined with a host of economic, social, and psychological issues.

From colonial times through the 1840s, China and the Chinese remained almost entirely at the periphery of Euroamerican consciousness. During this time, there was a small contingent of American traders and missionaries at Canton (modern Guangzhou); in addition, a very few Chinese had come to the US as students, servants, or marooned seamen. These direct contacts, however, took place at the margins of both cultures, and left the mass of Euroamericans untouched. The thriving trade with China, however, brought lacquerware, silk, tea, porcelain, and an indirect image of China into the homes of many ordinary Euroamericans. They had also inherited some hazy concepts of the land and its people from the tales of Marco Polo and Sir John Mandeville, the reports of Jesuit envoys, and the hopeful fantasies of Enlightenment philosophers. Present still further in the background lay the perpetual European wariness of invading hordes from the East. As America freed itself from colonial status and began to expand and develop, however, it had far more pressing concerns than China and the Chinese. When the land and its people occurred to Euroamericans at all, the predominant attitude was a mild and innocent curiosity.

It is no surprise, therefore, that the early years of America's existence saw the Chinese practically unrepresented onstage at all. They appear in only one legitimate play and perhaps five isolated burlesques: if scripts for the burlesques ever existed at all, they have completely vanished. *The Orphan of China*, which has survived, had its American debut in Philadelphia in 1767, and was revived occasionally until the turn of the century. The original text is an actual 14th-century Chinese work, which passed through many French and

English versions. The script performed in the colonies was written by the English playwright Arthur Murphy, and owes its images of China and the Chinese more to the prevailing dramatic style of heroic tragedy than to anything else. Although an interesting text in its own right, its British origin bars it from inclusion here.

During the first four decades of the nineteenth century, the relationship between China and America remained static. Euroamerican drama reflected this situation, and China and the Chinese simply had no images in Euroamerican drama at all. With the outbreak of the First Opium War in 1839, however, the situation changed forever. Because the fighting began at roughly the same time the mass print media began to develop, it attracted a great deal of publicity. Eager to attract readers, the new periodicals sent back regular reports of the conflict from the field. Because of their greater racial and cultural affinity with the British, Euroamericans overwhelmingly supported England, despite the morally superior position of the Chinese. Playwrights capitalized on popular anti-Chinese sentiment by creating several Opium War plays, some of which dramatized actual incidents from the battlefield. For example, *Yankees in China* (1842) depicts the Chinese as mere bodies to be hurled from the battlements of conquered Canton by triumphant Westerners. Unfortunately, not a single Opium War playscript has survived. From secondary accounts, it seems clear that while their literary quality was not particularly high, they featured spectacular stage effects which would have appealed to their predominantly working-class audience. The unavailability of even a single specimen of this type of play is regrettable.

The next important event in the Sino-Euroamerican encounter was the discovery of gold in California in 1848. This caused a geographically-based division among Euroamericans in their attitudes toward the Chinese. Residents of the East Coast still had no direct contact with them, and therefore continued to picture them as mere exotics. The first text presented in this volume is a scenario from a pantomime entitled *Kim-ka!*, which shows China and the Chinese as material for a fairytale. As the nineteenth century proceeded, this image eventually faded and lay dormant for decades. It did reappear, somewhat transformed, in the early years of the twentieth century. *Kim-ka!* therefore has more in common with the plays at the end of this collection than with those in the middle.

Meanwhile, Euroamericans traveling west to California in search of gold encountered many Chinese who had sailed east for the same reason. For the first time, large masses of ordinary Euroamericans and Chinese met face to face in the same territory. By the mere fact of their existence, the Chinese presented a large and complex psychological problem to Euroamericans. The two populations differed in physical appearance, language, culture, religion, dietary habits, and in almost every other imaginable particular. The Euroamerican adventurers found themselves completely unprepared for strangers who were so totally strange. The rough-hewn, active, hard-drinking types who ventured to the goldfields could not have been expected to be models of racial tolerance, and indeed, they proved not to be so. Even so, the initial predominant attitude Euroamericans displayed toward the Chinese was friendly curiosity, often mixed with mild patronization. As time elapsed, however, toleration receded and hostility grew. Many Euroamericans felt that California's bounty, though considerable, was limited; they resented the success of the often more skilled and better organized Chinese miners. Confident in their perceived and self-proclaimed racial superiority, they began to oppress the Chinese legislatively and to assault them physically. Outnumbered and for cultural reasons not as aggressive as the Euroamericans, the Chinese tended not to resist. Instead, they withdrew into the security of urban Chinatowns or small villages. Euroamerican hostility manifested itself in assaults committed against individual Chinese, mass expulsions from rural mining areas, a discriminatory tax, and even the legal deprivation of the right of the Chinese to testify in court.

Even with this great change in the logistics of the encounter, Euroamerican playwrights took a long time to present versions of the Chinese onstage. This perhaps reflected a natural human tendency to ignore matters which may prove upsetting, in the hopes that they will ultimately disappear by themselves. In addition, Euroamericans had more pressing concerns, i.e., the events leading up to the Civil War, the conflict itself, and its aftermath. For these reasons, China and the Chinese continued to exist only as significant absences in Euroamerican drama not only through the 1850s, but even into the 1870s.

By this time, however,"the Chinese question" could not longer be ignored. A number of economic and social factors, for which the Chinese themselves bore no responsibility, generated a widespread anti-Chinese animus in the Pacific Coast states, which eventually influenced Federal policy. Overt anti-Chinese racists, no longer content with merely wrecking individual laundries or even destroying whole Chinatowns, sought legislative action against the Chinese collectively at the highest level of government. After several false starts, this animus eventually resulted in the Chinese Exclusion Act of 1882, the first immigration law in the nation's history to restrict entry on the basis of race. Repeatedly adjusted and reenacted, this morally reprehensible legislation eventually did achieve its desired effect of limiting the Chinese population in America.

Simultaneously reflecting and fueling these sentiments, dramatists began to incorporate Chinese characters into their works, especially into the popular melodramas designed to give the audience in the East a taste of life on the wild frontier. Instead of ignoring the Chinese as before, playwrights now created Chinese characters who were effeminate, clumsy, and powerless. Plays such as Bret Harte's *Two Men of Sandy Bar* and Bartley Campbell's *My Partner* toured all over the country, presenting this prejudicial image of the Chinese to Euroamericans who would probably never encounter a Chinese person in real life. Despite their popularity, no Western-frontier melodrama has been included here, because they deal mainly with the adventures of the Euroamerican characters. The Chinese are relegated to the margins of the plot, where they provide comic relief by their mangled English, outlandish queue and baggy clothing, mental confusion, and physical clumsiness.

Other playwrights of the 1870s and 1880s, who did not write frontier melodramas, created Chinese characters and placed them in more domestic settings. George M. Baker's *New Brooms Sweep Clean* does not contain an actual Chinese character, but rather an Irishman who disguises himself as one. The humor involved in this undertaking is hardly innocent, however, and the play rests on the assumption that its audience will concur with its message of Euroamerican racial superiority. M.T. Caldor's *Curiosity* takes place in a similar domestic setting, and it also depicts the Chinese as fundamentally inferior. Written in a less realistic style, Ambrose Bierce's short closet drama *Peaceful Expulsion* distributes its author's characteristic misanthropy toward not only the Chinese, but to all parties involved in discussing the issue. Nor was Bierce the only major author to discuss the Chinese. America's two leading writers of the period, Mark Twain and Bret Harte, collaborated on *Ah Sin*, which they hoped would succeed as a Western melodrama. Unfortunately, this piece not only failed commercially and critically, but it also caused a permanent rupture between the two men. The text, however, extends the limits of the frontier melodrama, as it gives its Chinese character more power and influence than any other play of its type.

Another representative play from this era is Henry Grimm's *The Chinese Must Go*. This piece derives its title from the tag-line of the former drayman and anti-Chinese demagogue Denis Kearney, and it displays racist invective at its most blatant and vehement. Gentler in tone but similar in sentiment, Emma M. Brewster's *A Bunch of Buttercups* creates an explicit racial hierarchy, with Euroamericans at the top and the Chinese near the bottom. Finally, T.S. Denison's *Patsy O'Wang* portrays the Chinese character as an amiable scamp, disruptive but not evil.

By the turn of the century, the hysterical opponents of the Chinese had won the day, and successfully cut off all but a trickle of Chinese immigrants. Most of the Chinese in the United States were men; as they aged without offspring, the Chinese population nationwide began to dwindle. Chinese found themselves isolated and confined, more or less involuntarily, to many urban slums across the country. These Chinatowns, especially those in New York and San Francisco, became tourist attractions, and the Chinese themselves slipped to a position of low visibility for many Euroamericans.

Events in drama reflected this change. No longer perceived as an economic threat, the Chinese now appeared onstage as quaint and hyper-refined. The Euroamerican audience could now afford to consider a much more positive portrayal of the Chinese, first supplied by a prescient playwright named Frank Powers. In *The First Born*, he acknowledged the real differences between Chinese and Euroamericans. He did not automatically regard the Chinese as inferior; if his play falls short of modern standards of racial equality, it was a clear advance over previous scripts. Even the 1900 Boxer Rebellion, which placed China at the center of world attention during and after the summer of that year, failed to shake this new image significantly. Several plays dealing with this event, which almost certainly portrayed the Chinese unfavorably, were produced; none had any commercial or critical success, however, and none was published.

Even in this new era, however, racism was far from dead. One surviving play, Joseph Jarrow's *The Queen of Chinatown*, set in New York City, does still demonstrate fear and hatred of the Chinese. It differs greatly from *The Chinese Must Go*, however, because the basis for its animus is socio-cultural, and not economic. Moreover, although he disliked the Chinese, Jarrow realized that they were an integral part of American society. He urged Euroamericans to avoid them, rather than expel them. Generally speaking, although anti-Chinese racism certainly still existed, it had largely lost its urgency, and playwrights could no longer rely on it to create commercially successful works. As the effects of exclusionary legislation took hold, the perceived menace of the Chinese began to fade in Euroamerican eyes; the dominant culture shifted its concern to the Japanese and immigrants from southern Europe. This newer, more favorable image of the Chinese continued through the early years of the twentieth century, and underlay the successful plays produced during that time.

Chief among these was a collaboration by J. Harry Benrimo and George C. Hazelton, *The Yellow Jacket*. This play scored a great success at its 1912 premiere, and was repeatedly revived throughout the 1920s. Its image of the Chinese remains stereotypical, but the content of the stereotype differs completely from that of its predecessors. Instead of being lower-class laborers or quaint buffoons, the Chinese in this piece are noble, self-sacrificing, and refined if good, and intelligent, cruel, and refined if evil.

In another development which would have been inconceivable two decades previously, the noted religious thinker and philosopher Paul Carus published a "dramatic poem" on the life of Confucius. Although its verse is somewhat stilted and its dramatic action static, *K'ung Fu Tze* presents the Chinese quite positively. Carus' piece was aimed at Westerners who found their own culture, philosophy, and religion unsatisfying, and urged them to consider Chinese alternatives. The Chinese themselves as the objects of missionary efforts appear in Jean H. Brown's *The Honorable Mrs. Ling's Conversion*. This unique text almost certainly reflects the personal experiences and hopes of its otherwise-obscure author.

Dating from the early 1920s, Shen Hung's *The Wedded Husband*, is somewhat of a landmark. It was the first of three plays written by American dramatists of Chinese descent which appeared in the literary quarterly *Poet Lore*. After seventy years of being a significant but silent presence in American life, the Chinese at that time began to write and publish their own English-language drama. The text is most significant, however, for its wholesale adoption of the Euroamerican culture's image of the Chinese, rather than any resistance to it. The concluding play in the collection, the commercially successful playwright Clare Kummer's *Chinese Love*, further romanticized the Chinese. Her work is one of two plays from the era to share that title, which indicates a reversion to a previous attitude.

In the mid-1920s, a radical development in technology took place which affected the entire position of drama in American culture. The rise of film in popularity and influence forever changed the ways in which images of all sorts arose, spread, and influenced popular thought. Amidst the general change, the stage lost its status as the primary site for the depiction of the Chinese. Because of this new relationship, this collection does not include stage plays featuring Fu Manchu and Charlie Chan. Both these characters did appear onstage, but their characters and the plays in which they appeared were back-formations from film.

All the plays selected for this volume all represent important steps in the evolution of the image of the Chinese within Euroamerican drama. In the interest of improved relations in the future, both Chinese and Euroamericans need to understand the content of these images, how they arose, what they signified to the playwrights who created them, and their function for the audience who viewed them. Having them all in one book should make research of this type easier for the scholar, as well as providing pleasure for the general reader.

1852 -- The Ravel Family -- *Kim-Ka!*

The Ravels were a performing troupe from France who settled in New York City sometime in the 1840s. Although the works they performed were called "pantomimes," the relationship of this piece to the classic British pantomime is tenuous at best. Virtually the only feature they share is the young lovers who must overcome an obstructive parent to get married. Most central features of the British pantomime such as the principal boy and magic bat are absent, although the bigheads survive in vestigial form as imperial statues. The extent of the spoken dialogue in performance is unclear; certainly, several of the scenes would seem to be difficult to understand if performed without speech. The Ravels were also known as innovators in performance, adding gymnastic and balletic elements to pantomime acting. It is debatable whether these changes extended the pantomime form or distorted it beyond recognition.

The text presented here is a scenario printed in or around New York City near the middle of the 19th century, and it is of interest for several reasons. Most importantly, it is the earliest surviving piece written in the United States dealing with the Chinese. The play was enormously popular; records indicate it was performed repeatedly in New York City from the 1850s to the 1870s, not only by the Ravels, but by other troupes as well. (The number and nature of its performances outside the metropolitan area, if any, remain a mystery.) Second, the name of one of its characters is almost certainly a topical reference: *Ke-ying* was the name of a Chinese junk which appeared in New York harbor in 1846, and instantly became a popular tourist attraction. The ship made a slow and well-attended tour up the coast to Boston, stopping at many ports along the way, before returning to China. Finally, *Kim-ka* presents a fairy-tale image of China which subsequently disappeared until well into the 20th century.

In terms of characterization, the most important contrast is between the handsome, bold title character and the puerile Emperor: the piece unambiguously favors the West over the East. The real strengths of the play, however, lie in its opportunities for pageantry and spectacle, which were almost certainly fully exploited in performance.

Kim-Ka!
or the
Misfortunes of Ventilator

CHARACTERS:

KIM-KA -Francois Ravel
PWAN-TIN-QUA -Antoine Ravel
VENTILLATEUR - Gabriel Ravel
KEYING - Jerome Ravel
LEI -Mlle. Flora Lehman

Chinese Ladies and Gentlemen by the whole Company.

Scene 1.

The stage represents a splendid Chinese tent, supported by richly carved columns -- the tent is gorgeously decorated. In the background a picturesque garden on the margin of a silvery lake, surrounded by a beautiful landscape; on the right, the ladies' porphyr baths -- on the left, a magnificent pavilion.

The tent has been erected for the purpose of celebrating the grand Festival in honor of the Emperor, and a grand divertissement is to take place in the imperial gardens. At the sound of music, a grand procession of the Court, consisting of Mandarins, Priests, Ladies, and of the People, bearing flags and banners enter -- the Emperor, Kim-Ka, and his beautiful daughter, the accomplished princess Lei, in magnificent palanquins are carried at the head of the procession by Mandarins and Ladies of the court.

The palanquins are set down and the Emperor takes Lei by the hand; saluting the guests, they ascend the throne erected for them under the tent. Keying, the prime minister, gives the signal for the opening of the festival.

Grand Pas de Trois Chinois.
By Mlle. Celestine Franck, M. Brillant, and M. Collet.

Scene 2.

The Festival is interrupted by the sudden burst of a terrific storm. The Emperor and his suite retire into the pavilion. Keying and his secretary, the Mandarin Pwan-Tin-Qua, who are great lovers of astronomic observations, remain and arrange a telescope for the purpose of examining the terrific storm in all its grandeur.

At this moment they perceive a globe on fire in the clouds. The globe seen is a balloon on a new principle, invented by the celebrated French Aeronaut Ventillateur, who ascended in Paris with the intention of visiting London. Ventillateur's intentions have been disappointed by the terrific storm which broke forth at the moment of his ascension. Paris being the antipode of Peking, the balloon with its intrepid passenger has been carried by the raging storm over the latter city, where it has been struck by lightning. At the moment the balloon is seen, it is on fire. Some of the cords which attach the frail car to the burning globe are broken and Ventillateur is seen in the act of falling, his feet entangled in broken cords, and his head hanging downwards. The storm drives him across the spot where Keying and Pwan-Tin-Qua are making their observations; Ventillateur in his flight knocks them down and upsets them and their instruments. At last the bold Aeronaut succeeds in landing in safety, but afraid of the damage he has caused, he seeks for a hiding place.

Scene 3.

Keying and Pwan-Tin-Qua, being frightened, strike the alarm on the gong to call the people to their assistance. Several men and women appear in a great state of alarm. Keying and the Mandarin tell them that a monster has fallen from the clouds, and that if he is not immediately destroyed, he will cause great calamities to fall on the country. Keying describes the stranger as a monster of colossal height with immense limbs, and of a most repulsive appearance. Pwan-Tin-Qua, on the contrary, describes him as being short, and possessing immense strength. The men arm themselves to chase the monster, and led by Keying and the Mandarin, they follow Ventillateur's track. The ladies remain in anxious expectation.

Scene 4.

Ventillateur being chased by his pursuers, enters, and seeing the ladies, he appeals to their sympathy. The ladies, who expected to see a hideous monster, are astonished by the manly beauty of the adventurer. They turn him round and admire his fine proportions, but they are soon interrupted by the footsteps of his pursuers. The ladies immediately push the adventurer behind them and form a screen to hide him from his enemies.

Scene 5.

Keying and his followers enter. He is astonished to see the women there; he tells them it is not a fitting place for them, and that they must retire into the pavilion. They hesitate, afraid that Ventillateur will be discovered, but during the discussion, the adventurer has succeeded in hiding himself under a divan. The ladies, satisfied that he has escaped, no longer hesitate, and retire into the bathing pavilion.

Scene 6.

Keying tells the people to retire, and orders Pwan-Tin-Qua to call for refreshment and pipes. They sit down upon the divan under which Ventillateur has taken refuge. They take their pipes, but such an awful blow-up takes place that they are both astonished. But Keying's appetite being stronger than his fear, he calls for refreshments near the divan and commences to eat. His pleasure is soon interrupted by Ventillateur, who, tired of bearing his weight, suddenly rises and upsets him and the table. Keying strikes the gong and several men enter.

Scene 7.

Keying, Pwan-Tin-Qua, and the men attempt to seize him, but after many ludicrous failures, they manage to corner him near the ladies' pavilion. As they approach nearer, he backs near one of the windows and falls backward into the pavilion. The ladies in the pavilion are heard to scream, and such a running takes place that puts the audience into roars of laughter.

Scene 8.

A room in the pavilion, decorated with several statues of Chinese Mandarins, moving their heads. The beautiful Princess Lei is standing near the statues, absorbed in reflection. Hearing a noise, she turns her eyes and perceives the bold aeronaut. For the first time, she sees before her the man whose image has haunted her maidenly dreams. He is struck by her look of kindness and throws himself at her feet, tells her of his misfortunes and of the love and admiration he feels for her, and asks her protection. But unfortunately they are soon interrupted by the noise of someone approaching. The princess looks about for a hiding place for her lover, but alas, she finds none. A thought suddenly strikes her -- the mandarin statues being but shells, one of which will serve to hide the handsome stranger from the gaze of the intruder.

Scene 9.

Ventillateur has placed himself into one of the statues, when the Emperor enters, and he being surprised at finding his daughter alone, he bids her retire to the palace. After considerable hesitation and several signals to the mandarin that contains her lover, she retires.

Scene 10.

The Emperor being left alone, feels like all crowned heads in the same predicament, and for want of amusement makes faces at the mandarins. The Emperor is astonished at having them returned; his imperial dignity takes fire at the impertinence of a mandarin statue grinning at the brother of the sun. After several amusing scenes during which his majesty is pretty well pounded, the Emperor draws his sword and cuts off the mandarin's head. Stooping to pick the head up, the Emperor receives a blow from the mandarin statue. On looking up, he sees that head which he had just cut off still standing on the shoulders of the statue as before. Being superstitious, he believes in magic, and frightened, he rings for assistance.

Scene 11.

Several men enter, and the Emperor tells them of the extraordinary occurrences that have taken place. During the recital, Ventillateur comes out of the statue and makes his escape to the gardens. The Emperor gives orders to follow and arrest the fugitive.

Scene 12.

The Aeronaut is in the garden, attempting to escape, when he perceives the beautiful Lei, who is in the garden, watching as a guardian angel over the man she loves. He throws himself at her feet, begs her love and her protection against his enemies, takes her hand and is kissing it when the Emperor and his followers enter. Kim-Ka is astonished at the impudence of the foreign barbarian, and orders the guards to seize and chain him instantly. The guards after considerable trouble secure him. The princess and the ladies kneel to the Emperor to beg for the life of the prisoner. The Emperor refuses, but his daughter tells him that she loves the stranger, and that she will put an end to her existence if the Emperor does not give his consent to her union with him. Kim-Ka will consent on the condition that Ventillateur becomes a Chinese subject and has his head shaved. Ventillateur has no objection to become a Chinese, but objects totally to the shaving operation. He has worn his hair from childhood and will not part with it. The Emperor, enraged at his refusal, calls the executioners to take and confine him in the tub of punishment. The executioners retire to execute the sentence and soon return with the poor Aeronaut confined in the tub with his head and hands sticking out. The Emperor asks again if he will consent to have his head shaved. The prisoner refuses. A signal is given by Keying, and the imperial barber commences the operation of shaving the head of the unfortunate Aeronaut. The princess and her attendants are at the feet of the Emperor praying for the pardon of the unfortunate youth. The Emperor orders the executioners to throw the tub and its contents into the lake. The executioners are in the act of throwing it into the water when the bottom slips out. The Aeronaut in falling out trips up the heels of the executioners, and flings them into the water to cool their ardour.

Ventillateur being now free, thinks that the joke has been carried far enough, and that it is more pleasant to marry a princess even if she be a Chinese one than to take a cold bath shut up in a tub. He throws himself at the Emperor's feet and consents to all the conditions proposed. The Emperor, now in good humor, gives him the hand of the princess, and they are all made happy by the Emperor, who orders a

GRAND DIVERTISSEMENT

In which are introduced a Grand Pas de Quatre by
Mlle. C. Franck, Bertin, V. Franck, and Mme. Mazetti,
and a Pas Comic Chinois by M. Gabriel Ravel and
Mlle. Flora Lehman.

TABLEAU FINALE
TERMINATING WITH A GRAND DISPLAY OF
CHINESE FIREWORKS.

1871 -- George M. Baker -- *New Brooms Sweep Clean*

Although this short piece contains no Chinese character per se, it does feature a Euroamerican who disguise himself as one. It is highly significant that Euroamericans in plays of this period always had the option of disguising themselves as Chinese, and members of other non-white races as well; almost invariably, they appeared as comical characters rather than as evil ones, as in this piece. By contrast, plays in which a Chinese assumes the guise of a Euroamerican are quite rare; moreover, such a disguise is almost never humorous, but is undertaken to achieve some villainous end. The difference in attitudes toward disguise thus reveal strong anti-Chinese feeling.

Beyond the fact of the disguise, its content reveals much about prevalent Euroamerican attitudes toward the Chinese. In his new identity as "Jing Jimalong," Pat Regan appropriates the most obvious and stereotypical Euroamerican preconceptions of the Chinese, with both implicit and explicit commentary on how, in his view, they reflect Chinese inferiority. Most prominent of the Euroamerican clichés are those regarding the Chinese diet and the strong contrast between the Chinese and Irish dialects. In the world of this play, this contrast is not value-neutral; everything Chinese is presented as inferior.

The author shows some knowledge of the Chinese by giving his disguised character a real Chinese phrase to say. His repeated "Ki I" would nowadays be rendered as *keyi*, which translates roughly as "It's possible." His assumed name, however, is an utter impossibility according to actual Chinese nomenclature.

Finally, the social context of this piece must be mentioned. The subtitle of the collection from which this piece is taken (*The Social Stage*) notes that its component plays were "for home recreation, schools, and public exhibitions." *New Brooms Sweep Clean* was clearly not intended for the professional stage; therefore it was probably more influential in reflecting Euroamerican attitudes toward the Chinese than in forming them.

New Brooms Sweep Clean

Costumes

TESTY, *light pants, white vest, dressing-gown, black wig, black side-whiskers, wrinkled face.*

FRED, *modern suit.*

JACOB, *dark suit, grey wig.*

TIM, *overalls tucked into heavy boots, blue striped shirt, blue coat with brass buttons, red cropped wig, hat.*

SWIPES, *gray coat, gray vest, grey knee-breeches, top boots, long white neckerchief, black hat, gilt band, light-cropped wig, light side-whiskers.*

JING (*as a Chinaman*), *blue blouse, loose yellow pants fastened at the ankles, white stockings, heavy brogans, flesh-colored skull-cap (can be made of unbleached cotton like a night-cap, made to fit close to the head; color with flesh ball, cut holes on each side for the ears to appear, and it will be tight), a long black cue [queue], very red face, black about the chin and over the lip to have the appearance of being unshaven.*

Scene: TESTY'S *study. Writing-table, C. Small book-case with books, R.C. Mantel, with plaster bust, vases, and ornaments, C. Chair at table. Stool, R.C. Chairs, R. and L. Writing materials, paper, &c, on table.*

Enter FRED, *R., followed by* JACOB.

Fred. You really surprise me, Jacob. After twenty years' service, my uncle turns you adrift in your old age. It's impossible!

Jacob. It's true, sir, I assure you. Turned adrift, after twenty years' service -- and hard service too -- because I took the privilege of an old servant to tell him the truth.

Fred. Ah! What was the truth you told him?

Jacob. That he was making a donkey of himself. He was too old to *transmogrify* himself by putting on a black curly wig and dyeing his whiskers.

Fred. But why did you tell him so?

Jacob. Because I couldn't help it. The idea of that old gentleman trying to deceive the world at his time of life! He's as grey as a badger, and as bald as a new-born baby. Soon he'll have all the young ladies after him.

Fred. Perhaps he wants a wife.

Jacob. Then let him get one honestly. I don't believe in obtaining goods under false pretenses.

Fred. Neither do I, Jacob. But he's his own master. I'm sorry for you; but I do not see how I can help you. If he wants to marry, it's none of my business.

Jacob. But, Mr. Fred, I think it is your business. He's *gallavanting* after a widow. I know that. He's had Mr. Tubbs, the lawyer, here, draw up a will or a settlement; and I heard him say, "Now, Master Fred, you must take care of yourself."

Fred. Still, I say it's none of my business. If he chooses to marry, let him. I have taken care of myself so far; and, though I might reasonably expect, some time, to have a share of his riches, I can do without.

Jacob. That's very true, Mr. Fred. Still, you shouldn't let your uncle fall a victim to the schemes of such an adventurer as Mrs. Shoddy.

Fred. Mrs. Shoddy! Is that the lady my uncle intends to marry?

Jacob. That's the lady he is *dyeing* for. Yes, sir; *dyeing* by inches. He's commenced with his whiskers.

Fred. She *is* a scheming adventurer; and my uncle must not make a fool of himself.

Jacob. That's what I say, sir; and that's what I made bold to tell him. He took offense, and turned me off.

Fred. But, Jacob, you must not go. I'll see my uncle; and fortunately, here he is. Don't let him see you.

Jacob. I'll take care of that, Mr. Fred. (*Exit, L.*)

Fred. What a transformation! The old gentleman must be very far gone.

Enter TESTY, *R.*

Why, Uncle Noah! What a change! Have you "renewed your youth like the eagle?"

Testy. Oh, bother your nonsense! What is it to you?

Fred. Why, uncle --

Testy. Shut up! If I choose to make a change in my personal appearance, is it any of your business? I have had trouble enough with that confounded Jacob Trusty, and I don't want to be bothered by you.

Fred. I beg your pardon, uncle; I meant no offence, I assure you. I am delighted to see you looking so young again. But, uncle, Jacob tells me you have discharged him.

Testy. Yes, I have discharged him; and I have discharged Patrick, and Sally Greaser -- an impudent set who take advantage of long service to insult me.

Fred. Patrick! You don't mean it, uncle: he's the best servant you ever had. And Sally Greaser too. Why, there's not her equal in the city as a cook. Her soft-shell crabs are perfectly splendid.

Testy. Hang her, and her soft-shell crabs! She's an impudent hussy. I've turned her off, and I don't mean to have another woman in the house. I'll have a Chinese cook.

Fred. A Chinese cook! That's a novel idea; but where in the world will you find one?

Testy. That's my business. Fortunately I have friends, sir -- yes, sir, friends, who will see that I do not suffer for servants. I'll teach them better manners than to contradict me. I won't have it. I'll let them know who is master here. I'm going to commence with a new set this very day.

Fred. A new set?

Testy. Yes, a new set. I'm going to turn over a new leaf. "New brooms sweep clean." With a new set recommended to me by a lady who knows something about housekeeping.

Fred. A lady; pray, may I inquire who she is?

Testy. Mrs. Shoddy.

Fred. Mrs. Shoddy? -- (*Aside.*) So the schemer is at work. -- (*Aloud.*) But, uncle, are you not afraid to give a lot of new servants control of the house?

Testy. Afraid? No, sir. I shall have nobody but whom Mrs. Shoddy recommends. I have the greatest confidence in her; and, whoever she sends, I will employ.

Fred. Ah, uncle! Be careful of your "new brooms." They may sweep cleaner than you will like.

Testy. Well, sir, it's none of your business, as long as I like it. You *may* be owner of this property some day, and then you can do as you like with it. While it is mine, I shall exercise the same privilege.

Fred. Certainly, uncle. I've no more to say. Good day. (*Aside.*) It's too bad. The old gentleman will be swindled by that adventuress. I must know what is going on. Can't I manage to get a "new broom" into the house? There's the Chinese cook. I don't believe Mrs. Shoddy has one to send. At any rate I'll be beforehand. I'll send one myself. 'Twill be a capital joke. He will take any one whom Mrs. Shoddy sends. How shall I get her recommendation? I think I can manage it.

Testy. Well, sir, what are you muttering about in that corner?

Fred. I beg your pardon, uncle. I thought you had gone. I was thinking where I could find you a Chinese cook.

Testy. You needn't trouble yourself. I'll keep my eyes open for one.

Fred. (*Aside.*) And so will I. And I'll keep an eye on these new brooms of his too. (*Exit, R.*)

Testy. (*Sits at table.*) There's another impudent fellow. He'd like to say something saucy, I know; but the fear of the consequences deters him. It's no use, Master Fred: my money goes to Mrs. Testy; for Mrs. Shoddy will not consent to the change on any other conditions. Bewitching widow! I'd sacrifice life itself for her. (*Takes paper from drawer.*) The settlement is all ready. So, Master Fred, your chance for the riches of old Testy are decidedly slim. (*Takes out another paper.*) What's this? My bonds! Good gracious! I forgot to lock them up last night. That's very careless in me, to leave ten thousand dollars of Uncle Sam's indebtedness in this loose manner. (*Knock, R.*) Hallo! Who's that? (*Puts papers in drawer.*) Come in.

Enter JOHN SWIPES, *R.*

Swipes. Hi beg your pardon sir, Hi 'ave ha note from Mrs. Shoddy.

Testy. Mrs. Shoddy? Let me have it. (*Reads.*)

"My dear Mr. Testy," -- Her *dear* Mr. Testy! Bewitching widow! -- "I promised to send you some good servants. The bearer is an excellent coachman, one to be trusted, who never breaks anything except horses. He will suit you admirably."

"Ever yours, Cecelia Shoddy."

Ever yours! Delicious widow! -- So, sir, you are a coachman.

Swipes. Yes, sir; Hi'm ha coachman. 'Ave 'ad hexperience hin the haristocratic families hof the Hold World, hand hi flatter myself hi can drive.

Testy. Well, sir; your name.

Swipes. Swipes, sir; Handrew Swipes, son of Hoscar Swipes hand Hanastasia Swipes; birthplace, Hessex, Hingland; hage --

Testy. Never mind your age. You will suit me exactly. I engage you at once. You don't drink?

Swipes. Never; hexcept hon hextraordinary hoccasions, hand then honly hale.

Testy. You'll find your horses in the stable. As soon as possible, have the carriage at the door: I wish to take a ride.

Swipes. Hi'll do hit hat once. (*Exit, R.*)

Testy. An English coachman. That style will suit Mrs. Shoddy. If he is as fond of his horses as he is of superfluous *h*'s, he will do admirably. (*Knock, L.*) Hallo! Who's that? Come in.

Enter TIM, *L.*

Well, what do you want?

Tim. If yer plaze, sir, yer honor, I have a letther from Mrs. Shoddy.

Testy. Mrs. Shoddy? Let me have it. (*Reads*)

"My dear, dear Mr. Testy" -- (Two dears this time! Charming widow! She's dearer than ever!) "I have again the power to serve you. The bearer is a worthy and capable servant who will admirably suit you."

"Your devoted CECILIA."

My devoted Cecilia! Ravishing widow! Young man, your name.

Tim. Tim Regan, if yer plaze, sir, yer honor.

Testy. You are recommended to me as a worthy and capable servant.

Tim. O sir! yer honor, shpare me modesty.

Testy. What are your particular qualifications?

Tim. Which?

Testy. What can you do?

Tim. Ate, dhrink, and slape, sir, yer honor.

Testy. Ah, humorous, I see.

Tim. Not much. I had the masles once, I think, sir, yer honor.

Testy. Pshaw, man! Can you keep a room tidy?

Tim. I can, that, just; or a pig-sty, eather, sir, yer honor.

Testy. That's all I want. I engage you at once.

Tim. Thank yer, sir, yer honor; and the wages?

Testy. Forty dollars a month.

Tim. Forty --

Testy. You will go to work at once. Get a duster, and brush up my room. I shall expect great things of you, you are so highly recommended by Mrs. Shoddy. Go into the next room, take off that coat, put on a linen duster you'll find there, and come back here.

Tim. To be sure I will, sir, yer honor. (*Exit, R.*)

Testy. Well, I must say that Mrs. Shoddy has not been particularly nice as to the outward appearance of the individual she has selected to be my body-guard. He looks more like a hod-carrier than a gentleman's valet. But can I doubt her? -- my chosen one; the idol of my soul; the bewitching, beautiful --

Enter JING JIMALONG, *L. He stands grinning at* TESTY, *with the forefinger of each hand pointing up á la Chinese.*

Who the deuce is that?

Jing. Muchee purty well? Ki I!

Testy. As I live, it's a real live Chinaman. Oh! I see the beautiful hand of the divine Mrs. Shoddy in this.

Jing. Mee muchee big cookie, Ki I!

Testy. Ah, indeed! and who sent you here?

Jing. Muchee fine lady; muchee big bunchee on her back; muchee pig-tail round her head; muchee fine eyes; muchee little feet; muchee fine all over -- Ki I!

Testy. Her description exactly. What an intelligent foreigner! I know I shall like him. So you can cook?

Jing. Ki I!

Testy. Well, I don't want any "Ki I's" cooked here; that may do for your country. Can you cook bread?

Jing. Ki I!

Testy. Meat?

Jing. Ki I! Muchee ebery ting.

Testy. Capital, capital. He'll do. What an angel Mrs. Shoddy is! My friend, you wait here a moment, and I'll find somebody to show you to the kitchen. I'll take you into my service. You shall cook me a Chinese dish at once. I'm going to ride, and I'm always hungry when I return. (*Exit, R.*)

Jing. Be jabers! Here's a foine sitivation for an Irishman: rigged up like an owld woman, and jabbering like a Tottenhot. It's all the doings av Mr. Fred. "Pat," says he --"Anan," says I -- "Would yez be afther kapin' yer sitivation that my uncle took from yez?" says he. "To be sure I would, " says I. "Then come wid me." And thin he took me to his room; and, bedad, this is the consequince. I'm made a Chinaman widout naturalization intirely. "And thin," says he, "Pat, it's a little time I have to tach the language. Say, 'Muchee' and 'Ki I!' to all the owld gentleman says, and whativer yer own intilligence may bid yez." But, bedad, it's afraid I am av the owld man: if he finds out the desate, I'm a ruined Chinaman intirely. Muchee, Ki I!

Enter TESTY *with* SWIPES, *L.*

Testy. Swipes, just show this individual into the kitchen.

Swipes. Certainly hi will, Why, hit's a celestial!

Jing. (*Aside.*) A which is it? Begorra! What's that he's calling me?

Testy. Yes, it's my new cook. Take him along.

Swipes. Come this way. What ha cook! What can you cook?

Jing. Ki I! Ki I!

Swipes. His that hall? What a blarsted country that China must be! (*Exit, R.*)

Jing. Musha, I'm in for it! (*Exit, R.*)

Testy. What a novelty. I've got the start of my neighbors, thanks to dear Mrs. Shoddy. I've no doubt I shall find something nice on my return.

Enter SWIPES, *R., followed by* TIM.

Swipes. The carriage is at the door, sir. (*Exit R.*)

Testy. All right. Now, Tim, get my coat and hat in the next room.

Tim. All right, sir, yer honor. (*Exit, L.*)

Testy. (*Takes off his dressing-gown.*) I've got a trio of new servants, and they all *look* smart. That last lot thought I couldn't do without them, did they? There's nothing like a change. "New brooms sweep clean."

Enter TIM *with coat and hat.*

Just help me with this coat. (*Puts on hat and coat.*) Now, Tim, have everything in order on my return. (*Exit, R.*)

Tim. All right, sir, yer honor. Faith, here's a sthrake av luck. Intirely out av a sitivation, I dropped in to say me cousin, Biddy O'Honey, who lives wid Mrs. Shoddy. Biddy had a bit iv a shindy wid' the lady's own man; and, whin Mrs. Shoddy sinds Biddy to fetch him a note for Mr. Testy, Biddy pops it into my hand, and says, "You go, Tim: he'll niver be the wiser if you give it him, and you'll profit by the place. Shure, it's my duty to look after my own frinds furst." So here I am, ingaged on another man's karacther. It's little I know about the work, for hod-carrying's my perfession. Ah, well, the owld gint said, have everything in ordher. Faith, I'll do that same. (*Takes a duster and fiercely brushes table, sending papers flying in all directions, and upsetting the inkstand.*) Oh, murther! I've upset the ink. There's a black stain on my karacther. (*Takes* MR. TESTY'S *handkerchief from the pocket of dressing-gown, and wipes up the ink; puts handkerchief back.*) Jist as good as new. (*Picks up papers.*) The ould gint has covered his papers with pot-hooks and scrawls. They're no good, sure. (*Tears up papers.*) Now for the drawers. (*Takes out will.*) "Last will and testament." Sure, that's no good. Here's the last of that. (*Tears up will. Takes out coupons.*) Picters for his ould gint's baby. (*Throws them on the table.*) I'll finish my dusting. (*Brushes mantel, knocking off the bust and vases.*) Oh, murther! Here's a crash among the fine arts. What will I do? (*Knock, R.*) Who's that? Come in wid yer.

Enter JING, R.

Tim. Och, murther! What's that? It's a cannible, or a -- or a -- vhat is it?

Jing. Faith, I'd jist like to know what a Chinase dish is, onyhow, afore I'd cook it. Bedad! I must scrub up my jography, shure. Faith, thim fellers cook rats and mice and puppies! That's it. Where will I find a puppy? (*Sees* TIM.) Och, murther! If that ain't my own brother Tim. What will I do? He'll find me out, and raise a breeze, sure. Och, murther! Why was I born to die a Chinaman? (*Sits on stool, with head bent down.*)

Tim. By my sowl! That's one av them fellers that come from the bottom av the world. It's a Chinaman. Musha, whist! Vhat's your name, I'd loike to know?

Jing. Ki I!

Tim. Faith! now, is it? And where did yez come from?

Jing. Ki I!

Tim. Vhat's that? Is it a Dutchman yez are, or a Roosian, or a Proosian?

Jing. Ki I!

Tim. I belave yez, honey. Poor owld feller: he's deaf, dumb, and blind. Faith! Have yez a small taychist about yez, for it's my owld woman that's fond av the wade?

Jing. Ki I!

Tim. Get owt av that, ye dirty blackguard! By my sowl, if yez

"Ki I" again, I'll thread on the tail av yer hair. Away wid yez!

Jing. (*Aside.*) Begorra ! I'd loike to punch his head for him, the thaif. (*Aloud.*) Ki I! Ki I! (*Exit, R.*)

Tim. By me sowl! That owld chap looks enough like me brither Pat to be his own cousin! Chinaman, is it! Begorra! It's sorry manners he has, onyhow. (*Knock, L.*)

Enter FRED, *L., disguised as an image-vender, with a basket containing images, vases, &c.*

Fred. Imagees! Imagees!

Tim. What's that? Images!

Fred. You buy my imagees? Ver sheep; ver sheep.

Tim. Faith, it's not a sheep I want at all, at all. Have yer a bust of St. Patrick or O'Connell, sure?

Fred. No, no! Ze leetle Nap. See. (*Showing bust of Napoleon.*)

Tim. Faith, it's all the same. How much?

Fred. You buy, eh? Tree dollar; ver sheep.

Tim. Sheep, is it? Three dollars! Faith, it's deer. No, I've niver a cint.

Fred. No moneys! Den you no buy.

Tim. Hold on, Parleyvoo! I'll trade wid yer. Begorra ! I'll sind off some uv the owld gint's books. He'll niver rade thim all. (*Takes down a book.*) "Paradise Lost." Lost, is it? Faith, it's found once more, thin. Whist! Sh --! This for the little Nap -- hey?

Fred. (*Aside.*) My uncle's much-prized Bunyan. [*Sic.*]

Tim. It's something about bunions. I'm something av a corn doctor, and I know it's good. Is it a trade?

Fred. For ze leetle Nap? Yes. (*They exchange.*)

Tim. Now for the vases. What will I do fur thim?

Fred. Here's de vases. Ver rich. Two dollar. Ver sheep, ver sheep.

Tim. Will you have some more larnin', Parleyvoo?

Fred. (*Takes up the coupon bonds.*) Sharming picturs! Ver fine!

Tim. Oh! You like them, do you? Faith, give me the vases and they are yours.

Fred. For ze vases? Too sheep, too sheep. Ver well: you have ze vases. (*They exchange.*) (*Aside.*) Ten thousand dollars! My poor uncle!

Testy. (*Outside, R.*) Oh murder! Murder! Tim! Tim!

Tim. The owld gint. Begorra, here's a row! Cooming, cooming, sir, yer honor. (*Exit, R.*)

Fred. My uncle! I'll slip away. His new broom has made a clean sweep here. Wonder how he will like it. (*Exit, L.*)

Enter TESTY, *R., his clothes muddy, his hat knocked over his eyes, supported by* TIM.

Testy. O Tim, Tim! That coachman -- he's murdered me!

Tim. And left you spacheless, the dirty blackguard!

Testy. Upset me in front of Mrs. Shoddy's house. Bring me my dressing-gown. (*Puts it on.*) Here's a pretty situation. (*Takes out his handkerchief, wipes his face, leaving ink-stains upon it.*) Why, what's this, Tim? (*Looks around room.*) What have you been doing, you villain? My bust ruined! My papers destroyed! Open drawers! The will gone -- and my coupons -- (*Seizing* TIM.). You scoundrel, what have you done with my coupons?

Tim. If you plaze, sir, yer honor, I've been claning up a bit.

Testy. Cleaning up! Cleaning out, you mean. Where's my money?

Tim. Money, is it? How should I know?

Enter SWIPES, *R.*

Testy. O you villain! Back again, are you? You've been drinking.

Swipes. Honly ha little hale.

Testy. Didn't you tell me you didn't drink?

Swipes. Honly hon hextraordinary hoccasions. This was one, when hi got ha new place. Hi took ha little hale.

Testy. Which upset me as well as you. I'll make another hextraordinary hoccasion for you. Go! I discharge you.

Swipes. Go, without warning? This his han hinsult.

Testy. I give you warning that if you are found in this house in five minutes, I'll give you to the police.

Swipes. Hi won't go without my pay. Hit's haudacious. (*Takes off his coat.*)

Tim. True for you, honey; stick to that.

Testy. And you, Tim: I'll hand you over to the police at once.

You've robbed me.

Tim. Rob, is it? Begorra! There's an insult to an Irish gintleman. (*Takes off his coat.*)

Testy. What are you about?

Tim. About to have satisfaction, you owld blackguard!

Testy. Come, come; none of this. I'll hand you both over to the police.

Swipes. (*Threateningly.*) Pay hup, hor hover you go!

Tim. (*Shaking his fist.*) Robber, is it?

Testy. Do you dare threaten? (SWIPES *and* TIM *seize* TESTY *and shake him.*)

Enter FRED, *R.,* JACOB, *L.*

Fred. Hallo, uncle! What's the matter?

Testy. Fred, you are just in time. In a moment I would have fallen a victim to the violence of a drunkard and of a robber.

Fred. Why, these are two of your new servants.

Testy. No, they're not. They're both discharged. One has robbed me, and I want the police. Robbed of ten thousand dollars!

Fred. Which I can restore. Here are your coupons, uncle, safe and sound. I think they have depreciated in value, as Tim gave them to me for a pair of vases.

Tim. Sir, yer honor, I niver set eyes on him bafore.

Fred. Oh, yes, you did! Imagees?

Tim. Begorra! It's the Parleyvoo.

Testy. I've had a narrow escape. Thanks to you, Fred. Jacob, you'll resume your old situation at once; that is, if you have not found a new one.

Jacob. No, sir. I went to see Mrs. Shoddy to ask for a place, but she was in trouble.

Testy. In trouble?

Jacob. Yes. It seems about a year ago, she ran away from her husband, taking all his money. He's found her out, and this very day arrived to take her home again.

Testy. Her husband? A widow with a husband! Oh, horror! My hair is turning white.

Jacob. I told you, sir, that dye wouldn't stick.

Testy. Fred, I think you'd better come and live with me. I don't believe I shall ever marry. I'm getting too old.

Fred. (*Aside.*) "A hungry fox is passing by --" (*Aloud.*) Thank you, sir; I'll come with pleasure. But what about these new servants? (*A dog is heard yelping outside, L. Then a crash of crockery. JING runs in, R.*)

Jing. Och! Murther, murther, murther! It's kilt I am, intirely. (*Shakes his fist off, L.*) Yez murthering thaif av the world. Git out av that! Away wid yez!

Testy. What is the meaning of this? It's my new Chinese servant, Fred.

Fred. With a brogue like a wild Irishman.

Testy. You imposter! What does this mean? Speak, quickly.

Jing. (*Aside.*) Oh, murther! I've let the cat out of the bag! (*Aloud.*) Ki I! Muchee Ki I!

Testy. That won't do. What is the meaning of that "Ki I"ing downstairs?

Jing. (*Aside.*) Vhat shall I say? (*Aside.*) Me try cookee bow-wow; bow-wow no likee cookee him. Bow-wow muchee Ki I! Me muchee Ki-I too -- bow-wow muchee run into closet: muchee crockery, -- bang, --bang, --bang, muchee pieces all breakee. Muchee, --muchee, --muchee, --and be jabers! That's what's the matter intirely, or my name's not Pat Regan; and bother yez blasted Chinese, for it's nearly broke my jaw.

Tim. Pat Regan! Be my sowl! I recognize the vice of affection in my bones. (*Seizes JING'S pigtail, and pulls off skull-cap.*) It's himsilf intirely. O Pat, Pat! How could yez? Is it yerself that's disgracing owld Ireland by going over to China? Begorra! Ye's sowld yer birthright for a mess of broken china. Be my sowl, I'm pale wid blushing for yez.

Jing. Aisy wid yer blarney, Tim, or it's a batin' ye'll git.

Testy. Patrick Regan.

Jing. Sir.

Testy. What is the meaning of this masquerade? Didn't I discharge you this morning?

Fred. Let me speak for him, uncle. I alone am to blame; for I dressed him in the costume, and instructed him in the language of a Chinaman.

Testy. You did, you scamp! And what for, pray?

Fred. To assist you in your endeavors to procure "new brooms," and also to outwit Mrs. Shoddy.

Testy. Well, if that is a specimen of your proficiency in the Chinese language, the sooner you are sent as ambassador to the Celestials the better.

Fred. Uncle, let Pat have his old place: you can't do better. He won't contradict you again, will you, Pat?

Jing. Faith! Not muchee.

Testy. Shut up! Don't let me hear any of that lingo, or out of this house you'll go: for the present, you may take your old place.

Fred. And what's to be done with the other servants?

Tim. Begorra! That's what I'd like to know.

Swipes. You've crushed my 'opes, hand hi want my money.

Testy. Pay them, and send them off. I'll take back the old ones; for I am convinced, from my unhappy experience of the last half-hour, that, despite the old proverb, *new brooms do not always sweep clean.*

Disposition of characters:
R., PAT, FRED, TESTY, SWIPES, TIM, *L.*

1873 -- M.T. Caldor -- *Curiosity*

Like the previous piece, this short skit was also expressly written for performance by amateurs. It is a charade; each episode portrays a syllable of the title, and the final section presents the word as a whole. The author has imitated Bret Harte in the name he has chosen for his Chinese character. "Ah Sin" first appeared in Harte's poem "Plain Language From Truthful James," which, known colloquially as "The Heathen Chinee," became wildly popular. This poem tells a story of a cheater who is himself cheated. Although in fact it expressed sympathy for the Chinese, the public persisted in reading it as an anti-Chinese tract, to the point that Harte expressed public regret that he had ever written it. The responsibility for this was partly his own, however, as he muddled the question of the poem's sympathies by giving his Chinese character a name with such clear derogatory overtones ("Ah Sin" = "I Sin"). Because Harte's piece was a great hit, it was only natural for other writers of the era to attempt to capitalize on its success by imitation, as Caldor did here.

Curiosity seizes on the most obvious differences between Chinese and Euroamericans, and exploits them for comic effect. There was a serious point behind this laughter, however. The author has exerted considerable ingenuity in constructing situations that would clearly reinforce the sense of racial superiority among the play's performers and audience, and evoke a cruel type of merriment that would be wholly unacceptable today.

Curiosity

A Charade of Five Syllables

CHARACTERS

MRS. WOEBEGONE. *Cap, spectacles, and apron with long strings.*

MRS. SPRIGHTLY. *Any lady's costume.*

THE GRAND DUKE. *Must be tall, and well wrapped up with fur collar.*

RUSSELL. *English sporting suit, whip.*

AH SIN. *Chinese hat and long cue. Wide loose trousers and blouse.*

FIRST SYLLABLE: "CUE"

MRS. WOEBEGONE *dusting table and chair. A knock at the door. She opens it, and* MRS. SPRIGHTLY *comes in, tiptoeing in, with short, jerky ways in speech and gestures, illustrating her name as* MRS. W.'S *solemn face and long-drawn syllables confirm hers.*

Mrs. W. O, my dear Mrs. Sprightly, how do you do? Come right in.

Mrs. S. How do you do, Mrs. Woebegone? Why, I'm afraid you're not very well, you look so forlorn.

Mrs. W. Very well? In the name of distress and perplexity, how *could* I be well? O, Mrs. Sprightly, I am so tired -- so perplexed -- so everything! Do you know I haven't got but this one pair of hands for all the work in this house? Bridget's cousin is going to be married, and her sister's husband's sister's child is going to be waked, and she's gone to both places at once, I expect. And Dinah's taken offence because she was set to clean up after the "white trash," as she calls it. And she's left too. She's gone to find a place where there are other respectable colored individuals. And here I am all alone. O dear! O dear! What ever will become of me! And Mr. Woebegone *so* particular about the turn of his roast beef and the shine of his shirt bosom.

Mrs. S. Why, my dear creature, there's no need of your being so cast down. Haven't you heard the good news that rejoices the hearts of all the housekeepers in the land? No more ruling of helpless mistresses by lady Bridgets or saucy Dinahs. Is it possible you haven't read in the newspapers about the great revolution taking place? About the coming man who is to relieve all our perplexities? There, there, don't fret any longer. I'll just send word down to the agent, who is my friend, you know, and he'll send you up one promptly from the ship-load that came yesterday.

Mrs. W. I don't understand a word you're saying. But if there's any relief, do let me have it at once.

(MRS. SPRIGHTLY *is hastily writing a line, which she folds up, and carries out, returning again promptly.*)

Mrs. S. There! I've sent the word to Mr. Careful, and I know he'll send *Ah Sin* along promptly.

Mrs. W. Send *a sin* along! Haven't I sins enough down in my kitchen? What do you mean, Mrs. Sprightly? I am afraid you're losing your mind, getting to see less --

Mrs. S. Celestial. That's it, exactly. That's what they call 'em. Hark! There he comes now. I knew Mr. Careful would be prompt.

Enter AH SIN, *the Chinaman, who salaams to them.*

Mrs. W. (*Holding up both hands.*) What in the name of all the heathen is this?

Mrs. S. A heathen, certainly; but just ask him into your kitchen, and see if you don't find him a faithful one. That is, of course, after you've shown him what to do.

Mrs. W. O, I must show him, must I?

Mrs. S. To be sure. But then it's only for once. After that he understands perfectly, and you have no more trouble. He takes his cue, I may say.

Mrs. W. I should say so. That's it hanging down behind, isn't it? To think of my having man-help in my kitchen, with back hair hanging down in that shape.

SECOND SYLLABLE: "WRY"

Mrs. W. (*Again welcoming* MRS. SPRIGHTLY'S *arrival.*) O, Mrs. Sprightly, I'm so glad you've come! Sit right down, sit right down, and let me tell you the great honor that's come to me. I knew something splendid would come when I got the post-office appointment. What do you think, the *great* Grand Duke is coming here to call on me!

Mrs. S. The Grand Duke. Bless me, that is news! Why don't you send round and tell the neighbors? We ought to have a band, and speech-making, and a great dinner. And it would never do to have him miss a ball.

Mrs. W. La sakes, it's only a friendly call on me. I shan't make any great fuss about it. I don't want him to think I ain't a staunch republican. I'm only just going to give him a little refreshment. I've heard how he's very fond of a new drink. I can't tell you the foreign name for it, but it's made of honey and everything nice and delectable. And I've got the receipt, and Ah Sin knows how to make it, and he's going to bring some in.

Mrs. S. O, Mrs. Woebegone, how fortunate you are. I'm sure you never ought to say another word about your bad luck, and your unfortunate star. Dear me! How I should like to see the great Grand Duke.

Mrs. W. And so you shall. I'm going to let you stay here in this room when he comes. And O, Mrs. Sprightly, I want you to watch his beau-ti-ful expression. Haven't you seen in the papers what a handsome mouth he has? And they do say that this wonderful drink leaves it in the sweetest shape, a great deal more charming than the old talk about prunes, prism, and that stuff. Such a *sweet* expression. Mind you take notice of it. Mind you don't lose the expression.

Mrs. S No, indeed, I shan't; you needn't think I shall. Hark! There's somebody coming now.

Mrs. W. O, my! If it should be the Grand Duke. Sin, Sin, mind the door.

(She runs up and down in a flutter of agitation. MRS. S. retreats behind a curtain, or some tall chair.)

Enter GRAND DUKE, *a tall person, well wrapped in furs.* MRS. W. *makes an extravagant obeisance. The* DUKE *behaves with great dignity. Their conversation is carried on in pantomime.* AH SIN *enters promptly with the waiter, and glasses filled with the new beverage, which he hands first to the* DUKE, *who politely insists upon the hostess receiving it first, and takes the second himself. They both bow before the glasses, and drink, but pause suddenly, making the most horrible faces.*

(MRS. S. *puts her head from her retreat to say --*)

Be sure you mind the expression!

(MRS. W. *rushes at* SIN.)

Mrs. W. O, you wretch, you stupid! You've put in vinegar, instead of wine!

(GRAND DUKE, *with exaggerated wry expression of lips, takes abrupt leave.*)

THIRD SYLLABLE: "OS"

(MRS. W., *supposed to be standing outside her door in the street.*)

Mrs. W. I must confess I have a passion for foreign folks. Ever since that visit of poor, dear Alexis, I've been an envied woman in this town. I shouldn't wonder now if I had a call from this Englishman that is down to the tavern. The world-renowned Russell, they call him. The Squire said he was famous most of all for his profound sagacity, and his strict accuracy in letter-writing. I don't know exactly what he means, but he's famous, and I know he's an Englishman. Why, what's all that noise?

(*Enter* RUSSELL, *overcoat on, whip in hand; he runs along swiftly.*)

Rus. Stop him, stop him. Whoa, whoa!

Mrs. W. (*Catching hold of his coat, and holding him.*) Here, Mister, what's the matter?

Rus. My 'os, my 'os. I've lost him; he's run away when I was in the 'ouse ordering 'am and heggs for dinner. Catch him! Stop him! I've lost my 'os.

(*He pulls away from her hold, and rushes off.*)

Mrs. W. (*Looks around her in perplexed astonishment.*) Lost his 'os. That's queer English. What under the sun is it he has lost? I'll run down to the tavern, and see.

FOURTH AND FIFTH SYLLABLES: "I," "TIE"

MRS. WOEBEGONE *and* AH SIN.

Mrs. W. And now, Ah Sin, have you set the table?

Ah Sin. Me set him very muchee well.

Mrs. W. Very muchee well! That's neither English nor Chinee. I would try to talk in one of the other. To begin with, you must not be saying "me" all the time. I've told you over and over again to say "I." You poor little heathen, I should think you'd see for yourself how much respectable folks use that little nominative, first person singular. I won't say it isn't conceited, but if you don't think well of yourself, who else is going to? Now mind how you answer me! Have you set the bread to rising?

Ah Sin. (*Gesticulating to suit his talk.*) Me roll him, me pound him, me put him in the pan. He way up -- *so* high.

Mrs. W. There -- just hear him. I never shall teach him to talk in any other way than in that outlandish fashion.

(Runs out as he finishes.)

(She sits down to her knitting, and knits languidly, yawning; presently she nods, and finally falls asleep. AH SIN *steals in, takes her long apron strings and ties her to the chair. He stands a moment making all sorts of grotesque gestures of roguish delight, and then taking up a book, throws it down violently just before her. She starts up, chair and all.)*

Mrs. W. Goodness gracious! What noise was that? And, merciful sakes! What ails this chair? Dear, dear! Now whoever has done this mischief? It can't ever be that innocent heathen Chinee.

Ah Sin. (Putting in his head.) No me, no me. Missie, *I* tie.

THE WHOLE WORD: "CURIOSITY"

The post office. Boy brings in the mail-bag to MRS. WOEBEGONE, *and goes out. She takes off her spectacles to wipe them, puts them on carefully, and with a very consequential look unlocks the bag, and takes out the contents, looking at each one sharply. The last she comes upon is a square parcel, which she turns over and around, and even puts to her nose.* AH SIN *and* MRS. SPRIGHTLY, *unseen by her, are watching.*

Mrs. W. Well, now, here's a parcel from abroad, as sure as I'm alive, and it ain't for me. It's for Mrs. Jemimy Sprightly. Who could have sent it to her? And what is it? It beats all I ever heard tell of. Jemimy had a second cousin who went over the seas. I shouldn't wonder if 'twas from him. Mebbe he's made his everlastin' fortin' and sent Jemimy half of it. I do wonder now what's in here.

(She turns it over and looks at it wistfully.)

Dear me. I shouldn't wonder if Jemimy would take it, and keep it, and never breathe a lisp about it. O, dear! Like as not there's di-monds in it. It ain't heavy enough for gold, certain. I wonder if somebody couldn't seal that all up again. I've got plenty of wax -- I'll --

(Under her fingering the seals give way.)

There! It's come open. So I can't help it, can I?

(The watchers make amused gestures while she slowly removes the paper wrappings.)

Mrs. W. (Continues.) And then, mebbe, it's a mistake. Who knows but that it's a present from the Grand Duke, and meant for me, only he's got Jemimy's name by mistake. It's more'n likely to be a snuff-box, all set round with jewels. I should be sure, if it wasn't for that horrid vinegar in the drink. But he wouldn't lay that up. He knows't was that Ah Sin's fault. I do believe it's a snuff-box. I -- will -- open -- it.

(She pulls off the wrapping, touches the spring, and up flies into her face out of his box, a -- Jumping Jack. She screams and drops it. In rush AH SIN and MRS. SPRIGHTLY, clapping their hands.)

Mrs. S. That's the way people betray themselves. Now, Mrs. Woebegone, you must confess you have been led into great indiscretion, before all these people, by indulging your -- will somebody tell me, what troublesome trait of character?

(The box of the Jumping Jack should be covered so that the audience will not suspect what it is, and may be as surprised as MRS. WOEBEGONE.)

18?? -- Ambrose Bierce -- *Peaceful Expulsion*

This short closet drama presents a satirical look at the effects of the Chinese in the United States on Euramericans of different classes. Although Bierce does employ some of the devices of other writers who denigrated the Chinese, i.e., the meaningful name and the pidgin speech, the play does not satirize them exclusively. Instead, the author distributes his well-known detestation of <u>all</u> humanity evenhandedly. True, the Chinese receive a drubbing for their physical and cultural characteristics, but the patrician Euroamerican politician is a cynical manipulator, and the workingman an ignoramus. Overshadowing them all is Satan, whom Bierce supposes immensely enjoys all the strife and chaos created by "the Chinese question." Buried beneath the spite and invective is a valid point which most of the writers on the Chinese either misunderstood or ignored; for decades after the gold rush, California had more work available than there were people to do it, and the Chinese did supply cheap and diligent labor.

Even in such a short piece as this, Bierce demonstrates an attentive ear and good craftsmanship with regard to linguistic variation. Each of his characters uses distinctive and appropriate vocabulary, syntax, and accent. The piece is a caricature, but the individual portrayals are sketched vigorously, vividly, and precisely.

Peaceful Expulsion

DRAMATIS PERSONAE

MOUNTWAVE, *a Politician*
HARDHAND, *a Workingman*
TOK BAK, *a Chinaman*
SATAN, *a Friend to Mountwave*
CHORUS OF FOREIGN VOTERS

Mountwave.   My friend, I beg that you will lend your ears
(I know 'tis asking a great deal of you)
While I for your instruction nominate
Some certain wrongs you suffer. Men like you
Imperfectly are sensible of all
The miseries they actually feel.
Hence, Providence has prudently raised up
Clear-sighted men like me to diagnose
Their cases and inform them where it hurts.
The wounds of honest workingmen I've made
A specialty, and probing them's my trade.

Hardhand.   Well, Mister, s'pose you let yer bossest eye

Camp on my mortal part awhile; then you
Jes' toot my sufferin's an' tell me what's
The fashionable caper now in writhes --
The very swellest wriggle.

Mountwave.   Well, my lad,
'Tis plain as is the long, conspicuous nose
Borne, ponderous and pendulous, between
The elephant's remarkable eye-teeth.

(*Enter* TOK BAK.)

The Chinese competition's what ails *you.*

Both. (*Singing.*)

O pig-tail Celestial,
O barbarous, bestial,
  Abominable Chinee!
Simian fellow man,
Primitive yellow man,
  Joshian devotee!
Shoe-and-cigar machine,
Oleomargarine,
  You are, and butter we are --
Fat of the land are we,
  Salt of the earth;
In God's image planned to be --
  Noble by birth!
You, on the contrary,
Modeled upon very
  Different lines indeed,
Show in conspicuous
Base and ridiculous
  Ways your inferior breed.
Freak of biology,
Shame of ethnology,
  Monster unspeakably low!
Fit to be buckshotted,
Brickbatted, boycotted --
  Vanish -- vamoose -- mosy -- go!

Tok Bak. You listen me! You beatee the big dlum
An' tell me to go Flowly Kingdom Come.
You all too muchee fool. You chinnee heap.
Such talkee like my washee -- belly cheap!

(*Enter* SATAN.)

You dlive me outee clunty towns all way;
Why you no tackle me Safflisco, hey?

Satan. Methought I heard a murmuring of tongues
Sound through the ceiling of the hollow earth,
As if the anti-coolie cues -- ha! friends,
Well met. You see I keep my ancient word
Where two or three are gathered in my name,
There am I in their midst.

Mountwave.   O monstrous thief!
To quote the words of Shakespeare as your own.
I know his work.

Hardhand.   Who's Shakespeare? -- What's his trade?
I've heard about the work o' that galoot
Till I'm jest sick!

Tok Bak.   Go Sunny school -- you'll know
Mo' Bible. Blime by pleach -- hell-talkee. Tell
'Bout Abel -- mebby so he live too cheap.
He mebby all time dig on lanch -- no dlink,
No splee -- no go plocession fo' make vote --
No spendee money out of clunty fo'
To helpee Ilishman. Cain killum. Josh
He catchee at it, an he belly mad --
Say: "Alle Melicans boycottee Cain."
Not muchee -- you no pleachee that:
You all same lie.

Mountwave. This cuss must be expelled. (*Drawing pistol.*)

Mountwave, Hardhand, Satan. (*Singing.*)
For Chinese expulsion, hurrah!

> To mobbing and murder, all hail!
> Away with your justice and law --
>   We'll make every pagan turn tail.

Chorus of Foreign Voters.

> Bedad! oof dot tief o'ze world --
> Zat Ivan Tchany vos got hurled
> In Hella, da debil he say:
> "Wor be yer return pairmit, hey?"
> Und gry as 'e shaka da boot:
> "Zis haythen haf nevaire been oot!"

Hardhand.

> Too many cooks are working at this broth --
> I think, by thunder, 'twill be mostly froth!
> I'm cussed ef I can sarvy, up to date,
> What good this dern fandango does the State.

Mountwave.

> The State's advantage, sir, you may not see,
> But think how good it is for me.

Satan.

> And me.

Curtain.

1876 -- Bret Harte and Mark Twain -- *Ah Sin*

Although a difficult play to grasp at first reading, *Ah Sin* marks an important step in the evolution of the stock Chinese character. As previously depicted in Bartley Campbell's *Across the Continent*, Joseph A. Nunes' *Fast Folks of California*, and Harte's own *Two Men of Sandy Bar*, this character was invariably a single Chinese man of menial status, who spoke broken English, behaved stupidly or outlandishly, and, most important, remained at the margins of both his society and the main plot of the play. *Ah Sin* retained all the characteristics of this stereotype except the last. Harte and Twain wrote their play with a particular actor in mind. His name was Charles T. Parsloe, and he had won great applause for his portrayal of a stock Chinese character in *Two Men of Sandy Bar*. The co-authors purposely made their Chinese character the center of their play, thus setting this piece apart from all previous and subsequent frontier melodramas. Although a daring step artistically, this may have doomed their effort to commercial and critical failure. It is unlikely that a theater audience assured of its own racial superiority would have been comfortable with Ah Sin's ability to determine the destiny and happiness of so many sympathetic Euroamerican characters.

There may have been other reasons for the play's failure as well. Neither Harte nor Twain had much sense of theatrical economy, so their play is a dense network of plot lines, interesting characters, and digressions. During its brief tour, *Ah Sin* underwent virtually constant revision by Twain, who remarked that the more he cut away, the more the play improved. All efforts to make it a success failed, however, and the script was thought for a long time to be lost. An amanuensis copy eventually surfaced; quite likely it was never performed exactly as reprinted here. Despite its critical and commercial failure in its own time, *Ah Sin* is an important historical document, and it has received some modern critical commentary.

Reprinted by permission of Richard A. Watson and Chase Manhattan Bank, as trustees of the Mark Twain Foundation, c/o Chamberlain, Willi, Ouchterloney & Watson, 15 Maiden Lane, New York, New York, 10038
Thanks also to the Mark Twain Collection (#6314), Clifton Waller Barrett Library, Special Collections Department, University of Virginia Library

Ah Sin

ACT 1ST.
Scene.

Music at rise of curtain. FERGUSON, BOSTON, MASTERS, 8 *others; miners discovered on side hill at work --* BRODERICK *discovered in foreground working on his claim. Animated picture -- when music stops,* BRODERICK *throws down rock impatiently.*

Broderick. Always the same! Red earth, pebbles, and black sand, but never a show of the yellow gold. I'm sick of breaking a half acre of stone to get half a loaf of bread out of it; and, like as not, I've prospected the whole hillside just to make way for some fool to strike his pick into the one lucky spot.

Ferguson. That's so! Blessed if I point another pick. (*Throws down his tool; some of the others stop work.*)

Broderick. But I say, lads -- if there's a scarcity of gold, there are fools enough in camp, and here comes one -- York! the gentleman capitalist, the dandy scientist!

Masters. Hang him!

Broderick. His gentility is an insult to the camp. As to his science! Well, hold on; maybe I might get something out of him there!

Enter YORK *R.1.E. in hunting costume with gun and game bag -- crosses towards L.2.E. not noticing* BRODERICK.

Broderick. Hallo, York!
York. (*Stopping angrily, aside.*) Confound his familiarity! (*Aloud, carelessly.*) Good morning! (*Going.*)
Broderick. (*Aside.*) Snob! (*Aloud, leaning on his pick.*) I suppose now you're ruffled at my hailing you that way?
York. (*Indolently.*) Oh no! Why should I be? It's vigorous and chaste --
Broderick. (*Impatiently, aside.*) Hang his airs! (*Aloud.*) You're looking for game -- so am I! Good! We'll swop information; now if I should tell you where you could flush a flock of quails in the chaparral yonder, perhaps you'd show me how to bag something out of this claim?
York. It is a fair offer, but you will excuse me if I plead press of time and decline it. Good morning. (*Exits L.2.E.*)
Broderick. Humph! I'll get even with this gilt-edged prig, one of of these days. (*Takes up a handful of dirt.*) Confound it, this thing that's called a pocket claim is nothing but just a lottery with a thousand blanks in it and one big prize. I might as well give up the game. I wonder if Plunkett's got anything to drink? (*Knocks on* PLUNKETT'S *door L.2.E.*) Nobody at home, I guess. (*Pushes open door and looks in.*) Hello, what's this? (*Reaches in and takes out photograph.*) York's picture, flattering likeness of the puppy too. What a mug it is. Great friends, Plunkett and York! A liar and a snob. (*Throws picture on stump.*) It's a well-matched team. (*Looking into cabin again.*) Next thing I oughter run across is a picture of old Plunkett's daughter that he brags so much about -- No, but I reckon here's the *original.* (*Takes out bottle and drinks -- smacks his chops.*) Fine girl! Charming girl! I'll bet something that this is the only child that the gabbling old humbug has got. (*Drinks again.*) Pity but the family was larger! (*Music -- crash R.H. as if carriage breaking down.*)
Boston. (*Coming down C. -- dropping shovel.*) Hello! Boys, what the mischief was that?
Masters. (*Dropping pick and running down the rocks.*) Boys, it's the stage coach broken down -- There go the horses -- Hi there, whoa! (*All the miners drop tools and run down rocks and off R.*)
Broderick. The stage coach broken down, eh? I'm glad of that; it

never brought *me* any good. Hello! (*Looks off R.1.E.*) There's that old liar Plunkett and with a woman in tow. I wonder who she is? One of his family come from the states may be. I don't want to meet any more of the Plunkett tribe. I'll step aside! (*Goes R.2.E.*)

Plunkett. (*Outside.*) This way, miss, look out for the mud there, that's it -- ah, here we are!

Enter PLUNKETT *and* MISS TEMPEST *R.1.E.*

Plunkett. (*L.*) The stage will be repaired in a short time and you'll be on your road again same as if nothing had happened. Don't worry a bit, miss.

Miss Tempest. (*R.*) Oh, I am so much obliged to you for your kindness. So this is the gold region, eh? Rather a desolate place to pass one's time, I should imagine.

Plunkett. Oh, it's pleasant enough here, miss; we have any quantity of amusement. Hardly a night passes but we have a ball, oysters and champagne suppers and all that --

Broderick. Lie number one for the old fool! Oh -- he'll sling his yarns now -- as many as she wants. (*Exits.*)

Miss Tempest. Indeed? But let me ask the name of him who has so befriended me.

Plunkett. Certainly, miss, with pleasure; indeed you honor me by asking the question. I am Abner Plunkett, pretty well known in this region, proprietor of the Goddess of Liberty Mine, yonder.

Miss Tempest. Ah, a rich one, I hope?

Plunkett. You've hit it the first time miss -- it's awful rich, miss -- ah, miss, I am afraid I have forgotten the name.

Miss Tempest. (*Laughing.*) It is *so* easy to forget what one does not know. I am Miss Tempest of San Francisco! (*Removing veil.*)

Plunkett. (*Amazedly.*) What! The rich Miss Tempest? The heiress of Judge Tempest; the famous belle?

Miss Tempest. (*Sighing.*) I am afraid you're right. I'm all that sort of thing.

Plunkett. But my dear young lady, this is no place for you -- Not, you understand, that anybody in Deadwood would dare to-- to-- to--

Miss Tempest. Pardon me, my good friend, if I continue my explanation. You see, when the stage broke down on the hill beside your camp, my maid was with me and we were both on our way to the next settlement. I think they call it -- (*X. L.*)

Plunkett. Columbia?

Miss Tempest. Exactly, Columbia -- to meet my father Judge Tempest, when you offered your help. I was glad of the opportunity of learning for myself something of the ways and manners of the miners and also glad, considering my unprotected state -- to find in the first one I met -- a gentleman.

Plunkett. Oh dear, miss, you flatter me -- If any scoundrel -- (MISS TEMPEST *furtively examines photograph on log R.C. Exhibits surprise, delight, and a purpose.*)

Miss Tempest. A moment, Mr. Plunkett; I think I can therefore trust to you keeping this episode a secret.

Plunkett. (*With effusion.*) You do me honor, miss; you do me great honor, and yet you only do me justice too. In the matter of keeping a secret, you can rely on Abner Plunkett as you'd rely upon a corpse -- an old corpse, miss -- a mummy!

Miss Tempest. I believe you. (*Aside.*) I wonder if I could trust the good-natured extravagance of this man?

Plunkett. You have never been in this locality before?

Miss Tempest. (*Glances at photo again.*) Yes, once. (*Looking around and after a moment's hesitation -- aside.*) I *will* trust him! (*Aloud.*) Two years ago, a brave man seized my runaway horses and saved my life. A crowd surrounded the carriage, and in the confusion the stranger spirited himself away without waiting to receive our thanks or even disclosing himself.

Plunkett. You saw him?

Miss Tempest. (*Languidly.*) Only for a moment -- (*Aside, sighing*) I wish I hadn't!

Plunkett. And he saw you?

Miss Tempest. No! That's the worst of it! It was dark in the carriage. He might at least have waited to know whether it was an old or a young woman he had saved. We advertised for the wretch but to no purpose.

Plunkett. A singular case, miss, but not without a parallel. Why, I remember once on the plains I stopped a vast herd of buffalo; two thousand, I should judge. They were dashing down on a carriage *full* of women and children -- I up with a big buck --

Miss Tempest. (*Hurriedly*) I know -- the policeman told me all about it -- But -- (*Picking up* YORK'S *picture from log.*) Who is this?

Plunkett. That -- ahem! (*Aside.*) York's picture. (*Aloud.*) That, Miss Tempest, is a -- a-- my son, my only boy --

Miss Tempest. Your son. (*Aside.*) I'm sure this is the likeness of the face I saw for an instant from the carriage window -- (*Aloud.*) Where is he? Does he belong here?

Plunkett. (*Complacently.*) No. He was here a year ago, but he's gone, and confidentially, miss, he is *engaged* to one of the finest and richest heiresses in New York.

Miss Tempest. (*Aside.*) This man's son! In New York and (*X.R.*) engaged. Can it be the same? Yet (*Looking at photo.*) this is the face. (*Aloud.*) Mr. Plunkett, I've taken a great fancy to your son's picture. Let me tax your generosity as I have taxed upon your kindness further -- give it to me -- you have the substance, let me have the shadow -- but stop -- let us make it a fair exchange. Here is my photograph. It flatters me, no doubt.

Plunkett. (*Inspecting it.*) Jingo! The living image! I will wear it next my --

Miss Tempest. There is a condition attached to this gift, a fancy of mine -- I want you to send this picture to your son the day he is united to--

Plunkett. Miss Grace Astor Livingstone of Madison Square, New York.

Miss Tempest. Miss Grace Astor Livingstone. It may not be able to recall to him the face of one to whom he once did a service, but you will assure him that gratitude for that heroic service and appreciation of his rare modesty have prompted me to send it. (*She goes downstage sadly.*)

Plunkett. (*Aside -- lays the picture down on board by his window L. H.*) Oh, the mischief! What have I done? (*Inspecting her furtively, aside.*) I wonder if she sees through my -- my bit of imagination and is chaffing me.

Miss Tempest. (*Aside and inspecting him furtively.*) I wonder if this son and this wildly promising mine aren't creations of the same prolific imagination? I must find out.

Enter BOSTON *R.1.E.*

Boston. The stage coach is ready, miss. (*Exits R.1.E.*)

Plunkett. If you will allow me, miss, I will see you safe in. (*Crossing to R.1.E.*)

Miss Tempest. Thanks with pleasure. (*Exeunt both R.1.E.*)

Re-enter BRODERICK *L.2.E.*

Broderick. I couldn't make out what that inspired liar was saying to the young lady -- no truth, I'll be bound -- (*Sees the photo of* MISS TEMPEST.) By Jingo, what a face -- a regular angel in a pullback and the latest Parisian fixins. If I could -- hell, here comes that everlasting Chinaman, of course. He's always around! (*Gets in L. corner.*) Pictures nor nothing else safe while the heathen's around. (*Puts picture in window.*)

Music. Enter AH SIN *carrying carpet bag and umbrella.*

Broderick. (*L.H.*) Here, you slant-eyed son of the yellow jaunders, what *you* been up to?

Ah Sin. Walkee bottom side hillee -- stage bloke down -- plenty smashee upee. Plunkee plenty helpee, plenty makee allee rightee -- Plunkee velly good man.

Broderick. Oh, very good man. When you see him, tell him I drank his whiskey to keep you from stealing it, you sinful old sluice robber -- shabbee that?

Ah Sin. Me no sabbee sluice lobber. Me washee-washee.

Broderick. (*Aside.*) If I leave that Chinaman here, he'll dip into Plunkett's cabin -- it's just like that godless race. Well, it will serve Plunkett right and teach him that his trust in these pagans is misplaced. (*Going,* AH SIN *following him.*)

Ah Sin. You wantee washee-washee? One dollar hap dozen -- me plenty washee you.

Broderick. (*Going.*) Get out, you jabbering idiot. (*Exits over rocks.*)

Ah Sin. Me no sabbee giblet -- (AH SIN *looks cautiously after* BRODERICK *and then returns to cabin and takes a drink, coughs.*)

Ah Sin. (*Spits out whiskey.*) No goodee, makee belly allee same like a fire. (*Goes to claim.*) Onee, twoee, fivee, 'levenee, eightee holee, muchee holee, no goldee. (*Takes up pick and commences to dig in* BRODERICK'S *claim.*) Too muchee workee, no good for Chinaman. (*Picks up a piece of gold and comes downstage jabbering Chinese.*) Come back tonightee, catchee plenty goldee, mally Ilish girl, go back to China. Allee same. (*Goes up and steals cup.*) Broderick, he come now. (AH SIN *sits down on log R.C. Re-enter* BRODERICK *L.4.E.*)

Broderick. You here yet -- you moral cancer, you unsolvable political problem -- what's up now?

Ah Sin. Waitee telly Plunkee you dlink whiskey so me no stealee him.

Broderick. Look here, my lad, there's a smell of sarcasm about that remark, perhaps there's more satire in your system. I'll shake it out of you before it *sours* -- (*Seizes and shakes* AH SIN, *the cup falls out, etc.*) Oh, you've been stealing, have you? (*Cuffs him with his open hand,* AH SIN *not resisting, only shielding his head with his arms.*)

Ah Sin. Me no stealee him -- cup he lay around loose, me pickee him up -- me good Chinaman.

Broderick. O certainly, of course you are a *very* good Chinaman! (*He beats him.*)

Ah Sin. (*Runs up rocks at back, jabbering frantically in Chinese.*) You wantee washee-washee? (BRODERICK *runs after him and both exit L.*)

Enter YORK *reading letter R.2.E.*

York. (*L.1.2.*) What the deuce has Plunkett got to write to me about? (*Reading.*) Only lend me this fifteen dollars and take the mine; I enclose deed. (*Enter* AH SIN.) Poor old Plunkett! And here (*Opening letter.*) is the deed that would make me heir to all this man's illusions. Well, well, I'm *mighty* sorry for the old man, but for this once I've *got* to refuse him -- fifteen dollars -- that's all I've got in the world; it costs me exactly that to order my new shirts; no money, no shirts. The old man's managed to borrow about all my old ones; I can't go *shirtless* to accommodate *any*body. Not a single penny *this* time, old fellow. (*Goes to cabin -- knocks.*) He is not here! (*Turning to drink from barrel -- sees* MISS TEMPEST'S *photograph in window.*) Hallo! By Jove, this is a strange flower to be found blooming here! What a lovely face! (*Continuing rapturously gazing on it -- looking*

furtively around.) It's like profanation but (*Kisses it.*) I do it rev--
(*Kisses it.*) reverently, oh, reverently, as if (*Kiss.*) it were a pagan's
idol and I were (*Kiss.*) the meanest and the humblest pagan among all
her host of adorers. (*Kiss.*)

Enter PLUNKETT, *who sees this last kiss.*

Plunkett. (*Aside.*) Hello, but he's got it *bad*, got the *picture*
too. Well 'ats all right, it *belongs* to him. (YORK *is still adoring
the picture and hasn't discovered* PLUNKETT.) But if he asks
questions, what'll I-- She told me to keep still about today's talk.
(YORK *discovers PLUNKETT and is confused.*)

York. Oh is that you? Tell me (*Feigning indifference.*), is this
yours?

Plunkett. That? Oh yes -- it's mine.

York. But, I mean, who does the *original* belong to?

Plunkett. (*With simplicity.*) Belongs to me.

York. (*Astonished.*) To *you?*

Plunkett. (*With unruffled calmness.*) Certainly. That is my
daughter.

York. Your daughter?

Plunkett. Of course. You've heard of me speak of my daughter
often. This is the one.

York. (*Trapped into animation.*) Why, she's divi-- a-- a--
(*Confused again.*) very good looking. (*Music.*)

Plunkett. Yes -- yes -- she's well enough, though nothing to
what her mother was at that age. Born rich, but didn't spoil her. She's
as lowly and as simple as a cauliflower. Say, how's stocks today?

York. Stocks? What kind of stocks?

Plunkett. What kind? Why, *mining* stocks of course -- the Mary
Ann, for instance.

York. (*Absently.*) Yes -- oh yes -- certainly. (*Intent on
picture, musingly.*) Oh, she's tip-top --

Plunkett. Top of the heap, hey? By George, I *said* it a week ago.
I *did* that very *thing*; now that's *beautiful.*

York. Oh, *most* beautiful.

Plunkett. Now all she wants is the right sort of *handling* -- but
she's never *had* it.

York. What! It isn't possible.

Plunkett. It's just as I tell you. Oh the leather-headedest job 't ever was.

York. And yet what a perfectly exquisite result. It seems incredible.

Plunkett. Well, it *does*. But it's *so*. First they'd *crowd* her every way they could think of for a spell --

York. Oh, that was so unwise -- and such a pity.

Plunkett. Yes, it was a pity -- and there wasn't any sense in it, and next they'd let up and just entirely neglect her for a spell.

York. Oh, shameful, brutal. (*Aside.*) Poor child; poor child!

Plunkett. That's just what *I* said. Brutal --*that* was my word; why, looky here, I'll tell you what they done once -- you see, they'd *sunk* on her about a thousand feet -- (YORK *begins to stare at him.*) straight down perpendicular -- (*Illustrating.*) an air shaft you know --

York. (*Interrupting.*) An air shaft?

Plunkett. Yes -- an air shaft --

York. An air --

Plunkett. (*Interrupting in a loud voice.*) Yes, an *air* shaft, you ass! Are you deaf? Sunk an air shaft on her 'bout a thousand feet, then they drifted south three hundred feet and couldn't find anything.

York. (*Idiotically.*) Couldn't *find* anything --

Plunkett. (*Loud.*) That's what I said -- couldn't *find* anything -- so they cut across from wall to wall -- she was about thirteen foot wide there-- and timbered her up so she wouldn't cave in -- just stopped her up, you know, till she was as empty as a jug -- and then what did these everlasting fools do but put in a *blast* -- 'bout two ton of nitroglycerine -- and by George, when that blast went off if it didn't lift her vitals! Well, sir, of *course* her hysting works were out of order.

York. (*Interrupting.*) *Who* are you talking about?

Plunkett. Who? I ain't talking about any who -- I'm talking about the Mary Ann.

York. The Mary Ann?

Plunkett. Yes -- the Mary Ann. Who'd you suppose I was talking about?

York. I supposed you were talking about your daughter. (*X.L.*)

Plunkett. (*Stares at him about a minute.*) What have you been eating?

York. I don't know. Why?

Plunkett. Well, it's -- well, it settled on your mind; if it had settled on your stomack 'twould a' *killed* you. But say, never mind my chaff -- I wouldn't hurt your feelings today. I've heard about you're being busted and I'm mighty sorry. Of course, I wouldn't said a word about borrowing money if I --

York. (*Interrupting eagerly.*) Not a word of that, not a word! It's a *pleasure* to me to lend it, a pleasure. (*Forcing the $15 on the reluctant* PLUNKETT.) There, take it -- Yes, I assure you I can spare it to *you.* (*X.L.*)

Plunkett. But --

York. But you *must* take it, for *her* -- for *my* sake. Now, not a word, not a word! (*X., aside.*) He's got a noble face. I can just begin to notice the resemblance now, but at *first* -- (*He is looking at the picture.*)

Plunkett. (*Interrupting.*) Put that in your pocket, York, if you want it.

York. Oh, thank you; thank you. (*Seizing both his hands.*)

Plunkett. (*With effusion.*) Don't mention it. Once more, York, you've done nobly by me. It's like you -- it's like you, York. Take the mine -- it is yours. You've got the deed. Thank Heaven it has fallen to one worthy of it. Come, come, take a drink on it and then we'll have a game of cards.

York. (*Xing R.*) You'll have to excuse me, I hardly ever drink and I don't know how to play. But I see your friend Broderick coming. Look out, old friend, and take good care of yourself. Don't be too friendly with that man.

Plunkett. Too friendly? I ain't.

York. And don't you quarrel with him either. He's got a bad eye, couple of 'em. Good night. (*Shake hands.*)

Enter BRODERICK *L.U.E. As* YORK *Xes stage he meets* BRODERICK *and the two look at each other,* YORK *sassily and whistling carelessly. Exit* YORK *gazing on picture.* BRODERICK *proceeds to gather up moodily his pick, shovel, etc.*

Plunkett. (*Aside R. H., observes him as he gathers up his tools.*) York's right -- it ain't wise and it ain't worth while to be quarrelling with a body's next door neighbor; poor devil, he's out of luck; looks a good deal cut up about his ratty old mine. (*Aloud.*) Here, Broderick, what's the use of our splitting up this way; an unpleasantness between two men like *us* can't have but one end. (BRODERICK *leans on his pick to listen.*) *Bloodshed* and *Death!* (BRODERICK *smiles amusedly.*) You know me -- you know what I am when I get started. You know what I did in the Mexican War.

Broderick. (*Comes down L.H., sarcastically.*) *Every*body knows it, Plunkett. We all know how you carved a regiment to pieces single-handed.

Plunkett. (*R., pleased.*) No -- but did *you* hear about that?

Broderick. (*L.*) Why, it's common talk in the camp, some of your other exploits too, like that one where you surrounded a battalion of the enemy all by yourself and took every man prisoner!

Plunkett. (*Still more pleased.*) By George, I didn't think a little circumstance like that would be remembered. But I did it! By the great hocus-pocus, I did that very thing. Lots of people that are dead now were there and saw me do it. (*Aside.*) Hang it, I begin to like Broderick.

Broderick. You are a dangerous man, Plunkett, this camp knows it. It is notorious that when you shouldered your gun in the War of 1812, England give in and hung out a white flag.

Plunkett. Well, upon my sacred honor, I supposed that these things were doubted --

Broderick. Doubted -- why, my dear friend, nobody ever doubts *your* word. The rivers of blood which you shed in the American Revolution --

Plunkett. (*With effusion.*) Confound it, Broderick, I've always misunderstood you, and I'm sorry for it. (*Rises up and approaches* BRODERICK.) Any amends I can make -- here -- we've both been in starvation luck lately and have about forgotten what a square meal is. But I've made a raise. (*Showing money.*) And if it'll be of any favor to you to divide, why divide it *is*.

Broderick. (*Aside.*) Oho, this is luck! Divide? Yes -- I'll borrow half and win the rest. (*Aloud.*) Plunkett, there's mighty good stuff in you. I've always said that; and if you don't mind lending me --

Plunkett. Here -- Help yourself, and welcome -- (*They divide.*) Come -- baptize the new dispensation. (*Gets bottle from cabin window. Passing bottle, they drink.*) Hang it, when I came over with Columbus, I --

Broderick. Oh, come!

Plunkett. Well, never mind about that. It wasn't a matter of any consequence anyhow. Columbus said if I had such a thing as a deck of cards about me --

Broderick. And had you?

Plunkett. My friend, would I start on a voyage to a degraded and savage land without the appliances of Christian civilization? *No* sir -- I *had* them.

Broderick. Got them yet?

Plunkett. Would I lightly throw away such a memento? (*Produces a greasy old deck.*)

Broderick. (*R.*) Yes -- I see, it's the same old pack -- would you like a little game of draw?

Plunkett. Man, I'm fairly suffering for it. (*They seat themselves. AH SIN comes on about now.*)

Broderick. Here -- cut for deal. (*They cut.*) My deal. (*He deals.*) Ante and pass the buck. (*They ante -- the buck is passed to* PLUNKETT.)

Plunkett. (*Examines hand.*) Give me three cards. (*Discards and takes them.*)

Broderick. My hand's no account. I'll take a book. (*Discards his hand and deals himself a new one; slips it under his thigh and fetches up another hand.*)

Ah Sin. Broderick hab got cold deck. Plunkee goodee me -- no likee see Broderick swindly him.

Broderick. What do you do?

Plunkett. I bet ten cents. (*Shoving up a dime.*)

Broderick. I see your ten and go you ten better. (*Shoving up a couple of dimes.*)

Plunkett. I raise you twenty-five --

Broderick. I call you -- what you got?

Ah Sin. Bimeby Plunkee pilee all gonee -- Plunkee he no got a cent.

Plunkett. Two pair and a jack -- what you got?

Broderick. Oh, nothing much -- *only* a trifling little diamond flush. (*Rakes in the money.*) Ante and pass the buck. (*They ante --* PLUNKETT *begins an elaborate shuffle of the cards. AH SIN betrays an intelligent purpose, shows revolver, slips out just as* PLUNKETT *has got the hands dealt out. AH SIN fires a shot outside. Both jump without looking at hands.*)

Broderick. What's that?

Plunkett. There's a man for breakfast! (*Exeunt both R.3.E.*)

Music -- Enter AH SIN *-- goes to table and looks at cards -- looks at* BRODERICK'S *hand.*

Ah Sin. Two littlee tenee -- two littlee twoee -- velly good hand. (*Looks at* PLUNKETT'S *hand.*) Two littlee fivee -- (*Disgusted.*) Some Mellican man no can deal -- don't know how. (*Goes upstage and shuffles cards -- watching off R. occasionally -- picks out four kings and gives them to* BRODERICK *and then gives four aces to* PLUNKETT.) Him all litee now. (*Looks about jabbering in Chinese, tries to put pistol in his waist, but not having time, puts it in the barrel and conceals himself. Re-enter* PLUNKETT *and* BRODERICK.)

Broderick. (*Resuming former position.*) Didn't you think you heard a shot? (*Looks at hand and shows furtive signs of delight which he immediately suppresses.*)

Plunkett. I *know* I heard it, and it wasn't twenty steps from where we're -- (*Aside.*) My soul, what a hand! (*Looks at his hand and shows signs of delight which he tries to suppress.*)

Broderick. (*Aside.*) Oh, but I'll sweat him this time, if I can only draw him on to bet.

Ah Sin. Broderick he likee hand, velly good hand -- Chinaman deal allee same like poker sharp.

Broderick. (*Dissimulating.*) Consarn it, I don't seem to have any luck. Give me four cards. (*Discarding.*) Never mind, no use to try to improve such a hand as this. (*Aside, exultingly.*) There ain't much lie about *that.* (*Takes back his discard.*)

Ah Sin. Him old smarty from Mud Springs.

Plunkett. (*Pretending disgust.*) Hang it all, this is just a specimen. I never *could* hold anything.

Ah Sin. Allee same Plunkee -- allee same -- he allee time plenty lyee.

Plunkett. I guess I'll take three cards -- I'll take four. (*Hesitating with discard in his hand.*) No, bother it all, I might draw all night and I couldn't better such a confounded hand as this. (*Aside.*) Oh, no, I reckon not.

Broderick. (*Aside.*) Now, old man, if you'll just stand up to the rack, I'll skin you of everything you've got in the world. (*Aloud, reluctantly*.) Well, I guess I'll go ten cents. (*Puts it up*.)

Plunkett. (*Reluctantly*.) Well, I don't know -- yes -- I'll do it. I see that and raise you twenty-five.

Broderick. Oh, you're there, are you! All right! I come in and *more*. I go a dollar better.

Plunkett. Oho, bluff's your little game, is it! You can't scare me with your little old deuces *and* I see your dollar and go you five better.

Broderick. I bet I *will* scare you; come, I see your five and go my pile better! Come in if you dare.

Plunkett. (*Getting excited.*) I see your pile and go you -- (*Looking around feverishly.*) go you my *clothes* better, every stitch I've got in the world.

Ah Sin. Plunkee he no gottee clothes, he no can take a walkee.

Broderick. Good, I see your rags and go you my pick, shovel, fuse, powder, cabin better.

Plunkett. (*Rising.*) I see it all, pick, shovel, fuse, powder, cabin, and go you my -- wife better.

Ah Sin. He got him now.

Broderick. I see your wife with my grandmother.

Ah Sin. Stand off.

Broderick. And go you my scurvy old Branch Bank of England mine better.

Ah Sin. De debbil! Dere go my rich mine.

Plunkett. (*Aside.*) I've sold my mine to York, but no matter. (*Aloud.*) I see your American Branch of the Bank of England and slap up my old Goddess of Liberty mine against it. I call you! What have you got?

Broderick. (*Throwing down hand.*) Ha! ha! ha! *Four kings*, beggar! What you got? (*About to rake in the pile.*)

Plunkett. *Four aces*, my child.

Tableau. The men stand and lean over staring into each others' faces. PLUNKETT'S *fingers slowly closing upon the pile and* BRODERICK'S *fingers retiring from it.* AH SIN *doing dumb show of enjoyment of it, and exits.*

Broderick. (*Sarcastically.*) I wish you joy of your winning. Take your new claim, and take it with all the heartbreak and trouble it has given me. If you get anything out of it but disappointment and despair, why, you've found another lead than I have.

Plunkett. Aye, old man, but the case has changed. That mine belongs to a lucky man now. (*Puts barrel and stools L.C.*) You understand? A *lucky* man, and before that luck gets cold I mean to try it once more. The moon is up and there's light enough to put in a pick, so I'll do it, if only to take formal possession. (*Goes to cabin and takes up pickaxe.*)

Broderick. (*Aside.*) The besotted old fool is really going. (*Aloud.*) All right, old man, go on, there are whole bonanzas of poverty and beggary down in that hole somewhere. Don't get disheartened, you won't have to dig deep to find them. (*Sarcastically.*) Why, a man of your luck ought to strike them in forty-eight hours. (*Aside.*) And with all my heart I hope he will. (*Exit R.1.E.*)

Plunkett. (*At mine.*) They say hereabouts that when a miner is at the point of making a strike, the blood leaves his cheeks, his heart stops beating, his hands are cold and his limbs grow weak. Pshaw, a few good blows will bring back warmth and strength. Eh! What's that? I thought I saw something moving by that tree. No, 'twas only a shadow. Well, here goes. (*Strikes pick deep in earth.*) The soil seems loose here. What! Why, what's this? (*Reaching down.*) I can't withdraw the pick -- it is wedged in a mass of something (*Tugging and grunting.*) so heavy -- that -- Here now -- quiet, old man, don't tremble so -- be steady. What -- yes -- a pocket! A fortune! Thank Heaven, I am a pauper no longer! (*Drops on his knees beside hole.*)

Broderick. (*Xing rapidly to C.*) Hold on there!

Plunkett. Hold?

Broderick. Strike another blow in that claim and you shall suffer for it.

Plunkett. You would not dare to --

Broderick. Dare! Do you think me so blind as not to see through this poor juggle? You stacked the cards there to win this from me.

Plunkett. (*L.*) It's a lie -- and you *know* it's a lie!

Broderick. (*R., starting.*) A lie -- You are an old man, don't tempt me.

Plunkett. Yes -- a lie! -- The whole camp shall know it.

Broderick. And if they *did*, who will believe the champion liar of Calaveras (*pronounced Cal-e-va-ras*) County against a man of truth? No, no, go home, old man, and I'll forgive you, and say nothing of this vile attempt at robbery. (*Music.*)

Plunkett. I am an old man, Silas Broderick -- But since I am -- I can more readily put the few years left me at stake to-night for my rights. Ho! York! Masters!

Broderick. Be still -- or I'll strangle you. (*Struggle continues -- downstage to table. In struggling,* PLUNKETT *falls, overturning barrel and pistol rolls out on floor --* PLUNKETT *seizes pistol and fires a single shot, missing* BRODERICK, *who wrests pistol from his hand.*)

Broderick. (*Aside.*) Another shot may alarm the camp! (*Aloud to* PLUNKETT, *who is rushing at him with stool upraised.*) Ah, will you! Take that! (*Striking* PLUNKETT *with the butt of pistol;* PLUNKETT *breaks from him and runs up to C. to rocks, calling "Help!" -- ""Help"* BRODERICK, *following, overtakes him -- and throws him over cliff C.*) What have I done! Plunkett! Plunkett! (*Looking down.*) No answer! Great Heaven, I have killed him. That shot will bring the whole camp here in five minutes. How to get away without suspicion? Oh, what's this? (*Looks down upon his jacket and looks around.*) Blood stains -- his blood! (*Strips off jacket.*) I mustn't be seen here with this -- I have it. (*Hides jacket in chaparral R.3.E.*) I'll return for it tomorrow. Ah, footsteps, a figure coming this way. (*Exit R.1.E. Enter* AH SIN *slowly -- goes to bush and gets jacket. Re-enter* BRODERICK.)

Broderick. That infernal Chinaman -- curse him; I must have that jacket or I am lost. If I could frighten him into silence or, better still, fasten the crime on him. Hello! John.

Ah Sin. Good day, John. You want washee-washee?

Broderick. Yes, I want some washing done, but look here --

Ah Sin. One dollar hap dozen.

Broderick. Yes, but you washee-washee, what?

Ah Sin. Me washee--washee *him.* (*Shows jacket.* BRODERICK *retreats downstage until he reaches the stump of tree R.H. and secures in his hand a pick, which he holds behind him as he cautiously approaches* AH SIN. AH SIN, *watchful of him, yet seemingly preoccupied, continues to draw articles from carpet bag, a few silver spoons, a chicken, a pair of stockings, a tablecloth, and finally, as* BRODERICK *approaches him closely and raises pick, a revolver which he cocks and accidentally as it were (chord) covers* BRODERICK *with it --* BRODERICK *halts and drops his pick noisily.*)

Broderick. (*C.*) Look here, Ah Sin, you're a smart fellow.

Ah Sin. Me sabbe smart.

Broderick. A right smart fellow, but if I took a fancy to one of those articles, that jacket, what would you say it was worth? Shabbee, John?

Ah Sin. (*L.*) No like sellee -- How much you give? (AH SIN *is still taking rubbish from the inexhaustible carpet bag all through this.*)

Broderick. Well, perhaps three hundred dollars might satisfy the owner.

Ah Sin. Me talkee with man jackee belongee.

Broderick. No -- you answer now.

Ah Sin. Me takee five hundred.

Broderick. Enough! I haven't got five hundred dollars -- but my share in the Heart's Delight mine is worth more than that -- will that do? (AH SIN *hands jacket to* BRODERICK.) It's mine. The river's the place for this. John, got any paper in that store house of yours?

Ah Sin. Yesee, me gotee everything.

Broderick. Here, tie this up for me; that's the proper thing to do when a man buys anything from you, eh? Ha! Ha! (*As* AH SIN *ties up package,* BRODERICK *goes upstage and picks up stone.*) Here, put this stone in to make it seem as if it was something valuable! Put a string around it.

Ah Sin. Stlingee costee too much money. Ten cent for stlingee.

Broderick. I won't pay for the string.

Ah Sin. No hab got ten cent for stling? Then me lend um stling. (*Ties up bundle, and gives him the package --* BRODERICK *unseen by* AH SIN *throws package in river. Significantly:*) Good day and goodbye, Ah Sin. (*Going R.*)

Ah Sin. Goodbye, John. You satisfly?

Broderick. Yes, perfectly satisfied!

Ah Sin. No go back on Chinaman?

Broderick. (*Laughing.*) Not likely to! (*Exit.*)

Ah Sin. Me satisfly too! (*Comes downstage, fumbles at sleeve, drops cards, which he puts his foot on, fumbles at his sleeve and finally produces bloody jacket, furtively looking around.*) He forgettee jackee!!

(*Ring quick on word.*)
Curtain.

ACT 2ND.
Scene.

Lapse of 3 months. Deadwood. The Chinese quarters. Rude board table on rocks, on which are piled shirts, etc., on river bank. Music -- AH SIN discovered -- song -- speech. Business -- ironing, etc. Enter YORK looking at his watch.

York. (*L.2.E.*) Three o'clock! In my impatience I'm here before the stage coach -- Why, there's Ah Sin! Poor chap, since the mysterious disappearance of Plunkett, he has withdrawn himself from the camp. I wonder if he hasn't a pretty good notion of what went with him? If I could only make him talk -- I've got it. I'm wanting a servant -- a good excuse for pumping him -- (*Aloud and going upstage.*) Ah Sin!

Ah Sin. Good day, John.

York. (*C.*) Good day.

Ah Sin. You wantee washee-washee?

York. (*Aside.*) Confound him, his only belief is in the universal uncleanliness of the American people. (*Aloud.*) I say, John, do you know what's 'come of Plunkett?

Ah Sin. Me sabbee. Maybe Plunkee go with pretty lady.

York. No -- no -- washee to-day, John. But I'm looking for a servant, a good honest Chinaman, to be a head waiter at my ranch. You know the kind of man I want.

Ah Sin. All litee. Me sabby. Mellican man too muchee chin-chin, Chinaman plenty workee.

York. (*With great significance, looking at* AH SIN.) I have sent for the wife and daughter of your friend and benefactor, Plunkett. I have sent for them to come here so I might have some excuse for ferreting out the reason of his disappearance; you understand? (*Aside.*) His face is as unintelligible as a tea chest. (*Aloud.*) Well, I have determined to offer my house to these helpless women. (*Aside.*) No delight, no satisfaction, and yet his poor old benefactor would have *fought* for him. Well, it is the gratitude of the heathen.

Ah Sin. Missee Plunkee go to you.

York. Yes, and with this addition to my household, I shall need another servant, you sabbee?

Ah Sin. Me sabbee -- me sabbee -- Velly good man fo' you -- Velly good man fo' Missee Plunkee.

York. Suppose *you* take the place.

Ah Sin. Me washee-washee -- Pay better.

York. You can washee-washee all the same. Shan't want you except at meals.

Ah Sin. Me sabbee meal time -- Chinaman likee meal time. You pay six dollar a week?

York. Yes -- Is it a bargain?

Ah Sin. All litee, John, I come to-morrow noon -- no can come to-day.

York. (*Going.*) That's bad, but I'll get along some way. (*Aside.*) I've done a good strike! (*Goes up.*)

Ah Sin. (*Aside.*) May be me mighty poor servant -- don't know how. Well, me watchee-watchee -- do everything see Mellican man do -- pretty soon me learnee -- (*Goes into house.*)

Enter BRODERICK *and* MINERS *L.U.E.*

Broderick. (*Stopping.*) Boys, I've changed my mind.

1st Miner. What's the matter *now*?

Broderick. It's not fair for me to help question Ah Sin. I *hate* him; I'd see something suspicious in every answer he made.

2nd Miner. You're over-squeamish, Broderick. You were *sound* when you suggested this examination of him, and as for *hating* the Chinaman, why --

3rd Miner. (*Interrupting.*) Now you hold on. That's *manly* in Broderick. *I* say, let's 'tend to it ourselves.

1st and 2nd Miners. *All* right. (AH SIN *re-enters.*)

Broderick. (*Going -- aside.*) That wasn't badly done! (*Exits.* YORK *comes down.*)

1st Miner. (*To* AH SIN.) Looky here, my boy, there's a considerable suspicion around that *you* know what's become of old Abe Plunkett.

Ah Sin. No sabbee 'splicion. Me got 'gagement. Me go. (*Going.*)

2nd Miner. (*Restraining him.*) *No*, you ain't *going*, either. Things look bad *ugly* 'gainst you.

1st Miner. You bet they do.

York. (*Returning.*) Suspicions against *him*? What *are* they?

2nd Miner. What are they? -- (*Pause -- a little puzzled.*) Why, they are *suspicions*, of course.

York. But -- I mean the *particulars*.

2nd Miner. Well -- a -- he -- a -- he -- (*To* 3RD MINER) W--was there any particulars?

3rd Miner. Well, -- he -- a -- as I understand it, he -- a -- Oh, *this* ain't no time for conundrums!

2nd Miner. (*Relieved.*) That's the talk! You just come along, Ah Sin. If particulars is wanted, I judge we can milk 'm out of you with a rope's end, maybe.

Ah Sin. (*Taking refuge behind* YORK.) Me not done nothing, me good Chinaman.

York. If Ah Sin is suspected, let the law officers take up his case.

1st Miner. We can 'tend to his case ourselves.

York. There is no occasion. It is the law's business -- leave him to the law.

1st Miner. But don't I tell you we ain't *going* to leave him to the law.

York. I must insist -- If you take him I shall appeal to the law in his behalf. Your suspicion seems to be only a misty one at best.

3rd Miner. Come to look at it, it's *so*, boys.

2nd Miner. Rot it, *I* thought we had *particulars*, but I don't seem to see what's become of 'em. (YORK *signals* AH SIN *to slip away, which he does and exits into house.*)

1st Miner. Looky here -- let's go and get 'em -- and *then* take him.

2nd Miner. All right. Now, Ah Sin, you stay here till -- Why, he's gone. Mr. York, did you send him off?

York. He has only gone on an errand.

1st Miner. Mr. York, if Ah Sin escapes, you might wish you hadn't taken so much on yourself.

York. That may be, and may not. I'm willing to risk it. (*Exit R.1.E. The* MINERS *move off consulting together.*)

2nd Miner. It's just as you say -- It *is* sort of queer conduct on York's part. Blamed if it ain't. (*Exit* MINERS.)

Enter JUDGE TEMPEST *from rear R.4.E.*

Judge Tempest. (*C.*) Bother these mountain roads -- I wish I had taken the public coach and paid no attention to Mrs. Tempest's aristocratic requirements; she and Shirley must take the consequences for a while. Now I have only ten minutes to catch the up stage to keep my appointment at Fiddletown. What's to be done? Hang it, Ah! (*Looking around.*) Ah, here's a Chinaman -- I say, John.

Ah Sin. How do, John.

Judge Tempest. Do you know a Mr. York hereabouts?

Ah Sin. Me sabbee York, velly well.

Judge Tempest. (*Aside -- with impatience.*) The imperturbability of these Chinamen is insufferable. (*Aloud.*) Well, come here!

Ah Sin. You want washee-washee?

Judge Tempest. (*Furiously.*) No! Confound your washee-washee! Come here, I say. (AH SIN *slowly shuffles forward.*) Do you see that hill? (*Pointing.*)

Ah Sin. No sabbee hillee. Me washee-washee.

Judge Tempest. (*Seizing him by the collar.*) Blockhead! Look! There -- look! The other side of that hill lives Mr. York. Take him this note and you shall have -- a dollar. (*Handing note.*)

Ah Sin. Sabbee dollar.

Judge Tempest. (*Sarcastically.*) Of course you do!

Ah Sin. Mellican man no sabbee dollar?

Judge Tempest. What the mischief does he mean? Pshaw! Well, tell him the ladies are awaiting him on the summit of the hill. (*Blows horn.*)

Ah Sin. Mellican man plenty blowee hornee -- got some fish.

Judge Tempest. Hang it, there's the coach; why the devil don't you go? (*Hesitates, looking at* AH SIN, *who is regarding note quietly.*) Go, at once! (*Exit hurriedly, L.U.E.*)

Ah Sin. Bigee foolee, wantee Chinaman walkee-walkee -- Walkee-walkee topside hillee no good for Chinaman. York say he come bimeby -- all litee -- me waitee. (*Looking off.*) Mellican lady comee -- Plunkee wife -- Plunkee daughter, maybe --- me watchee all litee, John. (*Exits into house.*)

Enter MRS. TEMPEST *and* MISS TEMPEST *R.3.E.* MRS. TEMPEST *sinks exhausted on rock-bank L.*

Miss Tempest. (*C.*) I can go no farther; of all the insane projects of your father, this transcends everything. The idea of leaving us here!

Miss Tempest. (*L.C.*) I'm glad our carriage came to grief. It's so awfully romantic and all that sort of thing. Here we are, two helpless women waiting for a *man* to turn up.

Mrs. Tempest. (*Angrily.*) It's perfectly exasperating!

Miss Tempest. Well, you have no one to blame but father and yourself. It was all his fantastic idea that we should spend a day or two with this dreadful prodigy of his -- this poetical miner, this elegant stonebreaker -- this Mr. York.

Mrs. Tempest. My child -- why do you permit yourself to hate a man you have never seen?

Miss Tempest. Why am I asked to be *interested* in a man I have never seen? Mother, do you think I'm an imbecile? Do you think I don't know that this man, York, is the eligible person whom you have picked out for me? Do you think I have not fathomed the reason for Papa's discreet absence? For your own discreet *presence* on this occasion?

Mrs. Tempest. Heaven help the child! Why, he is the dear friend of your father. And you, why, you were willing enough to come a day or two ago.

Miss Tempest. (*Aside -- sighing.*) That was because I expected to find the original of my photograph -- Eh -- what -- (*Looking out at L.*)

Mrs. Tempest. (*Not noticing her daughter*) You must remember too, that this Mr. York -- has been to this moment, unadvised of our arrival. He has hardly got the note yet, which your father said he would send him.

Enter AH SIN -- *observing* YORK *coming -- and tearing up letter.*

Ah Sin. York come now, no goodee he catchee letter now. (*Exits R.2.E.*)

Enter YORK *L. U. E.*

York. (*Aside and starting.*) Heavens! 'tis she -- and the living image of the photograph! Plunkett has not lied! (*Business -- coming forward -- aloud.*) A thousand pardons, ladies, but surely the stage has arrived early -- I did not expect you for twenty minutes. (*Both ladies recoil.*)

Miss Tempest. (*Aside.*) 'Tis he! (*Aloud.*) The *stage*? There's some mistake. (*Keeps* MRS. TEMPEST *back with her hand.*)

York. (*With grave politeness, perceiving her perplexity.*) Pardon me, but I have not introduced myself yet. I am Henry York of Deadwood, at your service -- your correspondent, who invited you to visit the house of your father. (*Perceiving still further consternation among the ladies.*) I mean -- of course the house of your *late* father! (*Aside -- observing greater consternation.*) There, I've done it -- why the devil did I drag the missing father in?

Mrs. Tempest. (*Coming forward.*) But, my dear sir, we are --

Miss Tempest. (*Xes to C. -- holding her back.*) You must excuse her; the fatigues of the long journey have exhausted her. (*Aside.*) Be quiet, mother.

York. (*R. confusedly.*) I presume I am addressing the original of this photograph? (*Shows photo.*)

Miss Tempest. (*C. advancing and looking at photo.*) You are, sir.

Mrs. Tempest. (*L. struggling to get forward -- but held back by* MISS TEMPEST.) But really, I --

York. (*Apologetically.*) Then, Miss Plunkett, I ask your pardon again for reviving distressing memories. Let me beg you to allow me to withdraw a moment while I order a carriage to take you to your late father's home. (*Exits L.1.E.*)

Mrs. Tempest. (*Impulsively.*) What is the meaning of this masquerade?

Miss Tempest. Only this, he has mistaken you for the wife, and me for the daughter, of the gentleman who once befriended me here. I told you all about it. (*Aside.*) I didn't tell her who I mistook *him* for.

Mrs. Tempest. (*In alarm.*) But, my child, he will return in a moment and discover the mistake.

Miss Tempest. Not if you will help me. (*Going downstage.*) Mother, I've always been a good girl, haven't I?

Mrs. Tempest. Well -- perhaps a trifle wild and wayward and inconsiderate for one of your position. But, yes --

Miss Tempest. And my vagaries, as you call them, have never brought me to any harm?

Mrs. Tempest. Humph! -- Not as yet!

Miss Tempest. Then hear me. There's a little mystery here deeper than you see on the surface. I want to get to the bottom of it. (*Aside.*) I must know how he got that photograph. (*Aloud, emphatically.*) Mother, for twenty-four hours, at least, you must be Mrs. Plunkett.

Mrs. Tempest. (*Astonished.*) But, my child --

Miss Tempest. Calm your chaste emotions, my dear mother. There is no implied disloyalty to Judge Tempest. Your doting husband Mr. Plunkett is missing.

Mrs. Tempest. This is intolerable --

Miss Tempest. One moment, mother. You wish me to accept the hospitality of Mr. York. I will on only one condition -- that I shall do it as Miss Plunkett.

Mrs. Tempest. But what will this lead to?

Miss Tempest. To the arrival of my father a day later, and an explanation of this harmless sport; nothing more.

Mrs. Tempest. But if I should consent to entertain this folly, what am I -- what am I to call you? What is your Christian name?

Miss Tempest. He will furnish that. He will let that slip sometime. Meantime, dear mother, call me "My child," "My daughter," or (*Embracing her.*) "My darling." (*Aside.*) He'll understand *that.* (*Coquettishly.*)

Mrs. Tempest. Well, well --- of all your follies --

Miss Tempest. This may prove the most practical -- but hush -- here he is -- (*Re-enter* YORK.)

York. (*Bowing.*) A carriage is waiting for you at the foot of the hill. Ladies, let me lead the way for you. (*Exeunt omnes L.U.E. Music. Enter* AH SIN.)

Ah Sin. Plunkee got two wifee -- Mellican man no likee Chinaman hab two wifee -- Chinaman no likee wifee, sell wifee -- poor wifee got no home -- Mellican man no likee wifee, lun away, let poor wifee starve -- Mellican man too muchee -- clivilized. More Mellican lady comee -- me watchee. (*Goes to table and lights pipe -- sits.*)

Enter the PLUNKETTS *R.3.E.*

Mrs. Plunkett. (*Snuffling.*) My poor Plunkett! My poor, dear, sainted husband. (*L.*) Like enough this lovely scene was the very last his dear eyes ever tackled. (*Sobs.*)

Miss Plunkett. (*R.*) My, but this Californy's the land for me. I reckon there's no end of gold here, and fellows that want to get married! (MISS PLUNKETT *has gone upstage and looks at clothes on line -- then looks at a pair of shoes hanging up -- AH SIN goes to line, and snatches away shoes -- puts them in house.*)

Mrs. Plunkett. (*Continuing her rhapsody.*) No doubt he has set on these rocks a many and a many a time -- (*Stoops slightly and kisses the rock reverently.*) Roosted here and smoked his pipe and darned his socks and ate his beans and thought about us, so far away, and cried. (*Sobs.*)

Miss Plunkett. Fellows with loads of cash. Becky Simpson hadn't been to Californy a week 'till she married a hundred thousand dollars, with considerable of a man thrown in.

Mrs. Plunkett. (*Still sobbing and rhapsodizing.*) Dear me, dear me, to think *his* gaze has gazed on that cabin there and the mountains over beyond and maybe that mule yonder -- Maybe he *knowed* the mule, personally -- he was always fond of 'em, and as for jackasses -- Oh, they were like own brothers to him. (*Sobs.* AH SIN *has been poking around in the rear for awhile, observes that* MISS PLUNKETT *has dropped her handkerchief. He swipes, wanders away, puts it up his sleeve.*)

Miss. Plunkett. I wonder what sort of a man is this York that's sent for us? Like enough he's rich and wants us here so as to marry me, or mother!

Mrs. Plunkett. Poor dear, poor dear -- how it all comes back to me. The last time I saw him -- thirteen years ago. Little did I think when I shied the skillet at his head that it would be the last time I (*Sobs.*) I should ever see him dodge. When he said he was going away for ever and ever, little did I think that for the first time in his life his tongue missed fire and he was telling the truth. My child, my child. (*To her daughter.*)

Ah Sin. Plunkee got two childee -- heap difference -- other one high steppee stock -- 2:40 stock; this one plenty common stock, hossee car stock.

Mrs. Plunkett. Do you hear me?

Miss Plunkett. Yes, I hear you -- I hear you, mother, but I'm trying to study up whether that Mr. York's letters ever said whether he was rich or not, or whether --

Mrs. Plunkett. Oh, my child, how can you be so worldly when the whole scene is reeking with suggestifications of your poor, dear father, so to speak?

Miss Plunkett. Oh, bother all that, mother, *I* never saw him in my life -- Well, of course I *saw* him, but I don't think I ever had a real good look at him, you kept him humping around so!

Mrs. Plunkett. What do you mean, child?

Miss Plunkett. Well, you always had him up a tree or shinning for shelter under the bed. He wasn't ever still long enough for me to get acquainted with him.

Mrs. Plunkett. (Severely.) It is shameful -- shameful to hear a daughter talk like this, right here where the lastest -- Oh, if his dear spirit is here --

Miss Plunkett. But it ain't, mother. And it wouldn't stay if it was. And *I'm* not going to stay here either. Much Mr. York cares to meet us! Said he would be on hand when the stage came. *This* looks like it. *(X.R. -- to* AH SIN.) Young man, do you know Mr. York?

Ah Sin. (To MISS PLUNKETT.) Good day, John.

Miss Plunkett. (Indignantly.) My name is not John.

Mrs. Plunkett. (Chipping in.) A very dear and noble friend of my poor lamented husb --

Miss Plunkett. (Impatiently.) Never mind about that.

Ah Sin. Yes, me sabbee York.

Miss Plunkett. Well, he is expecting us. Doesn't know we have arrived? Would you mind going to find him?

Ah Sin. Can find in a minute, -- no hab got hap dollar for Chinaman? (MISS PLUNKETT *is looking around for her handkerchief.*) No hab got no can find -- *(To* MISS PLUNKETT.) You losee littee something, eh?

Miss Plunkett. (Gladly.) Yes. Did you pick it up? Give it to me!

Ah Sin. Know littee something if you see him?

Miss Plunkett. Certainly I'll know it. I could pick it out from among a million. Give it here.

Ah Sin. Maybe he belong to gentleman, no lady.

Miss Plunkett. Perfectly absurd -- any idiot could tell at a glance that it couldn't belong to a gentleman; I tell you it's mine! (AH SIN *gives* MISS PLUNKETT *a stocking rolled up and exits --* MISS PLUNKETT *lets it unroll -- flings it from her with a shriek and is about to faint -- when --*)

Miss Plunkett. Oh my, here comes Mr. York now: anyhow, somebody's coming -- (*Begins to furbish up her spitcurls and arrange her dress.*) Nice enough looking man -- Mother, we needn't seem to see him -- let *him* make the advances.

Enter BRODERICK L.U.E.

Broderick. (*Aside.*) They're not back *yet*! *Why* didn't I load them with particulars in the first place! (*Starts violently and shakes as with an ague.*) What was that! -- Nothing, nothing. Every sound blanches my cheeks and racks me with fear. Why, who are *these*? (*Regains his composure and steps forward C. -- lifts his hat.*) I see you are strangers, ladies, can I assist you in any way?

Miss Plunkett. (*L. aside.*) So it ain't Mr. York. (*Aloud.*) If you will be so kind. We are the wife and daughter of the late Abner Plunkett, who disappeared -- (BRODERICK *starts.*) Why, what is the matter, sir?

Broderick. (*Annoyed.*) Oh, nothing, nothing -- (*X.C.*)

Mrs. Plunkett. (*L.*) But you've turned so pale. Here -- take a smell of this -- (*Forcing smelling bottle on him.*) it'll fetch you. There -- I told you so.

Broderick. (*C. strangling -- aside.*) Oh, curse her. (*X.L.*)

Mrs. Plunkett. There now, set down a minute and you'll be all right again, sir.

Broderick. (*They both speak at once.*) Oh, it isn't necessary --

Mrs. Plunkett. I know them turns. If my poor husband was here (BRODERICK *shows signs of discomfort.*) -- but, poor dear soul (*Snuffling.*), he can't ever come anymore, for it's my belief some scoundrel murdered -- You *must* sit down, sir, you must indeed -- it's coming on worse'n ever. (*The ladies assist BRODERICK to a log L. and sit down one on each side of him.*)

Miss Plunkett. (*Aside.*) Goodness, what diamonds! Why this man must just simply roll in money. If he ain't married, I -- (*Aloud with a feeling look.*) If we knew where to send for your wife --

Broderick. I haven't any, ma'am.

Miss Plunkett. (*Dumb show of satisfaction -- aside.*) That took! (*Aloud.*) How sad at such a time to have no -- (*With a tender glance.*) Perhaps you are chilled -- will you let me -- (*She turns up his coat collar on the side that is toward her.*)

Mrs. Plunkett. (*Aside.*) Poor dear, to be in this state, and not got any pardner -- (*Aloud.*) You must take good keer of yourself when you have these turns -- Mayn't I -- (*She turns up her side of his coat collar -- she receives a covert savage glance from her daughter and returns it with interest.*)

Broderick. I'm a good deal better, now, thank you. Let me walk a little -- It will refresh me. (*Rises and walks -- aside.*) Vulgar cattle!

Miss Plunkett. (*Aside.*) He'll do.

Mrs. Plunkett. (*Aside.*) Poor thing, he needs a pardner, bad --

Broderick. (*Aside.*) It wasn't a false report then. York *has* sent for these people -- Damn him! They must not get into his hands -- I must get them into mine. (*Aloud -- coming forward.*) Ladies, your references to Mr. Plunkett, who was my dear bosom friend, have so affected me that I almost forgot I had a pleasant duty to perform by you.

Mrs. Plunkett. You, sir?

Broderick. Yes, my name is Broderick -- of whom your father may have spoken in his letters. My friend and neighbor, Mr. York --

Miss Plunkett. *Our* friend too; he is expecting us.

Broderick. Yes, I am aware of it. But he was called suddenly away from the camp an hour ago on business of the last importance, and he asked me to offer you the hospitalities of my house for a few days, until his return. Will you do me the honor, and the great pleasure, to accept?

Miss Plunkett. (*Aside.*) This *is* luck! (*Rising.*)

Mrs. Plunkett. (*Aside -- piously -- rising.*) Hear that! I do believe 'twas preforeordestinated beforehand! Because he needed a pardner.

Miss Plunkett. It is too generous of you, Mr. Broderick. If you are sure that we won't discommode --

Mrs. Plunkett. It's too generous, it is indeed. Why, it's like entertaining angels unawares. But if you are sure we won't disfranchise your arrangements?

Broderick. (*X.C.*) Don't mention it -- don't mention it, ladies. I shall be glad to throw my doors open to those who were dear to my old neighbor. I shall be only too selfishly grateful to replace the loneliness of my habitation with the cheerfulness of your society. Allow me to lead the way -- (*Bows himself out before them -- aside.*) Oh, this is the luckiest stroke! (*Exit L.U.E.*)

Miss Plunkett. (*Aside.*) Oh, if he were built of sugar, he couldn't wag a sweeter tongue.

Mrs. Plunkett. (*Aside -- piously.*) I feel as if I am going like a lamb to the slaughter.

MRS. *and* MISS PLUNKETT *exit L.U.E. Enter* AH SIN -- *picks up stocking and goes to table --* PLUNKETT *enters from house.*

Ah Sin. (*Pushing* PLUNKETT *into house.*) Go inee, go inee. Go to bedee -- I fetchee ginee -- (*Hands in gin.*) You wife catchee, you catchee plenty hellee -- (*Sits -- fills cup and drinks.*) Muchee goodee ginee -- me likee ginee -- Mellican men dlink whiskey -- Ilish man dlink whiskey, makee muchee go whoop (*Throws up his arms and loses cup.*) -- makee plenty fightee. (*Goes to fill cup and finds it gone.*) Allee same. (*Drinks from bottle.*) -- Me got nufee; Chinaman know when got nufee -- Some Mellican man no can tell. (*Puts away bottle.*) Feelee goodee, feelee allee same likee angel. (*Head nods.*) No can keep eye up -- me wantee go bye-bye. (*Stands up -- staggers to C. and then back to table -- gets up on table and goes to sleep. Music.*)

Enter FERGUSON, BOSTON, MASTERS, *and other* MINERS *excitedly L.U.E.*

1st Miner. Let's hang the scoundrel -- the yeller brute. (*All looking around excitedly for* AH SIN.)

Ferguson. Here he is --

Omnes. Drag him out -- Lynch him, etc. (*They drag* AH SIN *to C.*)

Ah Sin. Me no sabbee.

1st Miner. Come, it's no use your playing ignorance on this camp any longer --

Ferguson. (*R.*) You won't get off for want of particulars this time.

Ah Sin. Me no sabbee tickler.

Boston. You and York were last seen together in Plunkett's company.

Ah Sin. Me no sabbee Plunkee.

Ferguson. String him up. (*All make a movement.*)

1st Miner. Come, you know something about Plunkett, out with it! (*Threatens him.*)

    Ah Sin. Me no sabbee Plunkee.

    1st Miner. Here's York's pistol.

    2nd Miner. Found today on the river bank below the claim.

    Ferguson. You must know something about it.

    Omnes. Yes -- of course! (*All turn on* AH SIN.) Make the Chinaman confess what he knows of the affair --

    1st Miner. Look, here, John, you know all about Plunkett -- out with it or you'll swing with *York.*

    Ah Sin. Me no likee swingee -- swingee no good for Chinaman.

    Omnes. Out with it.

    Boston. You've got to talk.

    Ferguson. Yes, or hang.

    1st Miner. Talk and hang *both!* (*They all make a dive for* AH SIN *who scrambles between their legs and upsetting one or two of them -- jumps on table, seizes flat iron, shrieking and gibbering Chinese. Picture of consternation by miners. Quick curtain.*)

ACT 3RD.
Scene.

    Broderick. The suspicion against Ah Sin wouldn't stick. *Why?* Well, I suppose they want higher game. Very well. It's York or me, now; and the best man wins. I've got them started on his trail and everything seems to promise pretty well But what of it? To hang York will only give me *safety.* Nothing more. I am afraid, nothing more. There is that on my soul that will never wash --

Enter AH SIN.

    Ah Sin. (*Interrupting with a scream.*) Wash! Me washee-washee. You want wash?

    Broderick. (*Aside.*) Well, *safety* is *something.* I wish the evidence were a trifle stronger. I've got an idea -- in the egg -- and ready to hand, here is one of the devil's own chickens to hatch it. (*X.L. -- aloud.*) Here, Ah Sin, you remember my buying a certain jacket of you once?

    Ah Sin. Yes, me lemember.

    Broderick. Do you think you could furnish me a jacket of *York's* in the same condition as that one was?

Ah Sin. (*Aside -- X.L.*) What Mellican man up to, hey?

Broderick. You don't answer. (*X.R.*)

Ah Sin. (*Thoughtfully.*) Me got plenty jacket to wash fo' York, but no got any blood on 'em.

Broderick. Put it on, then! This is no time for mincing speeches. Come -- quick -- I'll give you three hundred dollars.

Ah Sin. (*Hesitating.*) -- Heap money -- heap money -- but --

Broderick. Five hundred! Is it a bargain?

Ah Sin. All litee, John. Me do it.

Broderick. (*Shakes hand.* AH SIN *surreptitiously wipes his hand on blouse, with the faintest perceptible show of disgust, which* BRODERICK *does not see.*) Good Chinaman! You shan't repent this. Now prepare that jacket at once -- bring it to me in your carpet sack quick as you possibly can. Go -- go!

Ah Sin. (*Going.*) All litee, John. (*Aside.*) Me quit washee-washee. Too slow. No pay. Me sellee bloody jackee all time. How me catchee blood -- me stealee chicken! (*Exits.*)

Enter FERGUSON, BOSTON, *and* 1ST MINER, *R.U.E.*

Broderick. You're too early, boys. I think you must be on the wrong track, *any*way.

Boston. I bet we ain't. York's the man! The minute you dropped that remark about him I *said* so -- didn't I, boys?

Ferguson. Yes; and didn't I?

1st Miner. And I too?

Broderick. Well, I'm sorry now I said anything if it has turned suspicion upon poor York. *I* never should have been acute enough to see what an ugly look that circumstance had.

Boston. I saw it in a minute.

Ferguson. So did I.

Broderick. I had supposed you were founding your suspicions upon some conduct of his when you wanted to question Ah Sin.

Boston. Oh, no!

1st Miner. No, nothing suspicious there.

Broderick. I though maybe his taking so much pains to shield the Chinaman and get him away --

Ferguson. (*Interrupting.*) Why *here*! I'd *forgotten* that! Don't you remember, boys, we *said* it was mighty queer conduct of York's!

Boston. Certainly! Remember it perfectly well, now.

1st Miner. Yes, indeedy. Come to put this and that together --

Ferguson. (Interrupting.) It looks worse and worse for Mr. *Y.*

Boston. Come along, boys, my mind's made up. We'll just *go* for *him.*

1st Miner. He's around here *some*where.

Broderick. Now, boys --

Ferguson. (Interrupting.) 'Tain't any use, Brod. He's the *man*; we ain't agoing to be argued *out* of it. (*Exit all R.U.E.* BRODERICK *rubbing his hands with satisfaction.*)

Enter MRS. TEMPEST *from L.2.E.*

Mrs. Tempest. Dear, dear me, what a muddle I'm getting into, representing another person, good heavens, what will I do when all is discovered? Well, Shirley drove me into the masquerade, and when the time comes to remove the masks she must stand the brunt of it. (*Goes to flower stand L. -- Music -- Enter* AH SIN *with dishes which he places on stump of tree, busies himself at table --* MRS. TEMPEST *observing him.*) So it seems Mr. York has made another addition to his domestic menagerie -- I hope this one is an improvement on the others, but he is a Chinaman after all and it's but hoping against hope. (*She stands at ease, sarcastically noting the frantic efforts of* AH SIN *to fix the table; presently she speaks to him gently.*) Wait a minute; stand still, please. (AH SIN *does so.*) There now, collect your senses and don't get frightened, you are doing very well. (*Musing aside.*) Poor afflicted creature, when he shakes his head it makes me nervous to hear his dried faculties rattle. (AH SIN *smiles blandly -- He struggles with table leaf.*) Wait please; let me show you. The table has a leaf, see? It has to be lifted up. (MRS. TEMPEST *lifts it up -- holds it a minute to let him see, then lets it fall.* AH SIN *lifts leaf -- holds it a minute, then lets it slam down. Aside.*) Well, upon my word, this mental vacuum is a Chinaman to the marrow in one thing, the monkey faculty of imitating. (*Aloud.*) Wait a moment; I'll show you the whole operation. (*She raises and fastens the leaf -- he raises and fastens the other one.*) Now spread your tablecloth.

Ah Sin. Tablecloth all same likee sheet. (*Gets tablecloth and places in center of table.*)

Mrs. Tempest. Come, let me teach you. (*She tries to spread it; it flies out of her hands and lights beyond the table on the floor* -- AH SIN *exactly imitates this performance and grins broadly at his success. Aside.*) Well, he has imitated that too. Looks as delighted over it as if he had done a miracle. (*Aloud.*) Give it to me. (*She spreads the tablecloth.*)

Ah Sin. (*Pats tablecloth.*) Allee samee like a feather bed.

Mrs. Tempest. Do it that way, next time -- Set your plates now. (*He sets a pile in the middle of the table and stands back.*) Oh, you innocent, is that all! You provoking -- But I won't scold you. (*Seizing a plate.*) Here, poor, neglected thing. *This* is the way to set a table. (*She flies around nettled, in spite of herself, sets one plate after another too near the edge -- they fall off.*) There -- (*Desisting.*) I *won't* lose my temper. (*He imitates her hurry and zeal -- touches plate after plate to table then slams it on the floor -- then stands back pleased.*) Oh, is there *nothing* to you but imitation?

Ah Sin. No hab got a cent.

Mrs. Tempest. (*Setting the plates right for his instruction -- Aside.*) Poor dumb animal, with his tail on top of his head instead of where it ought to be. (*Aloud to* AH SIN.) Surely you can't have had a very vast experience as a servant? (AH SIN *proceeds with his work.*)

Ah Sin. Me velly good servant for Plunkee -- Plunkee, he A-number one plopper man. You sabbee Plunkee.

Mrs. Tempest. (*Aside.*) Well I must keep up this imposture with everybody. (*Aloud.*) Alas, poor lost dear, he was my husband.

Ah Sin. Too bad he go die -- makee you heap sorry -- Plunkee got nother wife.

Mrs. Tempest. (*Aside.*) What shall I say now? Of course he had another wife -- his real wife -- this Chinaman suspects. (*Aloud.*) Ah, I am not alone in my heavy grief -- yes, he had another wife, several.

Ah Sin. Velly good man Plunkee, allee same like a Bligam Young.

Mrs. Tempest. Well, go and get the things ready.

Ah Sin. You got nufee?

Mrs. Tempest. Yes, quite enough -- go and get the things ready. (*Comic exit of* AH SIN *in house L.*) It is time that that giddy girl of mine, this fraudulent Mistress Plunkett, was back from her ramble -- I wonder what she really thinks of our Mr. York? York is evidently smitten, but she -- oh dear, I wish it were all over and the Judge here --

How stupid in him to tell her what he wanted her to do. -- Ah yes -- here they are coming down the road together, and actually pulling away from each other like a team going down hill. I wonder if the Judge's plan is going down hill too? Well, I shall only be in the way here. (*Exit into house.*)

    Enter R.2.E. distantly and embarrassedly YORK *and* MISS
    TEMPEST. YORK *beats the bushes with his cane --* MISS
        TEMPEST *pulls a flower to pieces.*

York. (*L.C. awkwardly.*) Well -- we -- are here!

Miss Tempest. (*R.C. mischievously.*) Had you any idea that a walk in this direction would bring us anywhere else? (*During the following speech* AH SIN *enters, and by the time* YORK *gets to "nature and beauty" and turns he finds himself face to face with the grinning Chinaman and utters an exclamation of vexation and disgust.* AH SIN *proceeds with his duties but is always in the way or between the lovers at critical places.*)

York. (*Aside.*) Can she be laughing at me? (*Aloud.*) No, I only meant -- that is -- Miss Plunkett -- I *confess* I had thought -- I mean I had *hoped* that in our little ramble through these calm sedate woods -- that in our mutual admiration of nature and beauty, that in our sympathy with the good and the true, we might perhaps have -- drawn -- a -- little nearer to --

Miss Tempest. To luncheon! (*X.R.*) We have! The table is already set. (*To* AH SIN -- *taking up cruet.*) -- No oil -- of course *something* would be wrong! Go and fill it! (AH SIN *exits.*)

York. (*Aside.*) She *is* laughing at me! (*Aloud.*) I -- beg your pardon -- Miss Plunkett.

Miss Tempest. (*Going to table and examining it.*) Excuse me a moment, but this Chinaman's glittering ignorance keeps one on the rack all the time, he needs so much watching. (*To* AH SIN, *who has returned with cruet.*) Ah -- you've got the oil.

Ah Sin. Yes, missee.

Miss Tempest. Very well. But I can't trust you. (*Smells.*) Pah! It's kerosene!

Ah Sin. Him velly good oil.

Miss Tempest. Now, *don't* you know any better than to put kerosene in a castor? Take it away and fill a clean cruet. (AH SIN, *going, tastes the kerosene and exits with hot bowels.*)

Ah Sin. Me sabbee, clean cluet.

York. (*Affectedly -- aside sadly.*) She is not only enjoying my discomfiture but is even laughing at my servants. (*Aloud.*) But you will admit, Miss Plunkett, that these little infelicities of our mountain life add a zest to -- to --is in fact the --

Miss Tempest. (*Examining table.*) Salt!

York. (*Aside.*) Confound it. (*Aloud.*) I meant that I owe perhaps to this very misfortune the felicity of being served by the fairest of hands -- of seeing you --

Miss Tempest. (*At table.*) Sugar!

York. (*Aside.*) This is too much! (*Aloud -- proudly.*) Miss Plunkett, you have twice checked me in an avowal that --

Miss Tempest. (*To* AH SIN *who brings fresh cruet straight to her with signs of vast satisfaction.*) Ah -- now you are sure you've got it right this time?

Ah Sin. Oh, him all litee now!

Miss Tempest. Well, you are a good boy. Now don't ever forget that there's only one kind of oil that's proper for a castor. (*Smells.*) Ugh. Why, what's this?

Ah Sin. (*Innocently.*) Castor oil. (*Goes off L.*)

Miss Tempest. (*Flings the cruet away -- turning and perceiving that* YORK *is going R.*) What! You're not going to leave me here alone. Is this your gratitude for my service as a housekeeper? (*Coming toward him with extended hands, archly.*)

York. (*Gravely.*) I was going Miss Plunkett. I *was* turning from you that I might better hide in my own breast a secret I had no right to disclose. I would have left you lest I should make an avowal that I *knew* was premature, that I *feared* was hopeless! I love you, Miss Plunkett! (*She starts -- he seizes her hand.*) If for the last few hours I have seemed strange and awkward in your presence, it was because I had this secret in my breast; because I learned too late that what I had deemed my duty to my dead friend --

Miss Tempest. (*Starting.*) Your dead friend!

York. Your late father, Miss --

Miss Tempest. My late father! (*Aside.*) Oh yes, twenty-four hours late; dear me. If he were only here.

York. That my duty to your father -- to your father's daughter, was not duty, but love! I know that honor, duty, even love itself, demanded that you should have known, long before this, that you were not receiving the hospitality of a host, but the devotion of a lover.

Miss Tempest. (*Agitatedly.*) You forget yourself, Mr. York. (*Aside.*) Dear me, I'm afraid I'm forgetting *myself* too.

York. No, Miss Plunkett. It is I who am remembering myself now. It is I who am recalling the man who loved you before he ever saw your face, who had, long before you knew him, dwelt upon your photograph, pictured you to his fancy -- loved you as an ideal.

Miss Tempest. (*Aside.*) Why, my goodness, that's the way I've been going on about *his* picture!

York. And yet, knowing this I brought you here, a helpless, fatherless girl -- only to take advantage of your gratitude, to press my foolish suit.

Miss Tempest. Pray -- release my hand, Mr. York.

York. (*Sadly*) As you will.

Miss Tempest. (*Embarrassedly.*) I have -- kept -- from *you* a secret. Two years ago, at the risk of your own life, you saved a woman from instant death, on the banks of the Stanislaus River.

York. (*Carelessly.*) Yes, I remember -- something of the kind.

Miss Tempest. I was that woman! (*Perceiving* YORK *start -- aside.*) What have I said! I'm going too far. (*Aloud.*) That woman's niece -- you understand -- she was my aunt.

York. (*Confusedly.*) Oh, that woman, she was your aunt?

Miss Tempest. Yes, my favorite aunt, a woman I loved as myself. (*Aside.*) Thank Heaven that's over. What shall I say? (*Aloud.*) Hear me, Mr. York, by that heroic act you purchased the right, the only right you have of making me listen to you here.

York. (*Stupidly.*) That woman your aunt?

Miss Tempest. (*Angrily.*) Yes, certainly. And if you'd really loved me -- my aunt -- I -- mean -- I -- mean -- if you hadn't been so stupid as to go away without looking in the carriage, you'd have found her out (*Sobbing.*) and me too -- long ago.

York. Yes, but how could I know the inestimable value of that old woman? (*Aloud.*) Then I am to understand, Miss Plunkett --

Miss Tempest. (*Hurriedly.*) Oh please, you're to understand nothing. Only go now and come back in half an hour, and I'll tell you all. Go, quick.

York. (*Going.*) Then, in half an hour I'm to come back.

Miss Tempest. (*Quickly.*) To luncheon.

York. (*Going.*) To luncheon -- *au revoir.*

Miss Tempest. (*Raising her voice.*) Mr. York!

York. (*Returning.*) Caroline!

Miss Tempest. Please don't call me Caroline.

York. I know I should have said *Miss Plunkett;* pardon me.

Miss Tempest. No, no -- call me Shirley; it's a pet name, my dear old aunt's pet name, that's all. Call me that -- for -- for -- my aunt's sake.

York. Shirley, dearest, bless you! (*Exit into house R.*)

Miss Tempest. (*Excitedly.*) What have I done? What have I said? Not content with foisting a wife and daughter upon him, I've added an aunt! An aunt! Oh, heavens, this is too much. Oh, I see it all -- it's in the atmosphere, it's in the *name!* It's that dreadful old story-teller Plunkett haunting the world again in *me* and *through* me. Why, I think I couldn't tell the truth if I died for it! (*Xes excitedly and goes up to summer house -- more seriously.*) In half an hour he'll return -- What shall I say? I'll tell him *all.* (*A pause.*) No, I won't tell him *all.* Umph! That photograph is *mine* -- not *hers.* It's me that he loves -- not Miss Plunkett. (*Goes up to summer house and throws herself on a settee upstage R.H.*)

Enter MRS. *and* MISS PLUNKETT, *R.U.E.*

Mrs. Plunkett. No, I won't hear another word! Don't talk to me, Caroline Anastasia Plunkett, (MISS TEMPEST *starts at mention of that name.*) on such frivolous and worldly topics when every *liniment* of the scene around fetches back your poor lost father. Mind, I don't object to your making a match with this rich, worldly man if you want to, though I wouldn't marry him though he was as rich as *Creosote* himself -- only don't harass *me* with it when I'm soaking my soul in memories of the departed.

Miss Plunkett. (*R.*) Oh yes, Ma, why didn't you soak your soul yesterday? Why didn't you soak your soul last night in your memories of the departed? Sour grapes! It's because you were trying your best to get him yourself. *There,* now!

Mrs. Plunkett. (*R.*) My child! Remember I am your mother. Such language to me is not respectable -- it is even irrelevant.

Miss Plunkett. Well, I can't help it if it *is* irreverent, it's truth. (*Tearfully.*) And the minute he gives you the cold shoulder you turn on him and talk harsh about him. I think it's just outrageous. *There,* now.

Mrs. Plunkett. (*With dignity.*) I am sorry if my simple effeminate attentions have seemed significant to him and to you, for I intended them to be, like all my conduct, entirely *in*significant. It more becomes my afflicted condition to consecrate myself to his sacred memory who is gone. (*Tearfully.*) Peace to his ashes -- poor thing -- But, as I said before, *you* may go on and make this match if you think best.

Miss Plunkett. Well, I *do* think best, Ma. And *he* does, if actions go for anything. A man don't moon around a woman that way for nothing. And sigh? When he takes in one of those monstrous sighs of his, you can hear his clothes give. I tell you, Ma, he is hanging out signals, and they're for me, too.

Mrs. Plunkett. But, Caroline, you haven't known him twenty-four hours yet. This is all premature.

Miss Plunkett. Premature! He must be worth a quarter of a million.

Mrs. Plunkett. Well, I won't make any more objections. One son-in-law will do as well as another, I reckon. I must try to be a good mother-in-law to him. The duties of a mother-in-law and the duties of a wife are about the same thing, I judge -- six of one and half a dozen of the other. With the experience I've had as a wife I reckon that when I'm needed on deck I'll be no mere huckleberry of a mother-in-law. (MISS TEMPEST *coming out of the summer house quietly -- unseen by the* PLUNKETTS.)

Miss Tempest. (*Aside.*) Twenty--four hours! These are the people he expected, the people *we* have anticipated. I must end all this *here.* (*Advancing L. aloud.*) I beg your pardon, ladies, but I believe I stand in the presence of Mrs. and Miss Plunkett, the wife and daughter of the late Mr. Plunkett of this place?

Miss Plunkett. (*Hurrying to her mother's side.*) Oh gracious, this is one of those stuck-up San Francisco quality. Look at her dress, it must have cost a bushel of money.

Mrs. Plunkett. (*To her daughter.*) Hush! It's the *eclat* of San Francisco.

Miss Plunkett. (*Sotto voce.*) 'Sh! Ma, you mean the *e*light.

Mrs. Plunkett. (*Continuing.*) Yes, miss, you see there the orphan child and here the stricken relic of the late deceased -- Two lonely, friendless, dissolute women.

Miss Tempest. My name is Shirley Tempest.

Mrs. Plunkett. What! You don't mean it! Not the daughter of Judge Tempest of San Francisco, that's got oceans and oceans of money, the great Pacific slope milliner, as they call him --

Miss Plunkett. (*Aside to* MRS. PLUNKETT.) Daughter of the Pacific slope millionaire! My!

Mrs. Plunkett. (*Effusively.*) I'm proud to know you. (*Curtseying.*)

Miss Tempest. Perhaps not. If you will retain your kindness for a moment, I may show you that I have unintentionally done you -- and especially that young lady -- a great wrong.

Mrs. Plunkett. Oh, don't mention it.

Miss Tempest. When my mother and myself arrived here yesterday, we were met by a gentleman -- in fact, the gentleman of whom you were speaking a moment ago. I grieve to say that I could not help overhearing that conversation.

Mrs. Plunkett. Oh, don't mention it.

Miss Tempest. That gentleman, I have every reason to believe, mistook us for *you,* and I am ashamed to say that I encouraged his blunder and, out of sheer frivolity, prevailed upon my mother to assist me in sharing his hospitality as Mrs. and Miss Plunkett. I should not have the courage to confess this foolish freak but that it enables me to assure you, from my own personal knowledge, of that gentleman's deep attachment to Miss Plunkett.

Miss Plunkett. (*Aside.*) I don't like this. So he's been receiving somebody else.

Miss Tempest. I expect him here in half an hour. I beg you will bear me company until I shall disclose in your presence my foolish imposition, and restore you to the protection of Mr. York, your admirer.

Mrs. and Miss Plunkett. York!

Miss Plunkett. He my admirer; I reckon not!

Miss Tempest. May I ask of whom you were speaking just now?

Mrs. Plunkett. Of Mr. Silas Broderick, our hospitable hostage.

Miss Tempest. (*Aside.*) I begin to see.

Miss Plunkett. (*Bridling, X.L.*) You can tell Mr. York we wouldn't take his hospitality with such a suspicion resting against him. (*Aside to* MRS. PLUNKETT.) The idea of his *mistaking* that starched-up thing for me!

Mrs. Plunkett. (Aside to MISS PLUNKETT.) Hush! (*Aloud.*) No, ma'am, we -- we couldn't accept no attentions from Mr. York, at present.

Miss Tempest. Well, come, let *us* at least be friends. (*Extending hand.*) and let me introduce you to your laggard friend. (PLUNKETTS *show signs of hesitation.*) Stay. (*Laughing.*) I have an idea; if I have personated you in the (*X. to C.*) sympathies of this man, it is only fair that you should personate me. Let me beg you to accept my hospitality to-day at luncheon, and you shall meet this sluggish friend, not as Miss Plunkett, but as Miss Tempest. He will show his loyalty to you, I'll be bound. (*Aside.*) If he does -- I'll hate him.

Miss Plunkett. (Half pleased -- half annoyed.) I'd -- like to, just to see him. Mr. Broderick will not be here. Yes -- we'll go with you.

Mrs. Plunkett. But what am I to be?

Miss Tempest. (Taking her arm.) You shall be *my* mother; but first let me introduce her to you. Come, Miss Plunkett, you must keep us company, and help me in coaxing our mothers to stand by us! (*The ladies go upstage L. and off.*)

Enter AH SIN -- *he carries a dish or something and puts it on table, then employs himself about table. Enter ladies as before with* MRS. TEMPEST *as* MRS. PLUNKETT.

Mrs. Tempest. Do you enjoy the mountain air, Mrs. Tempest?

Ah Sin. What! Missee Tempee!

Mrs. Tempest. I am sure *you* do, Miss Tempest; the roses in your cheeks speak for you.

Ah Sin. Plunkee one day -- Tempee next -- No sabbee. Mellican man all mixee upee. (*Exits.*)

Mrs. Plunkett. (With studied dignity and aristocratic grace and composure.) I *always* enjoy the mountain air, Mrs. Plunkett, because the temperature ain't so variegated as what it is down on the lower latitudes. The more equinoctual the temperature is, the better it suits my constitution and by-laws.

Miss Plunkett. (As MISS TEMPEST.) Mountain air suits *me*. There's inspiration in it. I can feel the poetry rumbling in my soul all the time.

Miss Tempest. (*Aside.*) I feel *him* coming! And, oh dear, I can't discover any pain about it, either.

Mrs. Tempest. (*Looking off -- looking at watch.*) I see Mr. York has that peculiar masculine virtue, promptness. He is here at the exact moment appointed.

Enter YORK *from house R.1.E.*

York. (*Aside.*) Some *strangers*, apparently.

Mrs. Tempest. Mr. York, I and my daughter have had the good fortune to secure a most valuable addition to our luncheon party. Let me present you to Mrs. Tempest of San Francisco. (YORK *shows great surprise but instantly recovers himself and bows with great deference.*) Also to Miss Tempest. (*He bows again.*)

York. (*Aside.*) It isn't possible that *these* people -- are -- (*Aloud to the elder lady.*) Am I right in my inference that I have at last the great pleasure of meeting the wife and daughter of my old friend Judge Tempest?

Mrs. Plunkett. (*In her new high-toned way -- for she is conspicuously trying to be the aristocratic personage she is representing.*) I too am mutually glad to say you are right, sir; and I am glad to say, too, that the mutuality of your pleasure in meeting *us* cannot be more mutual than the mutualness of our pleasure in meeting you.

York. (*Befogged.*) Beg pardon? -- My hearing seems defective today -- I am not sure that I exactly -- understood -- that -- is -- I -- would you mind --

Mrs. Plunkett. Saying it over? (*Smiling -- rather flattered.*) Oh, with pleasure. I was remarking that I was mutually glad to say you were right, sir; (YORK *listening with painful interest.*) and glad to say, too, that the mutuality of your pleasure in meeting *us*, could not be more mutual than the mutualness of our pleasure in meeting *you.* (*Pause.*)

York. (*Perfectly blank face and stupefied manner.*) Thanks, Madam, many thanks. (*Aside.*) Am I in my right mind?

Mrs. Tempest. I must explain that we sent to invite Mr. Broderick to join our luncheon party, but he was not in. (YORK *bows.*)

Miss Plunkett. He wouldn't enjoy society and cheerfulness today, anyway. He seems sad, and low, and sighs considerable. I think it's his -- his --

Miss Tempest. His mind! -- perhaps!

Miss Plunkett. Lor' no -- his liver!

Mrs. Plunkett. Now that makes my mouth water. You may talk about your sardines, and your ice cream, and your quails on trust, and blankmange, and your *pates* de foy grass, and your canary birds stuffed with onions -- (*Dumbshow of quickly concealed disgust on the part of* YORK *and the real* TEMPESTS.) and all the other indelicacies that we, that have got money, can indulge in; but as for me, give me *liver!*

Miss Plunkett. (*Impressively.*) That's good enough doctrine for me.

Miss Tempest. Ah Sin is a little slow with the fruit; I must hurry him a little. (*Goes up to house L.*)

Mrs. Plunkett. There's nothing like taking time by the *fetlock.*

> *Enter* AH SIN *with dish of fruit -- trips and falls.* MRS.
> PLUNKETT *screams. Comic business.*

Mrs. Plunkett. My goodness, what *has* the poor heathen done?

Ah Sin. (*To* MRS. PLUNKETT.) You likee him -- you likee him, you pick him up. (*Exit.*)

Miss Tempest. Don't mind him -- don't be afraid, dear Mrs. Tempest. Poor Ah Sin is harmless -- only a little ignorant and awkward -- (MISS TEMPEST *and* YORK *show great sympathy.*) My dear Madam, take some wine; it will restore you.

Mrs. Plunkett. O dear me, the thought of anyone being injured or killed reminds me of -- (*Hesitating -- she is nudged by her daughter's elbow.*) I had a poor dear friend whose brief sweet life was a *poem* to all that knew him -- *more* than that -- it was a *sermon*-- Just a rounded, complete and beautiful sermon, clear from the Doxology to the Malediction. But please let us change the subject -- I can't think of him without going into ecstasies of sensibility, perfect ruptures of emotion.

Miss Plunkett. Don't you be alarmed about her. (*This to the company.*) She'll soon come out of this! Pa says she's a little too sentimental for *her* age, and I reckon it's so, too. Pa tries to make me out so, too -- but he is mistaken. Whatever I am, I'm not one of the sappy sentimental sort. Excuse *me*, I'm no gumdrop.

York. (*Aside.*) And this chambermaid is the *divine* Miss

Tempest! Gumdrop! Ugh! This state of things is becoming intolerable.
I must contrive a change of some sort. (*Aloud.*) It is my pleasant
duty to make your time pass as little irksome as I can, ladies, and if
there is any diversion that I can offer ---

The Real Miss Plunkett. (*Interrupting.*) That's it! Let's have a
dance! -- let's have a good old rattling breakdown.

The Real Mrs. Plunkett. Laws, child, dance indeed! There ain't
enough men pardners.

York. (*Interrupting.*) Allow me -- I think I can offer a novelty.
My Chinaman is always meddling around the shows and picking up
something or other, and he mimics everything he sees there.

Miss Plunkett. Oh, call him in!

Mrs. Plunkett. That is the thing!

Mrs. and Miss Tempest. Oh, excellent!

York. Ah Sin!

Ah Sin. (*Outside.*) Me coming.

York. He will be a little diffident, maybe, but -- (AH SIN
enters.) Ah Sin, these ladies want to see what you picked up when
you used to go to the theatres in San Francisco. (AH SIN *smiles
largely and exits* -- YORK *exchanges wondering looks with ladies.*)
Why -- what does he mean by going off? Ah, here he comes again.
(*Enter* AH SIN *with carpet sack* -- *opens smilingly and takes out
gorgeous costume and odds and ends of dramatic properties.*) Well?

Ah Sin. Me pickee him up at theatre! (*General laugh.*)

York. Oh, you are too literal by half --

Ah Sin. Too little -- Mellican man say I fat enough to kill.

York. Too literal. Now the ladies would like to hear you do
some of the things you've seen at the shows.

Ah Sin. (*Shyly.*) Me no kin do such ting -- too muchee people
here.

York. (*Calls him* -- *whispers in ear* -- *only the word "Cash"
heard.*)

Ah Sin. Me singee littee songee. (AH SIN *sings song* --
Music. -- *Enter* BRODERICK, FERGUSON *and* MINERS *L.U.E.
The following dialogue very hurriedly and work up to climax.*)

Ferguson. (*Advancing.*) Beg pardon, ladies, but we don't want
to intrude here. We're only lookin' for this gentleman, Mr. Henry
York.

York. (*Quietly looking at* FERGUSON.) Very well, sir; your business?

Ferguson. I don't want to -- to --

York. (*Proudly.*) You can have no business with me that is not proper for ladies' ears. Go on, sir.

Ferguson. I am content then. We are here to arrest you.

York. (*Rising with dignity.*) For what? (*Coming C.*)

Ferguson. The murder of Abner Plunkett. (*Sensation -- ladies rise --* MISS TEMPEST *throws her arms around* YORK *protectingly.* MRS. PLUNKETT *faints.* MISS PLUNKETT *is startled.* MRS. TEMPEST *stupefied and indignant.*)

York. (*To* MISS TEMPEST *soothingly.*) This is all some dreadful blunder. One moment will clear it away -- Why, Broderick here can explain! He was last seen with the missing man. Speak up, Broderick; man, you remember! (BRODERICK *shakes his head solemnly.*)

Miss Tempest. There is some treachery here, some conspiracy, I am sure.

York. (*Amazedly.*) But at least Ah Sin here knows that I --

Ah Sin. Chinaman evidence no goodee.

York. (*Excitedly.*) At least, I must know the authority by which I am arrested?

Ferguson. (*Gravely.*) Certainly; by order of the highest authority in the land -- Judge Lynch!

FERGUSON *lays his hand on* YORK'S *shoulder --* MISS TEMPEST *falls upon her mother's bosom -- Comic business -- falling back for* AH SIN. AH SIN *sits on* MRS. PLUNKETT'S *knee -- she pushes him off and he falls against* BRODERICK, *who pushes him back to* MRS. PLUNKETT, *who catches him by the pigtail and pounds him with fan. Tableau.*

Curtain.

ACT 4TH.
Scene 1.

Marley's Hill (*in Scene 1.*) *A woodland landscape.* *Enter*
JUDGE TEMPEST *and* MISS TEMPEST -- MISS TEMPEST
excitedly -- JUDGE *following.*

Miss Tempest. Yes, I repeat it, it was all your fault. If you had
stayed with us, instead of leaving us unprotected to be picked up by any
passing stranger, this wouldn't have happened.

Judge Tempest. (*Expostulating.*) But if you will tell me what
possible connection there is between my leaving you alone and Mr.
York being arrested for murder?

Miss Tempest. (*Hurriedly.*) There, don't talk -- you're always
talking instead of acting! Oh, if I were only a man. I'd -- there -- there,
father, forgive me, (*Embracing him.*) but you see, dear, your habits as
a lawyer --

Judge Tempest. (*Interrupting.*) True! But my habits as a lawyer
have not blunted my perception as a father -- Shirley, my child, hear
me! You *love* this man! (*Putting his arm around her.*) There! I do not
blame you. Indeed, twenty-four hours ago I would have rejoiced at this.
But my experience of life teaches me that your lover --

Miss Tempest. But he isn't my lover -- it's Miss Plunkett that he
loves --

Judge Tempest. Well, the lover of Miss Plunkett *alias* Miss
Tempest, I grieve to say, is in a dangerous strait. The evidence that
might be frivolous and insufficient before a competent court will be
convincing to the rude law of this locality.

Miss Tempest. But father, you can -- you *will* save him!

Judge Tempest. (*Gravely.*) My child, your vigilance committee
knows that it must justify its irregularities by its final verdict. It has
to hang a man to show that it had the right to *simply* arrest him.

Miss Tempest. You terrify me, father.

Judge Tempest. Be assured, my poor child, I will do all I can. I
will go to the poor fellow now. They will admit *me* -- though they
deny all others. Have you any word of comfort to send him?

Miss Tempest. (*Impetuously.*) To send him? No -- I'll carry it
myself.

Judge Tempest. Why, my child, it's no place for you. *You* will not go there!

Miss Tempest. Will I grieve at home? Father, you know me better.

Judge Tempest. Let me persuade you. Think of that mob of rough men.

Miss Tempest. I don't care for them; I will go.

Judge Tempest. Child, what *good* can you do there? Your sex never reason.

Miss Tempest. When those we love are in danger? No -- thank Heaven, we act first and reason afterwards.

Judge Tempest. (*Aside.*) Confound it, I'm getting the worst of it. (*Aloud.*) They will not allow women there. They will not admit you.

Miss Tempest. They *shall* admit me.

Judge Tempest. Oh, folly, folly! But, my child, these are wild, rough miners --

Miss Tempest. They are *men*. And all men have hearts. (*X.L.*)

Judge Tempest. (*Perplexed for a moment -- then kindly.*) Shirley, I do sincerely feel for you; and if you could do the least good, I would yield. But you cannot. It is no place for a young girl. My arguments have all failed -- now I must use compulsion. You cannot go.

Miss Tempest. (*With gentleness but firmly.*) Father, try to forgive me, but I will go.

Judge Tempest. (*Surprised.*) Shirley, this is the first time you ever refused me obedience -- It does not become a girl to --

Miss Tempest. All my life, till this day, I was a girl, and a subject. To-day, I am a woman! (*X.R.*)

Judge Tempest. Then nothing can change your mind?

Miss Tempest. (*Calmly.*) Nothing, Father.

Judge Tempest. It will grieve me -- but you compel me to do it. I will oppose your entrance myself and I will take you home. You know me, my child.

Miss Tempest. (*Appealingly.*) Oh, father, father!

Judge Tempest. (*Embracing her.*) I must be cruel to be kind. Time is precious -- I must go to him. My darling. (*Kissing her forehead.*) You harbor no resentment against your father?

Miss Tempest. Oh, you know I do not -- *could* not.

Judge Tempest. There spoke my child! And you will obey?

Miss Tempest. (*Gently and firmly.*) No -- this once I will not obey.

Judge Tempest. (*Going -- aside.*) There spoke my own child again! But I mustn't seem to have heard it. (*Aloud.*) Keep your heart, my child -- wait at home 'till I bring you news. (*Exits.*)

Miss Tempest. Oh, there'll be no turning my father from his purpose; and that murderous pack will sacrifice the man whose life is dearer to me now than my own, and I shall not be near to -- But I *will* be there! Oh! What shall I do? What can I do? (*Exits R.*)

(*Change.*)

Scene 2.

Country Store. Bar C. Door of entrance L.H. Barrels, boxes, etc. -- Window back. Scene opens on Court. Two JURYMEN *are playing cards and several others looking on with interest.*)

1st Juryman. I go ten cents blind.

2nd Juryman. I see your blind and straddle it.

Masters. Gentlemen of the Jury, the evidence being all in now, let the prisoner be brought into Court and we will proceed to listen to the arguments of Counsel. (*Tremendous row outside.* BOSTON *jumps to door -- shouts --- "Dog fight! Dog fight!"*)

Boston. (*Running to door.*) Dog fight! Dog fight! Hands off -- fair play -- let 'em alone! (*To* MASTERS.) Five to one on the yaller pup!

Masters. Take it! This Court stands adjourned for ten minutes. (*Jumps down from counter. The whole crowd pile out with a yell --* JURYMEN *snatch up their cards and pocket them as they run out. Enter* BRODERICK.)

Broderick. (*Aside at bar.*) In a moment the Jury will return and I shall know the result. How I tremble! Nonsense! (*In nervous distress.*) Why don't that Chinaman come! Every second of time is important now and freighted with fate! One second too late may work destruction.

Enter the whole crowd, excited and puffing -- Prisoner comes, too -- Those JURYMEN *resume their cards.*

Masters. (*To* BOSTON.) You *won* the bet fair enough, but the *fight* wasn't fair on account of the yellow pup taking leg-holts. I'll pay you the amount tomorrow. (BOSTON *nods, as much as to say "All right."*) The court will now proceed to --

Boston. Just a moment, Judge. There's a little dispute here. I went ten cents blind, and Jake Miller saw it with a twenty, and then I straddled his blind, and it took him forty cents to make it good; and, by George, now he says it takes me eighty to come in.

1st Miner. Oh, that be hanged! Where'd you get your education, Jake Miller? The idea of its costing him eighty to come in on his own straddle.

Masters. (*Gravely.*) Mr. Miller, I am surprised that any man in a land where education is as free as the air we breathe should be so sunk in ignorance. A man straddles your blind and you -- in the broad light of the nineteenth century - proclaim that it costs him four times to come in on his own straddle! It is a spectacle to make one blush for his species. Such a man is not fit to sit upon a Jury and deal with the mighty matters of life and death. It is persons like you that have brought the Jury system into disrepute, and made the American Jury a synonym for ignorance and savage stupidity. You may retire from the box. Hank Williamson, take his place. (*The change is made.*)

1st Miner. That's it! -- Now there's sense in that.

Masters. A man that can't play poker is not fit to sit on a Jury.

1st Miner. Of course not.

Masters. Gentlemen of the Jury, the evidence is all in. (BRODERICK *hands* MASTERS *a flask -- He drinks and* BRODERICK *sends it to Jury.*) Thanks.

Judge Tempest. (*Rising.*) Your honor, I *must* protest, once more, against these irregularities. To pass a flask of liquor around --

Masters. Sit down, you're out of order.

Boston. Second the motion. Sit down, it ain't your turn.

Enter AH SIN, *who is prodded and pestered by people as he goes along. He protests with head shakes and a few Chinese words -- stoops or squats down where somebody will stand on his tail and tip wink to other spectators. A slight pause while AH SIN enters.*

Masters. (*C.*) Dry up, the whole lot o'ye -- Mr. Ferguson, if you're ready -- go on. (FERGUSON *rises.*)

1st Miner. Now, Fergy, toot your horn if you don't sell a clam.

Boston. (*L. corner.*) Turn on your gas, Fergy.

Ferguson. (*L. of table. C.*) Your Honor --

Masters. Hold on just a minute, Mr. Ferguson -- Which are you for? Prosecution or defense?

Ferguson. Well, I don't exactly know. I'm not familiar with law terms. But I'm going to put a blast under York, if I can.

Boston and 1st Miner. Bully for you -- that's the talk. (AH SIN'S *tail gets fast in something, or somebody is unconsciously standing on it. Tries to straighten up and can't -- jabbers frantically in Chinese.*)

Masters. Stand off the pagan's tail! Now you be quiet, or I'll pull your tail out and flog you to death with it.

Ferguson. Gentlemen of the Jury. You've seen yourselves that there is evidence enough to hang forty men. There had been a fight -- the ground torn up and the blood spots showed that; who fought that fight? York's pistol was found there with two charges shot off. Who generally carries Mr. York's pistol for him?

1st Miner. Good!

Ferguson. A handkerchief was found there, too. A *clean* one! -- Who does that suggest?

1st Miner. Good again!

Ferguson. I ask you to examine it. (*It is passed to Jury, who examine it with disgust --* BRODERICK *whispers to* FERGUSON *and pushes the dilapidated gloves before him.*) And a pair of unknown gloves found not fifty yards from the same place. (*Exhibits them and passes them to Jury.*) *Kid* gloves; you know this swell was always insulting the camp in every way he could think of, particularly by wearing kid gloves.

Boston. That's so every time.

Ferguson. There's another thing that looks mighty black -- he jumps Plunkett's claim, says he bought it. If he did, where's the papers for it? -- He says he lost 'em. Too thin! (*Sits.*)

Boston. You bet -- it's a blame sight too thin.

Judge Tempest. Your Honor, I *must* protest against these extraordinary expressions of opinion by Jurymen.

Masters. (*A trifle severely.*) Look here, my friend, who's trying this case if it ain't the Jury?

Judge Tempest. But these premature expressions of opinion are totally at variance with all custom and precedent.

Masters. Never mind -- you sit down. I reckon we've tried this sort of cases before often enough to know how to do it. If this man ain't guilty, I never saw a man that was, and if a *Juryman* can't speak his mind, where's your boasted freedom of speech your Declaration of Independence brags about?

1st Miner. Good! Had him there! (BRODERICK *sends box of cigars to* MASTERS *and Jury.*)

Masters. Go on, Mr. Ferguson.

Ferguson. Five or ten words more is all I want to say. Gentlemen of the Jury, look at the bare facts a moment. York was rich; all of a sudden he loses every dollar he's got and don't know where to turn to make a raise. He is frantic, crazy, perfectly desperate. That very day he stumbles on poor old Plunkett at the very moment that Plunkett has struck it rich. It was a lonesome place, nobody by to see the act -- he outs with his revolver, shoots the old man dead.

Judge Tempest. (*Rising impetuously.*) Come, come, *this* is not in evidence! Why, the very *fact* that nobody saw the act done is proof that nobody knows who *did* it.

Ferguson. (*Very calm, sarcastic manner.*) Look here, who's a making this speech, *I* would like to know. (*To Jury.*) As I was saying, when interrupted by this old Blackleg, he shoots the old man dead -- jumps the claim and has the effrontery to come calmly before this camp and say he *bought* the mine; and the heartlessness to come with new kid gloves and a new stove pipe hat on too -- mark that -- purchased with the proceeds of his crime. (*Audience shows rising excitement.*) There *was* a time when the man that dared to flaunt the contemptuous effronteries of kid gloves and a stove pipe hat in the face of this camp, did it at the peril of tar and feathers, a ride upon a rail, and *banishment!* (*The spectators surge forward, the Jury stand up -- Chorus of shouts.*)

Omnes. (*L.*) Hang him! Kill him! Shoot him like a dog! A rope! A rope! Fetch a rope! (*Grand struggle and pow-wow.*)

Masters. (*Springs up and points a huge revolver.*) Back, every devil of you! I'll kill the first man that lays a hand on him! (*They fall back muttering and shaking their heads -- MASTERS stands glaring on the crowd a while, then says with strong and pathetic indignation.*) *Confound* it, have I got to kill a man *every* time I sit on a case of this kind? (*Sits gravely down.*) Let the defense begin. (AH SIN, *in his fright, has climbed to the top of a conspicuous pile of boxes, starts to come carefully down and tumbles with a crash -- startled.*) What the nation did you get up there for!

Ah Sin. Me wantee *see* better.

Masters. Well, what did you come clattering down like that for?

Ah Sin. Me no got time be all day comin' down. (BRODERICK *whispers to* FERGUSON, *who springs up.*)

Ferguson. Hold on! Just a single word more! This prisoner has had a couple of women masquerading at his house for a day or two, passing themselves off for Plunkett's widow and daughter. It has been found that they are nothing of the kind. It's a suspicious business. What do you reckon in York's little game? Did he want that bogus widow to make him a deed to Plunkett's mine, hey? (*Sensation.*) And who *are* the imposters? -- the wife and daughter of no less a personage than -- that gentleman there! (*Pointing to* JUDGE TEMPEST. *Sensation.*)

Judge Tempest. (*To some friend near.*) Oh, what a *fatal* fool I have been! Now I would give the *world* if my daughter were here to throttle this calumny! (MISS TEMPEST *enters through door in R. flat impetuously through the crowd -- hat in hand, shawl half off -- very pale.*) Shirley, my child! (*She runs to him.*)

Masters. What means this? What is your name?

Miss Tempest. Shirley Tempest.

Ah Sin. Mellican lady goin' to heap lie some more! No can keep same name two day.

Masters. Were you known by that name in the household of Mr. York?

Miss Tempest. No.

Masters. By what name then?

Miss Tempest. Miss Plunkett.

Masters. What object had you in assuming that name?

Miss Tempest. (*Hesitatingly.*) Only -- a -- foolish girl's fancy. My father had brought us to meet Mr. York -- his old friend. The letter informing him of our arrival did not reach him. But Mr. York, seeking Miss Plunkett, who was due the same day, mistook me for that lady -- I -- I -- did not undeceive him.

York. (*Rising.*) May it please this Court.

Masters. Sit down, sir. (YORK *sits down protesting.-- To* MISS TEMPEST.) But what was your object, if you were the legitimate guest of Mr. York, in deceiving him in this way?

Miss Tempest. (*Greatly agitated.*) Oh, sir, I assure you it was only a mere fancy -- a foolish, girlish freak. (*Sobbing.*) He thought my photograph was Miss Plunkett's.

Boston. Oh, let up! Oh, give her a show!

Ah Sin. Givee her showee!

Masters. (*Gravely.*) Miss Tempest, consider one moment; upon your next utterance may hang the life of the prisoner. If you are really here in the interests of justice -- if you have come here, honestly, to clear his character, and your own, you will answer as honestly and frankly one question. What other motive had you in personating the woman in whom you knew he was interested?

Miss Tempest. (*Looking wildly round the Court.*) Because, because -- because -- I was -- (*Meeting* YORK'S *eye.*) Oh, spare me, sir; spare *him.* I implore you.

Masters. (*Gravely.*) Answer. Remember, his life may hang upon your next sentence.

Miss Tempest. Because -- I -- *loved* -- him! (*Drops her head in her hands. Sensation. Applause from Jury and spectators --* BRODERICK *turns away in anger.*)

Boston. Say that again, Miss, to *me*, and say it as you said it then, and I'll take *his* place under the gallows.

Judge Tempest. (*Rising.*) Again, I must protest against these constant intermeddlings of the Jury in --

Boston. Sit down, you old ass -- that girl of yours has said more in one minute than you have in sixty. (AH SIN, *who is standing with back against wall, slaps thigh and is in the midst of a prodigious laugh when he observes that there is a stillness and all eyes are on him -- slowly closes his wide mouth in shame.*)

Masters. Silence in Court! (*Silence, in which* JUDGE TEMPEST *embraces* MISS TEMPEST *and she whispers to him.*)

Judge Tempest. (*Rising.*) May it please the Court, may I have the privilege of examining this witness?

Omnes. Go on. Heave ahead, old man!

Masters. Go on.

Judge Tempest. Swear the witness!

Boston. Swear a *lady*! Doubt a lady's word -- Nonsense, go on! Go on!

Omnes. Yes, go on -- go on.

Judge Tempest. (Stupefied and shrugging his shoulders.) Well, I protest -- but --

Broderick. This is all very fine -- very pretty -- a put-up job between a father and daughter to humbug the Jury!

Boston. Oh, take a walk. (BRODERICK *sits down.*)

Ah Sin. Takee walkee topside hillee.

Judge Tempest. (To MISS TEMPEST.) By whose suggestions did you come here?

Miss Tempest. Nobody's but my own. You refused me permission to come. And -- and Mr. Broderick said I should not enter this courtroom, and *he* would see to it that I was prevented.

Broderick. (Aside.) Fool that I am! It serves me right.

Omnes. Broderick's a dog! Kick him out! Lynch him!

Judge Tempest. Mr. Broderick must answer for his officiousness. (*To* MISS TEMPEST.) How did you come to hold converse with Mr. Broderick?

Miss Tempest. I met him on the road, and in my distress I implored him to use his influence to save Mr. York. And he -- he --

Boston. Speak out, Miss -- don't you be afraid. What did he do?

Miss Tempest. He -- he -- insulted me with protestations of love! Said if I would discard Mr. York for *him*, he would see that York was set free. (*Breaks down and cries a little.*)

Judge Tempest. You scorned him -- of course, then he --

Miss Tempest. He said he would make my assumed name tell against the prisoner.

Judge Tempest. The whole conduct of the prosecution is of a piece with this. I will not shame your intelligence, your *manhood*, your magnanimity by defending a man who is so manifestly guiltless, or by attacking a prosecution which has so ignominiously failed.

1st Juryman. That's me -- shake!

2nd Juryman. And me too. She hasn't been treated right.

3rd Juryman. Count me in.

Ah Sin. Allee same me! (*They all get to shaking hands.* AH SIN *offers to shake with somebody -- is spurned contemptuously.* BRODERICK *whispers to* FERGUSON, *who springs up.*)

Ferguson. One word, Gentlemen of the Jury. Let us *acquit* him.

Omnes. Agreed! Agreed! Hurray!

Ferguson. Yes, let us acquit him --let us weep on his neck and welcome him back to our firesides -- *where he is so fond of coming to enjoy our society.* So very fond of it. Let's buy three or four gross of kid gloves so he can shake hands with us without -- without *catching* anything. Let's get him a dozen new stove pipe hats to take off respectfully when he meets us. And let's get him a hundred-dollar-forty-horse-power pair of spectacles so he can *see* us when he *does* meet us.

1st Juryman. Blamed if I vote not guilty!

Omnes. Nor I! Nor I!

Ferguson. Let's give him back the mine he stole from a poor afflicted widow and a stricken daughter who had never done him any harm! Let's forget -- if any of us *noticed* it -- that when the whiskey was passed to him from the Jury a while ago, he turned from it with the native air of a snob, because -- well, because he didn't feel worthy to drink *after such elegant gentlemen,* perhaps. (*He sits down.*)

1st Juryman. Guilty's the word for *me,* boys.

2nd Juryman. That's my style! Shake!

3rd Juryman. Goodbye, Mr. *York.* Shake!

4th Juryman. Guilty for *me,* and spell it with a big J, too.

5th Juryman. A big G, you flat head.

Spectators. Hang him! Hang him! Hang him!

AH SIN *starts for the pile of boxes, but is taken by the ear and led back again by* BRODERICK *who whispers to him and sends him out.*

Masters. Silence! The Jury can retire.

Boston. 'Tain't no use. The game's made. This Jury's unanimous for guilty. (*Sensation.* MISS TEMPEST *is about to rush forward to* YORK *when her father restrains her.*)

Judge Tempest. (*To* MASTERS.) It cannot be that this unparalleled outrage in the name of justice will be allowed to stand.

Masters. You had ample opportunity to prove the innocence of your client.

Judge Tempest. (*Indignantly.*) It is for you to prove him guilty. You have failed by every rule of law and evidence. (*Turning and appealing to spectators, who, meantime showing signs of dissent with the verdict, have gathered round him and his daughter.*) Hear me, gentlemen, I conjure *you* who have called this tribunal into existence, and without whose support it cannot continue to exist, not to let this verdict stand which is an insult to this defenseless girl.

A Juryman. Boys, there's something in that.

Another. Yes, blamed if there ain't.

Judge Tempest. You have wives, you have sisters, you have sweethearts -- You will not see this verdict recorded against this innocent man. (*Pointing to* YORK.)

All. No, we won't

Judge Tempest. I boldly invite a verdict. (*Sensation among Jury favorable to prisoner, during which* BRODERICK *starts up and goes downstage.*)

Broderick. (*Aside.*) No use holding back any longer. I must risk the Chinaman's evidence -- or these fools will give in. (*Aloud.*) One moment, Your Honor, I have another witness.

Masters. Who is it?

Broderick. Ah Sin.

Masters. A Chinaman cannot testify in this court.

Broderick. No, but he brings a witness more powerful than himself.

Masters. The mischief he does! Very well, then, let him come forward. (*Enter* AH SIN -- *with bag and umbrella.*)

Ah Sin. Good day, John. Good day, evellyboddy. (*Jabbers a lot of Chinese.*) -- ti kelly kee chow.

Masters. None of your jabbering -- get up there.

Ah Sin. Topside? (*Comic business -- getting on box.*)

Masters. Yes, topside.

Broderick. Now, Ah Sin, show the Court what you found in the bushes near Plunkett's claim the night he disappeared. (AH SIN *opens bag, fumbles about, jabbering Chinese or singing -- slowly takes out jacket and hands it to* BRODERICK, *who hands it to* MASTERS.)

Broderick. There's the witness! The jacket worn by York on the night of the murder, stained with the blood of his victim. (*Deed falls from jacket on table as* MASTERS *examines jacket.* FERGUSON *reaches for it --* MASTERS *plants his foot on it.*)

Masters. Why, Broderick, this is not York's jacket but yours, and here's your name on the collar.

York. (*Rising.*) Villain!

Broderick. (*Glaring at* AH SIN.) Ah Sin! It's false. It's some trick.

Ah Sin. (*Pointing pistol at* BRODERICK.) You likee him, eh?

Masters. And here's the deed which has just fallen from the pocket of your jacket.

Ah Sin. Him belongee me. I findee him in York jackee.

Masters. (*Pointing to* BRODERICK.) Don't let him escape! (*All gather round* MASTERS, *examining deed.*)

Broderick. Devil take the Chinaman, he has put the rope around my neck.

Ah Sin. How muchee you give suppose shelliff no hangee you?

Broderick. All -- everything I've got in the world.

Ah Sin. You givee half rich mine.

Broderick. Yes, and $10,000 to boot.

Exit AH SIN *hurriedly -- excited dumb show of fury among Jury and spectators has been going on while* AH SIN *and* BRODERICK *were talking -- Upon* AH SIN'S *exit the row breaks out furiously. They surge forward around* BRODERICK *and lay hands on him, drag him toward front.*

Voices. Hang him! Hang him like a dog!

Broderick. Have mercy! Have mercy!

Voices. A rope! A rope! (*The rope is brought and one end thrown over a hook; and three or four drag* BRODERICK *toward it -- he struggles with all his might, crying --*)

Broderick. Mercy! Give me one little instant to prepare!

Voices. Not an instant! Hang him!

Ah Sin. (*Enters with* PLUNKETT.) Hi! 'Nother witness! Plunkee!

Broderick. Alive?

Plunkett. Ya'as, boys, it's me.

Boston. (*Coming forward with outstretched hand -- stops suddenly.*) I say -- how do we know but what you're lying now?

Omnes. That's so -- that's so.

Plunkett. No more lying, boys -- I've reformed. As George Washington said to me -- (*All laugh --* MRS. PLUNKETT *enters, followed by* MISS PLUNKETT.)

Mrs. Plunkett. There's my poor dear Plunkett. (*She runs towards him -- he tries to shrink out of sight. General shout from miners, hand shaking, and "Hurrah for* AH SIN!")

Curtain.

1879 -- Henry Grimm -- *The Chinese Must Go*

By the 1870s, a worsening economy in the West had exacerbated anti-Chinese racism. The situation in San Francisco was especially tense, as it held the largest single concentration of Chinese in North America. In fear of losing their livelihood and whipped up into a racist hysteria by demagogues such as the former drayman Denis Kearney, Euroamerican workingmen congregated in associations known as "Anti-Coolie Clubs."

This text dates from just after the most intense period of such activity, and it contains the most overtly racist portrayal of the Chinese ever to have survived in American drama. Grimm's verbal vitriol and stereotypical attitudes make the play difficult reading today, as he blasted the Chinese with every accusation that he could possibly imagine. Crude in characterization and clumsy in plot, the play nevertheless powerfully conveys the emotions of its time.

If this play was ever performed, the most likely venue was the meetings of the Anti-Coolie Clubs, where it would have been performed by amateur actors. The audience would have applauded it for reflecting their own racist and populist sentiments. In 1879, a small advertisement in the leading San Francisco newspaper offered the play to theatre managers; apparently, all declined, as there is no subsequent record of a performance at an established theatre. It was, however, later performed at a theatre in Tucson, where it was a great success. With the passage of the 1882 exclusionary legislation and the consequent cooling of passions on Chinese immigration, the play became a period piece and sank into oblivion. Although dead as a text for performance, its extreme racism has attracted some recent critical attention.

I wish to thank the Bancroft Library for its gracious permission to reprint The Chinese Must Go.

The Chinese Must Go

DRAMATIS PERSONAE

WILLIAM BLAINE, *A Tailor*
DORA BLAINE, *His Wife*
FRANK BLAINE, *His Son*
LIZZIE BLAINE, *His Daughter*
CAPTAIN JULIUS TURTLESNAP
REVEREND HOWARD SNEAKER
JACK FLINT
SLIM CHUNK PIN
AH COY
LAM WOO
SAM GIN
MANDARIN
POLICEMAN
EXPRESSMAN

ACT I.
Scene -- A kitchen.

SAM GIN *washing dishes;* AH COY *smoking his opium pipe.*

Ah Coy. I tellee you, white man big fools; eaty too muchee, drinkee too muchee, and talkee too muchee.

Sam Gin. White man catchee plenty money; Chinaman catchee little money.

Ah Coy. By and by white man catchee no money; Chinaman catchee heap money; Chinaman workee cheap, plenty work; white man workee dear, no work -- sabee?

Sam Gin. Me heep sabee.

Ah Coy. White man damn fools; keep wifee and children -- cost plenty money; Chinaman no wife, no children, save plenty money. By and by, no more white workingman in California; all Chinaman -- sabee?

Enter FRANK BLAINE.

Frank. Damn such luck; can't borrow a cent to save my life. Money is getting as scarce as flies about Christmas. I must have some. Losing three games of billiards, one after the other, with this flat-footed Jack Flint is a shame. (*To* AH COY.) Why don't you work?

Ah Coy. Your mother no payee me last month; no payee, no workee -- sabee?

Frank. How much does she owe you?

Ah Coy. Six dollars.

Frank. All right, John; I get it for you. (*Aside.*) If I squeeze the six dollars out of the old man that Chinaman has to pay me commission, that's business. (*Pulling* SAM GIN *by his queue, exits.*)

Sam Gin. Damn hoodlum. What for you foolee me all the time?

Enter LIZZIE.

Lizzie. Has my brother been here, John?

Sam Gin. Your brother damn hoodlum, he pullee my tail all the time.

Lizzie. They are all trying to pull you back to China, John. Oh, how nervous I am this morning.

Ah Coy. You like smoke opium?

Lizzie. Yes, please.

Ah Coy. Drinkee too much coffee; no good, makee too muchee shaking -- sabee?

Enter WILLIAM BLAINE, *takes the pipe out of his daughter's mouth.*

William. What! Are you smoking this dirty pipe again? (*To* AH COY.) Get out of my house, you miserable dog.

Ah Coy. I wantee money.

William. Take that (*Striking* AH COY *with the pipe.*), you breeder of ruin and desolation.

Ah Coy. I make you pay. (*Exit.*)

Enter DORA.

Dora. What's this noise about? What's the matter?

William. The matter is that you are too damned fond of sitting in the parlor rocking yourself in the chair and reading trash instead of looking after your household affairs. There, I caught our girl again smoking that nasty Chinaman's pipe.

Dora. Poor thing! She is sick.

William. Is it a wonder? She has nothing else to do but to get sick. I told you a thousand times, why the devil don't you make her work?

Dora. Why the devil don't you make Frank work?

William. Haven't I been hunting for a place for years? Isn't every factory and every store crammed with those cursed Chinamen?

Dora. Excuses! Excuses!

Enter LAM WOO, *bringing washing.*

William. (*To* LAM WOO.) What do you want?

Lam Woo. Me bringing wash.

William. Wash yourself to hell; I got no money.

Lam Woo. Your wife owe me sixteen dollars. You no got money, I keepee washee. (*Exit.*)

Dora. John! John! (*Following him.*)

William. Sixteen dollars for washing. Oh, Stockton! Stockton! I am coming.

Enter FRANK.

Frank. Father, a gentleman down in the store wants to see you.

William. Stockton! Stockton! I'm coming. (*Exit.*)

Frank. Stockton! Stockton! I am coming. What's the matter with him? Is he cracked? Shoo fly, don't bother me. Well, I knocked down four bits anyhow while I attended to the store. But that isn't enough; I must get more. Where? There. (*Pointing to his sister, who is fast asleep in a chair.*) Fast asleep. I bet she has been smoking opium again. How pale she looks. (*Feeling her pockets.*) Not a cent in it; as dry as a city treasury. Lizzie! Lizzie! (*Shaking her.*) Wake up, wake up.

Lizzie. What is it? Oh, I am so tired.

Frank. That forty-year-old lover of yours, Captain Julius Turtlesnap, was down in the store not more than five minutes ago.

Lizzie. What did he want?

Frank. He is coming to see you this afternoon. Don't be too cool with him, sis. He is a man of influence, and has more money than brains.

Lizzie. This afternoon I won't be at home. Reverend Howard Sneaker is coming by the four o'clock train, and we are going to receive him.

Frank. Sneaker's a fraud; look out for him. Stick to Captain Julius Turtlesnap. Why, girl, you struck a regular bonanza in that man. Got four bits, sis?

Lizzie. I have not, Frank; but I will get you some to-morrow when I see my old sweetheart.

Frank. Thank you, thank you. (*Kissing her.*) Such a sister and such a lover ought to live for ever. (*Exit.*)

Enter DORA BLAINE, AH COY, LAM WOO, *and* SLIM CHUNK PIN.

Dora. Thank heavens, my husband isn't here.

Slim Chunk Pin. Madam, I am an agent of the powerful Six Companies, and I herewith order you to pay this Chinaman for his washing, and this Chinaman for his services; and mark you, if you don't, your life won't be safe a minute.

Dora. What shall I do? What shall I do?

Slim Chunk Pin. Go and sell your gold watch and chain. We will wait here till you return. Go!

Dora. Oh, heavens! Oh, heavens! (*Exit.*)

Ah Coy. White people damn fools. Too muchee eaty, too muchee drinkee.

Slim Chunk Pin. Dry up, will you? You are too muchee smart, too muchee sassy. This is the sixth time in eight months we have furnished you with a situation, and now you are on our hands again. If we had all such chickens as you, the importation of coolies would be a bad speculation. You have not half paid your passage money yet.

Ah Coy. Me like heep work.

Slim Chunk Pin. Shut up, you rat-smasher. Mind, now, if you don't improve you will get your wind cut off one of these days. We didn't import you to lose money; we can have that easier by gambling in stocks. (*To* AH COY.) Look at Sam. He fulfills his contracts with the Company like a man, and saves money besides.

Ah Coy. Sam Gin been here many years; white people plenty money then. White people no money now. Chinaman take too muchee money to China.

Slim Chunk Pin. Stuff and nonsense; what do you know about it? Don't the mines produce as well as ever? We can do without the white people altogether. Why should we allow them always to skim the cream from the milk; we have submitted to it long enough. In ten years more, California will be ours. Sam Gin!

Sam Gin. Master.

Slim Chunk Pin. How much money have you saved?

Sam Gin. Three hundred dollars.

Slim Chunk Pin. Wouldn't you like to have a washhouse for yourself? You know I am the man who has to say about that.

Sam Gin. I much likee washhouse.

Slim Chunk Pin. All right. You shall have one.

Lam Woo. Too muchee washhouse no good; me no make money.

Slim Chunk Pin. Because you trust a crowd like these people here, you fool. Sam, if you start a washhouse you will need a nice-looking China girl; white people like to see them -- sabee?

Sam Gin. How muchee two?

Slim Chunk Pin. One is enough for the present.

Sam Gin. How muchee one?

Slim Chunk Pin. I bought a fine lot of girls at Hongkong. (*Looking around and seeing* LIZZIE BLAINE *asleep.*) What the matter with her?

Ah Coy. She like smoke opium pipe all the time.

Slim Chunk Pin. Here is the letter. (*Reads.*)

"Friend Slim Chunk Pin -- By the last steamer we received an order from you for two dozen choice girls, between the ages of twelve and fifteen. We feel happy to accommodate you with the required number, but are very sorry to charge you ten dollars apiece more than the last lot we sent you; a good article is very scarce at present in the market, the producers in the country holding back their goods waiting for better prices. We will ship them by the next outgoing steamer, dressed as formerly in men's clothes, and hope that they may arrive in as good condition as they will leave this port.

Respectfully yours,

Ping, Pang, Pung, & Co.

Wholesale and Retail Dealers in Females

Hong Kong, Dec. 6, 1876"

Well, Sam, would you like to have one?

Sam Gin. How muchee one?

Slim Chunk Pin. The price depends on her age. How old do you want her to be?

Sam Gin. Twelve years.

Slim Chunk Pin. Look, that old rascal! He likes something tender. Well, I sell you a nice-looking girl for $200, cash on delivery.

Sam Gin. $200 too muchee money.

Slim Chunk Pin. That is cheap, Sam, depend on it. Some years ago, we used to get $1000 for a good-looking Chinese girl.

Sam Gin. I take one.

Slim Chunk Pin. All right, I will pick you out a good one; but you must know, Sam, that I always pack my girls in a box when I deliver them, to prevent other Chinaman from running away with them, sabee?

Sam Gin. I sabee.

Slim Chunk Pin. When I send the box you must have the coin on hand -- sabee?

Sam Gin. Me catchee the money.

Slim Chunk Pin. Well, it takes that woman a long time to sell her watch. Somebody is coming.

Enter FRANK.

Frank. Stuck again. Lost every cent; Jack Flint, you are too sharp for me. (*Looking up and seeing the Chinese.*) Halloo! What do you want?

Slim Chunk Pin. I am an agent for the powerful Six Companies, and am ordered to see that these Chinamen are paid.

Frank. Get out of here, powerful quick, you slave-dealer.

Slim Chunk Pin. I won't.

Frank. Take that with you. (*Beating them out.*) That's the way to make them go.

ACT II.
Scene -- A parlor.

William. My son is growing up in idleness, and idleness is the source of all mischief. As his father, it is my duty to impress the habit of working upon him; without it he cannot prosper. Work is the root of all lasting prosperity. Owing to the large immigration of coolies, it is almost next to impossible to find any kind of work suitable for a boy of his age.

Enter FRANK.

Frank. Well, father, here I am. Mother said you wanted to see me.

William. So I do.

Frank. Well, what is it?

William. I have found a place for you, Frank.

Frank. What sort of a place?

William. Bootblack.

Frank. What! Bootblack! Did you call me into existence for no other purpose than to black other people's boots? Why didn't you leave me where I was? A bootblack! Ha! ha! ha! Father, you mock me.

William. That's the only sort of work I know of which is not monopolized by the Chinese.

Frank. And there is little danger that it ever will be. They are too much afraid to touch a white man's boot -- it might hurt them somewhere. No, father, bootblack is no go.

William. You ought to do something, Frank, and quit running around with other boys in the streets from morning till night. What will become of you if you are not able to support yourself? It is my duty as your father to see to it.

Enter LIZZIE.

Lizzie. Why, father, it is high time to dress yourself. It is almost three o'clock; you know Mr. Sneaker will arrive by the four o'clock train.

William. That's so, child. I will be done in a minute. (*Exit.*)

Lizzie. Well, Frank, what's the matter? You make a face as if you had swallowed six pounds of sauerkraut.

Frank. Nothing, nothing, sis; let that pass. Father means good, no doubt, and he may be right, too. So you are going to receive Mr. -- What's his name?

Lizzie. Rev. Howard Sneaker. Father is an old schoolmate of his, and he invited him to stay at our house during his sojourn in the city. Frank, all the papers are full of him.

Frank. He must be a bad character if that's the case; most papers have a great appetite for rogues. Beware, sis; I heard of this Mr. Sneaker, before. Don't you know he is a bulldozer?

Lizzie. You are a fool, Frank; didn't you read in the papers how warmly he was received in Salt Lake City?

Frank. He ought to have salted down there forever; that would have relieved all decent people of the foulest hypocrite that ever existed.

Lizzie. You are down on him, Frank.

Frank. I hate him.

Lizzie. Why?

Frank. A man, who under the pretension of teaching the doctrine of Jesus Christ, sneers at the poor laborer that the rich may look with a more favorable eye on him, is, in my eyes the meanest fraud possible. Listen. (*Enter* DORA BLAINE, *unobserved.*) And in my eyes the meanest creatures are those who intrude themselves as public teachers, and lie and slander, blackmail and curse, to favor those who fill their purse.

Lizzie. You are a fool.

Dora. What ails you, Frank?

Frank. I am a fool, madam; your daughter just now said so.

Dora. Come, Lizzie, let's go. Leave that fool alone. Come, papa is downstairs already. Take care of the house, Frank. (*Exit* DORA.)

Lizzie. If my lover should come, tell him to call this evening, please. (*Kisses* FRANK *and exits.*)

Frank. Should come -- he will come; he told me so this morning. There is money in that man, sure; can't I get some out of him? Of course, I can. Lizzie and I are twins. I will put on one of her dresses. (*Exits and returns with a woman's dress which he puts on.*) Hurrah! The Chinese must go. (*Goes before a looking glass.*) Ain't I a lovely girl? Lady Nature, why didn't you make me a girl so I could kiss all the boys in town? (*Bell rings.*) Somebody is coming. I must see who it is. (*Exits and returns with* CAPTAIN JULIUS TURTLESNAP.)

Frank. Father, mother, and brother all went to see Mr. Sneaker.

Captain Julius. And why didn't you go, darling?

Frank. I don't like him.

Captain Julius. Why not?

Frank. I am not very fond of parrots. I hate them.

Captain Julius. May I ask why my darling hates parrots?

Frank. I hate them, Captain.

Captain Julius. Don't call me Captain again. Call me Julius, as you always do. (*Kissing him.*)

Frank. I hate them, Julius, because they are in my opinion nothing else than lazy chatterers.

Captain Julius. Very good, my darling. (*Kissing him.*)

Frank. The sparrow, the nightingale, the eagle -- in fact, every other bird has to look around for his food, except the parrot; he stands on an elevated position and produces -- what? A pile of noise.

Captain Julius. Pretty good, pretty good; so my darling thinks (*Kissing* FRANK.) that Mr. Sneaker is a good-for-nothing noisemaker.

Frank. I didn't say that; he must be good for something, else he wouldn't be in this world.

Captain Julius. Well, what's he good for?

Frank. I know of a French lady on Dupont Street who lost her parrot last week. It is my honest opinion Mr. Sneaker would fill that place to perfect satisfaction.

Captain Julius. Good! good! good! (*Squeezing and kissing* FRANK.) My sweetest sweetheart.

Frank. Don't squeeze me so; don't, please. You are worse than Mr. Sneaker. Shall I sing you a little song?

Captain Julius. By all means, let's have a song.

Frank. You must take a little whisky before I commence. Won't you?

Captain Julius. I would take anything from such a girl.

Frank. (*Getting a bottle and glasses out of the cupboard and filling the latter.*) Here we are, genuine blue grass whisky. The Chinese must go.

Captain Julius. For ever and ever, amen. (*Drinks.*) Good stuff, that. Do you know, darling, why it is called "blue grass whisky?"

Frank. Because if you take too much it makes you feel blue, and if you take too much you go to grass.

Captain Julius. First rate, first rate. Give me another. Thanks. (*Drinks.*)

Frank. Take another. In good company, always take three.

Captain Julius. Girl, you will make me drunk. Well, go ahead. (*Sings.*) "I once loved an Irish girl, and she was funny and frisky."

Frank. I am sure she loved her whisky.

Captain Julius. (*Sings.*) "Haul away, haul away, Joe." Give us another. Thanks. (*Drinks.*)

Frank. (*Aside.*) Now, if that doesn't bring confusion into his wit department, we will have a dry season, sure.

Captain Julius. Give us that song, girl.

Frank. All right. Here we go --

> Mr. Sneaker
> Is a speaker,
>> Sixty dollars he makes a day;
> And he always eats lucullish,
> It's no wonder he feels so bullish,
>> Like a bull among the hay.

(*Repeat.*)

Mr. Sneaker
Is a speaker,
        But he doesn't like the poor;
A dollar a day, he tells the nation
Keeps the laborers from starvation;
        That's enough, he knows it sure.

Mr. Sneaker
Is a speaker,
        People think him awful wise;
But if you look a little closer
You will find this speech composer,
        Has got fat by telling lies.

Mr. Sneaker
Is a speaker,
        In the far East, there he lives,
There he loves and there he kisses,
All the women and the misses,
        Gold he takes and love he gives.

Mr. Sneaker
Is a speaker,
        Chinese, Oh, he loves so well;
If he would only take the notion,
Do us the favor to cross the ocean,
        There, perhaps, he might find a hell.

(*Knocking at the door.*)

    Captain Julius. I ain't drunk. Give us another. Who's there?

    Frank. Come in. (*Enter* POLICEMAN *and Chinaman.*) I bet that's one of the new fellows; he knocks at the door. Green at the business.

    Policeman. I am ordered to arrest Frank Blaine for committing an assault and battery on those Chinaman. Here's the warrant.

    Frank. Don't lean against the wall, please; the color of your coat seems to be on the war path. Look (*Rubbing his hand on the coat.*), how easily it parts from you; what sort of a color is it, anyhow?

Policeman. Indigo, Miss Inquisitive. (*Aside.*) Fine girl. I ain't married yet.

Frank. Indigo. But the dickens, that's the wrong name. It doesn't go *in*, it goes *out*. Man, next time patronize white labor.

Policeman. Let's talk about business, miss. Where is your brother?

Frank. In his pants.

Policeman. Where are his pants to be found?

Frank. In the country; they needed fresh air.

Policeman. I have orders to search the house, and I will do so.

Frank. Help yourself. If anything should be missing I will hold you responsible. (*Exit* POLICEMAN *and Chinaman.*)

Captain Julius. What did that fellow want?

Frank. He is looking for a gentleman, but not for a fool.

Captain Julius. Did he say that I am a fool?

Frank. He did.

Captain Julius. What! I! I! I! a fool! Thunder and blue grass whisky. I'll fight him. I a fool?

Frank. You'll get arrested if you do.

Captain Julius. I don't care a snap. Give me your hand. I'll fight him like a man.

Frank. If you insist on fighting, all right. Let me take care of your gold watch and purse. They don't like such things at the police station. (*Taking his watch and purse from him.*) Now you are ready for him. (*Aside.*) And I go to call the policeman to arrest him. (*Exit.*)

Captain Julius. I fight any man in the country, even Ben Spoonfritz. (*Enter* FRANK *and* POLICEMAN.)

Frank. Take that drunken fool out of the house, please. I don't know him. He came up here to annoy me.

Captain Julius. I pound snuff out of you, you blasted blister. Call me a fool.

Policeman. Come along, old rooster. (*Taking him by the collar and dragging him out.*)

Frank. Blessed are those who have a good stomach. (*Counting.*) Twenty, forty, sixty, about eighty dollars, all gold. Not a bad strike. Well, he can stand it. I never robbed a poor man yet; that's the reason I am such a poor hand in the stock business. (*Knocking at the door.*)

Who is that? Come in.

Enter REV. HOWARD SNEAKER.

Rev. Howard. Does Mr. William Blaine live here?

Frank. He does.

Rev. Howard. You are his daughter, I suppose?

Frank. I am.

Rev. Howard. Your excellent father knows me well, sweet daughter.

Frank. (*Aside.*) Should he be that impudent fraud. (*Aloud.*) What is your name, sir?

Rev. Howard. (*Handing his card.*) Your father is no doubt waiting for me at the depot; therefore he cannot be here for an hour. (*Sitting down.*) We must take all the comforts we can in this world, my daughter. Come, sit on my lap, and let me kiss you for your father.

Frank. (*Aside.*) It's him. (*Aloud.*) Excuse me, I never sat on a man's lap before, except papa's.

Rev. Howard. There's no sin in that, child. Did not our Saviour always take the children on his lap? Come, come, don't be foolish.

Frank. (*Aside.*) I hate to touch that villain; but, never mind, I must see how far he will go. (*Sitting down on his lap.*)

Rev. Howard. God created man and woman to enjoy each other in this beautiful world. (*Kissing him.*)

Frank. (*Aside.*) He is getting hot, the old rooster. (*Aloud.*) How is it, sir, you didn't meet my father at the depot?

Rev. Howard. Very simply, child. I came into town by a different road than they expected. I sometimes change my road to avoid the crowd which always awaits my arrival. I am sorry to have deceived him.

Frank. (*Aside.*) He has done nothing else all his life but deceive people.

Rev. Howard. Has your father any more such handsome daughters as yourself?

Frank. I am his only daughter, sir.

Rev. Howard. When I and your father were schoolmates at the college, he used to be very fond of girls -- a regular Don Juan -- many innocent girls he deceived.

Frank. (*Springing to his feet and tearing off the woman's dress.*) You lie! Out of here, you villain!

Rev. Howard. By heavens! What a fool I was. A deceiver deceived.

Frank. Go! I won't dirty my hands on such a contemptible cur like you. Take that, you bummer. (*Kicking him out.*) All religious frauds must go.

ACT III.
Scene -- A drawing room.

DORA BLAINE *dressed to go out..*

William. To tell the truth, dear, I doubt very much if Mr. Sneaker will come. You know how Frank hates him, and I am afraid he handled him rather roughly that afternoon, although he doesn't say so.

Dora. And I tell you that he will come if I go and invite him. All the world knows that our sex has great influence over him.

William. If they are young and pretty.

Dora. So you think me old and ugly.

William. No, Dora, no. To me you are as young and as pretty as when I first met you; but everyone has his own taste.

Dora. Only think what an honor it will be to our house when all the papers state that the celebrated lecturer, Rev. Howard Sneaker, has dined with us.

William. It would be a splendid advertisement, and might draw customers to my store. As for the honor, I don't care a pinch of snuff.

Dora. Oh, you egoist.

William. Can't help it, dear. We can't live on air. Nature itself is an egoist; it takes everything back again; and if it had been my office to fix things in this world --

Dora. There was never a thing done yet that a fool, in his opinion, could not have done better.

William. I would not have given the man a stomach; the nourishment we need might be inhaled with the air. We all could afford to be angels then; now, most men are nothing else than slaves of their stomach, and many a man sells body and soul -- turns actually a slave -- only to satisfy the craving of his stomach. This very cause brings those hordes of Chinese to our shore; and if we allow the surplus millions of their country to invade ours, they will degrade us to the same level.

Dora. The old story, the egg wants to be smarter than the hen. Bill, you ought to be ashamed of yourself to talk in that way. Did you forget what Mr. Sneaker said in his lecture yesterday? Instead of discouraging the coming of the Chinese, we ought to encourage them, and divide with them the blessings of our country.

William. Well, Mr. Sneaker can afford to say so. If that pious fog-producer was compelled to earn a day's wages by bodily labor, he would have a different opinion on this subject. It is very easy for a man who has never earned a day's wages in his life to go around and blow about the brotherhood of man as long as he can fool the fools out of sixty dollars a day.

Dora. Are we not all sisters and brothers?

William. Let me tell you a little story about that. In early times in this state, I met while on a traveling tour two half-starved creatures on the road. I divided with them everything that I had; when night came on, we all slept under my blanket. The next night, I thought they took a little more of the blanket than they had a right to; the third night, they took still more; and on the fourth night, they left me in the cold altogether. When I remonstrated with them, they told me to go. I then saw I had made a mistake and left; but I will never divide my blanket with two men again.

Enter LIZZIE.

Lizzie. Mamma, if you go out, please order some flour and butter at the grocery. I used all we had this morning.

William. Come here, Lizzie.

Lizzie. What is it, papa?

William. Would you like to marry a Chinaman?

Lizzie. What an idea, papa!

William. That settles the question. Oil and water won't mix; the lighter material will always be on top, and any one who believes that it will mix is a fool. (*To* LIZZIE.) Go and mind your business.

Lizzie. Are you mad, papa?

William. I am, because your mother talks such nonsense.

Lizzie. O, look, papa, Thomson's cow is in mamma's garden

again.

William. Serves mamma right. I bought that piece of ground, united it with my own, hired a man to cultivate it, and plant vegetables in it, on the promise of your mother that she would take care of it and protect it; and look how she has kept her promise. The whole place is full of weeds to the utter ruin of the vegetables.

Dora. If the vegetables can't compete with the weeds, they deserve to be ruined.

William. You talk like an old woman.

Dora. Haven't the weeds as much right to grow there as the vegetables? Isn't this a free country?

William. Free country! Ha! ha! You make me laugh and sick at the same time. Let us look at the free country a little closer. What was growing here when we first came?

Lizzie. Sagebrush, papa.

William. Sagebrush; very well. Now let me tell you a little fable. It once happened that a strong wind blew a few grains of corn into a field of sagebrush. The corn found a fertile soil; it prospered, but ruined the sagebrush. Afterwards, another wind came from a different direction and blew the seeds of the weeds among the corn. The weeds increased very fast, and the corn disappeared.

Dora. If the seeds destroyed the corn, it was the will of the Creator who created them both; and if the Chinamen drive us out, it is His will, and we ought to submit to it.

William. Go! Go! to a college where they manufacture fools, and leave the Creator out of this game. He has nothing to do with it. I have a stomach; on weeds I cannot live; therefore, they must go. (*Exit.*)

Dora. Your papa caught the Chinese fever very bad. Lizzie, when Frank comes, tell him to go to the grocery, and let him order whatever you need. Give him this dollar to spend. That's sure to keep him all day in the beer saloon. Have a good dinner ready. I am going after the Reverend Howard Sneaker. He will dine with us to-day. That will turn all our neighbors green with envy. Good-bye. (*Exit.*)

Lizzie. Good-bye, mamma. I am not going to give that dollar to Frank to spend for beer. I will buy him something useful with it. (*Washing dishes and singing.*)

>My father is a tailor,
>A tailor is he;

And he hates like a poison
   The Heathen Chinee.

Mr. Sneaker is a preacher,
   A preacher is he;
And he made lots of money
   Out of the Heathen Chinee.

Enter FRANK.

Frank. Good morning, sis; your singing relieves me of the necessity of asking you how you feel. You are rosy, like the morning. (*Kissing her.*)

Lizzie. Do you know, Frank, whom I have to thank for it?

Frank. No doubt Dr. Sassafras.

Lizzie. Not Dr. Sassafras. I didn't take any of his pills yet. I have to thank you for it.

Frank. Me?

Lizzie. Yes, you; and no one else. You caused the Chinese to be turned out of the house; that compelled me to do the work. Work cured my sleeplessness, and gave me an appetite. I am healthy like a fish, can sleep like a bear, and eat like a lion.

Frank. If that's the case, it will be prudent to keep one's distance.

Lizzie. If all the girls in the United States would try that remedy, it would raise the price of flour fifty per cent.

Frank. And would turn all the flowers of the land into floursacks.

Lizzie. Leave off joking and drink your coffee, you bad boy. It is your own fault if the coffee is cold.

Frank. Cold coffee never makes me hot; but to remain cool by a cup of boiling hot coffee is sometimes difficult.

Lizzie. Do you wish any more rolls?

Frank. No, thank you, sis.

Lizzie. Do you know, Frank, that one of our late Chinamen has opened a washhouse?

Frank. Where?

Lizzie. Right across the street.

Frank. Which Chinaman is it?

Lizzie. Sam Gin.

Frank. Is it possible?

Lizzie. He is going to get married, too; that is, he bought himself a girl for $200. The China steamer which came in last night has her on board.

Frank. How do you know all this?

Lizzie. Last week, when the agent for the Six Companies was here, I overheard the whole transaction. Of course, they thought me fast asleep.

Frank. I will watch that fellow, and will have him arrested for selling women.

Lizzie. You can't.

Frank. Why can't I?

Lizzie. Because you wouldn't see anything of the girl. She is to be delivered in a box.

Frank. In a box? You are joking.

Lizzie. No, no; it is fact.

Frank. I must see Jack Flint about that. He was born and brought up in Hongkong by English parents; knows their customs and language. There might be something in it. (*Exit.*)

Lizzie. Off he goes, bound to make mischief. I wish I hadn't told him; besides, I forgot to tell him to order the groceries. I must have them. Well, I will get my shawl, and order them myself. (*Exit.*)

Enter CAPTAIN JULIUS TURTLESNAP, *in old and ragged clothes.*

Captain Julius. Such devilish fine girl playing me such a devilish mean trick. I can't think it possible it was she. Could I have dreamed all this? No! These rags on my back prove the fact. No more blue grass whisky for me; I would sooner go to grass at once. I am chilly; a cup of coffee would do me good. Somebody is coming; perhaps it is my darling. Will she recognize me? I look like a bummer. (*Enter* LIZZIE.) Good morning, my sweetest sweetheart; you don't know me. I am your most obedient servant, Captain Julius Turtlesnap.

Lizzie. Julius! In such a condition.

Captain Julius. And all your own fault.

Lizzie. My fault?

Captain Julius. Didn't you make me drink?

Lizzie. You insult me.

Captain Julius. (*Aside.*) I must have been dreaming; it wasn't she. (*Aloud.*) Didn't you take care of my watch and purse?

Lizzie. No!

Captain Julius. Let me explain, darling. I got drunk, was arrested and locked up with a dozen more drunkards; next morning when I awoke, my new suit, lately made by your father, was gone, and, instead, these rags surrounded my body.

Lizzie. So, my future husband gets drunk in company with bad women. I must take that into consideration.

Captain Julius. Don't be hard on me, darling; I wasn't in any woman's company. I swear to it. I dreamt about you all last night.

Lizzie. Very flattering to be dreamt about by a drunken man. Sit down and take a cup of coffee; I suppose that is what you need most.

Captain Julius. Lizzie, you are an angel.

Lizzie. If I was, I would fly at you. I will go down and tell my father to bring you a new suit. (*Exit.*)

Captain Julius. (*Sitting with his back to the door, drinking coffee.*) A good woman is the greatest bonanza a man can strike in this world. Like a sound ship, she will carry you through the biggest storm; that is, if you know how to handle her.

Enter DORA.

Dora. This infernal Mr. Sneaker. Such an insult; telling me to my face that my house is a den of robbers and cutthroats. Oh, why was I not born a man! (*Seeing the* CAPTAIN.) Who is that man? A thief! A thief!

Captain Julius. Woman, woman, what a blessing.

Dora. (*Seizing a broom and striking* CAPTAIN JULIUS *over the head with it.*) Wait! I will bless you.

Curtain falls.

ACT IV.
Scene 1. -- A street corner.

Frank. Glad I met you, Jack; I have some fine news for you.

Jack Flint. How fine? Perhaps as fine as a trade dollar, 900 fine; but nobody will take it.

Frank. The Chinese take it.

Jack Flint. The Chinese are nobody.

Frank. The Chinese are nobody; notwithstanding, they get the best of us in a terrible manner. How much money do you think those pigtails suck out of this state every year?

Jack Flint. Damned if I know.

Frank. Five million dollars. Now, what is money?

Jack Flint. Money is like honey; it sweetens life.

Frank. You wasted your dimes in a candy store, I see. Let me tell you, if I take a four-bit piece, buy meat and flour with it, digest it, it turns into blood; therefore, money is blood. Now, what would you think of a man who would allow a lot of parasites to suck every day a certain quantity of blood out of his body, when he well knows that his whole constitution is endangered by this sucking process; mustn't he be either an idiot or intend self-destruction? And suppose those Chinese parasites should suck as much blood out of every state in the Union, destroying Uncle Sam's sinews and muscles, how many years do you think it would take to put him in his grave?

Jack Flint. Don't talk me to death, for heaven's sake. If you wish to breed wisdom, go to Congress.

Frank. You insult me by such a proposition.

Jack Flint. Excuse me; I didn't intend to ruin your reputation. Let's talk about business. Give me that news you were in such a hurry with just now.

Frank. That's so, Jack. You always told me you understood the Chinese language. I will give you a chance to prove it.

Jack Flint. I not only speak it, but can read and write it besides. Ain't I half a Chinaman myself, born in Hongkong? What has that to do with your news?

Frank. A great deal; let me tell you. One of our late Chinese servants has opened a washhouse; this Chinaman, while still in our employ, and an agent of the Six Companies had a conversation which my sister overheard. The substance of this conversation was that the agent sold a girl twelve years old to our Chinaman for $200; the girl will be packed in a box when delivered. The bargain is cash on delivery. There ought to be some money in it if we use the opportunity.

Jack Flint. Of course there is. Do you know the agent's name? We must know it to make out the bill.

Frank. I can easily find that out.

Jack Flint. Go and do so by all means. I will go and hunt for a box. Meet me at my room. (*Exeunt.*)

Scene 2. -- A Chinese washhouse.

The rear part represents a temple; the four idols of Fire, Water, Air, and Earth are represented; Chinese prostrated before them; a MANDARIN *standing in their midst.*

Mandarin. Thou whose order the fire obeyest, I humble pray thee to protect this house, and all its inmates, against conflagration. Thou who commandest the water, I humbly pray thee to guard this house, and all its inmates, against inundation. Thou who rulest the wind, I humbly pray thee to defend this house, and all its inmates, against its fury; and, thou who holdest the fate of all creatures in the hollow of thy hand, I humbly pray thee to look with a pleasant eye on this house, and all its inmates, that they may prosper and be happy for ever and ever. (*Then addressing the Chinamen.*) Now, children, arise and feed the idols with the choicest of the season. If you wish to retain their favor they must be pleased.

Chinamen arise and put rice, fruit, sweetmeats, chickens and tea in front of the idols.

Mandarin. Our idols are fed; and I am done; be merry now and have some fun.

Some Chinese beating a tin pot; others burning firecrackers.

Mandarin. Sam Gin, you owe me six dollars.
Sam. Gin. Here, master, six dollars.
Mandarin. Thanks; take care of my idols; let no one touch them. I will send for them this afternoon. Farewell.

Enter JACK FLINT, *dressed like a Chinaman, and an* EXPRESSMAN *carrying a box.*

Mandarin. There comes a box, Sam. You see my prayers have done you some good already.
Sam Gin. Heep good, master. (*Exit* MANDARIN.)

Jack Flint. (*To* EXPRESSMAN.) Wait for me outside.

Expressman. All right. (*Exit.*)

Jack Flint. Master Slim Chunk Pin ordered me to deliver this box to you, and receive $200. Here is his writing.

Sam Gin. Open box; me likee see. Me no likee old girl; too muchee tough. (*Opening the box.*)

Jack Flint. How do you like that for plum pudding? Fine piece of meat, eh? Best girl in the lot.

Sam Gin. He! he! he! Me like plenty of fat.

Jack Flint. Let's take her out; she must be tired of lying in that narrow box. Take her by the feet; I take her by the arms.

Sam Gin. Wait; I gettee chain; she run away.

Jack Flint. Don't you see both her hands and feet are tied? How can she run? Take her out; I must have the box. Now. (*Taking out* FRANK BLAINE *dressed as a Chinawoman.*) Where's the money? Let's have it.

Sam Gin. I gettee money. What for you lookee at my wife? (*To the other Chinamen.*) Go out, all of you. (*Exit Chinamen.*) Don't let her run away; I gettee money. (*Exit.*)

Frank. He is gone. What now?

Jack Flint. In the first place, let me cut the ropes (*Taking out a knife and partly cutting the ropes.*) so you can easily break them; then, when the old fool is counting the money to me, you go on tiptoe, but don't make any noise, and take down one of those idols; they are hollow inside; then you creep behind him, and as soon as I have the last dollar in my hand, you pull it over his head; then take that chain and chain him. That done, we decamp as quick as possible.

Frank. How can I run in the street in such a dress?

Jack Flint. Not necessary; the wagon is waiting outside for us. He is coming; stand so that he can't see the cut in the ropes.

Enter SAM GIN.

Sam Gin. My good money; my fine money. Me no likee part with money. (*Crying.*)

Jack Flint. Don't cry like a fool. Come, down with it; I can't wait here six months.

Sam Gin. Me heep likee that girl. O, my good money. Here $200.

Jack Flint. Count it; it might be more, you know.

Sam Gin. O, my good money. (*Counting 20, 40, 60, a sigh when he reaches 200. FRANK has taken up an idol, steps up behind him, and puts it over his head, then chaining him.*)

Jack Flint. Well done; come, quick. (*Exeunt.*)

Sam Gin. O, my good money! (*Tries to run, and falls down.*) O, my fat girl!

Curtain.

1881 -- Emma E. Brewster -- *A Bunch of Buttercups*

Many of the pieces intended for amateur performance featured explicit comparisons among people of different races and nationalities. These comparisons always expressed a hierarchy with white Americans of British descent at the top and the Chinese near the bottom. This short piece is an example of how the "natural" assumptions of one period can strike later sensibilities as completely unacceptable.

The Chinese character is marked not only by his accent, (as are all other characters except the "real Buttercup"), but also by his stereotypical slanted eyes, created by the performer's fingers. Part of the audience's enjoyment of the piece may have come from the fact that the Chinese character follows directly after the Irish one. The animosity between the Irish and the Chinese was an established fact, and the actors may well have expressed or commented on it physically in performance.

A Bunch of Buttercups

CHARACTERS
Four women, two men, one little girl.

Music: "Buttercup's Song"

Enter, L, a pretty DUTCH GIRL, *in national costume, with basket of laces on her arm. Sings:*

> I's galled leedle Pootergub,
>> Dear leedle Pootergub,
>>> Dough I gant nefer dells vy.
> Poot shtill I's galled Pootergub,
>> Dear leedle Pootergub,
>>> Schveet leedle Pootergub, I.

Passes off, R., as enter, L., DARKY WOMAN *Sings:*

> Dis chile am called Buttercup,
>> Dee leetle Buttercup,
>>> Dough I doesn't never know why;
> But still I's called Buttercup,

> Lily-white Buttercup,
>> Mos' lubly Buttercup, me.

Passes off, R., as enter, L., IRISHMAN, *in national costume.*
Sings:

> It's meself that's called Boothercoop,
>> Dear little Boothercoop,
>>> Though it bothers me head to tell why;
> But the ladies (bless 'em!) are afther callin' me
>> Boothercoop,
>> Schwate little Boothercoop,
>>> Arrah! It's mesilf that's the Boothercoop bh'y.

Passes off, R., as enter, L., CHINAMAN *(hold the outer corners*
of eyes up with fingertips, to give them obliquity.). Sings:

> Mi am alwiz callee Buttleclup,
>> Dee leedle Buttleclup,
>>> Allee samee mi nevee'll dell why.
> Steel mi am callee Buttleclup,
>> Dee leedle Buttleclup,
>>> Sweedee leedle Buttleclup, mi.

Exit, R. Enter L., SCOTCH LASSIE. *Sings:*

> I am callit wee Buttercup,
>> Dear little Buttercup,
>>> I hope none will spier o' me why!
> For I'm always call't Buttercup,
>> Bonnie, bright Buttercup,
>>> Wee, blinkin' Buttercup, I.

Exit R. Enter, L., old FRENCH TAMBOURINE WOMAN.
Speaks:

Von leedle twenty-five cents, dear messieurs and sweet ladies! Von
leedle twenty-fife cents for de pauvre orphans whose farder and mooder
die in der last war. Oh gif to me for der loof of sweet charitee, for --

(*Sings and dances to tambourine*) --

> J'suis jamais call Buttercup,
>   Chere petite Buttercup,
>   Dough I navair tells you pourquoi;
> Mais still je suis Buttercup,
>   Chere petite Buttercup,
>   Most charmante Buttercup, moi!

Twenty-fife cents, most charitable messieurs and mesdames! (*Exit, L., jingling tambourine and speaking as she goes.*)

The various exits and entrances being through the near entrances, enter now from R.U.E., LITTLE GIRL *dressed in green and yellow, to represent a buttercup blossom. Buttercup hat, made of yellow board cut in ten scallops to represent ten petals, green sepals turned back over crown, green stem hanging over. Pink hose, green slippers. Basket of buttercups and grasses. Runs down, sings:*

> I'm the real little Buttercup,
>   Dear little Buttercup,
>   I'm thinking you all can tell why.
> For I'm called little Buttercup,
>   Dear little Buttercup,
>   Sweet little Buttercup, I.

Enter, R.U.E., actors in reverse order, headed by TAMBOURINE WOMAN. *Form in semicircle around* LITTLE GIRL, *sing in concert their various stanzas.*

Curtain.

1895 -- T.S. Denison -- *Patsy O'Wang*

This domestic farce most closely resembles the earlier *New Brooms Sweep Clean*. Although the situation is different, in both plays, a household is disrupted by the addition of a "Chinese" character. More pointedly than the previous play, however, this text emphasizes the contrast between the Chinese and the Irish, clearly in favor of the latter. *Patsy O'Wang* is also noteworthy for its presentation of Mrs. Fluke's fears of being poisoned by her new Chinese cook, which may have accurately reflected the unspoken anxiety of many Euroamerican women. In addition to its overall negative evaluation of the Chinese, the play also satirizes pro-Chinese Euroamericans in the person of Miss Simper, who is presented as a laugable contrast to the more level-headed Euroamericans. Finally, it is noteworthy that the title character ends the piece as an Irishman who hopes to enter American politics. He can therefore achieve not only assimilation but even power in a way absolutely denied to the Chinese of the time and for decades thereafter.

One literary influence on the play may have been Robert Louis Stevenson's *Dr. Jekyll and Mr. Hyde*, which had been published nine years before. Although the play lacks the philosophical elements of Stevenson's novel, the central plot device is quite familiar.

The author's original stage directions contain some interesting comments on the appropriate stage portrayal of the Chinese (always by Euroamerican actors) at the time. Therefore, the relevant portions of this preface have been reproduced along with the play.

Patsy O'Wang

An Irish Farce With a Chinese Mix-up

SYNOPSIS AND HINTS TO PLAYERS

The key to this capital farce is the remarkable transformation of which CHIN SUM *is capable. Born of an Irish father and a Chinese mother and brought up in barracks at Hong Kong, he has a remarkable dual nature. Whiskey, the drink of his father, transforms him into a true Irishman, while strong tea, the beverage of his mother, has the power of restoring fully his Chinese character.* DR. FLUKE *employs* CHIN *as cook, on the hearty recommendation of his old friend, Major Barker. Unfortunately for the doctor,* CHIN *gets at the whiskey bottle through the carelessness of* MIKE, *who in his way is no less a character than* CHIN SUM *himself. . . No instructions can be given here concerning the Chinese part, except that the timbre and tones of the Chinese voice are very peculiar, and can be learned only by listening to Chinamen. The Chinese dialect as written here (and elsewhere in America) is at best but a poor imitation, but good enough to be funny, which is the only object in view.*

Scene -- DOCTOR FLUKE'S office.

Main entrance L., private consultation room R., massage and electric room entrance D.F.R.C. Table C. with old papers and magazines. Small bookcase with books, or shelves with bottles at option, by flat L.C. Diploma on wall. Sign on door "DR. FLUKE, hours 12 to 4." Settee R.

Mrs. Fluke. (Discovered as curtain rises.) Well, Dr. Fluke, I shan't take the responsibility of having a Chinaman in the house.

Dr. Fluke. My dear, don't be absurd! There's no responsibility in the case. Out in California, you know, people are charmed with Chinese cooks. Why, your sister couldn't be induced to part with Weak Lung.

Mrs. Fluke. Maria always was eccentric.

Dr. Fluke. But you know, darling, we have tried everything but the Chinese -- Irish, Swede, German, French, African, Yankee -- that's so as we haven't had any Hindoos yet nor Cannibal Islanders.

Mrs. Fluke. Dear me! It makes me weary to think of it. Why can't we get along with Nora?

Dr. Fluke. (Sarcastically.) Or transform Mike into a cook?

Mrs. Fluke. Now you are absurd, Henry. I'll wash my hands of the whole affair.

Dr. Fluke. My dear, that is just what I wanted you to say.

Mrs. Fluke. Indeed, then you needn't have asked my opinion at all.

Dr. Fluke. I am sure this Patsy O'Wang is a treasure.

Mrs. Fluke. (In astonishment.) Patsy O'Wang! Patsy doesn't sound very Chinese.

Dr. Fluke. But he has a history.

Mrs. Fluke. Oh indeed! That's rather a doubtful accomplishment for a cook.

Dr. Fluke. Quite the contrary! Harriet, I tell you that I've found a treasure. Let me read you what Major Barker says in his letter recommending Chin Sum.

Mrs. Fluke. Chin Sum! I thought his name was -- what barbarous name did you say?

Dr. Fluke. (*Laughing.*) Patsy O'Wang! But that's only a nickname. The Chinese of it is Chin Sum. Now, Chin is the son of a wild Irish officer in the tenth Artillery stationed formerly at Hong Kong. His mother is a pretty Chinese girl.

Mrs. Fluke. (*Surprised.*) Well, did you ever!

Dr. Fluke. My dear, I admit that there is a slight flaw in his pedigree. (*Looking at letter.*) But let me skip all that. Major Barker speaks of him in the most extravagant terms -- (*Reading.*) "The best cook I ever saw," "the most obedient servant," "the most affectionate creature," (*Triumphantly.*) isn't that enough?

Mrs. Fluke. I suppose so, since apparently it is all settled.

Dr. Fluke. There's more.

Mrs. Fluke. Never mind, skip it.

Dr. Fluke. Eh, what's this? "Never under any circumstances let him taste a drop of whiskey."

Mrs. Fluke. Humph, then you'll have to keep him and Mike apart.

Dr. Fluke. (*Reads to himself.*) Really, that is surprising.

Mrs. Fluke. What's surprising?

Enter NORAH, *L.*

Dr. Fluke. Nothing, my dear. (*Reads.*) The remedy is --

Norah. If you plaze, sor, the Chinee cook has come.

Dr. Fluke. All right, Norah, show him his room and then take him to the kitchen. My dear, will you install him?

Mrs. Fluke. No indeed! You may do that, Henry, till he gets a start. Decidedly I feel nervous with a Chinaman in the kitchen. Who knows but he may poison us all.

Norah. (*Re-enters with card.*) If you plaze, Mrs. Fluke, Miss

Simper's at the dure.

Mrs. Fluke. Show her in, Norah, at once. (*Exit* NORAH, *L.*)
Now she will be trying to convert him.

Enter MISS SIMPER, *L.*

Mrs. Fluke. I'm delighted to see you, Miss Simper.

Miss Simper. Thank you! I just run in for a minute. Good
morning, Dr. Fluke.

Dr. Fluke. Good morning, Miss Simper. How charming you
look. That tonic benefited you greatly. Shall I change the
prescription?

Miss Simper. (*Hastily.*) No, thank you, I have come today in
the interest of the missionary cause.

Mrs. Fluke. Won't you step back into the parlor where we can
talk at leisure?

Miss Simper. Oh no, I'm in a dreadful hurry. The African
Argonauts meet at eleven and I preside. We start our first worker to
Ashantee tomorrow. At four p.m. the Mongolian Mediators have a
meeting, and at eight p.m. is the debate in which we shall answer the
Cannibal Calumniators.

Dr. Fluke. You are a very busy bee, Miss Simper.

Miss Simper. No, I've resigned from the Busy Bees;
concentrating, you see. They say you have a new Chinese cook, Mrs.
Fluke.

Mrs. Fluke. Not I. He's the Doctor's importation. Talk to him.

Miss Simper. (*Enthusiastically.*) Oh Doctor, tell me all about
him. My heart bleeds for all the millions of Asia who sit in outer
darkness.

Dr. Fluke. My dear Miss Simper, he is a gold nugget. He will
be a capital acquisition in your mission school. So intelligent, so
docile, so affectionate, so -- so --

Miss Simper. Just so. Oh, I'm perfectly delighted. Doctor, does
he -- ah -- has he doffed the Chinese garb yet and donned the raiment of
civilization?

Dr. Fluke. Blessed if I know. I'll call him in and introduce him
at once. (*Rings.*)

Miss Simper. Do so. I was just going to ask that very favor.
I'm sure he will agreeably surprise us all.

Dr. Fluke. He will. (NORAH *enters L.*) Bring Chin Sum here.

Mrs. Fluke. I hope the wretch doesn't smoke opium.

Dr. Fluke. Harriet, don't expose your ignorance. That is done in *joints.*

Mrs. Fluke. What kind of joints?

Dr. Fluke. Blessed if I know, bamboo joints possibly. I hear the Chinese do most everything with bamboo except to fight Japan. They did that in their minds.

Enter NORAH *followed by* CHIN.

Dr. Fluke. Chin Sum, I want to introduce you to my wife; by the way, I think I will call you Patsy. Wife, our new servant Patsy O'Wang. (MRS. FLUKE *surveys him in silence.*)

Patsy. (*Puts left hand to heart and bows.*) Velly much glad see Missee Fluke.

Dr. Fluke. And this is Miss Simper, a mission young lady.

Patsy. Velly nice mission gull.

Miss Simper. (*Blushing.*) Mr. O'Wang, you're *so* gallant. Promise me to come to Bible class next Sunday.

Patsy. Sooh thing!

Miss Simper. How intelligent!

Patsy. Leadee all same Biblee in Flisco?

Miss Simper. I don't understand him. (*Turns enquiringly to* DR. FLUKE.)

Dr. Fluke. Yes, Patsy, they read the same Bible as they do in Frisco.

Patsy. Sing velly nice hymn-song all same day?

Dr. Fluke. Yes.

Patsy. Chin Sum make be school boy next Sunday all same day.

Dr. Fluke. (*Looks at watch.*) Patients will be coming soon. Patsy, I'll show you the kitchen and tell you what to prepare for dinner today. After that, Mrs. Fluke --

Mrs. Fluke. Oh dear!

Miss Simper. How charming! How childlike!

Patsy. (*Grins.*) All samee like big man-shile? No catchee what say.

Dr. Fluke. Patsy, go into the kitchen, I'll be there in a minute. (DR. FLUKE *goes into office and changes coat, putting on light jacket, hanging coat in office. Follows* PATSY *out L.*)

NORAH *and* MIKE *heard D.F.*

Mrs. Fluke. Here are the attendants getting the baths ready. Come into the house. It may be all right, but I'm afraid.

Miss Simper. What, afraid of Chin! I shall call him Chin, poor boy. I think those Chinese names perfectly lovely. So brief, so simple, so childlike. Chin! Just think! *So* expressive.

Mrs. Fluke. (*As they go, L.*) And those horrid stories of rats and opium.

Miss Simper. I don't believe a word of it. (*Exeunt, L.*)

Enter MIKE *and* NORAH *from D.F.*

Norah. What do you think, Mike, of havin' a Chinee cook in the house?

Mike. Ah Norah, it's an outrage, that's the whole blissid truth. To think of a blackgyard haythen cookin' for dacint people.

Norah. It's a disgrace, I'll give notice, I will --

Mike. I'll not ate a bit o' his dirthy cookin', faith I'll not.

Norah. But what'll ye do? Them that works must eat.

Mike. (*Winking.*) Oi'm all right as long as free lunches hold out.

Norah. Free lunches ye'd better let alone, Mike.

Mike. Norah, it's not the lunches that afflicts me. It's what goes with thim.

Norah. Last time you know, Dr. Fluke said you'd have to leave if you got drunk again.

Mike. It's a bit of charity the Doctor needs. Ivery mon has some wakeness.

Norah. And woman is weak too, so just carry out that box of bottles for me, I'll have to wash them here. The Doctor has some of his truck in the library.

Mike. He'll be blowin' the whole place up yit with his dinnymite and farmacopy. (*Brings out bottles and sets box L. up.*)

Norah. Mike, ye'd better get ready for Mr. Boyler. He'll be here pretty soon for his electricity and that Englishman will want his bawth. (NORAH *washing bottles.*)

Mike. Faith, it's enough to try the patience of ould Job himself. Begob, Job never was docthor's assistant. I regret I iver intered the midical profession. Ivery toime I look at ould Boyler he sez, Mike, ye've hurt me rheumatiz again.

Norah. Mike, you are too strong, you must be careful.

Mike. Faith, I handle him just like a new born baby, or like the egg with the chick unborn. But the ould badger's that tender I'm mortally afraid he'll go all to pieces in the bath thub.

Norah. Mr. Boyler complains to Doctor Fluke that you are too rough.

Mike. Too rough, is it! Faith, he'll have to be packed in cotton nixt. The Docthor was after tellin' me to stretch Boyler's limbs gently like, and I tuk hold av his arm with one hand and his shoulther with the other like this, and pulled like this, sort o' bracin' mysilf loike with one fut forinst the tub. I'm a thafe if some jint or other didn't snap like a pistol. I was so scared that I dropped the ould bundle in the wather hid over ears. I thought he was goin't to exshpire right there in me hands.

Norah. (*Laughing*.) What did he say?

Mike. I don't know what he intinded to say. He sthrangled.

Norah. Why, was he under the water so long as that?

Mike. No, indade, it wasn't the wather. It was the strong language. He is that way sometimes when his emotions overcome him. When the ould sinner gets to swearin', he can't stop till he sthrangles. After that he's very paceable for a shpell.

Norah. But he's awful good in spite of his rough ways. He gives you many a quarter.

Mike. That he does, and I couldn't think more of an only child if I had wan, nor an only father ayther, for that matter. I'm prayin' for him night and day. If he survives these baths and the alictricity an' the drugs and the plasthers, it'll be a great triumph of the midical profession. There he comes now, I hear his cane on the walk.

Enter BOYLER, *L., limping and twisted with rheumatism.*

Boyler. Good morning, Mike, good morning, Norah.

Mike. Mornin', sir. Begob, ye're spry as a kittin this marnin'. I thought it was the milkman whin I heerd yez.

Boyler. Mike, try to be careful today. You rubbed my right side yesterday till I think you started all my ribs.

Norah. Do be gentle, Mike.

Mike. I'll be as tender -- as tender as a shpring chicken. It's alictricity, sor, today?

Boyler. So it is, I forgot.

Mike. The Docthor said yez couldn't stand another bath today. (*Catching himself.*) I mane ye're improvin' till yez don't nade it. (*Leads* BOYLER *into D.F. to operating room.*)

Norah. (*Washing bottles.*) Such dirty bottles. The labels ain't half soaked off and half of them look greasy. (*Sound of machine humming.*)

Boyler. (*Offstage, groans.*) Oh! Mike, that's too strong.

Norah. Poor man, I wonder if it does him any good?

Enter PATSY O'WANG, L.

Patsy. Ilish gal! Monnin', Nolee.

Norah. (*Looks up.*) What's that?

Patsy. All samee nice day.

Norah. Go back with yez to the kitchen.

Patsy. Chin Sum want see.

Enter MIKE *from D.F.*

Mike. Yez want to see? All right, ye shall see. This (*Points R. door.*) is the Docthor's private consultinotion room. Nobody but himself and patients and mimbers of the profession like misilf go in there. (BOYLER *calls "Mike."*) Back there is the operating room. Whin ye git hurted that's where they saw yer leg off.

Patsy. (*Startled.*) What time saw leg?

Mike. Ony toime.

Patsy. Who leg?

Mike. Begob, onbody's if they can pay for the job. (BOYLER *impatiently calls "Mike, Mike!"*)

Mike. Comin', sor.

Patsy. (*Sees machine through door.*) What machine? All samee lope loun wheel.

Mike. (*Scratching his head.*) I'm thinkin' it would take a Frinchman or a Dago to talk to the haythen.

Patsy. Lope loun wheel. (*Makes sign of turning.*)

Mike. He wants to turn a bit. Begob, yez may turn awhile.

Norah. Be careful, Mike. The Doctor wouldn't like it. (*They enter D.F.*)

Mike. (*Voice heard.*) Turn aisy loike. It's great shport. (PATSY *turns machine.*)

Re-enter MIKE.

Norah. Doctor wouldn't like your litting the Chinee boy meddle here.

Mike. I've a bit of an arrant. He may turn till I get back. (*Exit. L.*)

Norah. Worry now! These be a bad lot of bottles. (*Drops one and breaks it.*) There, I've broken one. (BOYLER *groans "Hold, that's too fast." * PATSY *turns faster.* BOYLER *yells "Stop!" Chinaman does not understand.* BOYLER *screams in pain "Stop, you scoundrel!"*)

Norah. Oh dear, there they go. I knew there would be trouble. (*Calls D.L.*) Mike, Mike, come quick. Where is the Doctor? He ought to be here. (*Runs out D.L.*)

Boyler. (*Gets up, and crash of chair upsetting.*) You Mongolian idiot. (*Comes out D.F.*) Where is that rascally Irishman? (PATSY *follows out, looks puzzled.*) John, you are a fool.

Patsy. (*Grins.*) My name not John. Name in Chinee Chin Sum. Melican name Patsy O'Wang.

Boyler. Stop your chatter, you mummy, you saffron-colored rat catcher! Where is that rascal of a Mike? When I get well it'll be a bad day for him. I'll murder that man yet. (*Dances around.*) How my nerves thrill, oh, oh! (*Seizes left leg and dances around on right.*) The liniment! No attendance here. I'll sue Fluke for damages. Here, you moon-faced Mongolian monkey! What are you grinning at? Do you see that bottle of liniment? (*Points with cane to bottle on shelf.*)

Patsy. Heap bottle, one time, whichee?

Boyler. That one! Bring it and rub me, I'm on fire.

Patsy. Melican man hot like old boy; all bun up.

Boyler. I'll die in this infernal torture chamber. (*Roars.*) Bring the bottle! (*Enter D.F. growling and holding leg.*)

Patsy. (*Takes brandy bottle, uncorks, smells.*) Um! Hong Kong blandy! Make toddy likee time in Hong Kong. Dlink heap toddy.

(*Takes drink, rubs stomach.*) Velly good.

Boyler. Hurry up, you! What on earth are you doing?

Patsy. (*Takes bottle of liniment, enters D.F. Rubs* BOYLER, *who gives grunts of satisfaction.* PATSY *runs out, takes another drink, rubs stomach; runs back again, rubs* BOYLER. *Business ad lib.*)

Enter MIKE *suddenly, followed by* NORAH, L. *They surprise* PATSY *with bottle.*

Mike. Put that down, ye haythen!

Patsy. Ilishman dlunk! (*Runs back and turns handle furiously.*)

Norah. Do ye hear that, Mike? That Chinaman's goin' to ruin the place! Oh, do stop him.

Mike. Let the haythen airn his wages. (*Piercing shrieks from* BOYLER.)

Norah. Oh Mike, do stop him. He'll kill Mr. Boyler.

Mike. (*Unconcernedly.*) Faith, that's nothin'. That's the way the ould badger goes on ivery day if I only touch a bit av a sore spot. A good shakin' up'll benefit him greatly. I think he'll be ready nixt for the bat's liver oil.

Norah. Merciful heavens! Did ye say bat's liver oil?

Mike. Bat's liver oil, I said. (PATSY *comes out to make sneak for bottle,* MIKE *turns and sees him.*) Hould on there, Patsy! The Docthor and meself have institooted a regular coorse.

Boyler. Mike, where are you!

Mike. Here, sor. (*To* NORAH.) First comes the hot bath, nointy noine degrays Farenhot, followed by pullin' the limbs, on the injy rubber plan. (*Business of stretching patient's arm.*) Nixt is the alictricity an' liniment. Then comes that bat's liver oil.

Norah. An' what will be next?

Mike. That's a saycret like the Kaly cure.

Norah. Tell *me*, won't you, Mike?

Mike. Yiz, if yez won't tell onybody. (*Approaches her and puts up hand to her ear, then in a very loud distinct stage whisper.*) Sand paper!

Norah. Go 'long with yez. (*Slaps him.*)

Boyler. (*Inside.*) Murder! Oh! oh! You infernal scoundrel. (*Great racket of* BOYLER *getting out of chair.* PATSY *comes out flying with* BOYLER *after him. They come down C.* BOYLER *strikes* PATSY *with cane.* PATSY *grabs at cane and pulls* BOYLER'S *wig off. Runs with it into office R., and closes door as* BOYLER *throws cane after him.*)

Mike. Thank God he's cured! He's throwed away the cane. (BOYLER *clutches at* MIKE'S *throat,* MIKE *dodges.*) Aisy sor, aisy, ye're all right now.

Boyler. (*Speaks with difficulty.*) You villain! My leg is on fire. (*Makes after* MIKE, *chases him round the table.*)

Mike. I belave it, sor. It's a very lively leg, Mr. Boyler. (*They stop,* MIKE *next L.,* BOYLER *R. of table.*)

Boyler. (*Trying to speak, but cannot for rage and excitement.*) Oh, you -- you --

Mike. Aisy sor, careful sor. Won't ye step into the office and write a bit of tistimonial for the inshtitootion? (BOYLER *shakes his fist at him, speechless.*)

Norah. Oh dear, we're all ruined. He'll tell the Doctor.

Mike. Whist, he's stranglin' now. It is the profanity. He's often took that way. (PATSY *in office utters a loud whoop.*)

Norah. Where *is* the Doctor? Everything's going to ruin. (*Runs out L. Another whoop in office.* BOYLER *frantically rubbing lame leg.*)

Mike. That haythen is gettin' gay. I'll tache him a lesson he won't forget soon. I'll tache him to stay in the kitchen. (*Goes toward office door.*)

Boyler. (*Recovers speech.*) I'll have you arrested, you villain, for malpractice.

Mike. Malpractice! What sort o' practice is that?

Boyler. You are a pair of knaves. (*In excitement puts down lame leg.*)

Mike. What a wonderful cure. Beautiful! I'll just kape this stick as a tistimonial.

Boyler. None of your insolence. I'll sue Doctor Fluke for damages, and as for you and that Chinaman, I'll have you put in jail. (*Going L.*)

Mike. A beautiful cure, sor. Ye walk as straight as -- as straight as -- the moral law. Ye'd make an illegant drum-major.

Boyler. (*Snorts.*) Drum-major! (*Going.*)

Mike. Won't yez take yer hat, sor? (*Exit* BOYLER, *limping very little.*) Now I'll just settle with John Chinaman, bad cess to him.

Enter PATSY *suddenly from office.*

Patsy. Whoopee! Feel good! Allee same day feel bully. (*Jumps from floor and kicks his wooden-soled shoes like an athlete.*)

Mike. (*Starting back.*) Faith, I think he's possissed. (PATSY *still clutches wig in left hand, seizes cane from table and jumps up again. Comes down with a whoop and makes a lightning shillelah pass at* MIKE'S *head.*)

Mike. The divil's in him. I'd bitther call the Docthor. (*Starts L. slowly at first with* PATSY *advancing. They keep eyes on each other and* MIKE *gradually gets in a panic. He suddenly darts for door just at* PATSY *throws an empty bottle from table at his head. Bottle breaks outside with a crash.*)

Patsy. (*Comes down C.*) It's a bad head I have. Where am I? What am I? (*Thinks a moment.*) Is this Hong Kong? No, this is America. (*Looks round.*) A doctor's shop. I was this way once before in Hong Kong when I got drunk in the barracks. Whiskey brings out the Irish in me. But they put me back. What did they give me? I can't remember. My head's all confused. (*Hands to head.*) Well, I won't be a Chinaman. I won't take a blessed drop of anything but poteen. I'll get rid of this Chinese dress. I hate it. (*Notices wig.*) Just the thing! (*Coils pig-tail up carefully on top of his head and puts on* BOYLER'S *wig. Looks in hand glass that is on shelf.*) Not so bad! Old coat, I'm done with you, too. (*Throws off Chinese tunic. Gets* DOCTOR'S *coat from hall inside office and puts it on. Looks in glass.*) Not so bad a fit, though a bit too long in the tails. (*Walks across stage.*) Well now, ain't I good enough Irish for New York, or Chicago, or Cork ayther? (*Sees shoes.*) Look at the bloody shoes. (*Kicks them high in the air.*) Off with ye. Cow leather's good enough for me. (*Goes in office and comes out with* DOCTOR'S *shoes. Puts them on.*) Now me toilet is more to me likin'. (*Struts admiringly.*) Let that ould bear come back, an' the Doctor, and his man. I'll thrash the whole crowd if they lay hands on me.

Enter MRS. FLUKE, *L.*

Mrs. Fluke. A patient? The Doctor will soon be here. Have a seat, sir. (*Notices oddity of* PATSY'S *appearance. Starts.*) Oh! Who are you?

Patsy. Don't be alarmed, madam. I'm Patsy O'Wang. I'm the new -- No, indeed, I'm *not* that.

Mrs. Fluke. The new cook, and crazy! Oh dear, I knew there'd be trouble. Oh, *why* doesn't Dr. Fluke come!

Patsy. Madam, you are not well. (*Politely.*) I beg you to be seated. (*Points to chair by table.*)

Mrs. Fluke. He's very polite, at any rate. (*During this dialogue,* MRS. FLUKE *has been getting closer to door L. and at last darts out suddenly, to surprise of* PATSY.)

Patsy. There goes another! It's not much confidence the new mistress has in me. They're puttin' a job on me. What is it they gave me before? I'd give a thousand dollars if I could only think of it. (*Enter* DR. FLUKE *L., followed by* MRS. FLUKE, NORAH, MIKE, *and* MISS SIMPER. PATSY *runs into office R. and locks himself in.*)

Mrs. Fluke. Doctor Fluke, I told you something would happen.

Dr. Fluke. Pshaw, nothing has happened. Mike let him have whiskey.

Mrs. Fluke. I told you so. The very thing he shouldn't have had.

Dr. Fluke. I'll cure him quick enough, and Mike, you are very careless.

Mike. I'm very sorry, sor, but I didn't let him have the whiskey. Do yez think I'd be wastin' good liquor on a Chinaman?

Mrs. Fluke. But he's got it now, and what will you do, I'd like to know?

Dr. Fluke. I'll just give him the remedy spoken of by Major Barker.

Mrs. Fluke. What is the remedy?

Dr. Fluke. (*Claps hand in pocket.*) Where is that letter? Here's a go! (*Turns over papers on table looking for letter.*)

Mrs. Fluke. Have you lost the letter?

Dr. Fluke. It seems so. (*Business of diving his hands into his pockets.*) Oh, I have it!

Mrs. Fluke. Read it then!

Dr. Fluke. I mean, I know where it is. I changed coats.

Mrs. Fluke. And Patsy has the coat on!

Dr. Fluke. Well, that is a situation!

Mrs. Fluke. (*Hysterically.*) Now he'll murder us all!

Dr. Fluke. Nonsense! Major Barker says he's the most affectionate creature.

Mrs. Fluke. Major Barker, fiddlesticks.

Miss Simper. I am sure that Major must be right. I think the Chinese have such lovely dispositions.

Mrs. Fluke. Miss Simper, you and the Doctor fatigue me with such twaddle.

Doctor Fluke. Mike, suppose you go into the office and ask him for my coat.

Mike. If you plaze, sor, I think my appearance excoites him a bit.

Miss Simper. Oh, let me go. (*Starts.*)

Mrs. Fluke. Miss Simper, are you out of your senses? (*Pulls her back.*)

Doctor Fluke. I will go in.

Mrs. Fluke. (*Pulling him back.*) Henry, do you want to be murdered?

Doctor Fluke. (*Petulantly releasing himself.*) Let me alone. (*Goes toward door, knocks.*) Patsy! Patsy!

Mrs. Fluke. Oh, rash man! Henry, I know we'll all be killed in our tracks.

Miss Simper. Let me reason with him!

Mrs. Fluke. Oh, you silly goose. Do be quiet, won't you? What *can* he be doing? (*All listen.*) It's as quiet as the grave. I'll bet he's taking poison in his desperation. Or hanging himself, maybe.

Mike. There's a noice bit of rope on the pulley machine.

Mrs. Fluke. We'll all be killed yet, I know. Miss Simper, save yourself. (*Shoves* MISS SIMPER *and* NORAH *out, L.*)

Dr. Fluke. Harriet, there isn't the slightest danger.

Mrs. Fluke. Dr. Fluke, why do you stand there like a post? Why *don't* you send for the police before that Chinaman does anything desperate? He is crazy and so are you.

Dr. Fluke. Humph! He's drunk!

Mrs. Fluke. He's crazy. Mike, run for the police.

Dr. Fluke. Mike, stay where you are, to assist me.

Mrs. Fluke. What *are* you going to do, Henry?

Dr. Fluke. Going into that room. (MRS. FLUKE *throws up her hands and then suddenly lays hold of* DR. FLUKE'S *coat tails.*)

Let me alone. (*Breaking loose, raps on door;* MRS. FLUKE *runs to door L.*) Patsy! Say, Chin Sum!

Patsy. Sir.

Dr. Fluke. Will you let me in?

Patsy. No.

Dr. Fluke. I don't want to arrest you.

Patsy. (*Voice indistinctly.*)

Dr. Fluke. I give you my word of honor, yes, I'll send them all out.

Mrs. Fluke. Indeed, I won't go out and see you killed.

Dr. Fluke. Harriet, how could you see me killed if you went out? (*Voice again through door.*) Yes, I'll send them *all.* Mike, go at once. Harriet, please go. He won't open the door till you all go. He is afraid we'll take him to jail.

Mike. Sarve him good and roight, I say.

Mrs. Fluke. Yes, he ought to be jailed for acting that way. (*Exit* MIKE *to operating room D.F.*)

Dr. Fluke. (*Leads* MRS. FLUKE *out L. She, protesting; returns to office door R.*) Just hand my coat through the door, please. (*Door opens and coat is pushed through.*) Now for the remedy! (*Eagerly opens letter, reads.*) "Affectionate creature."

Mrs. Fluke. (*In door L.*) Stuff!

Dr. Fluke. Hum, "most confiding" -- yes, it seems so. Oh, here it is.

Mrs. Fluke. (*Entering, eagerly.*) What is it?

Dr. Fluke. Harriet, why do you interrupt? Oh, here it is! "If he ever gets under the influence of liquor, he labors under the strange delusion that he is an Irishman."

Mrs. Fluke. How absurd! He's crazy, I'd call the police.

Dr. Fluke. (*Petulantly.*) My dear, will you allow me? This is a very curious case. "The remedy is *tea*, plenty of strong *tea*." How very simple. (*Rings bell.*) I'll give him enough tea to settle him in short order.

Enter NORAH, *L.*

Norah. What is it, sor? Is he still violent?

Dr. Fluke. Peaceful as a lamb! He wants tea.

Norah. Tay is it! Did yez iver --

Mrs. Fluke. As well try a pinch of salt.

Dr. Fluke. Don't stand there talking, Norah. Bring the tea at once. Plenty of it! Strong! Just throw about half a pound into the tin pot and fill it with hot water.

Norah. The tin pot houlds a gallon, sor.

Dr. Fluke. (*Impatiently.*) Will you obey orders? Go! Run! (*Exit* NORAH *grumbling, L.*)

Mrs. Fluke. Tea! The idea!

Dr. Fluke. (*Pacing floor, excitedly.*) This is a great case. I'll write it up for the medical journals. A wonderful case --

Enter BOYLER, *L., angry.*

Boyler. All humbug, sir.

Dr. Fluke. What's that? Oh, it's you, Mr. Boyler.

Boyler. At last I've found you out, Dr. Fluke!

Dr. Fluke. So it seems. Why bless me, if you ain't cured. Walking without a cane!

Boyler. Humbug! I said.

Dr. Fluke. But it's a fact!

Boyler. You can't hoodwink me, sir. You're a charlatan!

Dr. Fluke. Don't be unreasonable!

Boyler. Unreasonable! Oh, I *can't* stand that. (DR. FLUKE *laughs.*) Gad, sir, you are actually laughing at my misfortunes. Do you call yourself a gentleman?

Dr. Fluke. Cut all that! What do you complain of? You are cured.

Boyler. Confound your cure. You first maltreat me, outrage my feelings, and then laugh at me.

Dr. Fluke. When has all this happened?

Boyler. Every day for a month, Dr. Fluke. First you put a Hercules in the shape of a wild Irishman to rub me in the bath. He breaks every bone in my body by installments. Then he pummels me by degrees into a jelly.

Dr. Fluke. Well, what did you expect, Mr. Boyler? This isn't a kindergarten, and your rheumatism was a very obstinate case.

Boyler. Obstinate case! Let me say, sir, you are a butcher and that Irishman is an executioner. To crown the indignity, you set a crazy Chinaman to give me the electrical treatment. He runs a stream of liquid fire through my leg.

Dr. Fluke. Which cured you completely!

Boyler. Will you let me speak, sir? When I protest, the heathen doubles the quantity. Why gad, sir, it was something terrific. I saw the constellation of Orion in broad daylight.

Dr. Fluke. Ah, it *is* a fine machine! A beauty!

Boyler. (*Laughs.*) There you are wrong, for I smashed it to bits.

Dr. Fluke. (*Startled.*) What's that you say? My fine machine ruined? I'll have damages, Mr. Boyler.

Boyler. Damages! I shall sue you for $10,000 damages.

Dr. Fluke. Do it, sir, do it! It'll make my fortune. It will advertise the greatest cure of the age. Nothing like a lawsuit for advertising purposes. Won't you oblige me by breaking something else? Just upset those shelves, won't you? Throw my instrument case out of the window.

Boyler. I'll not do it. I won't gratify you. A gentleman can find other ways of avenging an insult. And then there's my wig, too.

Dr. Fluke. Where?

Boyler. Where? Do you doubt my word? (*Takes off hat and exposes shiny bald head.*) Do you see that?

Dr. Fluke. I see the head-piece but I don't see any wig.

Boyler. (*Emphatically.*) No, sir, you don't see any wig. Your crazy Chinaman snatched it off my head and exposed me to the indignity of going home barehead in the public street.

Dr. Fluke. You shouldn't go out barehead, you may catch cold. I'll not be responsible if you disobey orders.

Boyler. And whose fault would it be?

Dr. Fluke. Yours, of course.

Boyler. Why, hang your assurance, Dr. Fluke.

Dr. Fluke. I disapprove of your indiscretion.

Boyler. (*Excitedly.*) Fluke, I don't think I ever saw quite such monumental effrontery as yours. That wig cost me one hundred and fifty dollars, one of the very best make by the celebrated Toupee.

Dr. Fluke. Oh, we'll not haggle about trifles. I'll credit it on the bill for the electric machine. That cost five hundred dollars.

Boyler. (*Gesticulating.*) Credit it on the bill! That's cool! Why, confound your insolence! I've a mind to cane you on the spot.

Dr. Fluke. But you can't, you see. You have no cane. You are cured.

Boyler. (*With a roar.*) Oh, this man will put me crazy if I stay here much longer. You'll hear from me again, Dr. Fluke. You are a quack. (*Bolts toward door as -- enter* NORAH, *L., with tray, milk jug, sugar bowl, spoons, and plate of crackers.* BOYLER *runs against her and sends things flying as he exits.*)

Norah. Well, did yez iver see such a cyclone! (*Commences picking up things around the stage.*)

Enter MIKE *carrying big tin pot full of hot tea.*

Mike. Begorrah, it was lucky I was carryin' the tay pot or there'd been a Noah's flood o' tay.

Norah. Must I get more crame, Docthor?

Mike. It's aisy to pick that up with a spoon.

MRS. FLUKE *and* MISS SIMPER *appear timidly at door, L.*

Dr. Fluke. Bother the cream. It's the tea I want. Put the things on the table. Now I'll get him to come out.

Mrs. Fluke. Henry, do you think he'll hurt you?

Miss Simper. The idea! Poor abused thing!

Dr. Fluke. Clear out, you women. Do you want to frighten him? (*Exeunt* MRS. FLUKE *and* MISS SIMPER.) Mike, go in the operating room to be ready for emergencies. (MIKE *enters D.F, and peeps out from time to time, as do the two ladies, L.*) Norah, you be ready to serve the tea. I'll drink some to make believe. Be cool, don't lose your head.

Norah. (*Arranging tea things.*) Yis, sor, but I can't guarantee to kape me head if that ould cyclone blows in again.

Dr. Fluke. (*Knocks at office door.*) Patsy, come out, please. It's nearly dinner time. (*Voice indistinctly inside.*) What's that? Yes, I'm all alone, that is, Norah is here, too. (*Door opens cautiously.* PATSY *looks out, then comes out enveloped in* DOCTOR'S *ulster and muffled to the ears with* DOCTOR'S *neckcloth. Wig frowzed till he looks like a fright. As he appears, heads at other door disappear.*)

Dr. Fluke. (*Starting back.*) Why Patsy, are you cold? I feel decidedly too warm.

Patsy. I think I took a bit o' cold in the ears, I'm subject to sore throat.

Norah. (*Aside.*) Crazy as a June bug.

Dr. Fluke. Chin Sum, do you like tea?

Patsy. My name isn't Chin Sum; just Patrick O'Wang, if you please.

Dr. Fluke. What is the *O* for, Patrick?

Patsy. The *O* shows I'm the son of me father.

Dr. Fluke. We have tea served. Sometimes we take a light refreshment an hour before dinner. Patsy, do you like tea?

Patsy. (*Aside.*) Tea! (*With wink.*) I'm onto their scheme. I'll take a drop, weak if you please, one lump of sugar.

Dr. Fluke. (*Is at L. of table, seats himself facing front.*) Norah, place a chair. Be seated, Patsy. You must be tired.

Patsy. Your honor, I couldn't sit in your presence. (PATSY *is at R. of table.*)

Dr. Fluke. Very well, as you please. Norah, pour the tea. Give me a small cup. For a cold it should be drunk copiously. You had better take several cups, Patsy.

Patsy. Very well, sir, I like tea myself. (DR. FLUKE *chuckles to himself.* NORAH, *rear of table, hands* DR. FLUKE *a small cup, then a large one to* PATSY. *Latter has a large hot-water bag under his ulster with rubber tube and small funnel, all found in office. The collar of the ulster must be very high and stand well forward. The funnel is held by the left hand partially enveloped in a large silk handkerchief. Under pretence of coddling his throat,* PATSY *keeps his left hand up under his chin to keep the funnel concealed. As he drinks, he turns away to R. from the* DOCTOR, *back to audience, pours tea down funnel. As he hands cup to* NORAH *he thrusts his left hand beneath the ulster, the top button of which is unbuttoned. Repeat with each cup.*)

Dr. Fluke. (*Sipping tea and nibbling a cracker.*) How do you like the tea, Patsy?

Patsy. (*Smacking his lips.*) It's capital tea, Doctor.

Dr. Fluke. Norah, fill his cup. He wants several cups to break his cold. Then I'll put you to bed, Patsy, and give you a good sweat.

Patsy. All right, sir. (*Drinks as before.*)

Dr. Fluke. (*Aside.*) It's working! Obedient already.

Norah. Will yez have some more tay, Docthor?

Dr. Fluke. (*Impatiently.*) No, fill Patsy's cup. Don't you see it's empty? (PATSY *drinks.*) How do you feel now?

Patsy. Better already, Doctor.

Dr. Fluke. Have another! There's nothing like tea. Why, it will cure every ill that flesh is heir to. Norah, fill his cup.

Norah. I'm pourin' as fast as I can, sir. What a dale o' tea he do hold.

Patsy. (*Handing back cup.*) Very nice tea, Norah.

Norah. I could do a dale betther with plenty o' tay and more time.

Dr. Fluke. Norah, why don't you fill his cup instead of talking? (*During this drinking the people at the door enter and look on with increasing astonishment.*) How do you feel now, Patsy?

Patsy. Much better, sir.

Dr. Fluke. Head clearer?

Patsy. Well, it's not as thick as putty an' it's not as clear as a June mornin'.

Dr. Fluke. Try a few more cups, keep it up. Norah, don't you see his cup is empty? Pour him another.

Norah. The mon'll explode purty soon a-drinkin'. He's swellin' already. (PATSY *takes cup.*)

Dr. Fluke. Hold your tongue. The charm's working already.

Norah. Faith it's time, the tay pot's impty.

Dr. Fluke. (*Jumping up surprised.*) Empty! Why girl, it holds a gallon.

Norah. An' he's drunk it all. The poor bye must have the stomach of an ostrict or a dodo.

Dr. Fluke. Patsy, do you mean to say that you have drunk a gallon of tea?

Patsy. Faith, I think it's nearer a barrel.

Dr. Fluke. And how do you feel?

Patsy. Like an irrigation canal! (*During these last speeches,* MRS. FLUKE, MISS SIMPER, *and* MIKE *gather round back of table, L.*)

Mrs. Fluke. Doctor Fluke, you'll kill that man with your experiments.

Miss Simper. Poor dear man!

Dr. Fluke. Silence, ladies. This is a most extraordinary case! (PATSY *stands perfectly still, facing them, left hand to throat as before.* DR. FLUKE *takes him by the shoulder and turns him round.* PATSY *does not resist but makes a very wry face.*) A remarkable case. Why, I've hypnotized him.

Mike. Begob, I think he's paralyzed!

Mrs. Fluke. What makes the horrid creature act so? He's got a wild look. (PATSY *rolls his eyes. Women retreat toward door.*)

Norah. I think he's drownin', I do.

Dr. Fluke. (*Severely.*) Patsy, why don't you speak? What ails you?

Patsy. A bit o' queerness here. (*Rubs stomach with right hand.*)

Dr. Fluke. How's your head?

Patsy. Me head's all right. It's me stomach.

Dr. Fluke. Do you still imagine you are an Irishman?

Patsy. I am, sir, Irish to the bone. (*Leans forward as if in pain in stomach. Rubs stomach with right hand and squirms. All this time he has been holding his throat with his left hand and concealing the funnel.*)

Mrs. Fluke. Says he's Irish. He's crazy, Henry. I told you so. He'll murder us all. (*Movement of all but* DR. FLUKE *toward doors as before.*)

Norah. I give notice, Mrs. Fluke. I'll not live in the house with a crazy mon.

Mike. Nayther will I. I give up me job. It will be hurtin' the profession to mix with loonytics an' Chinese.

Dr. Fluke. (*Irritated.*) Hold your tongue, Mike. This is a most extraordinary case!

Mike. Indade it is! First he's a haythen Chinee. Then he takes a drop too much an' goes wild an' pulls the clothes aff other people and says he's an Irishman, bad luck to him. Another dram'll turn him into a Dago, I belave. I quits today, Doctor. (*During this time* PATSY'S *uneasiness is increasing; finally he begins to prance around. Movement toward doors as before.*)

Dr. Fluke. Where is your pain, Patsy?

Patsy. (*Groans.*) Me stomach feels all queer like.

Dr. Fluke. (*Puts hand on* PATSY'S *stomach.*) And no wonder. Why, it's hot as fire! And distended like a balloon.

Mike. (*Nods to ladies, with wise look.*) He's dishtended!

Dr. Fluke. Mike, get the stomach pump in the office. Norah, a basin, quick! (MIKE *runs for pump.* PATSY *makes for door, L. Ladies scream and disappear.*)

Patsy. Faith, I'm on fire!

Dr. Fluke. (*Seizes him.*) We'll fix you in a minute.

Patsy. Aye, Doctor, you've fixed me already.

Dr. Fluke. (Holding to PATSY *who struggles toward door L.)* Quick, Mike! (MIKE *reappears with pump.*)

Patsy. You'll never put that thing down my throat. (*Renews attempt to escape.* DR. FLUKE *grabs at his throat and catches rubber tube. Ulster comes open. Pulls out bag of hot water and all gaze in astonishment.*)

Mike. By the powers, you've pulled the sthomick clane out av 'im. (*Pause.*) Is that what it looks like? I niver seed one before.

Mrs. Fluke. (In door.) Oh, horrors!

Mike. Hadn't yez better put it back, Docthor? He may nade it.

Dr. Fluke. (Is so astonished that he holds the bag by the tube for a few seconds. Drops it in disgust.) What does this mean, you rascal?

Patsy. (Determinedly.) It means you can't fill me up with tea and turn me back into a Chinaman. They did that trick in Hong Kong!

Dr. Fluke. (Crossly.) What are you now? Irish or Chinese?

Patsy. Irish forever.

Miss Simper. (Sentimentally.) Dear me! I'm so disappointed. I did hope we had got a real Chinaman.

Dr. Fluke. But confound you man, I hired you for a Chinaman. A bargain's a bargain.

Patsy. That bargain is off.

Mike. (Throws down pump.) Then I'm aff, too. Two Irishmen in wan house is wan too many.

Patsy. Keep your place, Mike, I can do better. (*All dress stage, women L., men R.*) I'm in America now, the land of opportunities. I'm goin' into politics. Me ambition is to be an alderman and die beloved and respected by all.

Mike. Begorray, the ambition of it!

Dr. Fluke. Very well, Patsy. Since you are going to have influence, let us part friends. (*They shake hands.*)

Mike. Inflooence! Faith, I'll niver vote a shplit ticket, half Irish, half Chinay.

Dr. Fluke. Patsy, you have had a strange history.

Patsy. I'll recount it if you please, Doctor.

"Patsy O'Wang," *Song. Air "Pat Molloy."*

My father was a hooligan, me mother was Chinay
And I was born in Hong Kong town ten thousand miles away.

Me father was a sojer in the tenth artilleree,
He took me to the barracks there in Hong Kong by the sea.
Me Christian name was Patsy and O'Wang me name Chinay;
An' while they all took toddy I drank nothin' but green tay.
One day I brewed the punch meself an' then I tried the same;
Hooray! It touched a vital spot, it lit the Irish flame.
True son of ould Hibernia, I struck for higher pay.
I swung it like a gentleman, I drank no more green tay.
But all good luck must have an end, there comes adversitee.
They sent us to Ameriky ten thousand miles by sea.
We sailed and sailed the ragin' main forever and a day.
The boundin' ocean made us sick, they dosed us with green tay.
For twenty hours or more I lay, that poison did me rack;
I rose a haythen Chinaman, a queue hung down me back.
Me almond eyes were set askew, me queue twirled round me pate,
They called me Chin, I made the duff and boiled the Captain's
    mate.
A fool for luck, the proverb says, a fool O'Wang must be,
But now I'm turned true Irishman, bad cess to all Chinee.
And in this free Ameriky I'll have a word to say;
I'm goin' into politics, I'll drink no more green tay.
And for the moral of this tale, I'm sure it's very plain:
When tipple stirs your blood too much, you'd better just abstain.

R.   *L.*

MIKE, DR. F., PATSY, MRS. F., MISS S., NORAH

Curtain.

1897 -- Frank Powers -- *The First Born*

In its depiction of the Chinese, this play is the exact antithesis of Grimm's piece. *The First Born* contains the most sympathetic portrayal of the Chinese by far to appear on the American stage in the nineteenth century. Unlike most Euroamerican authors, who based their Chinese characters merely upon scanty acquaintance or received opinion, Powers spent several weeks living in San Francisco's Chinatown. The script is therefore sprinkled with phrases in Cantonese, the meanings of most of which are clear from the context. Besides being an acute observer, Powers largely lacked the racial animosity so characteristic of the period. He noticed the full range of Chinese life, including opium, immigration fraud, and prostitution, but he did not automatically assume the Chinese were evil or inferior. As a result, his characters resemble actual Chinese more than the creations of any of his predecessors and most of his followers. Even his "highbinders" (petty criminals) are believable figures. A further sign of Powers' racial tolerance is the fact that he directed his gentle satire at not only the Chinese but his fellow Euroamericans as well. Even so, he continued the tradition of humorous names for his Chinese characters.

The play was a strong critical and popular success when first staged in San Francisco. It had a long initial run, and David Belasco assisted in revising it, after which it continued to attract good crowds. It was later staged in both New York and London, and revived repeatedly in San Francisco during the next twenty years. The enthusiastic reception that *The First Born* received indicates that the Euroamerican theatre audience was ready for a drastic upward re-evaluation in its opinion of the Chinese. In addition to its enlightened attitude, the piece has far greater literary and dramatic value than any other play of its type. Perhaps alone of the scripts in this volume, *The First Born* could possibly be presented successfully today.

The First Born

CAST OF CHARACTERS

LOEY TSING, *a bond woman*
CHOW POW, *a Chinese nurse*
CHAN LEE, *wife of* CHAN WANG
DR. POW LEN, *a Chinese physician*
CHAN WANG
HOP KEE, *a pipe-bowl mender*
CHUM WOE
KWA KEE, *a restaurant vendor*
DUCK LOW
WAY GET, *a Chinese guide*
MAN LOW YEK, *a Chinese merchant*
SUM CHOW, *an employee of* MAN LOW YEK
CHAN TOY, *the first born of* CHAN WANG
Visitors, Sightseers, Highbinders, etc.

Scene 1

Scene: Chinatown, San Francisco. At back, Joss House of the Ning Yung Association. On the left, the clothing store of MAN LOW YEK *and barber shop of Yee Hing. The architectural characteristics of these buildings are as follows: Temple of Bing Tung Association -- Two-story brick structure with practical balcony, stairway ascending. Chinese lanterns decorate projecting roof above balcony. Clothing store of* MAN LOW YEK *-- Two-story building with verandah attachment, extending slightly into street. A railing made of wooden pickets painted green encloses the verandah. Plants and shrubs in small flower pots are seen through pickets, arranged in Chinese fashion. In the Left corner of this shop is a narrow hall with open door and stairway ascending. Barber shop of Tong Yung -- One story high, practical door, and window looking into street. Provision store of Fong Get & Co. -- the wares of this store, (dried fowl, salted fish, Chinese vegetables, boxes of imported Chinese goods, eggs, etc.) are scattered about in abundance. On the left of this store, upstage, a stairway descends to wood cellar of Ah Him & Co. Wash house of Yee Hing -- one story, door practical. Window disclosing laundry man at work. Wash house roof.*

As curtain ascends, the following characters are discovered: HOP KEE, *a pipe bowl mender, seated on his low stool behind his work box at the corner of* MAN LOW YEK'S *store. A Fortune Teller behind his table, Right of stairway leading to Ning Yung Temple. Through window of barber shop, a Chinese barber at work. Through window of wash house, a Laundryman at work. On roof of wash house, a Chinese hanging out clothes. Fong Get in his store Right. Music.*

At rise, when curtain is midway between footlights and proscenium arch, two Chinese workmen start from L.U.E. and exit through store of Fong Get & Co. As Workmen exit into store, a Chinaman, well groomed and shaven, enters from barber shop, goes to Fortune Teller and buys a fortune stick. Another, dressed in worn jeans, comes up from wood cellar with wood racks filled, which he carries by means of a pole, Chinese fashion, across his shoulder; he goes off L.U.E. Two young women, followed by an old Amah, enter from R.U.E., cross, and enter store of MAN LOW YEK. *The two Workmen re-enter from store of Fong Get & Co., carrying between them by means of a pole a chest of tea. Two Chinese of the Highbinder type enter leisurely from L.U.E. and look through window of* MAN LOW YEK'S *store. A Laundryman, dressed in white blouse and jean trousers, enters from L.U.R. with immense bundle of clothing tied up in a sheet carried resting on the nape of his neck. He crosses to laundry door, calls to those inside, "Ning-na, Ning-na." ("Open, open.") The door opens, letting out a chatter of Chinese words. He enters and the door is closed. A Chinese enters from store of* MAN LOW YEK *with a neat parcel. He crosses and goes off R.F.E. The two Highbinders who have been looking at him through window scrutinize him keenly, and follow him off R.1.E. Two Chinese enter from R.U.E.; one stops at Fortune Teller, buys fortune, and exits L.U.E. The other goes into barber shop; as he enters, he is greeted with "Ha low, Ma." Two Highbinders re-enter from R.F.E., and stand in front of barber shop. Two young women and old Amah re-enter from store of* MAN LOW YEK *and exit R.U.E. carrying parcels.* WAY GET *comes from R.U.E. preceded by well-dressed official. They cross to* MAN LOW YEK'S *store. Official points to bare spot on wall of store.* WAY GET *crosses and pastes up bulletin. Official and* WAY GET *exit L.U.E. The two Highbinders look after him and then come down and regard bulletin. Door of laundry opens and a Chinese laundryman enters with large baskets filled with clean laundry, exits L.U.E. The two Highbinders slowly leave bulletin and peer into* MAN LOW YEK'S *store, standing in doorway. A voice from behind counter,* SUM CHOW, *speaks Chinese, "Kee hi gow do moon how suey." ('Stand from that doorway.") The curtain music, Chinese in character, is continued until the action described has taken place, lasting one and three-fourths minutes. As it ends, the pipe bowl mender,* HOP KEE, *is heard crooning a Chinese ditty. Enter from the store of* MAN LOW YEK, SUM CHOW, *a well-dressed employee of the latter. He goes to* HOP KEE, *squats on his knees, watching the work of the pipe mender.*

Sum Chow. Well, Hop Kee, have you finished with my pipe bowl?

Hop Kee. In a few turnings, respected sir, your admirable pipe-bowl will be ready for you. Rarely have I bored through such metal. It seems to have contempt for my augur.

Sum Chow. Your tools are dull.

Hop Kee. Then devils have gotten into my tool chest, for I sharpen them every morning. No, Sum Chow, I think the reason lies in the excellent material of your pipe bowl. If curiosity was not condemned by the classics, I would ask how you came by a pipe bowl fit for a mandarin.

Sum Chow. That sort of curiosity will not improve your trade, my inquisitive pipe mender. I will return in a few moments for my pipe bowl. (*Rising.*) When I shall expect it finished.

Hop Kee. It shall be, respected sir. (SUM CHOW *goes into store of* MAN LOW YEK. *Two Chinese children,* CHAN TOY *and* KIM POON, *heard off R.U.E. "Hila, hi la, hi la," and laughter five seconds. They enter from the right and run playfully across stage off left. Laughter five seconds. One of them,* CHAN TOY, *returns as though playing at hide and seek and hides at the right of* HOP KEE, *exclaiming "Kim Poon, Kim Poon!"*)

Hop Kee. Son of Chan Wang, who permitted you to be abroad in the streets? Are you not afraid the evil spirits will gobble you up? Where is the Amah who takes care of you?

The child responds with suppressed laughter. HOP KEE *seizes the child and with mock severity strikes him with his open palm gently on the back. The boy breaks away and runs into the street, laughing and exclaiming "Ee - ee - ee."*

Hop Kee. The Gods preserve us. The boy takes after his mother. Like her, he will be a runaway. Go home, naughty boy. (*Makes slight movement towards child who runs R. and onto sidewalk, colliding with* LOEY TSING, *a Chinese woman of the demi-monde class. She is rather fashionably dressed. He runs around her, clutching his garments. She turns towards him and he dodges away again.*)

Loey Tsing. Come, beautiful one, tell me your name.

Chan Toy. Chan Toy.

Loey Tsing. Are you not the first born of Chan Wang? (*Boy laughs.*) Come, pretty boy, see what I have for you. (*Fetching from her clothing strips of coconut wrapped in leaves. The child comes slowly toward her.*)

Hop Kee. (*Arising from his stool.*) Chan Toy. (*The child stops, then comes to* HOP KEE, *keeping his eyes on* LOEY TSING.)

Loey Tsing. Why, Hop Kee, I would not harm the child.

Hop Kee. Are you a fit person to bestow gifts on this boy? What shall I say of this to Chan Wang, his father, and a member of my Tong?

Loey Tsing. Tell him his child met a woman almost as bad as its own mother.

Hop Kee. Hush! (*Crosses Center to* LOEY TSING, *leaving boy.*) Have you no shame in the presence of the child?

Loey Tsing. Oh, come. The boy must hear the truth someday.

Hop Kee. But not from you. Unfortunate one, pass on, and leave the child in peace.

Loey Tsing. My time is my own, most excellent mender of pipes.

Hop Kee. And your tongue is the devil's.

Loey Tsing. It never harmed this child or you. You have such friendship for the boy, and yet you serve the man who stole his mother.

Hop Kee. Silence, shameless woman. (*To boy.*) Run to your home, motherless one, and close your ears to the evil of the street.

CHAN TOY *runs off R.U.E. hiding behind corner of wash house. When* HOP KEE *turns,* CHAN TOY *sneaks to Center of stage, and shaking his fingers at* HOP KEE, *runs quickly off L.U.E.*

Loey Tsing. And you do not know, Hop Kee, that your Tong has declared a boycott against Man Low Yek?

Hop Kee. If it has, I shall learn of it. It needs no boycott to keep me from being false to my friends. (*Pause -- looks up.*) What meant you when you said I serve the enemy of Chan Wang?

Loey Tsing. (*Looking at the pipe bowl in* HOP KEE'S *hands.*) You are mending his pipe bowl, most virtuous friend.

Hop Kee. (*Pause, looks at pipe bowl, then at* LOEY TSING, *then back at pipe bowl.*) What, this pipe bowl? 'Tis the property of Sum Chow.

Loey Tsing. 'Tis the property of Man Low Yek.

Hop Kee. (*Pause -- looks up.*) Man Low Yek?

Loey Tsing. Yes, Man Low Yek. Do you think I could ever forget that pipe bowl or its owner, who brought me, a slave girl, from the province of Shantung and sold me to a life of shame?

Hop Kee. Sold you?

Loey Tsing. Yes, sold me to make way for the Canton woman, Chan Lee, the runaway wife of Chan Wang and mother of Chan Toy, sold me for a woman who committed the rarest crime known to her race, "a deserter of her child."

Hop Kee. Man Low Yek, the respected dealer in clothes?

Loey Tsing. Yes, Man Low Yek, official of the Six Companies, a member of the Sam Yip Association, the respected merchant, Man Low Yek, who stole the wife of Chan Wang.

Hop Kee. Speak softly, unhappy one, the shop of Man Low Yek is here. Its doors are open and its servants have ears.

Loey Tsing. I fear not the Canton dog nor his slaves.

Hop Kee. (*Looks around R. and back.*) And 'tis Man Low Yek who is responsible for the loss of Chan Wang's wife? 'Twas he who enticed her from her home? (*Pause -- looks up.*) But where did he take her?

Loey Tsing. To the north -- to a city of the white devils in a province called Oregon.

Hop Kee. Ah, that is the reason Man Low Yek is absent from the city so often. He goes to see her. He is in Oregon with another man's wife.

Loey Tsing. He has been bold enough to bring her back with him, on one or two occasions, but she is never allowed to remain here long, for fear she might be recognized.

Hop Kee. What a wicked woman she is, to return in sight of the home she has deserted -- perhaps a longing to see the child brings her here, who knows. She may still love the boy, she is his mother.

Loey Tsing. The woman who deserts Chan Wang, let alone her child, for Man Low Yek, is not only wicked, but the greatest fool among us. Believe me, Hop Kee, he will grow tired of her. These Canton women have no manners and are too loud of voice; he will sell her as he sold me. I wonder that a man of Chan Wang's spirit can submit so easily to his disgrace. Of what use is your Tong, and where are your hatchet-men?

Hop Kee. Our Tong knows best its own affairs. Chan Wang was never heard to complain.

Loey Tsing. Perhaps he did not think she was worthy of it. She must have been troublesome and expensive. What a fool he was to marry a woman from the province of Quong Tong.

Hop Kee. How wise he would have been had he married a woman from the province of Shantung.

Loey Tsing. He might have been spared the fate of a deserted husband. But Chan Wang is a fool. If he was not, he would never allow his child to run around in the streets where his runaway wife, Chan Lee, can see her son.

Hop Kee. Why, what would she do to the child?

Loey Tsing. What any woman would do if she were a mother -- steal her child. She might take Chan Toy to Oregon, and Chan Wang would mourn the loss of his first born.

Hop Kee. Is Chan Wang's wife now in the city?

Loey Tsing. Of course she is. (*Going R.*)

Hop Kee. How do you know this?

Loey Tsing. Is that not Man Low Yek's pipe bowl?

Hop Kee. You have said it is.

Loey Tsing. I also say he is here to smoke his pipe and the Canton woman Chan Lee is here to light it up for him. How do I know? (*Pause -- looks up.*) Look at the roof of his house. (*Pause -- HOP KEE comes to her.*) Does Man Low Yek decorate in that fashion to honor male guests? (*Pause.*) Those flowers are intended for a woman.

Hop Kee. (*Seeing* SUM CHOW *come out of store.*) Hush.

Sum Chow. Well, is my pipe bowl finished, Hop Kee?

Hop Kee. (*To bench for pipe bowl.*) It is, respected sir. (*Giving him pipe bowl and receiving money in return.*)

Loey Tsing. Your pipe bowl, Sum Chow? Your master's pipe bowl, you mean.

Sum Chow. Indeed. Who is this woman?

Loey Tsing. You have forgotten me, it seems. You knew me well enough when I was of Man Low Yek's household, and you were my servant.

Sum Chow. I your servant? You must be insane. You the mistress of my master's household, and with such manners? As they say in the foreign devil's tongue, "too thin." (*Laughs and exits into store L.*)

Hop Kee. (*Goes to his work box.*) Pass on, child, and leave me to my work. I have heard nothing but troublesome news today.

Loey Tsing. (*Crossing L., giving him money.*) Buy prayer papers, Hop Kee, and pray for Loey Tsing at the shrine of the God of Fortune.

Hop Kee. Wronged one, the God of Fortune has rarely heard my prayers. I will pray for you both to Quan Kong, who is a kindlier Joss than me. Go your way in peace. (LOEY TSING *exits, L.F.E. A pause of three seconds, and* CHUM WOE *and Companion enter from R.U.E. and cross to bulletin board.* WAY GET *follows from same entrance, stopping at Fortune Teller's table.*)

Hop Kee. What strange beings they are. "Tell nothing to a woman" is a wise proverb. (CHUM WOE *turns towards* WAY GET *and calls "Way Get, hi la."* WAY GET *answers and comes to bulletin board. Two Chinese enter from R.U.E. and* WAY GET *motions them to bulletin board.*)

Hop Kee. Chan Wang's wife here in the city with Man Low Yek. Ha!

CHUM WOE *calls to* HOP KEE, *"Hop Kee!"* HOP KEE *does not hear.* CHUM WOE *then goes to him and says "Hop Kee! Fidee!" ("Hurry up.")* HOP KEE *replies "Met-how-low?" ("What is it?")* WAY GET *calls to* HOP KEE *"See Yip, san man chee." ("Read about the See Yip society.')* HOP KEE *calls out "See Yip?"* WAY GET *replies "Chan gore!" ("Sure!")* HOP KEE *gets up from stool and goes to bulletin board.* WAY GET *calls to Fong Get "Way ah, Fong." Fong leaves store and crosses to bulletin board. Two Chinese come from wash house and join crowd at bulletin board. Two more come from barber shop. The following dialogue occurs among* WAY GET, CHUM WOE, HOP KEE, *Fong Get, and others. As Fong Get crosses to bulletin board,* KWA KEE *enters from R.U.E. carrying Chinese basket full of poultry. He goes to Fong Get's store, crying out as he enters to Fong Get "Way ah, Fong." ("Come here, Fong.") Fong Get replies "Chan gore!" ("Sure!") An old Amah enters from L.U.E. carrying pail; she goes to Fong Get's store, picks out vegetables and sausage, then calls "Fong Get!" Fong leaves bulletin board and goes to his store, sells vegetables and sausage to Amah, who goes off.* KWA KEE *comes from inside store immediately after and crosses to bulletin board. A Chinese Ragpicker enters from R.U.E. with pole, baskets, and rag hook. He gathers a rag in front of Fortune Teller's table; he sees a stocking that has dropped from roof of wash house and picks it up. The laundryman on roof sees the action and calls to him "Chee la!" ("Drop that!") Immediately, another laundryman enters from wash house, takes stocking away from him, and the same conversation takes place between them. Ragpicker goes to* HOP KEE'S *stand, picks up rag there. The following talk occurs between* HOP KEE *and Ragpicker:*

   Hop Kee. (*Very angry.*) Chee la! Chee la! ("Get out! Get out!")

Takes rag from him. Ragpicker goes off L.1.E. The conversation around board grows louder and climaxes at the first sight of DR. POW LEN, *who enters R.U.E.* HOP KEE, *seeing him, hushes the talk down to a murmur, and tells* CHUM WOE *to ask the* DOCTOR (*done in pantomime.*) CHUM WOE *answers in pantomime, and turning, says to* DOCTOR.

   Chum Woe. Illustrious Doctor.

From the time HOP KEE *says "Chan Wang's wife here. . ." until the cue "Illustrious Doctor," the action described must not occupy over one minute and three quarters. At the cue "Illustrious Doctor," laughter and Chinese exclamations, "Hi la, hi la" off L.F.E. from* CHAN TOY *and* KIM POON, *lasting five seconds.*
   CHAN LEE'S *face peers from roof, looking towards audience, wearing anxious, puzzled expression. This action of* CHAN LEE *lasts five seconds, then laughter from* CHAN TOY *and* KIM POON *is repeated for five seconds, after which they enter from L.F.E. running upstage and off R.U.E., crying "Fi di lah."*
   At the beginning of the last bit of laughter, CHAN LEE *quickly turns her face Left, sees* CHAN TOY. *Her face becomes mingled with love, fright, and anxiety. She gasps "Oh!" as* CHAN TOY *passes beneath her; she involuntarily reaches down and exclaims "Chan Toy! Chan Toy!", the first scarcely an aspirate, the second clearer and more passionate. She goes to farther end of roof, following with her eyes the children* CHAN TOY *and* KIM POON, *playing in the distance.*

   Chum Woe. Read to us, the characters are difficult to our unlearned minds.
   Dr. Pow Len. (*Adjusting his glasses, crosses Right.* CHAN LEE *retreats from view.*) 'Tis a proclamation from the lofty Chen Yen Ming, Consul-General at this port. (*Reads.*) We inform the Chinese residents of this city that the boycott declared against Man Low Yek and

others of the Sam Yip Association is contrary to the laws of this country, and we wish to warn members of the See Yip Tong that his celestial majesty, our Emperor, is displeased with their conspiracies and will take swift vengeance on their relatives in China, if this way against the Sam Yip merchants is not stopped. Chen Yen Wing, Consul-General. Third Moon, Sixteenth Day.

Chinese around bulletin board murmur lasting five seconds; then HOP KEE *commences dialogue addressing* DR. POW LEN. CHUM WOE *comes to Left of Center.*

Hop Kee. A boycott against Man Low Yek? Most learned Doctor, when was this boycott declared?

Dr. Pow Len. Constant study of the Classics, industrious Hop Kee, has taught me the folly of street gossip. Yet, to answer you calmly, the See Yip Association yesterday, I am told, launched a boycott against Man Low Yek and other merchants of the Sam Yip Association.

Hop Kee. What power has the Consul-General to interfere with the doings of the See Yip Tongs?

Dr. Pow Len. None whatever, but being learned and wise, he makes clear to them that the laws of this barbarous country forbid the boycott. (WAY GET, KWA KEE, *and four other Chinese draw near to hear* DR. POW LEN *discourse.*)

Chum Woe. And what about the grievances of the See Yips? (WAY GET *and* KWA KEE *murmur "Ho la."*)

Dr. Pow Len. He says nothing of that, though he undoubtedly believes they should be redressed by law.

Chum Woe. What law? The law of the white devils? Of what use is that to a Chinaman? (*Murmur a little louder: "Ne goy la."*) Are wealthy men of the Sam Yip Association to be permitted to break up the See Yip Tong without resistance? (*Murmur: "A low man wur."*) Has the Consul-General taken into consideration that fact?

Dr. Pow Len. He has no doubt taken them all into consideration, my inquiring friend. The excellent Chen Yen Wing is a man of noble ancestry, schooled in the wisdom of the Philosophers, who alone can impart that judgment which is necessary for the guidance of men. For has not the great Ho Wang, who flourished in the Seventh Dynasty, said, "Wisdom shall be given to him who meditates upon the past?"

(*Murmur: "Ne go ti yat."*)

Chum Woe. I cannot discuss this question in so learned a manner, but it looks as though our Consul-General was acting with partiality.

Dr. Pow Len. You should not discuss these questions without the deepest meditation, then perhaps you would not to readily question his judgment. For when the great Li Hung Chang was commanded by the Emperor to travel to the four corners of the world, and shed the light of his lofty wisdom upon the barbarous inhabitants of lands, he repaired to the tombs of his ancestors, spending hours there in profound meditation, and departed only when the omens proved favorable to his journey. (*Murmur: "Zai yat."*)

Chum Woe. There are others higher in power than Consul-General Chen Yen Wing. (*Murmur: "You la."*) We shall appeal to our ambassador. (*Murmur: "Kuey lar."*)

Dr. Pow Len. That would be the proper way to redress your wrongs. A petition to the eminent Yung Yang, setting forth the grievances of your Tong, written in the classic Mandarin. (HOP KEE *grunts.*) For any other dialect would be offensive to the literary tastes of that lofty man. For 'tis said that while a student, the sight of an essay written in any but the classic Mandarin would suddenly bring upon him an agitation of the heart so grievous as to compel him to industriously peruse the three thousand essays of the great Mug Wow, in order to ease the shock to his good taste. (HOP KEE *grunts.*)

Chum Woe. If Consul-General Chen Yung Wing isn't careful how he treats the See Yip Tong, the shock he will receive will compel him to issue his proclamation in some other world. (*Crowd murmurs.*)

Dr. Pow Len. Even that might not be distasteful to the literary habits of the excellent Chen Yen Wing. (CHAN LEE *enters from roof.* WAY GET *shakes fortune box.*) A secretary in ordinary to the celestial gods would be a position far more preferable than a Consul-Generalship at this port. (*Murmur while one counts three.* DR. POW LEN *crosses to store and speaks to* FONG GET.)

Dr. Pow Len. Ho la pang yow.

Fong Get. Ho la.

Dr. Pow Len. Ho sang ye.

Fong Get. Ho sangge ye.

Sound of children laughing and crying "Hi la, hi la" heard off R.U.E. Enter children. Flower and abduction business, lasting 30 seconds.

Chow Pow. (A Chinese nurse, heard offstage Right.) Chan Toy. (CHAN LEE *clasps child.*) Chan Toy. (CHAN LEE *looks Right.*) Chan Toy? (CHAN LEE *takes child quickly up stairs.*) Chan Toy!

Hop Kee. That is the Amah looking for Chan Wang's son.

Chow Pow. (Offstage Right.) Chan Toy! Chan Toy!!

Hop Kee. The boy is lost.

Dr. Pow Len. Whose boy?

Hop Kee. Chan Wang's. Here comes the woman who takes charge of him. (CHOW POW *enters Right, calling.*)

Chow Pow. Chan Toy, Chan Toy!

Hop Kee. Hold your tongue, foolish woman. What is the matter?

Chow Pow. (Crying.) Good friend, I have lost my charge, Chan Toy -- he has wandered into the City. I cannot find him anywhere. White devils have stolen him, good pipemender, for they love beautiful things, and he was a beautiful boy.

Hop Kee. Silence! Would you tell the enemies of his father he is lost and then expect to find him?

Chow Pow. Ah, good friend, what shall I do? If he is not found, his father will kill me. (HOP KEE *goes upstage and speaks to* WAY GET *and* HOP KEE. *Exit* HOP KEE, *L.U.R., and* WAY GET, *L.1.E.*)

Dr. Pow Len. Where was the child seen last?

Chow Pow. Alas, learned man, I know not. He was an active child and ran from my side an hour ago to play games in the street.

Hop Kee. (Comes forward.) Why, he was here a short time ago.

Chow Pow. Oh, excellent Hop Kee, tell me where he is, the only son of your friend, Chan Wang, the first born, the beautiful Chan Toy.

Hop Kee. Be quiet, woman.

Dr. Pow Len. Where is Chan Toy's mother?

Chow Pow. (To Doctor.) Speak not of her, the woman who deserted her child. She is far from here.

Hop Kee. Chow Pow, it would be a blessing to your master,

Chan Wang, if you were far from here. (*Looks towards store of* MAN LOW YEK, *then, as if struck with an idea.*) Chow Pow, go find Chan Toy's father and send him to me.

Chow Pow. Oh, I dare not, good pipe-mender, for he will beat me.

Hop Kee. You go with her, Chum Woe, and prevent harm. (*Exit* CHOW POW *and* CHUM WOE *R.U.E. Re-enter* KWA KEE *R.U.E. and* WAY GET *L.1.E., speaks to* HOP KEE *and exits R.U.E.*)

Dr. Pow Len. I have just thought of an excellent remedy for a case of this kind. A powdered tiger's tooth, mixed with oil of the green snake, and sprinkled on the spot where the boy was last seen, will keep the devils from him during his absence. It is a compound that has ever been helpful in cases of this kind. The tooth contains courage, and the oil, cunning; these qualities combined are certainly a match for all devils. The omens have acted strangely of late, for did I not this morning discover three white spots on the second fingernail of my right hand, which was undoubtedly a portent of this disaster to Chan Wang? I will go at once and prepare the compound.

Hop Kee. Illustrious Doctor, run and do so.

Dr. Pow Len. Excellent Hop Kee, the drug shall be prepared calmly and quickly, though I will not sacrifice my dignity by running.

Hop Kee. (*Goes into the street, looks up at the roof of* MAN LOW YEK'S *house, calls softly "Chan Toy, Chan Toy."*) The hallway door is closed -- could she have taken the child from the street through that door? Loey Tsing is right. The mother is there, though no one but a woman would have guessed it. She has stolen the child. Else where could he have gone? What an unhappy day for Chan Wang. It was an ill omen when I mended the pipe bowl for Man Low Yek. Surely no harm will come to the boy, for he is beautiful and therefore beloved of the gods. Did I think otherwise, I would, old as I am, with my tools in my hands, follow the example of the great Tong King, and create such a tremendous and awful noise that it would frighten the kidnappers out of their wits, and they would quickly give up the child. It surely is a prosperous day for evil spirits. They may have crawled into my tool chest from the garment of Sum Chow. It's just as well to be precautious and frighten them away. (*Music. Lighting punk sticks and sticking in corner of his table.*)

Chan Wang. (*Offstage.*) Chan Toy. Chan Toy.

Hop Kee. The gods preserve me from an angry man, here comes the child's father.

CHAN WANG *enters hurriedly from the Right, dragging by the wrist* CHOW POW, *who is frightened and weeping. A small crowd led by* CHUM WOE *follows them. It increases in size, and from now on until the end of this scene, everybody concerned in this act is on the stage.*

Chan Wang. Point out to me the one who last saw my child.

Chow Pow. Merciful master, it was this mender of pipe bowls, the virtuous Hop Kee.

Chan Wang. Hop Kee, brother of my Tong, where is my boy, my first born?

Hop Kee. Friend and brother, I cannot with truth answer that question.

Chan Wang. But this faithless woman says you saw him here.

Hop Kee. So I did; he was here playing games upon the street. (*Crosses to Center.*) Chan Wang, consider me a friend. I can speak more, but it will be only the speech of suspicion.

Chan Wang. Then speak.

Hop Kee. What I shall say concerns our private affairs. Shall I speak before all these people? Would I be your friend and tell to the street your household affairs?

Chan Wang. Yes, tell them to the world, I care not. I want my boy, my beautiful child, my Chan Toy. Friends -- (*Turning upstage.*) or enemies -- (*Grunt from one or two at back.*) you all know my shame. I am the deserted husband Chan Wang. (*Turning downstage.*) Not long ago in this cursed land, I was robbed of my wife by a man of my own race. My household shrine was desecrated by the Cantonese dog Man Low Yek. I speak thus to loosen the tongue of this man, my friend, who would be spared the telling of a painful tale. People of my race, from whatever province you come, to whatever Tong you belong, if any of you hold feud against me, I ask that you harm me not -- until my child is found. Now, Hop Kee, speak.

Loey Tsing. (*Crossing.*) Hop Kee, I will save you the trouble. Chan Wang, your wife is in the City, so is Man Low Yek. They have taken your child.

Sum Chow. (*He has been standing in the hallway door,*

coming down.) The woman lies. She is of impure morals and is unworthy of belief. Man Low Yek does not steal children, he is no thief.

Chan Wang. You lie, you Canton slave. He steals wives. (*Rushing across stage.*) Yek, come forth and meet me.

Hop Kee. (*Intercepting him.*) Friend Chan, do not start the fury of the Tongs at this time, let us find your child. (CHUM WOE *takes hold of* CHAN WANG.)

Chan Wang. (*Struggling.*) My boy is with that faithless woman, Chan Lee. (*Starts toward door, is held back by* HOP KEE *and* CHUM WOE.)

Hop Kee. (*Rustling him upstage.*) Chan Wang, the foreign devils will arrest you and what will become of your child?

Chan Wang. (*Struggling.*) While you hold me here, Man Low Yek, the Canton dog -- the coward laughs at me. He stole my wife, he would steal my child. (*Struggling fiercely.*)

Chum Woe. (*Releasing* CHAN WANG.) I'll call the hatchetmen of our Tong.

Hop Kee. Madman, would you commit murder?

Chan Wang. Let me go -- let me go to my child.

Breaks away and rushes to hallway door, following SUM CHOW *upstairs. The crowd gathers quickly around hallway door. A few surge back from the house.* HOP KEE *runs up hallway, calling "Chan Wang." Sound of breaking door.* HOP KEE *calls again, "Chan Wang."* CHAN LEE'S *voice heard calling frantically, "Chan Toy -- Chan Toy."* HOP KEE *calls for the third time, "Chan Wang." A voice from crowd,* CHUM WOE *cries, "They're on the roof." Dull thud of falling body, then frantic scream from* CHAN LEE. *Pause two seconds. Then Ragpicker murmurs for five seconds. A pause of two seconds and* KWA KEE *murmurs for three seconds. A pause of two seconds and* WAY GET *murmurs for three seconds.* HOP KEE *in a hushed tone says "The child has fallen -- he is hurt." Murmurs, faint, lasting two seconds. Then* CHAN WANG'S *voice calling frantically, "Chan Toy, Chan Toy." At this point the crowd becomes silent, motionless, remaining like so many statues, until* CHAN WANG *comes down hallway stair and breaks through them, carrying child under his left arm. Stops in the center of the stage; the child hangs limp. Calls his name and shaking him in his frantic efforts to wake the boy from death, at last laying him on the stage.*

Chan Wang. (In agony.) Chan Toy -- Chan Toy -- My beautiful one. Speak -- speak.

Dr. Pow Len. (Who has entered during CHAN WANG'S *struggle in the house, examines the child and says:)* Unhappy man, your beautiful child is with those who love him best, the gods.

Chan Wang. Unfriendly gods, give back my child. There are no thieves in heaven, though there be upon this earth. Steal not his life, celestial gods, but give him back to me.

Hop Kee. Chan Wang, friend and brother, come from this place -- they will bring your child.

Chan Wang. No. Let no one dare to touch my child. Chan Toy -- Chan Toy.

Hop Kee. Brother of my Tong, do not start the fires of a feud here in the streets. Let us leave this place of evil, for devils invest the house of Man Low Yek.

Chan Wang. Man Low Yek -- Man Low Yek. Come forth and look upon my child, that I may roll your head at his feet. May the gods of the celestial heaven be a stranger to you and your kin. May you live until you meet the father of Chan Toy -- Chan Toy -- Chan Toy. My beautiful, my first born, my motherless one, my Chan Toy. *(Ends sobbing.* CHOW POW *takes up the death keen, rocking to and fro over the body.* CHAN LEE *rushes frantically from the hallway and throws herself toward the body of* CHAN TOY. CHAN WANG, *seeing her, raises his knife to kill her; he is held by* HOP KEE, CHUM WOE, *and others.* DR. POW LEN *holds the mother from the body of the child.)*

Curtain.

Scene 2.

Scene: An alleyway in Chinatown. Doorways leading to gambling houses and opium dens in the building between center and right of stage. A row of windows, latticed, cross the lower part of the second story. One of these windows is lighted. On the left of the stage, an open doorway and window disclose a Chinese domino room filled with Chinese. The air in this room is dense with tobacco smoke. Chinese are playing dominoes on a small table.

Discovered: HOP KEE *in Domino room, with others playing dominoes.* CHUM WOE *squatting at D.F.L. Keeper of gambling den squatting at door F.R.H. Fat Toy cries five times at the back of flats.*

At rise of curtain, Fat Toy continuing fifteen times longer. No. 1 enters from L.2.E. Two Chinese cross to Right and exit L.2.E. No. 2 enters from R.1.F. One Chinese crosses to 2nd D.F.R.H. Looks right and left and then exits into D.F.R.H. No. 1 enters from L.2.E. Two more Chinese enter. One crosses to L.M. and exits L.2.E. One takes tray from L.H. and carries it off L.2.E. Chinese clamor outside R.U. -- 16 bars. Banjo in. HOP KEE sings. Clicking of dominoes.

Kwa Kee. (*Off. L.2.E.*) No me ah Buck Lum. (*Fat Toy cries ten times.* KWA KEE *outside.*) No me a Buck Lum. Woe me due chee chee Buck Lum. (*Fat Toy cries five times. Gamblers exit.*) Did you attend the funeral, Chum Woe? Tell us of it. Was it worthy of the noble Chan Wang?

Chum Woe. It was, corpulent sir. 'Twas a pageant worthy of a mandarin. The prayer papers thrown away would keep devils crawling through their holes for a thousand years, before they could reach the soul of the beautiful Chan Toy.

Kwa Kee. What has become of Chan Wang since the burial?

Chum Woe. His friends have not been able to tell. I hear that he passes his time in the Ning Yung Temple praying for his boy.

Kwa Kee. What an unhappy day it was for poor Chan. How did the boy meet his death?

Chum Woe. No one exactly knows, but it is supposed the mother hid the child on the roof. A struggle took place there, and the child must have fallen from the landing to the floor below.

Kwa Kee. What has become of Sum Chow?

Chum Woe. He has not been seen since that day. Chan Lee, the wife, has been spirited away again. Man Low Yek is alive and well. The funeral has almost beggared Chan Wang, and the law officers are on the lookout for him.

Kwa Kee. Why, he had committed no crime against their laws.

Chum Woe. No, but they are afraid he will.

Kwa Kee. What a barbarous lot the white devils are to arrest a man not for what he has done, but for what they think he will do.

Chum Woe. Man Low Yek is getting bold again. He gave a great feast the other night to the Consul-General, Chen Yen Wing, and swore to do all in his power to break up the See Yip Tong. He declared our association to be a band of conspirators, enemies not only of the laws of this country, but to our own as well, disturbers of trade, boycotters and murderers whose deeds have shocked the white devils.

Kwa Kee. Do you think he will convince the Consul-General?

Chum Woe. Chen Yen Wing needs little persuasion. We can only await the results of our leaders' conference with Ambassador Tung Yung.

Kwa Kee. Did Dr. Pow Len leave to attend the conference?

Chum Woe. No. He prepared the petition our leaders will present to the Ambassador. How fortunate our society was in securing the services of such an ancient, wise, and learned man. They say he is the greatest scholar in our quarter.

Arises and goes downstage R. A door to the right of the speaker opens softly and a Chinese head appears, looking about cautiously. He sees CHUM WOE and quickly ducks back out of sight, closing door. At the sound of the closing door, CHUM WOE turns quickly, looks at door, pauses, then turns to KWA KEE and says "Hoy." KWA KEE looks Right, and then replies "Ho -- ay." CHUM WOE goes quickly to door, looks off Right and Left, then opening door, calls "Hi la, hi la." DUCK LOW comes to door again and peeps out. KWA KEE, recognizing him, begins dialogue.

Kwa Kee. Come out into freedom, Duck Low. No one will recognize you, and here are only friends. (*Comes out.*) Chum Woe, this is the excellent Duck Low, who left the province of Chick Lee scarcely two months ago. 'Tis his first visit to the white devil's land.

Chum Woe. Talented sir. I am happy to know you, but how is this, you have not been in this country before? Did you come over in a tea chest?

Duck Low. No, respected sir. I came over in an immense junk, that swam the sea without a sail, propelled as I believed by some supernatural power. I landed in a province north of here, whose laws are more hospitable towards a Chinaman. At the advice of a laundry friend, I crossed over into this country disguised as an Indian, a savage race much favored by the white devils. This government, I am told, not only feeds and clothes them, but allows them to ride free passage throughout this land, while I, a subject of the oldest of civilized nations, would hardly be permitted to walk.

Kwa Kee. Cleverly managed, friend Duck Low, but your entry into this country was scarcely as wonderful as was that of the brother of our good Chum Woe.

Duck Low. Indeed. Let me hear of anything that has deceived these barbarous people.

Kwa Kee. Well, according to the laws of this country, every Chinaman residing here is expected to register his name in a big book, and have his portrait taken in order that he may be identified as a resident of this country; should he visit China and wish to return here, he must show his portrait to the law officers, so they will be able to tell he is not a newcomer, for these barbarians cannot tell us from each other. Our friend Chum Woe complied with the law, wrote his name in the big book and had his portrait taken, sent it to his brother in China, who with it passed safely into this country.

Duck Low. But how could he do so? Surely he was recognized.

Kwa Kee. Not a bit of it. They are as alike as two nuts. Chum Woe and his excellent brother are twins. (*Laughter. Fat Toy cries five times. Four bars are played on a Chinese fiddle back of scene.*) Here comes the learned Dr. Pow Len. (*As* DUCK LOW *steps into passageway,* CHUM WOE *calls him back with "Hi la, hi la."* DUCK LOW *comes back to doorway cautiously.*) Fear not, he is a friend. (*Enter* DR. POW LEN *from Right.*) Wise and ancient man, where are you bound?

Dr. Pow Len. My healthy friend, I have just left the bedside of the unfortunate Ah Woe.

Kwa Kee. What is his complaint, Doctor?

Dr. Pow Len. (*Crosses to* KWA KEE.) He suffers grievously from an indignation of the stomach.

Kwa Kee. Allow me to present to your wise notice Duck Low, a recent arrival from our native land.

Dr. Pow Len. Excellent sir, I welcome you. The vice of curiosity compels me to ask you, from what province of our beloved country do you come?

Duck Low. From Tien Tsing, respected sir, in the province of

Chick Lee.

Dr. Pow Len. A glorious province. 'Twas there the great Pow Poe, who flourished in the Third Dynasty, wrote his poem of eleven thousand verses. There also lives the illustrious Li Hung Chang who so startled the inhabitants of barbarous lands by asking an infinite number of questions which they were unable to answer. Sir, you are welcome. (*Crosses to Left Center.*)

Duck Low. I have ventured but yet into this vast city. But today, learned man, I saw a wondrous sight. 'Twas near the forks of two great roads, a lofty palace was in the process of construction. I distinctly saw a huge stone attached to a rope going upward in the air, to the very roof of the palace, but propelled neither by man nor beast. How now do you account for such a miracle, learned sir?

Dr. Pow Len. Simple enough. If you had entered the palace, you would have seen a terrible Chu-Chu monster, who, after being fed with fire, performs the task of hoisting the stone.

Kwa Kee. You will see stranger sights than that, Duck Low, if you remain here long enough. There is situated at the end of the land, an enormous bath house, where they keep a monstrous snake who sucks water up from the sea, and spits it out again into the bath house. (*Pause.*) In this place men and women bathe together.

Duck Low. Men and women -- together? Impossible! (*Turns to* DR. POW LEN.)

Dr. Pow Len. Such is the lamentable fact. (*Exits Left.*)

KWA KEE *imitates engine hoisting. Fat Toy cries five times. Laugh off L.2.E.* KWA KEE *cries "Bo wa chuck" outside. Enters, cries "No me ah Buck Lum," crosses Right.* HOP KEE *enters from D.F.L. H.* DUCK LOW *ducks back into house.*

Hop Kee. Here comes a party of sightseers, guided by the thrifty Way Get. Fi la. (*To C. house, goes in domino room Right.*)

Kwa Kee. Here, Chum Woe. (*Giving him money.*) Go and buy packages of punk sticks and stand in the doorway of Puff Gow's opium house. Refuse to let these vultures enter until Way Get makes them buy your punk sticks. Charge them double price.

Music begins in domino room. CHUM WOE *hurries off Right. Din as* KWA KEE *begins his restaurant cry of "No me ah Buck*

Lum. Call of "Ba wo chuck" outside.

Kwa Kee. Bo wa chuck, Buck Lum, Bo wa chuck. (*Enter* WAY GET *from Left, guiding a party of sightseers. Music, cries in domino room.*)

First Visitor, Male. Hello, John. Your boy? Nice little boy.
First Visitor, Female. What place is this?
Way Get. Gamblum loom. You sabee gamblum loom?
Second Visitor, Female. Do they gamble here?
Way Get. Yes-a-mum, gamblum all same 'Melican gentleman. (CHUM WOE *returns with punk sticks and stands in door about Center of stage.*)
First Visitor, Female. Why, look, there's little Sam Chow, one of the scholars from the Mission School, smoking and playing cards.
Way Get. You sabee Sam Chow? He heap smart little boy, go Mission School, make too much money gamblum. Bimeby, you make him preachy-man?
First Visitor, Female. Make preacher man? I should think not, the little wretch.
Kwa Kee. (*Entering from Right.*) No me ah Buck Lum. (WAY GET *and* KWA KEE *speak Chinese.* KWA KEE *crossing, "No me ah Buck Lum."*)
First Visitor, Male. What's he selling?
Way Get. Sellum Chinese soup.
First Visitor, Male. Will you have some soup? (FIRST VISITOR, FEMALE *shakes her head.*)
Kwa Kee. Wo me due chee chee Buck Lum. (*Exits Left.*)
Way Get. You like go see Joss House?
First Visitor, Male. What house?
Way Get. Joss House.
First Visitor, Male. Oh, you no sabee -- Joss House all same belong Chinaman God.
Kwa Kee. (*Outside.*) No me ah Buck Lum.
First Visitor, Male. Oh, you mean church.
Way Get. Yes. You come this way, I show you Chinaman make opium. (*Speaks in Chinese to* CHUM WOE.) What's the matter? This Chinaman speak for me. You buy punk sticks, then go inside.
First Visitor, Male. How much are they?

Way Get. Half dollar one piece. How many pieces you likes?

First Visitor, Male. Give us three.

Way Get. Doll hap. You come this way up stair.

First Visitor, Male. Up this stair? It won't hold any weight.

Way Get. Yes, heap strong.

Second Visitor, Female. It must be a difficult place to get in. Ain't we lucky to have him for a guide. (*They enter opium den.* CHUM WOE *leaves doorway and meets* KWA KEE. *They divide money and pass off,* CHUM WOE *going Right and* KWA KEE *going Left, continuing his restaurant cry.* LOEY TSING *appears at lighted window. She sings softly a Chinese love song. At its close, the orchestra commences the Chinese death keen which continues until the close of this act. Previous to this,* CHAN WANG *appears in the shadow of the doorway a little to the left and below the window of* LOEY TSING. *At the finish of her song, he utters, half audibly:*)

Chan Wang. Chan Toy. Chan Toy.

Loey Tsing. (*Startled, looking down.* What was that? (*Pauses, then softly calls.*) Chan Wang. Chan Wang? (*Recognizing him.*) Dear friend, why do you utter your thoughts aloud? Call not on your beautiful child, he is with the gods, and happier than you or I. (*Sighs and looks off Right.*) Chan Wang, the store of Man Low Yek is opposite us. He lives and thrives, while you and I are brought to sorrow and disgrace through him. 'Twas he that brought me from the rice fields of Shantung -- those fields that I shall never see again. 'Twas he that robbed you of a wife, 'twas he who stole your beautiful boy.

Chan Wang. Chan Toy, Chan Toy.

Loey Tsing. Unhappy friend, speak not so. Your voice sounds like a cry from the tombs. Think of him who wronged both of us. See, he sits there in his store among his friends. He smiles. He laughs. The Cantonese dog, who ruined my life and caused the death of your beautiful child.

Chan Wang. (*Passionately.*) Man Low Yek. Man Low Yek.

Loey Tsing. Good friend, forgive me, I meant not to stir your feelings. Friend Chan, no one in this barbarous land would feel more grieved at giving pain to your heart than Loey Tsing. 'Tis not my mode of life nor the shame of it that makes me say, I have thought of you softly, friend Chan, for a long time before your sorrow came upon you, when the Canton woman, Chan Lee, was your wife, and when she deserted you, I felt pleased, and yet I cursed her, not because she usurped me in Man Low Yek's household, but because she gave you sorrow. You never guessed my secret, dear Chan, and I thought it my duty to smother it in my heart, but I was a fool. I should have enticed you from your home as Man Low Yek enticed your wife from you, but it was not to be. I was born to lose all I ever set my heart on. Home, father, mother, brothers and sisters, self-respect -- all. (*Weeps.*)

Chan Wang. Peace. Peace. My sister in sorrow, the province of Shantung is still in China, and flowers yet grow there.

Loey Tsing. Yes, dear Chan, and the most beautiful in all the world. A breath from such flowers would ease the pain that lurks in my heart. Perhaps my father's boat is still in the river -- his boat that hauled the rice from the fields to Montedrin. He used to take me with him on that voyage. My brothers and sisters would wait upon the bank for my return. But they wait no more for me in Shantung -- for I'll never -- never see them again.

Chan Wang. Peace, my child, you may see them yet.

Loey Tsing. Oh, buy me, dear Chan, and take me from this cruel land. Take me to my home in beautiful Shantung. I will respect your household shrines and at the tomb of your ancestors I will pray for Chan Toy.

Chan Wang. Chan Toy. Chan Toy.

Loey Tsing. Oh, take me, Chan Wang, let us leave this land.

Chan Wang. Loey Tsing, you shall leave it, and go to your home in Shantung.

Loey Tsing. And will you go with me, dear Chan?

Chan Wang. If anything happens to me, pray for my child, my beautiful boy, my first born, my Chan Toy.

Loey Tsing. Oh, why do you speak so? Your words frighten me. There is vengeance in your heart. (*Turns, looks off Right.*) See, Man Low Yek is closing his store -- the shutters go up -- he is locking the door. Your friend Quoong Ling is with him. Celestial gods, he is coming this way.

Chan Wang. Loey Tsing, close your window.

Loey Tsing. Friend Chan, what does it mean? Man Low Yek is coming this way -- he enters the alleyway -- alone. (CHAN WANG *steps out a little from his position in the doorway.* LOEY TSING *notices the movement.*) Merciful gods! (*Quickly closing her window.* MAN LOW YEK *enters from Right and comes as far as doorway in which* CHAN WANG *is standing.* CHAN WANG *suddenly springs out into alleyway and strikes him two blows with a highbinder's hatchet, exclaiming "Chan Lee!" at the first blow, and "Chan Toy!" at the second.* MAN LOW YET *falls dead near doorway.* CHAN WANG *quickly picks up the body and throws it into the room. Closes door and resumes his position in the doorway.)*

Curtain.

1899 -- Joseph Jarrow -- *The Queen of Chinatown*

During the last twenty years of the nineteenth century, Chinese in the United States began to diffuse outward and eastward from the West Coast. Just as they had generally congregated in San Francisco right after the Gold Rush, they tended to cluster in other cities across the country. Boston and New York had had very small Chinese colonies since mid-century, but these now expanded greatly in size and population. In Euroamerican eyes, a Chinatown was a place of mystery and danger, somewhere to visit briefly for an exotic thrill on a slumming expedition. The text presented here is the only one which has survived that is set in New York City; the area of Mott, Pell, and Doyer Streets is still the heart of Manhattan's Chinatown.

Jarrow's image of the Chinese is nearly as negative as Grimm's, but his rationale for condemning them is cultural, not economic. This reflects historical reality, as the Chinese on the East Coast were such a tiny minority that they constituted no economic threat whatever. Jarrow's Chinese do not compete with Euroamericans for jobs, but they do run gambling joints, consume and provide opium, and abduct Euroamerican women. Moreover, despite Jarrow's condemnation of the Chinese, he recognizes that they are fully established in America, and that expulsion is not even to be attempted. Instead, he counsels Euroamericans to avoid them and the area in which they live.

One interesting feature of this text is the period slang spoken by the youths Columbia and Freckles. While some of the expressions are nearly incomprehensible today, their general meaning can be deduced from context. The many non-standard phrases must have greatly enlivened the piece for its contemporary audience.

The Queen of Chinatown

ACT I.

Scene: *Gambling room of* HOP LEE. *Square room with tables, chairs and Chinese paraphernalia. Signs displayed of the different games played, so arranged that they can be changed to signs reading different religious proverbs. Seated at the table are Chinese, white men and white women.*

Dan. Come, One Lung, ain't you going to pay me for that turn?

One Lung. What's a matta with you, me no pay for that, that no good.

Dan. What, you mean to tell me I did not win?

All. (*In chorus.*) Pay the man, One Lung. He won; that's all right.

One Lung. Me no pay; me no lose.

Dan. What, you mean to dish me out of my winnings? I thought this was a square game.

One Lung. Me play square alla timee; me pay when you win; you no win, me no pay, savey?

Dan. All right, if you don't come up with the money in a jiffy, I will smash your head and break up your swindling den in five minutes.

One Lung. Me no pay, me no swindle; me pay when you win; you no win, me no pay. (*Enter* HOP.)

Dan. You lie, you thieving Chinaman; I will take the cash out of your hide. (*Uproar in place.*)

Hop. What's a matta? What's a matta? (*Between the men.*)

Dan. Why, the rascal won't pay me what I won.

Hop. (*Talks Chinese to* ONE LUNG, *goes to table; pays* DAN $20.*) Me give you money; One Lung he make mistake; you make no fight.

Dan. All right, Hop; you're a square Chink. That's why I always like to play here, but I will be jugged if I will allow that devil over there to do me, that's all.

Hop. Sit down; have a dlink. (*Orders drinks, which are served.*)

Columbia. (*Calling offstage.*) Extra -- extra -- *World, Journal, Sun, News* -- Extra -- all about de great abduction -- Extra.

Dan. (*Going to table.*) Are you in love with your new Chink, Hop?

Hop. (*Sits R.*) Velly much; velly much; a peach.

Dan. Where did you put her?

Hop. (*A cunning smile.*) In a loof garden -- flowers, music -- plenty to eat and dlink.

Dan. (*Laughs.*) You've hidden the girl in some safe hole -- no doubt of that. Well, come up with the price.

Hop. (*Reluctantly.*) Beezie did the work. (*Turning away.*)

Dan. And I collect the dough. (*Decisively; fist on table.*)

Hop. (*Annoyed; vexed.*) Bling paper; an' order from Beezie.

Columbia. (*Offstage.*) Extra -- extra -- All about the big mystery -- de abduction -- extra.

Dan. (*Rising X. table, threatening.*) Do you hear that? I'll bring the cops from Mulberry Street.

Hop. (*Rising C., sharply.*) Sam Foy! Ah Fong! (*Two Chinamen go quickly to* HOP, *on his R. He speaks in Chinese hurriedly to them.*)

Dan. Hold on, Hop! I cave -- don't give me the hatchet -- I don't want any mix-up with your highbinders.

Hop. (*Cunning.*) You no want Chinese law?

Dan. No; nor any kind of law.

Hop. Velly well. (*Speaks Chinese again to Sam Foy and Ah Fong; they retire.*) Be good. If Beezie the Queen, say glive money to

Dan Driscol, velly good, me glive it.

Dan. You've got me cinched -- I'll go for Beezie and settle the matter tonight.

Hop. Velly well.

Columbia. (*Enter with papers.*) Extra -- extra -- All about de mysterious disappearance of a beautiful Mission teacher -- here's a chance for some of youse mugs to pick up a cool thousand. One Thousand Dollars Reward -- Extra -- all about de abduction. (*To* DAN.) Extra?

Dan. No, I read it yesterday.

Columbia. It's easy money, Dan.

Dan. Then put Hop onto it. (*Going to door C.*)

Columbia. Get into my game, Hop.

Hop. Go long -- you no bother me -- me busy. (*To gaming tables.* COLUMBIA *goes up, selling papers. Enter* JACK FOGARTY, *a man-of-war's man, in tow of* FRECKLES, *a bootblack. Sailor is half drunk.*)

Freckles. (*L. of* JACK.) Ship ahoy there, you land lubber, or we'll fill you full of cod-fish balls.

Dan. Why, I'll -- (*About to cuff* FRECKLES. DAN *remains at table up L., his eye on* JACK.)

Jack. (*Pulling* FRECKLES *on his right.*) Avast there, mate, my pilot's papers are government-stamped.

Freckles. And Dan won't want no run in with the government -- nit.

Jack. Nor anybody else since we sunk the Spaniards in Santiago Harbor and Manila Bay.

Freckles. Hip -- hip -- hooray -- Columbia. (*Slapping* COLUMBIA *on the back.*) Didn't we rattle their slats?

Columbia. (*Pointing to* FRECKLES.) Well, I want to know. Three cheers for the cabin boy of the *Olympia* -- the hero of Manila.

Freckles. (*Stopping cheers.*) After Dewey.

All. Hurrah! Hurrah! Hurrah!

Freckles. (*Pointing to* JACK.) Three cheers and a tiger for the hero of Santiago -- de real ting.

All. Hurrah! Hurrah! Hurrah!

Freckles. Tiger.

Jack. Pipe all hands to grog. (*Pulling out wad of money. All go up to drink.*)

Columbia. (*To* JACK.) Extra -- extra, sir. All 'bout de abduction of a beautiful young girl -- great battle in the Philippines -- de land forces wid the half of Dewey's marines knocked de niggers to smithereens -- casualties -- Aguinaldo captured -- His losses, one thousand killed, wounded and captured. Our army, three wounded -- our navy, nary a man. Everybody singing "Der'll be a hot time in de old town tonight." Extra, sir?

Jack. Well, blow me if you ain't a clipper. Can you sing as well as you jaw?

Freckles. Take it from me; she warbles like a sea gull. Dat ain't no dream either.

Jack. Hold hard, pilot -- what's your handle, sis?

Columbia. Columb for short; Columbia for long.

Jack. Columbia forever. Yer a trim little yacht, that can't lose nohow.

Freckles. Hah -- Rah -- Rah -- Hurrah. U.S.A. U.S.N. Hurrah; dum de dum dumb --------------- (*Break. Laugh.* COLUMBIA *joins in break.*)

Jack. (*Laughing.*) How much for de whole cargo? (*Papers.*)

Columbia. I ain't no Guinea -- make your own price.

Jack. (*Gives bill.*) Aye, aye, miss, here's a dollar -- here's another for a song, and let it be a merry one.

Columbia. (*Song and dance.* JACK *places paper on Table R. and all retire upstage; drink and start to gamble.*)

Dan. (*L. of table.*) Am I in this play, Freckles?

Freckles. Not on yer tin type. Dis time I passes yer up. You steer right away from here or I'll train my thirteen-inch gun on you -- (*Looking back at* JACK.) and he'll make you look like thirteen cents.

Hop. (*Back of table.*) Fleckles is light -- you glo. (*To* DAN.)

Dan. Where did you find him?

Freckles. At Chuck's, throwing his money away -- that reminds me, Dan, dere's an officer down dere wants a guide to show him troo de sights.

Dan. Thanks. (*Going.*)

Freckles. Keep de change -- it's all yours.

Dan. I'll be back soon, Hop. If Beezie runs in, tell her; so long. (*Exit.*)

Hop. Velly well.

Freckles. Hop, dere's a bad proposition -- he'll trow you yet.

Hop. Do you think so?

Freckles. Chee-o-eese it. Der's a streak of yellow in dat duck what gives me de rickets.

Hop. I watchee him. (*Going up.*)

Columbia. Did you get your percentage?

Freckles. Old gal, I'm on de hog -- bug house -- my nut's unhinged -- forget it.

Columbia. You're an easy mark.

Freckles. Cheese -- cheese -- forget it -- forget it. (*Calling.*) Hop, Hop. (HOP *comes down C.*) De cash.

Hop. How much?

Columbia. De regular ting.

Freckles. Dat's de stuff, Columbia -- make de real roar.

Hop. Five dolla. (*Handing it to* FRECKLES.)

Freckles. (*In disgust.*) Five bucks -- chuck it to me treasurer. (COLUMBIA *puts it in her stocking.*) Now a V for your poppa.

Hop. (*Chinese speech.*)

Freckles. Chee-e-eese, chee-e-eese, or I'll make you look like a two-spot, Jack! (*Starting upstage.*)

Hop. (*Catching him.*) Allee light. (*Giving money.*) You blingee back more, eh?

Freckles. Sure, Mike, but no cheap gazabo dealin's wid dis firm -- eh, Columb?

Columbia. (*Disgust.*) How did he ever cop us out for a charity graft?

Freckles. (*To* HOP.) Wouldn't that uppercut you? Are you on?

Hop. Me pay velly well.

Freckles. Right -- square goes -- if dis commission firm gets done up, it's got to be by somebody besides a counterfeit.

Hop. Allee light. (*Goes upstage.*)

Freckles. (*Admiring* COLUMBIA.) Columb, you're all right.

Columbia. (*Admiring* FRECKLES.) Well, I play no understudy to a low card, do I?

Freckles. Meanin' --

Columbia. Dat you're de real ting.

Freckles. And how do I stand?

Columbia. So dat I'll never toss you in de air.

Freckles. Your mitt. (*They clasp hands.*) Your mug. (*They kiss.*) Columbia, de pride of de nation.

Columbia. Columbia de gem of de ocean. (JACK *bursts into song "Columbia" singing one verse, assisted by crowd, loudly cheered by all.* FRECKLES *and* COLUMBIA *with flag do cake walk. Enter* DAN, *showing in* LIEUTENANT HARRY HILDRETH.)

Harry. (L.) Whose place are we in now?

Dan. (R.) Hop Lee's; this is the best known place in Chinatown.

Harry. What kind of games do they play?

Dan. Fan tan, policy, any old game.

Harry. I will pay you $20 on condition that you will show me everything worth seeing in Chinatown. I want to penetrate all the opium joints and if possible, I want to enter even the houses of Chinaman living with white women. (*Giving money.*)

Dan. What, you want to see the Chinks?

Harry. Are there many of them living here?

Dan. Well, I guess there are; some come and some go, every day in the week; they like this place.

Harry. What do you mean by some come and some go every day in the week?

Dan. Why, you see, my friend, they do a lot of business here with the Chinks and when they get too many of them they send them away.

Harry. Send some away, where to?

Dan. Why, to Frisco, or other cities.

Harry. Horrible. (*Aside.*) My poor sister. (*Aloud.*) Who is the head of this dastardly traffic?

Dan. Now you've got me; I don't know the bloke who does the business.

Columbia. (*Picking up papers from table R. To* LIEUTENANT.) Extra -- extra -- all 'bout the big abduction. (DAN *goes upstage and watches them gamble.*)

Harry. (*Watching L., aside.*) It is on everyone's lips, the abduction -- and the girl my only sister. God grant that she is safe, and that this night will restore her to me.

Freckles. (*Saluting, aside.*) You don't make de right play, Columb. Salute de Admiral. (*Saluting.*)

Columbia. Cert; day or night, any old time. (*Salutes.*) Admiral Dewey.

Harry. (*Saluting.*) Simply Lieutenant, my little patriot. (DAN *sits beside* JACK *and gambles.*) What is your name, little one?

Columbia. Columb for short; Columbia for long.

Freckles. (*Nudging her.*) Salute, you lobster. (COLUMBIA *salutes.*)

Harry. Columbia, the gem of the ocean.

Columbia. Nit; of Chatham Square.

Freckles. (*Slapping her on back.*) You gets an introduction to Beefsteak John's tonight for dat -- salute. (*Both salute.*)

Harry. And who might you be?

Freckles. Me, why, I'm a horrible Rube, one of dem fellows dat you want to get a crack at de minute you see him.

Harry. And your name?

Freckles. Freckles.

Harry. (*Laughing.*) You look the name, but not the Rube.

Freckles. Say, Lieutenant. I like your face. I want to sail in your ship. (*Putting down box and saluting.*)

Columbia. (*Putting down papers.*) A little of de same. (*Saluting.*)

Harry. (*Laughing.*) I can't arrange that, but you two can do me a great service -- if I could trust you.

Freckles. (*Picking up box.*) Pass de buck -- pass de buck.

Columbia. (*Picking up papers.*) I'll answer for Freckles. He adores dat uniform.

Harry. And you?

Columbia (*To* FRECKLES.) Wake up, it's up to you.

Freckles. Well, Lieutenant, if I ever rents a flat, dis is de party dat picks out de furniture -- see?

Harry. (*Laughing.*) Good. If you serve me, I'll pay you well -- far better than selling newspapers.

Columbia. All news is getting stale nowadays -- de only big extra lately has been de abduction.

Harry. And that is the kind of job I want you to work on for me.

Freckles. Is de gal in Chinatown?

Harry. I don't know. I want to find out.

Freckles. Have you said anything to Dan Driscol (*Pointing.*) about this?

Harry. No -- I was going to.

Freckles. Don't.

Harry. Why?

Freckles. Columbia, keep your peelers on Dan and Beezie. If she comes in de Lieutenant and yer steady is going to hold a council of war.

Columbia. Onto de game, in a minute. (*Retires upstage.*)

Freckles. If de gal is in Chinatown, dare is a couple of ducks what is likely to be next fer fair -- Dan Driscol and Beezie.

Harry. Who is Beezie?

Freckles. De Queen of Chinatown.

Harry. Ah. Then I must cultivate them.

Freckles. If they don't plant you first. Got much money about you?

Harry. A little.

Freckles. Den hide it. Between Hop Lee, Dan, and Beezie, you won't last till dessert time.

Harry. I'll attend to them. Why do you mention Hop Lee?

Freckles. Hop is de main squeeze of dis place and de tree have talked so much together lately. Beezie is expected here every minute.

Harry. (*X. down R., aside.*) I may be on the right trail -- who knows -- I'll wait.

Jack. (*At gambling table.*) Avast there mate, that's my bet.

Dan. Don't get gay, old ocean. I know my business.

Harry. Why, that's the voice of Jack Fogarty, my gunner's mate.

Freckles. Then get ready, he'll need help. Up you go, Columb, to de fighting top. (*Lifting her on to table R. -- confusion -- Chinese and American tongues.*)

Dan. (*Rising.*) Then I'll leave it to the dealer.

Jack. (*Rising.*) You'll leave the money to me, and no white-livered Mongolian junk will cross my bows without getting rammed. (*Putting money in pocket.*)

Dan. Give me that money. (*Drawing knife.*)

Jack. Clear decks for action. (*Clinching; they come down C. struggling. JACK bends DAN over his knee, chokes him. Hand R. on DAN'S knife hand. HOP and Chinamen extreme R.*)

Dan. (*Gasping.*) Give him the sand, boys. (*Crowd rush forward.*)

Harry. (*Stepping forward.*) Stand back. The first sand bag in sight --

Freckles. (*Besides LIEUTENANT, swinging his shoebox.*) Will get a broadside --

Columbia. From the combined fleet. (*Holding her papers aloft.*)

Jack. (*Holding* DAN.) Awaiting orders, sir.

Harry. Disarm the enemy.

Jack. Aye, aye, sir. (*Starts to get knife from* DAN.)

Hop. (*Chinese speech -- inciting crowd to action. During scene,* BEEZIE *arrives.*)

Beezie. (*At door.*) Let me pass; let me pass, I say. (*Loud exclamations from crowd.*)

Harry. Who is that?

Freckles. Beezie Garrity, de queen of Chinatown -- if she lets loose dere'll be hell.

Beezie. (*To* HOP, *as she bursts through crowd.*) You are having Dan killed, are you? (*Sees sailor is choking* DAN. *Screams and throws herself between knife and* DAN, *arms around him. Position of men is such that* DAN'S *life is apparently in danger.*)

Beezie. Are you all cowards, to stand by and see a man butchered? Hop Lee! Sam Foy! Ah Fong! help! Oh, you curs, is there one man in this room?

Harry. There is one man here.

Beezie. Then prove it -- for God's sake, save him, save him.

Harry. Jack --

Jack. Aye, aye, sir.

Harry. Have you disarmed the enemy?

Jack. Aye, aye, sir.

Harry. Draw away from the pirate.

Jack. Aye, aye, sir. (*Releasing* DAN, *who rests head on chair* L. JACK *goes R.*)

Beezie. (*C.*) Now, what does this mean? If I say the word, that man will never leave Chinatown alive.

Harry. You won't say that word.

Beezie. And who are you that assumes so much?

Harry. A Lieutenant of the U.S. Navy attached to the ironclad *Oregon*, at your service.

Beezie. Hop, who was to blame?

Hop. One man makee blet -- nother man claimee blet -- dat man.

Dan. He took my money.

Jack. You lie, you white coolie. (*Starts.*)

Harry. Hold hard, Jack.

Beezie. Did any one see the bet made?

Freckles. Beezie, I saw the whole play. De sailor played the card to win; Dan played it to lose. De card won -- nuff said.

Dan. You lying cub.

Freckles. Chee-e-eese, cheese -- (LIEUTENANT *and others go up. Exit* HOP *and Fong Sing.*)

Beezie. (*To* DAN.) Well, how do you stand?

Dan. A 20 spot.

Beezie. Where did you get it?

Dan. From the naval officer, to show him around.

Beezie. So. Where's my share of the $20?

Dan. Nonsense.

Beezie. If you throw me down in little things, Dan, you will in big things.

Dan. We're in no need of ready money -- Hop has a roll ready for us. I was on the lookout for you, so we could draw it.

Beezie. Ah! Hop wouldn't give it to you?

Dan. No -- you get it -- I want to win that $20 back.

Beezie. The money stays where it is. You promised me this was to be our last job -- we were to go away from Chinatown. Are you going to keep that promise?

Dan. What can we do on $500?

Beezie. Escape a living death.

Dan. Now, if it were a thousand --

Beezie. (*Anxiously.*) Yes?

Dan. Then I could see a way out of Chinatown.

Beezie. And you'll quit this accursed place the moment we have $1000 to the good?

Dan. So help me; on the oath of a highbinder.

Beezie. I'll remind you of that oath.

Dan. Beezie, get me $50 from Hop; I want to buck the tiger.

Beezie. No. I will not.

Dan. (*Roughly.*) Stop your fooling.

Beezie. Not a penny to gamble with.

Dan. (*Taking her by throat.*) Damn you; get me the money.

Beezie. Oh, Dan, don't. You are hurting me.

Dan. Will you get it? (*She shakes her head. He shakes her roughly. She moans.*)

Harry. What's this?

Jack. (*Standing over* DAN *with* DAN'S *dirk in hand.*) Awaitin' orders, sir.

Harry. Stand aside, Jack. I will handle this affair myself. Now, you whelp, if you have anything to say, be quick about it; for I am going to send you to a hospital. (*Murmurs from crowd.*)

Dan. Why do you interfere?

Harry. Because I am a man and you are a cur.

Dan. She belongs to me.

Harry. That may be, but this is one of the times that you become responsible to me for your cruel treatment of women. Jack --

Jack. Aye, aye, sir.

Freckles. Columb, somethin's doin' in de Navy, sure.

Columbia. Chee-e-eese -- Chee-e-eese.

Harry. I counted four turns in that stairway. If you stop at any one of them after I administer my last kick, I'll drag you back and begin all over again. (*Starts for* DAN.)

Beezie. (*Stepping between them.*) One moment, this is my affair.

Harry. Why -- I -- he --

Beezie. Choked me, yes, it is not the first time, nor will it be the last, I suppose.

Harry. Then --

Beezie. If it is my will -- pleasure -- call it what you may, to permit these pleasantries or attentions, whose business is it, sir?

Harry. I am at a loss to understand --

Beezie. The other half of the world, eh? The seamy side of life -- Why should you? Your environment has lifted you beyond our sphere; return to it and leave us to grovel in our despair, or happiness -- for we are happy at times, aren't we, Danny?

Dan. (*Rudely.*) Oh, come off.

Jack. Awaitin' order, sir. (*About to go for* DAN.)

Harry. Stand aside, Jack.

Jack. Aye, aye, sir.

Beezie. (*Aside.*) Go -- wait for me at Chuck's. (*Aloud.*) Go --

Harry. Let him depart; in deference to the lady's wishes. (BEEZIE *sinks on chair at table, inclining her head to the* LIEUTENANT *in acknowledgement of courtesy.* LIEUTENANT *X.R. in deep thought, sits. Gong sounds.*)

Freckles. (*At door.*) Look out Hop, slummers; a sky pilot and his flock. (*Signs change; all appear to read, smoke, write, &c. Enter* REV. PARKER, FRANCES, *Oliver,* MAMIE, NELLIE, *and*

BELLA.)

Reverend Parker. (*To* FRANCES.) Trust we may find a clue here. (*X. to* LIEUTENANT.) Who have we here, sir? (*Hand on shoulder.* FRANCES *is joined by* DAN *at door; she speaks earnestly, pleadingly to him;* MAMIE, NELLIE, *and* BELLA *scatter among the men, eagerly asking questions.*)

Harry. (*Rising*.) Well, you, Frank?

Reverend Parker. Harry, I did not expect you to get shore leave until tomorrow.

Harry. A New York paper --

Reverend Parker. I understand, then, that you know all?

Harry. That my dear sister has been abducted, yes.

Reverend Parker. I understand you reproach me.

Harry. I do -- I can't help it.

Reverend Parker. Mary was my promised wife, Harry.

Harry. All the more reason why you should have taken greater care of her.

Reverend Parker. I would sacrifice my life to find her. You are unkind.

Harry. No -- just -- Chinatown is no place for pure, beautiful young girls. In the name of God, you make them teachers in your Missions and in the name of the devil you furnish the bait to these yellow devils to -- Oh, I shall go mad. Have you no news of Mary?

Reverend Parker. None, as yet. I am deeply grieved. My own sister is engaged with me in this holy work.

Harry. Your heart and aim are all right, but the results prove the contrary. You will sacrifice Frances as you did Mary.

Reverend Parker. Heaven forbid that harm will reach either.

Harry. If so, there will be a terrible awakening for the villains.

Reverend Parker. Amen.

Harry. Frances, where is she?

Reverend Parker. There. (*Pointing upstage.* FRANCES *is shaking* DAN *by the hand and apparently pleading with him.* BEEZIE *looks at the pair just as* LIEUTENANT *and* REVEREND PARKER *look.*)

Beezie. (*Walks up to* DAN *and looks steadfastly at* FRANCES. FRANCES *withdraws her hand, which causes* DAN *to look round at* BEEZIE. *To* DAN.) Go. (*Exit* DAN.)

Columbia. Freckles, dere's trouble brewin' for de Mission teacher.

Freckles. Chee-e-eese -- chee-e-eese.

Frances. (*Seeing* LIEUTENANT.) Oh, Harry. (*Rushing to him.* BEEZIE *watching* FRANCES, *tears a flower to pieces as she returns to her seat.*)

Harry. You know that man, Frances?

Frances. I have met him many times while trying to enlighten the heathen. I was seeking his help for the rescue of Mary. Oh, isn't it terrible. (*Weeping.*)

Harry. The same danger threatens you, dear.

Frances. Harry.

Harry. And all young girls who are so imprudent as to enter this foul district.

Frances. Oh, brother. (*Turning to* REVEREND PARKER.)

Reverend Parker. All is not vile, Harry. You see here evidences of our work now. (*Pointing to religious signs.*)

Harry. Bosh -- this place belongs to Hop Lee -- do you know him?

Reverend Parker. Yes, he is a member of my Sunday-school class, and through his influence I hope to find your sister.

Harry. Nonsense; this gambling den belongs to and is run by Hop Lee.

Reverend Parker. Gambling den, you say. (*Looking round.*) Gambling den, this -- this place? (*Reading signs and pointing to same.*) Impossible -- you must be wrong.

Harry. Wrong?

Reverend Parker. But those signs?

Harry. Turn them over and you will see the names of the different games played here.

Reverend Parker. If this is true, 'tis no fit place for the ladies. (*Calls ladies.*) Come, ladies, we will go.

Frances. You will come with us, Harry?

Harry. Yes, we will go to your Mission and talk over some plan to rescue my sister. Frank, take the ladies, I will follow in a few moments.

Reverend Parker. The number is 11 Doyer Street.

Frances. Don't be long.

Harry. No. (REVEREND PARKER, FRANCES, MAMIE, NELLIE, *and* BELLA *exit. As* FRANCES *passes* BEEZIE, *the latter stares at her, causing* FRANCES *to notice it and gather up her skirts.*)

Harry. Freckles.

Freckles. Aye, aye, sir. (*Saluting.*)

Columbia. Aye, aye, sir.

Freckles. (*To* COLUMBIA.) Oh, come off; the conversation hasn't reached you yet.

Columbia. Wouldn't dat jar you?

Freckles. Awaitin' orders, sir. (*Saluting.*)

Harry. (*Laughing.*) Take Jack with you to 11 Doyer Street.

Freckles. De Mission?

Columbia. Goin' to Heaven, by gosh.

Freckles. What is dis gospel lay? I'm dead agin' it.

Columbia. Stop chewin' the rag and salute your superior officer. If he orders you to go to a Guinea synagogue, you've got to go or skip de service.

Harry. Columb is right. You must obey orders.

Freckles. De gang'll never get over it, and Jack is in de push, too. Well, here goes, but I'm dead agin' it, you hear me? (*Goes up to* JACK. LIEUTENANT *X. to* BEEZIE.) Had enough, Jack?

Jack. Aye, aye, pilot, where's the next port?

Freckles. De sky pilot shop.

Jack. What?

Freckles. De come up and be saved stand. You've got to stand de guff, ole salt horse. Orders from the Lieutenant.

Jack. Aye, aye, mate, but --

Freckles. Guess we's goin' into action, an' got to prepare for de planters.

Jack. The what?

Freckles. De undertakers -- go long, Columb. You can sing de doxology anyway, but I'll tell you, ole sport, just as I told the Lieutenant, I'm dead agin' the game.

Jack. Aye, aye, mates, heave ahead. (*Exeunt* COLUMBIA, JACK, *and* FRECKLES. JACK *singing "Columbia" as he goes.*)

Beezie. I like to hear you talk -- you are not going? (*As* LIEUTENANT *prepares to depart.*)

Harry. Yes, my friends await me.

Beezie. It is so seldom I meet such as you that it is hard. (*Rising.*) Go to your friends -- excuse yourself and then return here. I should like to have a few moments' conversation with you; in the meantime, keep a sharp lookout for Dan Driscol.

Harry. (*Aside.*) Ah. This begins to look like dangerous work, but Freckles told me to cultivate this woman and Dan Driscol -- in the interest of Mary, I'd brave dangers a thousand times greater. (*To* BEEZIE.) I shall return.

Beezie. Thank you. (*Exit* LIEUTENANT.) And with such men in the world, I am in love with a desperado. What a world, what a world. Ah! (*Enter* HOP and *Tong Sing*.) I have been waiting a half hour for you -- the money -- (*Impatiently.*)

Hop. Velly wellee; velly solly; here it is. (*Gives large roll of money.*) Dan wantee money, but me no givee him.

Beezie. Right; what have you done with the girl?

Hop. I mallied her.

Beezie. You lie, you yellow devil, you doped her and made her believe you married her.

Hop. No -- no -- me mallied her. Her name now Mary Lee, Hop's wife.

Beezie. And she is miserable, of course.

Hop. After she smoke opium, she velly, velly happy and love Hop velly much.

Beezie. The newspapers are full of her disappearance. The preacher and her friends are seeking her; if they find the girl --

Hop. No can take her, she my wife -- me keepee her, no one find her anyway -- no how.

Beezie. We'll see.

Hop. Beezie, you know Miss Flances teachee mission school?

Beezie. Yes, she was here a few minutes ago.

Hop. Fong Sing wantee her velly much. Pay big plice for her.

Beezie. Ha. How much?

Hop. Five hundred dollars.

Beezie. Tell him half down and I'll talk business.

Hop. Fong Sing! (*Fong comes downstage;* HOP *talks Chinese to him; Fong replies, winding up by handing* HOP *a roll of bills.* HOP *hands same to* BEEZIE.)

Beezie. Rest easy, you yellow devils, Dan and I will arrange the details; you shall have the girl (*Aside.*) because I hate her. (*Exit* HOP *and Fong Sing, chattering in Chinese. Enter* LIEUTENANT. *Crowd gradually disperses, leaving* BEEZIE *and* LIEUTENANT *alone.*)

Beezie. Ah, you have kept your word.

Harry. Did you doubt?

Beezie. No, I knew you would come.

Harry. Now for your news -- you have something to tell me.

Beezie. Yes, you must leave Chinatown and never return.

Harry. Impossible.

Beezie. Ah, because of the Mission teacher, Miss Frances.

Harry. (*Aside.*) They warned me not to mention my name or relationship to this woman. (*Aloud.*) Yes?

Beezie. You love her?

Harry. Yes, devotedly.

Beezie. Ah, she is a lucky woman.

Harry. Rather I am a lucky man.

Beezie. You love her; she loves you and I love a brute.

Harry. Which is incomprehensible to me.

Beezie. You have seen dogs love a brutal master? Well, some women are like dogs; dogs that lick the hands that beat them. I am such a one.

Harry. Such a love --

Beezie. Is one of the mysteries of Heaven or of Hades.

Harry. Your language stamps you as a woman of gentle birth.

Beezie. Thank you. I had almost forgotten it until tonight.

Harry. Why not cease your present mode of life?

Beezie. I have tried --

Harry. And?

Beezie. Failed.

Harry. And the cause?

Beezie. Society first, and opium. I am an opium fiend.

Harry. Truly?

Beezie. Yes.

Harry. But you have no symptoms visible of a confirmed smoker.

Beezie. (*Smiles.*) I smoke $1.25 worth every day of my life. They give me three years.

Harry. To live?

Beezie. Yes; deprive me of opium and I have all the symptoms you miss; my limbs refuse to carry me and my brain becomes a seething furnace of acute agony.

Harry. Terrible -- and the beginning of this life?

Beezie. A slumming expedition to Chinatown; a trial of the pipe for sport. I became fascinated; came again and again. Gradually, I lost lover, friends, family, all. Society turned its back upon me and now I have no other world.

Harry. I wish I could aid you.

Beezie. (*Turning.*) You can.

Harry. How?

Beezie. Take me out of this life.

Harry. Impossible.

Beezie. So says all the world.

Harry. You have Dan Driscol.

Beezie. (*Returning; leaning on chair at table R.*) Yes, he took care of me when the world turned me adrift. I love him for that. He uses me for crime, but he never permits me to suffer for opium. I am useful to him; he is useful to me, but if I were assured of proper protection in the sphere to which I once belonged, Dan would be willing to give up all claim on me. His love, though brutal, is unselfish. (*Tenderly.*) If I can be assured of life, I could obey you. Like a drowning man I grasp at a straw; like the doomed convict, I pray for a reprieve.

Harry. This is pitiful. I love --

Beezie. Frances Parker.

Harry. You know?

Beezie. That and more. You have a sister too, that you love. I heard all as I sat in that chair.

Harry. Great Heavens; you know where my sister is?

Beezie. I may find her.

Harry. You will restore her to me?

Beezie. Yes, if you will it.

Harry. You demand --

Beezie. Your protection, in return for your sister's honor, reputation, reason.

Harry. My God, are you a woman or a fiend in human form?

Beezie. No -- merely a human soul battling for life.

Curtain.

ACT II.
Scene 1.

Mission school, full stage. Seated at small tables are Chinamen, being taught by young ladies: MISS FRANCES *with* TONG SING. MISS NELLIE *with* HOP LEE, MISS MAMIE *with* One Lung, MISS BELLA *with* AH FONG. JACK *in chair L. of table.* COLUMBIA *down L. corner on floor. Supers about stage. Before curtain rises, a hymn is sung.*

Freckles. Dis is de toughest deal I've passed tro' in a month of Sundays.

Columbia. Freckles, you ought to have taken out an accident policy before yer risked yerself in here.

Jack. (*Roaring.*) Splice my main brace if the lass ain't sailin' right before the wind.

Freckles. Well, you hear me, an' dis is no pipe dream; if the Lieutenant don't show up soon, I'll ventilate dis atmosphere wid some large blue language.

Jack. Cheer up, my hearty. The Lieutenant is your commander, and all we have to do is obey.

Freckles. Well, dis is purty punk, sittin' here like bumps on a log.

Columbia. (*Pushing him.*) Gee whiz. Wasn't we on the go all last night and dis mornin' huntin' for the lost fairy. You ain't no hog, you ain't. You're only a sixty-foot car loaded down wid pork.

Jack. (*Roaring.*) Aye, aye, lass, in a stiff breeze.

Freckles. (*To* COLUMBIA.) Don't get gay, don't get gay. (*Sulking, to* JACK.)

Columbia. (*To* JACK.) There's something else eatin' Jack.

Jack. Spin the yarn, lass.

Columbia. Hop Lee paid him a bill last night with a counterfeit $5 bill.

Jack. (*Roars.*)

Freckles. Pass de butter; pass de butter.

Jack. Hop gave you that bill for steering me up against his game.

Freckles. How did you know it?

Jack. (*Wiping his eyes.*) Why, I played it into his bank. (*Laughing.*) See if there ain't a smell of tar on it, and a piece torn off the upper left hand corner.

Freckles. Wouldn't dat knock the laundry off of a schooner of beer? (*Examining bill, calming down, rising.*) Well, I thought I was a good mixer and could get next to de live ones, but old sea log, I'm worse'n one of them rah-rah boys with a big bunch o' hair.

Columbia. Or one of those saucy guys dat wears a big bunch o' ribbon.

Freckles. Pile it on; all I need is an umbrella, a grip, and a bunch of spinach (*Goat bus.*) to be a regular "come on." What'll I say when the gang gets on, to be done up by a Chink, aided and abetted by Old Neptune? I need de air.

Columbia. Try a balloon.

Freckles. Parson, me and my rag is shy on a feed. Do you mind if we hot foots it across de alley to float a couple of sinkers?

Columbia. If de Lieutenant comes a wire'll reach us on a fishing pole.

Reverend Parker. All right. (FRECKLES *and* COLUMBIA *go to door L.E.*) But Jack, go with them.

Jack. Aye, aye, sir. (*Goes to door.*) The lass is all right, but my pilot; I'm afraid I'll have to lift his papers and put him out of commission.

Freckles. Dat ain't no kid, neither. (*Exit* JACK, FRECKLES, *and* COLUMBIA. JACK *sings "Columbia."*)

Reverend Parker. Brethren: I desire to call your attention to the untoward disappearance of one of our beloved teachers -- Miss Mary Hildreth. The mystery of this lady's absence and the frightful grief into which it has plunged her family and friends is appalling. To our Christian Chinese friends I make a special plea for ardent effort. A standing reward of $1,000 is offered for the recovery of Miss Mary Hildreth. We will close this evening's lessons with the 14th hymn.

At beginning of address, DAN *has appeared at door; sees* HOP KEE, *and goes to him, conversing earnestly. At beginning of hymn,* DAN *joins* FRANCES *and Tong Sing joins* HOP. *About middle of hymn,* BEEZIE *appears at door, attended by a Chinaman, who shows himself at door and then disappears.* BEEZIE *notes* DAN *and* FRANCES. DAN *endeavors to kiss* FRANCES' *hand, which she repels.* BEEZIE *sinks on chair back of open door. At close of hymn, Chinamen,* DAN, *and Supers exeunt.*

Reverend Parker. Remember, any clue to the lost Mission teacher you will kindly report here at once.

Dan. Sure, parson.

Hop. Me help velly much.

Tong Sing and Ah Fong. Me too -- Me too.

Reverend Parker. Good night; peace be with you all.

All. Good night; good night.

Reverend Parker. (*About to close the door, discovers* BEEZIE.) Who have we here? (MAMIE *and* BELLA *bring* BEEZIE, *who is very faint, C.*)

Frances. (*R.*) That vile creature?

Reverend Parker. (*Severely.*) Frances, you are forgetting yourself. This stray lamb has come to the house of God.

Frances. (*Weakly.*) Where she would return good for evil.

Reverend Parker. Thank heaven; ladies, conduct her to the sitting room and give her every attention.

Nellie. Very well.

Bella. We will do our best.

Reverend Parker. Thank you. (*The young ladies conduct* BEEZIE *to room off R.* FRANCES *X. L.*) I see a ray of hope for the return of my sweetheart in that woman's face and words.

Frances. (*L.*) I am sorry, brother, that I so far forgot myself as to be harsh with a seeker after comfort, but how could I be otherwise? This woman's infamous proposal to Harry aroused all the feminine instinct in me against one who would rob her of love and life. (*X.R.*)

Reverend Parker. (*R.C.*) I understand, sister, I understand, but have I not a greater cause for anger?

Frances. (*Turning.*) True, but you are the greater Christian. (REVEREND PARKER *takes* FRANCES *in his arms and comforts her.*)

Harry. (*Enters in sailor's garb.*) Frances. (*She goes to him.*)

Frances. This costume?

Harry. Chief Devery advised it. How do I look?

Frances. Splendid.

Harry. Where are my assistants?

Reverend Parker. (*R.*) They are taking supper across the way. They will return shortly; what's the news?

Harry. (*Breezily.*) I have secured the co-operation of Chief Devery and the whole detective service. Every avenue leading in and out of Chinatown will be covered from this moment until my sister is found. In addition, fifty photographs of Mary have been placed in the hands of men assigned to conduct slumming parties; so that the inside as well as the outside of Chinatown will be under strict surveillance. Send for Jack and the boy and girl at once.

Reverend Parker. One moment, our search may be simplified by a new piece of good fortune.

Harry. What? (*Enter* MAMIE.)

Mamie. The woman is in a frightful state; her body is covered with bruises. She is on the verge of collapse from nervous prostration and pain.

Reverend Parker. Send for a doctor.

Mamie. She says she does not require a doctor; only opium.

Harry. What is the woman's name?

Reverend Parker. Beezie Garrity, the so-called Queen of Chinatown.

Harry. (*Taking Stage Left.*) Ah! She here?

Mamie. (*To* REVEREND PARKER.) We have the opium, sir.

Reverend Parker. (*Looks at* LIEUTENANT, *who nods.*) Give her sufficient to calm her.

Mamie. (*Exit hurriedly.*) Yes, sir.

Harry. What brought Chinatown's Queen here to-night?

Frances. (*Piqued.*) You.

Reverend Parker. Frances.

Frances. (*Tears.*) Well, I can't help it. (*X, sits table R.*)

Harry. (*Goes to her, pets her. To* REVEREND PARKER.) Did you tell her of my conversation with Beezie?

Reverend Parker. Yes.

Harry. You were in error. Such revelations are not for such pure, gentle ears.

Frances. Forgive me, Harry. I know I wrong you by this exhibition of weakness, but it is all so horrible.

Harry. (*Comforting her.*) Yes, yes.

Frances. And I should be the last one to add to your grief. (*Rising.*) Tell me how I can help to lighten it.

Harry. By placing implicit trust in me.

Frances. I will; Oh, Harry, that horrid man Driscol was here this evening.

Harry. Well?

Reverend Parker. (*L.*) I have noticed that he takes quite an unnecessary interest in you.

Harry. (*Gaily.*) Ha! Ha!

Frances. (*C.*) Now brother, I enlisted his sympathies in the interest of Mary. He has been diligence itself. He suggested to-night that the teachers go on a slumming expedition.

Harry. To be led by him?

Frances. No, by the Queen. (*Pointing to room off R.*) I refused.

Reverend Parker. And quite right.

Harry. Could he have had a motive?

Mamie. (*Enter.*) The woman is rapidly recovering and asks to see Lieutenant Hildreth.

Harry. Driscol had a motive and this woman must explain it.

Frances. (*Going to him.*) Harry!

Harry. Be patient, sweetheart. (*To* MAMIE.) Ask the woman to come here as soon as she feels able.

Mamie. She insists upon seeing you alone, sir.

Frances. (*Weeping.*) There, now.

Reverend Parker. Frances, this behavior is unseemly. (*Goes up C.*) Tell her, sister, and I shall retire as soon as she is ready.

Mamie. (*Exit.*) Yes, sir.

Harry. Be calm, Frances. There may be in this woman's heart a pity newly awakened, which may deliver my unfortunate sister back to us. (*X. with her L.*) Do you see no comfort or happiness in the prospect, the hope?

Frances. Forgive me, Harry. (*Drying her eyes.*)

Reverend Parker. (*Earnestly.*) And may justice, peace and mercy be meted out to and by this unfortunate child of the streets this night and for all time to come. (BEEZIE *has entered at beginning of* REVEREND PARKER'S *speech. She reverently bows her head.*)

Beezie. Amen. (*X. down R.* REVEREND PARKER *and* FRANCES *bow as they pass her and both exit R.*)

Harry. (*C.*) Pray be seated.

Beezie. Thank you. (*Sitting R.*)

Harry. You wished to see me?

Beezie. Yes, for a number of reasons -- reasons pertinent to you -- to myself.

Harry. (*Stiffly.*) I trust this is not a continuance of last night's interview.

Beezie. (*Pained.*) No.

Harry. I beg your pardon for speaking so warmly.

Beezie. I admire you for it. Such words proclaim you a man, one who will bestow on me his sympathy if he cannot his respect.

Harry. I beg of you.

Beezie. I understand -- Oh, so, well. Men are seldom fair to women, but you are fair, just. (*Pause.*) I want to beg your pardon for forgetting myself last night. Women of my class have no right to memories or hopes; both plunge us into extremes of delight and despair. When we awake from the transient dream, note the surroundings, see the ravages of desire upon our bodies and upon our souls, we try to shut out the terrible truth (*Hands to eyes.*), but truth will not down. (*Rising.*) The spectacle of an untimely end pierces the inward as well as the outward sight, and our only solace is to seek death instead of waiting for it. (*Upstage.*)

Harry. (*Takes Stage L.*) This is terrible; can this be the effects of opium?

Beezie. (*Hand on chair R., arousing herself.*) I suffered for the pain I caused you last night.

Harry. Suffered?

Beezie. Yes, a portion of our conversation was overheard by the man that loves me.

Harry. Driscol?

Beezie. (*Bows.*) After you left, he entered without a word and conducted me to my home. I knew what his silence meant, and somehow or other I did not care. First he removed my smoking outfit and then my opium, then he struck me, struck me, yes, beat me into insensibility. (*Sinking into chair.*) When I came to my senses, he sat there glaring at me, toying with a dirk. I begged him to kill me, but he simply shook his head. I asked him for liquor, he pointed to the water pitcher. I had been without opium too long and prayed to have it restored to me; he silently refused.

Harry. Monster.

Beezie. I had upon my person last night $750. You shall not know how I came by it, but when that sum should grow to a thousand he had promised to take me away from Chinatown forever. He robbed me of that money.

Harry. The hound.

Beezie. (*C.*) To fill my cup of misery, this fiend declared he loved Frances Parker, your fiancee --

Harry. This is too much.

Beezie. So I told him, but he declared he would have her.

Harry. (*Angry.*) And he demanded you should place her in his clutches.

Beezie. A yellow devil's fist. He threatens me with death and I expect it now any time. Still he refuses me opium until --

Harry. Until?

Beezie. I should conduct Frances and some of her women friends to One Lung's opium joint, to-night, if possible. That was my quest here to-night.

Harry. Driscol was paving the way.

Beezie. Yes, one of his Chinamen has not left my side all day. He is near that door now. His business is to keep me away from opium.

Harry. I now see how that drug is responsible for crime. Do you know where my sister is?

Beezie. Not now; they are going to move her to-night, but I have an idea that your best plan is to push through this slumming expedition. The safest place in Chinatown will be chosen, and I know of none so safe as One Lung's.

Harry. You really advise this?

Beezie. I do; you will find your sister by using Frances as a decoy.

Harry. (*Mental struggle.*) I will trust you.

Beezie. Oh, thank you, thank you. (*X.L.*)

Harry. I will arrange with Frances and party to start at, say, eleven o'clock. No harm shall befall them with the preparations I shall make; and now you must excuse me, as I wish to put my assistants on the street to note every white woman out to-night. How shall I ever repay you for your advice and help?

Beezie. By thinking kindly of me.

Harry. But let us trust your case is not so hopeless.

Beezie. (*Kissing his hand.*) This sympathy is paradise.

Harry. Your comfort lies in the satisfaction of meriting it.

Beezie. Yes, I shall merit your sympathy -- your regard, even your respect. In saving your sister and your love --

Harry. Frances, too?

Beezie. Yes, she too is sought by the monsters. In saving them, I sacrifice my life. (*Rising.*)

Harry. May Heaven preserve you. (*On his knee, kissing her hand.*) I am your debtor forever. (BEEZIE *sinks into her chair, radiant with happiness.*)

Scene 2.

Mott Street. Enter FRECKLES, COLUMBIA, *and* JACK.

Columbia. (*C.*)   Come here, you two fire-eaters, and stop chewin' de rag. (*They approach R. and L.*) Is dere any change comin' to e-e-ither of you?

Freckles. (*L.*) Not if old storm centre'll stop his yap.

Jack. (*R.*) Give us your flipper, pilot, I restores to yer yer papers.

Freckles. It sort o' crawls up my head piece dat you put him next.

Columbia. Say, I've got a license dis minute to give you a good swift punch. (*Squaring off.*)

Jack. (*Coming between them.*) Hold hard there, ship mates.

Freckles. (*To* COLUMBIA.) I passes you up.

Columbia. (*To* FRECKLES.) I'll change yer face.

Jack. (*To both.*) I'll report you to the Lieutenant if you don't change your manner. During time of war it's death, same as treason, to fight anyone 'cept for the enemy. What's the Army and Navy Rules and Regulations for, eh? I've a notion to throw you both overboard. (*Bus. for* FRECKLES *and* COLUMBIA.) Shake hands. (*They shake gingerly. To* FRECKLES.) Now give her a rousing good smack and a hearty hug.

Freckles. Not on your ironclad.

Columbia. Freckles is gettin' the harpoon fer fair.

Jack. (*Takes them by the shoulders and brings them together.*) At it, you young land pirates, or I'll put you in irons for the rest of your life. (FRECKLES *is compelled to kiss and hug* COLUMBIA.)

Columbia. More -- more. (*Hugging* FRECKLES.)

Jack. Obey orders, sir. (FRECKLES *laughs and hugs* COLUMBIA *again.*) Now you hug your superior officer. (COLUMBIA *and* JACK *hug. Jealous business by* FRECKLES.) Now, how do you feel?

Columbia. Out of sight. So does he; don't you, bub? You see, Jack, Freckles was four flushin' all the time.

Freckles. She's next. On de square, I never could get wise to a gal. You showed me up before her and me name was pants. Now I am back in de service and ready for orders -- feelin' like a forty-time winner.

Jack. Come then, to the Mission.

Harry. (*Enter C.*) Jack.

Jack. Aye, aye, sir.

Columbia. (*To* FRECKLES.) Salute, you forty-to-one shot. (FRECKLES *salutes.*)

Harry. I have learned that Miss Mary is to be moved from her present prison to another to-night. While 'tis but a rumor, I want you to have your eyes open, especially on Mott, Pell, and Doyer Streets.

Jack. Aye, aye, sir.

Freckles. Aye, aye, sir. (*To* COLUMBIA.) Salute, you lobster. (COLUMBIA *salutes.*)

Harry. Off with you at once; you are all supplied with whistles.

Jack. Aye, aye, sir. Bo'zens whistles. (FRECKLES *and* COLUMBIA *show whistles.*)

Harry. Blow sharply three times if you run across my sister. Should you learn of any news -- any rumor -- report it to the Mission without delay.

Jack. Aye, aye, sir. (FRECKLES *and* COLUMBIA *are about to slap each other's shoulders to salute. Then they salute together.*)

Harry. To your posts and luck go with you.

Jack, Freckles, and Columbia. Aye, aye, sir. (FRECKLES *exits R.1.E.,* COLUMBIA *L.1.E., Jack L.U.E.* BEEZIE *enters L.U.E., followed by Chinaman and meets* LIEUTENANT, *C.*)

Harry. (*To* BEEZIE.) Miss Frances and the ladies will be ready at the Mission, at eleven o'clock.

Beezie. I shall be there.

Harry. I cannot tell you how thankful I am.

Beezie. Sh! Be prudent, your life -- mine -- your sister's -- hang in the balance.

Harry. True, I shall be careful. (*Taking her hand.* DAN *appears at door of saloon and notes scene.*)

Beezie. Go, please, I expect Dan.

Harry. Very well. (*Exit R.U.E.*) You shall never regret your noble work. (BEEZIE *looks off after* LIEUTENANT, *puts her hands back of her head and walks down R. slowly, as if in a reverie; turning, she sees* DAN, *looking at her coldly.*)

Dan. (*Seated L., pause, dryly.*) Well?

Beezie. (*Goes to him L.*) I have done your bidding.

Dan. Good.

Beezie. I shall amuse Frances and party with music, song and dance; feast their feminine eyes with the curious draperies and elaborate costumes the place contains. If they like, they shall be permitted to put on Oriental dresses. Refreshments will be served. I shall smoke for their edification -- and my own -- I shall tempt them to smoke.

Dan. Fine.

Beezie. When Frances Parker becomes insensible to her surroundings, the attendants will carry her -- where?

Dan. Upstairs.

Beezie. Will Tong Sing be there?

Dan. Yes.

Beezie. You, too?

Dan. No.

Beezie. Ah, I see; you want the girl first in Tong Sing's possession to collect the other $250.

Dan. Yes.

Beezie. Then with our combined earnings, you will, after outwitting Tong Sing, revel in the society of Frances Parker?

Dan. No.

Beezie. You lie. (*Business.*)

Dan. I have listened; you have not bewailed the loss of my love. Why?

Beezie. (*Shrug.*)

Dan. Two days ago the fact that I might notice another woman would have crazed you. You have changed.

Beezie. For cause.

Dan. Yes; the Lieutenant.

Beezie. Don't forget your cruelty.

Dan. To get square with him I put up Tong Sing to covet Frances. To test you, I claimed I wanted her -- I don't. The play is a fifteen-year sentence. Now listen to me. Drop your Lieutenant -- stick to me -- a false move --

Beezie. And you will kill me.

Dan. You know your lesson. You can't get away from me, so

don't try. Now go and get ready for the slumming party.

Beezie. Very well. (*Exit R.U.E., followed by Chinaman.*)

Dan. I don't understand her; she's not the same Beezie. Well, I'll have her in shape just as soon as I finish with the Lieutenant. (*Exit.*)

Urchins quarrel C. Enter MRS. HUFFNAGLE.

Mrs. Huffnagle. Oh! (*Taking hold of one of the boys.*) Patrick Sullivan Huffnagle, into de house wid ye. I'll give ye all the fight that's comin' to ye -- go on. (*Giving him a slap and looking after him.*)

A CHINAMAN *has entered R.U.E. and is going off L.U.E. As he reaches C, one of the boys pulls his queue, and turning quickly, his basket strikes* MRS. HUFFNAGLE, *who counters on his face, knocking him down. Boys raise hue and cry amid laughter.*

Mrs. Huffnagle. Bad luck to ye, ye miserable heathen, I've a great notion to pound you to a jelly. How dare ye interfere wid a decent Irish lady whose decindints were Christians before you were born, ye omahdan, ye --

Chinaman. Melican boy velly bad.

Mrs. Huffnagle. Shut up, ye blitherin idiot, or I'll spread the map o' Chinatown all over your face, you round-faced, moon-eyed Mongolian heathen.

Chinaman. (*Chinese speech as he exits.*)

Mrs. Huffnagle. Shut up, shut up, ye yellow jacket. If I had a kettle o' hot water I'd drown ye, ye encycle-velocipede ye. (*After* CHINAMAN *exits.*) I'll bet a cint against a raw pickle, if I understood his talk I could have him pinched. Say, One Lung, what's all this jabbering about -- news from Chinee?

One Lung. Melican gal stole.

Mrs. Huffnagle. Now this is gettin' altogether too promiscuous. White fathers, brothers, and sweethearts will burn down Chinatown one of these days. What's the poor unfortunate's name?

One Lung. Mary Hildreth.

Mrs. Huffnagle. Souls alive. The sweet-faced Mission teacher. (*Taking off her apron.*) I'll not do a blessed hour's work again until she's found. (*X. R. to her house.*) Huffnagle! Huffnagle! (*To* ONE

LUNG.) Some one among your yellow brothers is at the bottom of this outrage. (*Enter* FRECKLES *and* COLUMBIA.) Huffnagle! (*To* ONE LUNG.) And all I ask is to have one crack at him. (*Looking about.*) Did any of ye see Huffnagle about? (*Boy points to saloon.*) Ah! Ha! One Lung, your news has just put me in the humor to interview me husband. (*Exit into saloon.*)

Freckles. Say, Columb, don't take no pointers from dat old buzzard. No lady as respects her old man would show him up by acting dat way.

Columbia. Bet you fifty kopecks she does him up.

Freckles. Can't go yer till I see his form. (*Enter* MRS. HUFFNAGLE *with her hands about* HUFFNAGLE'S *neck.*)

Mrs. Huffnagle. Come out; come out, ye drunken loafer.

Freckles. (*To* COLUMBIA.) You win -- a cinch.

Columbia. Ain't she a scorchalorem?

Huffnagle. (*On* MRS. HUFFNAGLE'S *left.*) For vy you make me dot saloon out yet?

Mrs. Huffnagle. I'll tell you soon enough, ye old varmint. (*Taking growler from him.*) You've drank the whole pint, haven't ye?

Huffnagle. It vas the leetlest pint whatever vas, yes --

Mrs. Huffnagle. If it wasn't for the news I've got to tell ye, I'd beat ye within an inch of yer life.

Huffnagle. Vy not, don't you miss it.

Mrs. Huffnagle. There's been another abduction, Huffnagle.

Huffnagle. I am affected, not.

Mrs. Huffnagle. The yellow devils have stolen another white girl.

Huffnagle. I know all dat -- about it -- yes --

Mrs. Huffnagle. What?

Huffnagle. Listen out -- dey talk about lost gal in the saloon. I listen out -- I have a glue, yes --

Mrs. Huffnagle. A clue?

Huffnagle. Sure! (*Pulls lady's shoe from pocket.*) Not.

Mrs. Huffnagle. You're a fool.

Huffnagle. So'm I -- (*Bus.*)

Mrs. Huffnagle. So ye are -- a woman's shoe a clue -- why don't ye mend it, instead of drinkin' yerself blind in the rum shop?

Huffnagle. Foolishness, dy name is vomans -- yes -- see? (*Taking paper out of pocket.*) $1,000 reward -- yes -- de abducted gal's broder vas a Navy officer whose ship vas lately in Rio Janiero.

(FRECKLES *and* COLUMBIA *have been listening.* FRECKLES *rushes forward. Enter* JACK.)

Freckles. Who brought you dat shoe?

Huffnagle. One of Hop Lee's servants.

Freckles. Give it to me. (*Snatches shoe and exits R.U.E.* MR. *and* MRS. HUFFNAGLE *grab at him.* COLUMBIA *hangs onto* HUFFNAGLE. JACK *restrains* MRS. HUFFNAGLE. MR. *and* MRS. HUFFNAGLE *raise loud cries of* "Thief! Thief!")

Jack. (*R., arms about* MRS. HUFFNAGLE.) Hold hard, hold hard.

Mrs. Huffnagle. That's what yer doin', ye old monster, let go of me or I'll scratch your eyes out.

Huffnagle. Och! Da basa buba. (*German speech.*) My customer's shoe -- not. My $1,000 reward -- not -- yes.

Columbia. Nit, that's what you mean -- everything's all right -- Jack.

Jack. Aye, aye, sir.

Columbia. Freckles' actin' under orders; dat shoe seems to be a clue and he's takin' it over to de Mission.

Mrs. Huffnagle. Come on then, Huffnagle, and claim your property.

Jack. Hold hard. (*Holding* MRS. HUFFNAGLE.)

Columbia. Hold hard. (*Holding* HUFFNAGLE.)

Huffnagle. Dot is my wife -- yes --

Jack. And a fine lump of a girl she is -- (*Hugging her -- she likes it and smiles.*) To prove that I admire your taste, mate, I'll salute the saucy frigate. (*Kissing her.*)

Mrs. Huffnagle. There now, stop yer jollyin' --

Huffnagle. (*Struggling with* COLUMBIA.) My wife, yes -- da moder of my children, yes --

Jack. How many?

Huffnagle. (*Still struggling.*) Four.

Jack. Here's one for each. (*Kissing her four times.* HUFFNAGLE *makes a fuss.*)

Mrs. Huffnagle. Ef anyone but an Irishman had taken such liberties, I'd have the law on him.

Jack. Aye, aye, lass.

Huffnagle. One good turn deserves another -- yes. (*Tries to kiss* COLUMBIA; *she slaps his face.* MRS. HUFFNAGLE *rushes over, swings* COLUMBIA *aside R.*)

Mrs. Huffnagle. Ye little hussy!

Columbia. Cheese; cheese.

Mrs. Huffnagle. If I catch you monkeyin' wid dat little fairy --

Huffnagle. Och! Gott! You -- yes -- (*Pointing to* Jack.)

Mrs. Huffnagle. Simply carried out an old Irish custom -- people from the same county in the old country greet each other that way. Youse Dutch never got to that high state of edication. Now -- (*To* JACK.) about the shoe --

Jack. Aye, aye, lass; if the shoe proves to be the clue Columbia speaks of, I promise you on the word of an Irishman that you'll get the reward.

Mrs. Huffnagle. Hurrah! Huroo!

Huffnagle. Another pint; I'll get it -- yes -- (*Exit into saloon.*)

Jack. Now, darlin', to celebrate our meetin' and the prospects of the $1,000 reward, give us a song. One of the good old sort.

Mrs. Huffnagle. Anything to please you, my buckoo.

Song, dances, and specialty. At finish of specialties, three sharp whistles are heard off L.U.E. During specialty, COLUMBIA *exits L.U.E.*

Jack. The little pilot, by Jupiter. Sea room, ye land lubbers, or I'll sink ye all into Davy Jones' locker. (*Breaking through crowd and rushing C. Great commotion, angry voices off L.U.E.* FRECKLES *heard to cry with pain.* MARY *screams.* COLUMBIA, *dress torn, hair awry, meets* JACK *up C. She screams.*)

Columbia. They have struck Freckles down. He found the owner of the shoe. Here she comes with Hop Lee. (*Enter* HOP LEE, *dragging* MARY *along roughly, a motley crowd at their heels.* COLUMBIA *rushes off L.U.E. and returns with* FRECKLES, *who has a cut on his head. His clothes are torn and his hat gone.*)

Jack. (*Blows whistle three times, confronting* HOP *and* MARY.) Hold hard there, you yellow Chinese pilot. Heave to, until I take a peep at your papers. (*Going down C.*)

Hop. Take your hland off me. Sam Foy! Ah Fong! (*Chinese speech.* COLUMBIA *and* FRECKLES *get between* JACK *and the Chinamen, who rush forward at* HOP'S *bidding. Chinamen and mob work L.* HUFFNAGLE *enters from saloon.)*

Freckles. Look out, Jack, they'll do you as they did me.

Jack. They will, eh? Clear decks for action. *(Pulling pistol.* COLUMBIA *blows whistle three times.)*

Jack. Good lass, there are two of us and one on the Hospital list, but the enemy must surrender.

Mrs. Huffnagle. Here's another for the right and the old sod.

Huffnagle. *(R.)* Und dere vas anoder one -- Huffnagle and the reward.

Freckles. *(Pointing to* MARY.*)* Look at her feet.

Jack. Right, by the eternal. Give up your white prisoner, you robbin' heathen, or I'll kill you like a mad dog. *(Great turmoil.* COLUMBIA *rushes upstage, blowing her whistle continuously.* DAN *at this point breaks through crowd and strikes* JACK *from behind. The* LIEUTENANT *arrives at the same time.* MR. *and* MRS. HUFFNAGLE *take care of* JACK, *and seat him extreme R.)*

Harry. *(Recognizing his sister.)* Mary! Found at last. *(She screams and rushes to him.)*

Mary. *(In his arms.)* Brother! *(Arrival of policemen.)*

Hop. I wantee dat man arrest -- he stluck me.

Dan. I too was assaulted by him.

Harry. But, officer, this Chinaman has abducted my sister.

Hop. This lady is my wife. *(Swinging* MARY *L. She screams.)*

Dan. Yes, I was present at the ceremony.

Harry. Ah, liars! *(Makes quick dash and grabs* HOP *and* DAN *each by throat by either hand. Dashes both to ground and is strangling them. Policemen pulls* LIEUTENANT *to feet.* HOP *and* DAN *each rise on one knee, gasping. Bell of approaching wagon heard. Three policemen rush on to take part in finish.)*

Hop. *(Grasping* MARY.*)* You come home with me. *(*MARY *screams.)*

Harry. *(Struggling with policemen.)* Mary!

Dan. *(To* LIEUTENANT.*)* And you go to the Tombs for to-night, at least.

Harry. Mary!

Mary. *(Being dragged away.)* Harry, brother, for God's sake, save me!

Harry. *(Struggling with two policemen who restrain him.)* Hop

Lee, Dan Driscol, as God is my judge, I shall kill you both! (*Struggling with policemen.* MARY *screaming as* HOP LEE *drags her away.*)

Curtain.

ACT III.
Scene 1.

Upper apartment.   Enter HOP LEE, *dragging in* MARY. *Charlie, a Chinaman, is with* HOP. *Charlie, L.*

Hop. (*L.C., throwing* MARY *to floor.*)   You glive Hop velly much trouble, see.

Mary.   You coward.   You will have trouble enough before you are through with this world.   (*Pause.*)   Release me now and I promise to stay my brother's hand.   (*On knees.*)

Hop.   He never find you.

Mary.   He has sworn to kill you.

Hop.   Me killee him first.

Mary.   (*Pleadingly.*)   He will pay you money.   Let me go. Please, please let me go.

Hop.   No, me likee you.   (*Approaching her.*)

Mary.   (*Rising; drawing back.*)   Ough! You filthy creature, don't you dare to touch me.

Hop.   (*Approaching her.*)   No?   Me teachee you better manners.

Mary.   (*Screams -- runs to window W.F.*)

Hop.   (*Clasps handkerchief to her mouth -- drags her back to bench, places her on it.   Charlie assists.*)   Me teachee you to scream and run away from Hop.   (*They strap her to bench.*)   The bastinate.

Charlie removes her shoes and strikes soles of her feet several times with bastinado.   MARY shows by twistings of her body the agony.   At finish, HOP unstraps and ungags her.   She does not move.

Hop.   She faint; velly good; she wake soon.   (HOP *and* CHARLIE *smoke opium.*)

Lower Apartment. At rise, MERCIDES *reclining L. attended by a Chinaman who is cooking dope pills. As curtain goes up, she is smoking. Female attendant serves* MERCIDES *tea.* SAM *cooks another pill.*

Mercides. (*Languidly.*) How many pills, Sam?

Sam. Two, Miss Mercides.

Mercides. I want more, about six more, eh?

Sam. Three makee plenty.

Mercides. All right. (*Enter* BEEZIE, *with* FRANCES, MAMIE, *and* BELLA.)

Mamie and Bella. How beautiful! How lovely!

Frances. (*R.C.*) How debasing!

Mamie. That heavy sweet scent --

Beezie. Opium.

Bella. There's a woman.

Beezie. You can speak to her -- there is no such thing as breach of etiquette here.

Frances. Frightful. (*The three approach her.*)

Mercides. Good evening, ladies, slumming?

Frances. (*R. of* MERCIDES; MAMIE *and* BELLA L.) Yes.

Mercides. It is great sport. I go about often. (*Lights cigarette.*)

Beezie. (*R.*) How much are you smoking now, Mercides?

Mercides. $1.25.

Frances. Why, what does she mean?

Beezie. She consumes $1.25 worth of opium every day. She will not live long. About four years at that rate.

Frances. If I could but save that poor soul.

Beezie. Try it -- the dope fiend does not object to sympathy. She will at least listen to you and thank you.

Frances. I will. (*Goes to* MERCIDES *and sits beside her; taking her hand, converses.*)

Mamie. It is all so novel and interesting.

Bella. And what a lovely costume she wears.

Beezie. Women cannot wear stays, my dear, when they indulge in this vice. Would you like to see the costumes?

Mamie. Yes, indeed.

Bella. I would love to put one on.

Beezie. Come with me, then. Miss Frances, we are going into the dressing room. (*At the door L., with ladies.*) Will you come?

Frances. Yes, I am useless here.

Beezie. No more so than science, my dear.

Frances. (*R. of* BEEZIE, *looking into room L.*) Women are smoking opium in there, too.

Beezie. Yes, in every room in this house women are hitting the pipe.

Frances. Dreadful! (*Exit* MAMIE, BELLA, FRANCES, *and* BEEZIE, *L.*)

Mary. (*Groans, moves, looks about.*) Oh!

Hop. (*Throwing her to the floor.*) You glive me great trouble, you savey? You no want Hop Lee? Velly well, me see. Charlie, you make a pipe ready.

Mary. (*Sitting up.*) No, no, please don't.

Hop. You no likee smoke, you no likee Hop; you no likee Chinatown. Velly hard to please. (*Picking up pipe.*)

Mary. Please don't make me use that, it makes me so ill.

Hop. You like him velly much after while, then you like Hop.

Mary. (*Rising.*) I won't touch that vile thing again. Oh, restore me to my family -- to my brother -- (*Crying.* HOP *lays down pipe and picks up bastinado.* MARY *in fear quiets down. Sits, then reclines.*)

Hop. (*Arranging pipe, both reclining.*) Ah! You ready to smoke now. (*Handing pipe to her, assisting.*) Smoke. (MARY *groans.*) Smoke -- quick -- (MARY *draws on pipe and blows out smoke, choking.*) Swallow smoke. (MARY *tries again, same result. Moans.*) You smoke velly bad; next pill you smoke, or (*Flourishing bastinado. Pause.*) Me heapee likee you.

Mary. Oh, if death would only come. (*She is forced to smoke at periods indicated.* MERCIDES *falls asleep and* SAM *carries her upstage and puts her in bunk.*)

Columbia. (*Offstage at back.*) You will tell ze -- vat you call him? Ah, ze coachman, to call in two hour.

Chinaman. (*Offstage.*) Allee light. Me tell him, me savey. (*Enter* COLUMBIA *dressed in long skirts, flashy, Frenchy.*)

Columbia. (*Aside.*) Wouldn't dat rattle yer slats? Well, I wonder. Where are dey? (*Looking about.*) Oh, dere's a woman. (*Looks at her.*) Dat's not Mary, nor Frances, nor anybody much, I guess.

Sam. You wantee smoke?

Columbia. Cert -- (*Catching herself.*) Certainment, Monsieur le Chinaman.

Sam. Allee light. (*Preparing dope.*) You wantee changee your dless?

Columbia. What? Talk about a half hook on the point of de jaw, I'll put a face on you that'll fade flowers. (*Catching herself.*) Don't mind me, Monsieur le Chinaman -- Mamzelle's little joke.

Sam. Ha! You actless?

Columbia. Me? Wouldn't dat frost you? Now dat's a fly Chink, an' dat's no Hungarian joke neither. If I ain't a actress, I've put on actress' clothes. If yer der real thing yer corset's got to be peeled. As I never wear dem, dat lets me out. But I'll take off dis lovely skirt, for it tangles me all up and I'll ruin it. (*Taking off long skirt.*) No use talkin', dat daughter of Mrs. Huffnagle do have ex-qui-site -- e-lab-o-rate outfits. (*Skirt is off and* COLUMBIA *appears in short petticoats.*)

Sam. (*Admiring, excited. Chinese speech.*)

Columbia. (*Business.*) I've knocked him a-twister fer fair.

Sam. You actless; me savey.

Columbia. Actress, sure. I can make Ellen Terry look like a Friday night amatoor. Come on with your double X brand of dope. (*Sits. Aside.*) I wonder where they are. (*Looking about.* SAM *prepares dope. Enter* LIEUTENANT, FRECKLES, *and* POLICE OFFICER.)

Policeman. A slumming party, Sam.

Sam. Allee light.

Columbia. (*Looking back.*) Hully gee. Me boss an' me steady.

Policeman. (*Turns over* MERCIDES *in bunk.*) Is this her?

Harry. (*Looking.*) No.

Policeman. There's another one. (*Pointing to* COLUMBIA. FRECKLES *in meantime has gone down C. and sees* COLUMBIA *just as she takes a whiff of the pipe and nearly chokes.*)

Freckles. (*Pulls* SAM *away.*) Dis is a nice deal, dis is. Choke, ye lobster, choke.

Columbia. (*Recovering.*) You told me it wouldn't hurt me if I didn't swallow it.

Freckles. (*Angry.*) Where's dat Chink? (*Turning.*)

Harry. One moment, Freckles. What are you doing here, Columbia? (POLICEMAN *and* SAM *converse R. Enter Charlie.*

SAM *addresses Chinese speech to him. Charlie exits.*)

Columbia. After you was arrested, I went to de Mission and told de parson. He was crazy, cause de girls had started to de opium joint with Beezie, so I thought I'd protect them, as you couldn't, so I borrowed dese duds and came fer fair.

Harry. You're a brave girl.

Columbia. How did you dish de cops? (*Enter Charlie, who in pantomime indicates to* HOP *who is below.* HOP *and Charlie carry* MARY *out of window onto fire escape out of view. Charlie returns, lies down and smokes.*)

Harry. I soon made my position clear at headquarters. Have you seen or heard of my sister?

Columbia. No, nor of Miss Frances.

Harry. (*X.C.*) Where can they be? (*To* POLICEMAN.) Does he know anything?

Policeman. No, but that is not strange; you never can get any news from these people.

Harry. Freckles, we are going to search the house. No harm can come to anyone, Columbia, so you two can stay here.

Freckles. Aye, aye, sir. (*Exit* LIEUTENANT *and* POLICEMAN *into room at back.*)

Columbia. (*L., reclining.*) How's your head, bub, hurt?

Freckles. (*Seated R. of her.*) De worst dat ever came up de pike.

Columbia. On de square. Oh! (*Solicitously.*)

Freckles. I thought I was up against de cold outside fer quits. I'll put you next. My light went out in de station house and I went to sleep with me face in a plate o' somethin' the doctor ordered. De Lieutenant and Jack stayed by me until I got back to Mulberry St., till I woke up.

Columbia. Don't you feel any better, now?

Freckles. I'm comin', but I feel as though I had a set o' coppers on me dat'd heat a four room flat, and my mouth feels like a Chinese family had just moved out of it.

Columbia. Never mind, bub, de Lieutenant'll send you out o' town, where you can live quiet and den you may see de flowers again.

Freckles. Cheese! Cheese! Chop de josh.

Columbia. Come, bub, cheer up, trow out your chest; you're not one o' dem easy winners what comes to a high jump and den quits. (LIEUTENANT *and* POLICEMAN *enter upper apartments; they note*

Charlie smoking, look about, converse, and exit.)

Freckles. (*Brightening up.*) Dat's de rag chewin' dere's music in, you can make book on dat. Did you cop out de Chink dat done me?

Columbia. I spotted him, and we'll trim him fer fair.

Freckles. Columb, put it dere, dare ain't no fairy as will ever have a drag with me but you.

Columbia. I feeds on de same fodder, Freckles. (*They embrace. Enter* BEEZIE, *L.*)

Beezie. I did not know you two were here.

Columbia. You can't lose us, Beezie.

Freckles. Say, queen, you don't find no johnny-jump-ups growin' along Pell Street, do you?

Beezie. (*Laughing.*) No.

Freckles. (*Goes up, looking about.*) Is Miss Frances and de oder Mission teacher here?

Beezie. (*X to dope lay-out L.*) Yes, I have been amusing them in that room. (*Charlie looks cautiously about; rises, goes to window and assists* HOP *to carry* MARY *back into room.*)

Columbia. How?

Beezie. Smoking hop. (*Reclining.*)

Freckles. Did Miss Frances smoke?

Beezie. No.

Freckles. (*C. to* COLUMBIA.) Is she on 'bout de riot?

Columbia. (*L.C.*) Search me. Tell her 'bout it. I'm goin' to see Miss Frances and spin de yarn; she ought to know. (*Exit L.* BEEZIE *prepares dope.*)

Freckles. Did you know the Lieutenant saw his sister to-night?

Beezie. (*Half rising, nervously.*) Then he has no more need of me and these girls had better go home.

Freckles. I say he saw her. They gonneft her right out of his arms.

Beezie. They?

Freckles. Hop Lee and his crowd, the cops and Dan -- dere was a riot an' de Lieutenant gets pinched.

Beezie. What? (*About to rise. Enter* DAN *upstairs; converses with* HOP; *they exit.*)

Freckles. Oh! He squared de Sergeant -- too easy -- de way I got in here to-night was wid him an' a cop. Dey searched de whole house.

Beezie. Which amounted to nothing. The Lieutenant was here;

he'll spoil all.

Freckles. Naw! He was togged out in one of de sailor get-ups --
an' me -- (*Big.*) we took chances on meetin' Hop and Dan.

Beezie. Now listen to me, Freckles, do you want to distinguish
yourself?

Freckles. Dey calls me Dewey.

Beezie. I've been thinking how you can serve the Lieutenant, and
no one else can do it.

Freckles. Dat's me; spiel.

Beezie. If Mary Hildreth is in this house, she is in the room
above. You must get a peep into that room.

Freckles. Easy if dere's a fire escape.

Beezie. It is difficult. The court-yard below is always crowded
with Chinamen; you must find some other way.

Freckles. I'll report it to de Lieutenant. He'll find a way. He'll
want to know that Miss Frances is here anyway.

Beezie. Go now. Tell the Lieutenant I have seen neither Hop nor
Danny in this house to-night; his only chance to find his sister lies in
an alarm -- an outcry and then get here quickly. Go!

Freckles. Sure! So long. (*As he goes up he sees D A N
approaching and rapidly snatches up* COLUMBIA'S *skirt, hops in a
bunk and covers himself. Enter* DAN *and* HOP.)

Dan. (*R.C.*) You brought the girl, Frances?

Beezie. (*Smoking.*) Yes, she's in the dressing room.

Dan. (*To* HOP.) The money.

Hop. (*C.*) Me wantee look. (*Goes up and peeps through
curtains L.*)

Dan. Hurry up; there's $250 coming.

Hop. But you have not done the job.

Dan. I'll do my part of the work, but I want the money now.

Hop. And if I no give it now?

Dan. I'll throw you down on both girls. (*Business for*
FRECKLES.) I'm not going to let you do me. Come on, Tong Sing
gave you the dough, for I saw it; the $250 or I quits.

Hop. You will do your part of the work. No lettee up till I have
Miss Flances, so I can turn her over to Tong Sing?

Dan. On the oath of a Highbinder.

Hop. Allee light, you no do it, you get de hatchet. You no do
Hop and live. (*To door, handing over money.*) Remember! (*Exit.*)

Dan. Well, how do you feel?

Beezie. You ought to know.

Dan. (*Tauntingly.*) Your friend -- lover, is in the Mulberry Street Station House.

Beezie. You refer --

Dan. To your Lieutenant. I just wanted to tell you, provided you had arranged any little surprise for me.

Beezie. Thanks for your consideration.

Dan. You don't play no tricks with me.

Beezie. What are you going to do with that money?

Dan. Give it to the poor. When I give it all away you can make more for me.

Beezie. And that has been your intention from the start?

Dan. Sure, you are a cinch; can't let a good thing like you slip. I came near losing you on the Lieutenant deal, though. Don't trifle that way again, and you'll have no trouble. You do what you're told -- no more. When you slip up I'll see that you have no more trouble. Now get those girls in here.

Beezie. What am I to do?

Dan. Nothing; the orders have all been handed out and you are not in them to-night.

Beezie. Ah!

Dan. Interference from you means a bullet from me -- enough said -- (*Exit.*)

Beezie. Death stares me in the face, but notwithstanding I shall baffle those wolves. (*Rising.*) As for Danny, the Lieutenant will attend to him. The Lieutenant. Ah! which is worse, a hopeless love or my present state? Heaven help me, I boasted that I would merit his regard, command even his respect. I shall do it. I was not wrong in my calculations. Hop Lee is in this house. Mary cannot be out of it. They will convey Frances to the same place. The Lieutenant must have every entrance guarded. The first signal of alarm, he will close in on the abductors and my revenge is complete. If Dan thanks me with a bullet, he will bless me with tender memories. (*Going up to door L.*)

Freckles. Dere'll be somethin' doin' pretty soon. Dere'll be a hot time in de old town to-night.

Beezie. Come, ladies, will you never tire of curios -- costumes? (*Enter* MAMIE, BELLA, FRANCES, *and* COLUMBIA. BEEZIE *and* FRANCES *go R.*)

Mamie. (C.) Oh, never.

Bella. Such lovely things.

Frances. Had we not better go now? (BEEZIE *takes* FRANCES *aside and converses with her.* MAMIE *and* BELLA *inspect smoking outfit L.*)

Columbia. I've been touched; de very skirt off me back. (*Looking about.*) If dere ain't a fairy back dere usin' it for a quilt. I won't make a holler, Oh no. (*Goes up to bunk, taking out a long hat pin, jabs it into* FRECKLES. *He grimaces in pain and* COLUMBIA *suppresses surprise; throws skirt back.*)

Freckles. (Whispers.) Dere's a dozen comin' to you for dat.

Columbia. Oh! But I'm so sorry -- I --

Freckles. Shut up -- listen. I'll stay here as long as I can. If I'm done up, use the whistle. That's the alarm agreed upon.

Columbia. All right, but won't you forgive me, Bub?

Freckles. (Covering up.) Go wan. (COLUMBIA *goes down.*)

Frances. I'm so frightened over it all.

Beezie. You are doing this for his sister -- for his sake. You are risking a great deal, aye, life itself. It will not be long now before the end, the climax, as they say in the theatres. Be brave; Lieutenant Hildreth is watching and guarding us all.

Frances. Oh! I haven't the strength. (*Tottering.*)

Beezie. Lie down a moment and we will enliven you with a song. You will recover shortly. (BEEZIE *has* FRANCES *lie down up R.C.* BEEZIE *reclines down L. and smokes.* BELLA *and* MAMIE *recline R.*)

Columbia. I'll cheer her up. (*Specialty. At beginning of specialty,* DAN *appears as female attendant; approaches with tea service. Pours drops of drug from bottle.* FRANCES *drinks first and is overcome.* MAMIE *and* BELLA *are served.* SAM *has moved screen which obstructs* FRECKLES' *view. Before finish of song, trap door opens above and rope with hook attached is lowered by* HOP, DAN, *and Chinaman.* SAM *attaches hook to* FRANCES' *belt and the three pull her up slowly.* FRECKLES *sees body of* FRANCES *when it gets above screen.*)

Freckles. What t'ell. (*Tumbling out of couch.*) I'm onto dere game with four feet. The Lieutenant. (*Exit hastily.* BELLA *and* MAMIE *have swallowed their tea and are asleep. At finish of specialty,* COLUMBIA *sinks down beside* BEEZIE *L.*)

Columbia. Come ladies, it's your turn now. (*No reply.*) I say it's up to you. (*No reply.* COLUMBIA *goes over to them R.*) Here, wake up; why, what's the matter with them? (*Looks in direction* FRANCES *was lying; screams.*)

Beezie. (*Arising.*) What is it?

Columbia. (*Pointing.*) Frances.

Beezie. My God! My carelessness. (*Throwing down pipe.*)

Columbia. The girls. (*Rushing to* MAMIE *and* BELLA.)

Beezie. (*Seeing tea cups.*) Drugged! (*In despair.*)

Columbia. (*Rushing to bunk.*) Freckles! Freckles! (*Pulling off skirt.*) Gone!

Beezie. Freckles. Where was he?

Columbia. In dat bunk. Maybe Frances went wid him.

Beezie. No, impossible -- blow the alarm.

Columbia. In a minute. (*Before she can do so,* DAN, *who has heard the order, jumps forward and wrests whistle from her and throws her in arms of* SAM, *L.,who also enters.*)

Dan. (*C.*) There, you little spit-fire, and now what have you got to say for yourself?

Beezie. That simply after this night's work we will be even.

Dan. A woman's threat. Bah! Stop that and come home with me.

Beezie. No, I am done with you.

Dan. You are? (*Laughing.*)

Beezie. I have been your partner, now you pose as my master; I am no slave.

Dan. I can prove my authority here as well as at home. (*Springs toward her.*)

Beezie. (*Pulling pistol.*) No you won't. I'm tired of submitting to your blows.

Dan. You would shoot me?

Beezie. As I would a mad dog.

Columbia. Dat's de stuff.

Dan. So that's your game, eh? I see when I must, I'll have to do you good. Come, Sam. (*Exit both.*)

Beezie. Quick, Columbia, put on your skirt and I shall also change. We must get these girls and ourselves out of this place at once. If Freckles failed to reach the Lieutenant I'm afraid Frances as well as Mary is lost. (*Going toward door L.*)

Columbia. (*Grabbing her skirt.*) Are you going to leave me here all alone with the doped ones?

    Beezie. Come, but be quick. (BEEZIE *and* COLUMBIA *exit.*)

When FRANCES *was drawn to upper floor, they laid her on the floor beside* MARY, *who is asleep.* HOP *and* Tong Sing *are present, gloating over their prey. This is the picture that* FRECKLES *sees when he is apparently lowered from the roof outside the window by a rope, alighting on fire escape. He beckons, and* LIEUTENANT *and* JACK *jump down beside him.*

    Harry. (*Jumping into room.*) Sister! Frances! Now, you yellow devils, I have cornered you. (DAN *has entered and gets to window in time to push* FRECKLES *back against* JACK, *and both are supposed to fall down the fire escape.* LIEUTENANT *fires and kills* Tong Sing. HOP *grapples with* LIEUTENANT *and* DAN *fells* LIEUTENANT *with club. At pistol shot, enter* BEEZIE *and* COLUMBIA.)

    Beezie. Heaven protect him. (BEEZIE *and* COLUMBIA *in each others' arms. At* DAN'S *appearance,* BEEZIE *screams.*)

    Hop. Quick, Dan, da rat pit.

    Dan. Good! (*Exit.* HOP *opens trap door above and* DAN *enters and opens trap door below.*)

    Hop. (*With dummy.*) Ready?

    Dan. Yes, let him go. (HOP *throws dummy.* BEEZIE *enters in time to see it drop through lower trap.*)

    Beezie. (*Screams.*) What have you done? (*Striving to look down pit.* DAN *locks trap door.*) For God's sake, tell me who was that man?

    Dan. Lieutenant Hildreth, the man you love. (*Throwing her L.*) The rat pit for him; the bullet for you. (*Firing on* BEEZIE, *who sinks to floor moaning.* DAN *exits quickly.* COLUMBIA, *screaming, supports* BEEZIE. HOP LEE *at shot downstairs makes for window.*)

End of Scene 1.

Scene 2.

Street. Enter FRECKLES *and* JACK, *rather shaken up.*

Jack. Hold hard, pilot. It ain't quite clear in my mind what happened.

Freckles. When we tree got on the fire escape, de Lieutenant went troo de windy into de room. I tried to follow, but Dan Driscol trew me against you, and de pair of us fell in de courtyard below, plump into 'bout a swarm o' Chinamen.

Jack. (*Alarmed.*) And de Lieutenant?

Freckles. (*Disgusted.*) We're forgettin' him.

Jack. (*Excited.*) He's in that house.

Freckles. De cops at once; quick.

Jack. Heave ahead, pilot, into the house, police or no police. (FRECKLES *and* JACK *rush L., meeting* BEEZIE, *supported by* COLUMBIA.)

Jack. Are you wounded, lass?

Beezie. Never mind me -- the Lieutenant's --

Jack. Yes, quick.

Beezie. Is in the rat pit.

Freckles and Jack. Rat pit?

Beezie. I know a way to get at him.

Jack. We'll cut through China to reach him.

Beezie. Quick, quick. (BEEZIE, JACK, COLUMBIA, *and* FRECKLES *exit L. quickly. Lights up back of scrim drop showing* LIEUTENANT *fighting rats.* HUFFNAGLE L. *mending a shoe, by the light of a lamp. Enter* BEEZIE, JACK, COLUMBIA, *and* FRECKLES, *down steps into cobbler's shop, hurriedly.*)

Beezie. (*Picking up axe and striking a partition; falls back exhausted; pointing.*) Strike -- cut -- the Lieutenant -- save him!

Jack. (*Chopping.*) Pilot, take her out of this; Columbia too; quick. Lieutenant, are you alive?

Harry. Aye aye, Jack. Quick, I'm getting weak.

Jack. Aye, aye, sir. (*Partition falls.* J A C K *drags* LIEUTENANT *into cobbler's shop, the rats following.*)

Harry. Thank God.

Huffnagle. Oh! De rats. (*In fright, throws lamp through opening into rat pit and exits quickly.*)

Harry. What have you done? My sister and Frances; they will be burned alive. Follow me, Jack, to the rescue, to the rescue. (LIEUTENANT *and* JACK *exit, as lamp explodes. Dark change to first scene. Shouts and orders are heard, fire and patrol bells. Fire seen coming through trap leading to rat pit. Whole place is on fire, upstairs and down.* FRECKLES *leads firemen to lower door and they save* MAMIE, BELLA, *and* MERCIDES. LIEUTENANT *smashes glass window of upper floor and leaps into room; passes out* MARY *to* JACK *at window and carries out* FRANCES *himself.*)

Curtain.

ACT IV.
Scene 1.

Huffnagle. Nine! Nine! Jams Jeens, Nine, Rats, yes. Listen I told you all out, so I vas in in the schop ven in comes some peoples; dey take mine axe and chops down de vall und out comes a man and a million tousand rats -- ugh!

Mrs. Huffnagle. Huffnagle, ef you tell me any more fairy tales I'll have you sent to Bloomingdale.

Huffnagle. Nine! Nine! It vas de truth.

Mrs. Huffnagle. Well then, there was a man, you say; who was he?

Huffnagle. De Lieutenant vat lost his sister.

Mrs. Huffnagle. Good gracious.

Huffnagle. Dat vas not de vorst, I vas holding a lamp vile dot sailor mans --

Mrs. Huffnagle. Fogarty -- Jack -- go on!

Huffnagle. Vas chop, ven de rats dey run on mine feet und legs, und I get excited, und drops de lamp in da rat-pit -- de lamp exploded.

Mrs. Huffnagle. And you killed --

Huffnagle. Nine, yes, da house caught fire und I vill go mit Sing Sing out yes --

Mrs. Huffnagle. So, you're a house burner too, are you? I heard the ingines go by, but I had no idea my husband started the fire. Come on here, ye old fool, till we see the extent of your infamy. (*Takes* HUFFNAGLE *by arm and is dragging him L., when* BEEZIE, *conducted by* FRECKLES *and* COLUMBIA *enter L.*)

Mrs. Huffnagle. (*R.C.*) Oh! You old reprobate; this poor creature is one of your victims.

Freckles. Stop yer yap, old century plan, and see what you can do for Beezie -- she's been shot.

Mrs. Huffnagle. (*Looking at* HUFFNAGLE *R.*) Och! Worse and worse. (*To* BEEZIE.) You're looking pale and weak, darlin', come into my daughter's house and we'll take a look at ye. Let us hope for the best. (*Going toward house.*) Freckles, run for Doctor West around the corner. Huffnagle, don't you stir away from this house on yer life. (*Exit* MRS. HUFFNAGLE, BEEZIE, *and* COLUMBIA *into house R.*)

Huffnagle. Und now I vas a murderer; mine Frau say I shot dot vomans. How I done it mitout a revolver, I don't know. First I have rats, ugh! den Jan Jeems; den I burn de house; den I shoots de vomans. I don't know what it is, but I am off my trolley tracks, yes. Mine Frau sends me to Bloomingdale; da insurance people send me to Sing Sing und de police send me to dot electric chair. Huffnagle, I sees dot finish of yours. You vas a cooked goose mitout any stuffin', yes. (*Dejected, sits R. Enter* FRECKLES *with Dr., whom he ushers into house R.*)

Freckles. Do you need de Doctor, what's eatin' yer?

Huffnagle. Rats -- yes.

Freckles. Don't' get gay, old skate factory, or I'll send you to --

Huffnagle. (*Rising.*) Bloomingdale, yes. (*Mimic crazy.*)

Freckles. De old chump's head-piece is twisted, de excitement's too much for Old Germany. Come along; I'll take yer over to --

Huffnagle. (*Weak.*) Sing Sing, yes.

Freckles. You want to sit down.

Huffnagle. In de chair -- yes -- mine Frau, she say I shoots Beezie.

Freckles. Come off, yer shy all round and you want to stop dis monkeyin'. Come wid me and I'll shoot a snipe into you and den you come wid me to de fire. Dere's a lot o'women in dat house wot's to be saved.

Huffnagle. But mine Frau?

Freckles. Never mind de old woman, she's all right. Come along.

Huffnagle. I vas all upside turned up, yet, yes. (*Exit* FRECKLES *and* HUFFNAGLE *L.*)

Mrs. Huffnagle. (*From house R.*) Huffnagle! Huffnagle!

(*Pause. She enters from house.*) Huffnagle! (*Looking round.*) Gone! Wait until I lay me hands on him. Just when he's wanted, he's anywhere but where's he wanted. (*Going to door.*) Columbia!

Columbia. Yes'm.

Mrs. Huffnagle. Come here. (*Enter* COLUMBIA.)

Columbia. She's not so bad, is she, Mrs. Huffnagle? She won't die?

Mrs. Huffnagle. No, darlint. The Doctor says the bullet just skinned her arm there. Thanks be to goodness, she's suffering more from shock than anything else. Columbia, you'll have to run to the drug store and get this tonic, as my rapscallion husband has disobeyed my orders and skedaddled. (COLUMBIA *exits with prescription.*) As I live, that looks like Huffnagle. (*Looking off L.*) I'll just make a sprint, as they call it, when I lay my hands on him, I won't do a thing. (*Runs L., but bumps against* HOP, *who enters with* DAN.) Out of me way, you yellow dog. Ye child-stealin' pirate. And as fer you, Danny Driscol, the electric chair is waitin' for you. (*Exit L., hurriedly.*)

Dan. She's heard.

Hop. (*Shaking head.*) No shoot -- velly bad.

Dan. Shut up, you scoundrel. You got me into this nasty scrape.

Hop. You went in with your eyes velly wide open; I want de gal; Tong Sing wantee de gal; me payee you and Beezie; Tong Sing, he pay too. What you kick for?

Dan. Stop yer gab. We've got to get out of Chinatown, and quick, too. As soon as the fire is over, there'll be a hot hunt for you and I.

Hop. Velly well, where we go?

Dan. That's the trouble; we're hemmed in; the police cover every street out of this hole. Look there (*Pointing L.*) and there. (*Pointing R. Both cower back. Enter Doctor from house R., exit R.1.E.*) Ah! He has left the door open. Any port in a storm -- come. (HOP *and* DAN *make for door;* DAN *pushes it open, and with exclamations of surprise, both fall back at* BEEZIE, *pale, her arm bandaged, appears in doorway.* HOP *falls back upstage; drops down R. when* BEEZIE *crosses C.*)

Beezie. Oh! You miserable cowards. Have you come to finish me? (*Walking C.*) Well, proceed, I will make no outcry.

Dan. (*L.C.*) Beezie! Yes!

Beezie. Yes, Beezie, the so-called "Queen of Chinatown." She who was your tool, and slave. She whom you sought to murder and who now defies you to finish her as the last deed of your infamous life. Coward, profligate, murderer -- strike --

Dan. (*Approaching her.*) You --

Hop. (*X. to* DAN. *Grappling with him.*) You no stlike.

Dan. What?

Hop. You no stlike -- me killee you, same as a dog, savey?

Beezie. And in these two men I have a protector and a murderer. (*Goes up.*)

Dan. Take your hands off, Hop. I didn't intend to harm the girl, though she done me.

Hop. You dlid her; you rob, beat -- I know -- Chinaman no beat gal 'less she lun away. You no good, savey -- you shoot. She say the word, Danny Driscol no shoot any more.

Dan. You mean what you say, Hop?

Hop. If Beezie say word, you no shoot any more.

Dan. I tell you I mean the girl no harm. Beezie, we're in a bad box; the cops are everywhere and if you don't help us out, we'll be caught like rats in a trap.

Beezie. Oh! (*Shuddering at the word "rats."*) What do you want of me?

Dan. For God's sake, help us out of this. Hide us somewhere; anywhere, until we can get out of Chinatown. You loved me once, Beezie; it can't be that you want me butchered?

Beezie. And these men are perhaps responsible for a score of lives.

Dan. No, Beezie, they are all saved; not a woman was lost in the fire.

Beezie. You swear to this.

Dan. Yes, we saw them carried out alive, didn't we, Hop?

Hop. Yes.

Dan. (*X.*) Do you want more crime? I swear I'll kill you before I'm captured. For the love you once bore me, Beezie, help me out.

Beezie. (*Aside.*) He would kill the Lieutenant. (*Aloud.*) I will, and if I am wrong, may I be forgiven. The rear of this house leads to the rear of Collin's Concert Hall; if you can lay low there a couple of days, you can easily escape. (HOP *and* DAN *enter house.*)

Dan. (*At door.*) And you will go with me?

Beezie. No, that chance has gone from you forever.

Dan. We'll see. (*Noise off L.*)

Hop. (*Pulling* DAN *in.*) You clome.

Beezie. Yes, quick. (*Sinking into chair or on doorstep. Enter* COLUMBIA *R.1.E.*)

Columbia. What on earth are you doing out here? I had to wait on the drug clerk; de dude had to watch de fire. Where is Mrs. Huffnagle? (BEEZIE *shakes her head wearily.*) At the fire too? Well, never mind, I'll fix this dose up for you myself. (*About to enter house.*)

Beezie. (*Stopping her, taking bottle.*) You need not mind. (*Looking at bottle.*) A teaspoonful -- (*Drinks. Enter* LIEUTENANT *and* FRECKLES, *hurriedly L.*)

Harry. Here she is, and not badly hurt, I trust.

Beezie. No, merely a scratch, the doctor says.

Harry. Thank Heaven.

Beezie. And your sister and Miss Frances?

Harry. Both well and safe. (*X.*) Likewise the other ladies; they are resting comfortably, and will be perfectly happy when they learn that you have escaped severe injury.

Beezie. I thank them and you.

Harry. Are you able to come?

Beezie. Is it far?

Harry. No, only to Collin's Concert Hall, on the other street.

Beezie. (*In alarm. Looking at door of house.*) Collin's Concert Hall?

Harry. Yes, the large dancing room has been given up to the ladies. They are so well that the noise and hilarity in the concert room has not even a bad effect on their nerves.

Beezie. (*Aside.*) In trying to save these men from death I have sent them to it. (*Aloud.*) Who is with the ladies at that place?

Harry. The Reverend Frank Parker and my gunner's mate, Jack.

Beezie. The sailor. And if he should meet Hop Lee and Danny Driscol, what would happen?

Harry. Simply murder. He too has sworn to kill them both.

Beezie. Quick, to the Concert Hall -- I mean, to the ladies!

Harry. There is something you are concealing -- something on your mind.

Beezie. There is.

Harry. Hop Lee and Danny Driscol?

Beezie. Yes! For my work in rescuing your sister and your love, I demand that they shall be permitted to go free!

Harry. Free from me, yes; but the law?

Beezie. We'll risk the law. Come, to the Concert Hall.

Scene 2.

Restaurant and Concert Hall.

At rise, men and girls are seated at tables drinking. MADGE *is playing "There'll be a Hot Time in the Old Town To-night." Waiters serve drinks.*

Huffnagle. (*Half drunk.*) Say, Madge, sing something 'bout home and mudder, yes.

All. Dat's de stuff. Let her go, Madge.

Madge. Say, what do you stiffs want for the price of a drink?

All. Go on Madge, don't be offish.

Madge. I've been thumping and yelping all night.

Huffnagle. Und not one yelp 'bout home and mudder.

Madge. I'm onto you, Huffnagle. You've had a run in with your Irish Princess. (*All laugh.*)

Huffnagle. Not yet, but I have what you call von run in comin', yes.

Madge. You'll get it, too. Now I'll go you on that song, if you'll also oblige.

Huffnagle. In a second, yes.

All. Good! Go ahead, old girl. (MADGE *sings "What is Home Without a Mother?" Song applauded loudly.*)

Madge. Now, old cobbler shop, it's your spiel.

All. Huffnagle! Huffnagle! (*Specialty by* HUFFNAGLE. *At finish, enter* MRS. HUFFNAGLE *with fire in her eye, followed by* FRECKLES *and* COLUMBIA.)

Mrs. Huffnagle. So you're here with the elite of Chinytown, while your poor wife is -- Ah! running the streets after you. Didn't I order you not on pain of yer life to leave the spot you were on?

Huffnagle. Freckles, say somethings. I vas too full of happiness to give out, yes.

Mrs. Huffnagle. Too full of lager, ye mean, you old Highbinder.

Freckles. Cheese; cheese; I made de old guy go wid me to save de women out of de burnin' building. (*Enter* JACK.)

Mrs. Huffnagle. And did Huffnagle save anybody?

Jack. Sure he did, me lass. I saw him carry out two girls with my own eyes.

Mrs. Huffnagle. Huffnagle, you're a hero!

Huffnagle. (*Stiff.*) You apprecianionation me not, yes.

Jack. And sure ye don't, Mrs. Huffnagle. Come, cheer the husband, me and the party wid one of yer own swate melodies.

All. Sure, go ahead, Mrs. Huffnagle.

Mrs. Huffnagle. I'll be plazed to honor the distinguished company here prisint. (*Curtsies and does specialty. At finish:*) Come on, ye old hero. You've got too much work on hand to be a sport. Good night, all.

All. Good night, good night. (*Exit* HUFFNAGLE *and* MRS. HUFFNAGLE. *All laugh. Specialty by* FRECKLES *and* COLUMBIA. *All are loudly applauded by company present.*)

Madge. (*Rising from piano.*) Good night. (*Exit.*)

Jack. Well, pilot, how are the lovers? (*Nodding to room L.*)

Freckles. Ask Columbia, she's ben there.

Columbia. Turtle doves, dat's it. Dere's de Lieutenant and Frances, but they ain't a marker to Miss Mary and the sky pilot, Reverend Parker. (*Enter* DANCER *from room R., screaming. Enter* LIEUTENANT *and* FRANCES, REVEREND PARKER *and* MARY, BEEZIE.)

Jack. What is it, Miss?

Dancer. There is somebody in my dressing room.

Jack. Then my lass, we'll see who it is. (*Rushing into room R.*) Throw up your hands, you devils!

Harry. Drive the fellows out, Jack.

Jack. Aye, aye, sir. (*Enter* HOP *and* DAN, *followed by* JACK.)

Harry. So, we have you at last.

Dan. Yes, but I'll have her before I go. (*Fires at* BEEZIE, *who falls.*)

Harry. A doctor, quick. What have you done? (MARY *and* FRANCES *catch* BEEZIE, *place her in chair C.*)

Dan. Finished her for sending me to a trap and then leading you to capture me.

Harry. You madman, Beezie made me promise to permit you to escape my vengeance and I gave my word.

Hop. (*Tries to stab* DAN. *They prevent him.*) Velly bad, no shoot.

Dan. Take that yellow demon away. (*X. to* BEEZIE.) Is this true, Beezie?

Beezie. (*In chair, dying.*) Yes, Danny, I could not exercise any influence over the police, but these good people listened to me. They, headed by the Lieutenant, agreed, thankful for the recovery of their loved ones, to condone your offence and mine.

Dan. (*Broken.*) And you did this for me?

Beezie. Yes -- I -- I -- loved you, once.

Dan. I thought you had given me the double cross. We couldn't get through here and we couldn't return to the street on account of the cops. I'm all broken up, Beezie girl. Forgive me if you can.

Beezie. I will, with all my heart. I will not survive this shot, but I have no malice. There is a brighter life and I have embraced it, though late; Danny, it is never too late; if you get out of this trouble, leave Chinatown forever. Be a better --

Dan. Live, Beezie, and save my life!

Beezie. (*Delirious.*) Oh! I am so full of pain; what is it? Why are so many people here? Ah! ha! ha! Oh dear! I am so happy! Where is the old home lawn, the orchard, papa, mamma? Coming, coming, papa, my new pony. Oh papa, you are so good to me. How I cantered through the lanes and the meadows. Ah! then I met him. Oh! Everybody said afterwards, what a pity. He petted, he fascinated me. I eloped and broke, ah, so many true hearts. He did not place a wedding ring upon my finger, and in desperation I left him and was alone in this great city. I worked, slaved, ah, how hard I slaved. I would have gone home, but I have no home. I fell ill and Danny found me and was good to me. I was near death's door and then Danny saved my life. Opium came into my world to deaden the agony of the past. Crime ensued to live. Oh, the reckoning. I became tired of it all and Danny promised to leave Chinatown with me. He broke his word, beat me, tortured me. I turned against him. (*To* LIEUTENANT.) Then you came, and with you a ray of hope. It too, died. Lost, hopeless, abandoned by all except him. (*Looking upwards and laying hand on* REVEREND PARKER.) I tried to repent. A life misspent; a life lost. You

(*Looking about at the* LIEUTENANT, REVEREND PARKER, *and the girls.*) are reunited, happy. My efforts were not in vain. Oh, I am going. Danny, you go before I pass away. (DAN *looks at the* LIEUTENANT.)

    Harry. Go! I gave her my word. Go, both of you.

    Dan. Good-bye.

    Beezie. (*Whispers.*) Good-bye. (DAN *and* HOP *move slowly to door and exit. Doctor enters at same time and approaches* BEEZIE, *who is seated in arm chair C. A cry is heard off at back, followed by two pistol shots.* JACK *and* FRECKLES *exit.*)

    Beezie. (*Rising, excited.*) What was that? (*Enter* JACK.)

    Jack. Danny was stabbed by the Chinaman.

    Beezie. My protector.

    Jack. And the Chinaman was shot by Dan.

    Beezie. My murderer. God forgive them and me. (*She dies.* FRANCES *in* LIEUTENANT'S *arms.* BEEZIE *in chair C.* COLUMBIA *in* FRECKLES' *arms. Doctor indicates that* BEEZIE *is dead.* JACK, *hat in hand, at back. Two Dancers and* MADGE *at back.*)

Curtain.

1912 -- George C. Hazelton and Harry J. Benrimo -- *The Yellow Jacket*

As the issue of Chinese immigration declined in importance after the turn of the century, playwrights began to focus on the Chinese in China. Despite years of commercial and diplomatic contact, the land itself was still remote from most Euroamericans, who thought of it as an exotic fairyland. Thus, even despite the decline and overthrow of the Qing Dynasty, significant challenges to Confucianism, and great strides in Chinese industry and technology, the image of China in Euroamerican drama remained static.

The Yellow Jacket is an interesting and important text for many reasons. One of the co-authors, Benrimo, had first acted the role of Hop Kee in *The First Born*, thus creating a significant connection between the earlier work and this play. Like Powers, the writers of this play had enough basic familiarity with the Chinese langauge to give their characters plausible names; the translations given in the cast list are substantially accurate, although today they would be romanized differently. In addition, *The Yellow Jacket* is also noteworthy for its use of Chinese stage conventions, such as the Property Man and the extensive use of symbolic mime, which caused the play to differ greatly from the pedestrian realism prevalent at the time. These conventions, coupled with the frankly presentational style, make it almost a precursor of Brecht in its use of "alienation effects," although it lacks any political content. Finally, *The Yellow Jacket* is not the first play dealing with the Chinese to link the issues of race and gender, but it does so most forcefully and explicitly. The (male) character of Daffodil underscores the Euroamerican perception of the East as passive and effeminate; the piece also has a heavily misogynistic subtext which presents women as victims and/or martyrs throughout. This is almost certainly the authors' comment on the incipient feminism which was then unsettling traditional gender roles in the West. *The Yellow Jacket* was first presented in New York in the fall of 1912, and enjoyed a successful run. It was later revived often during the 1920s.

The published version of the script includes a forward by the pioneering and eminent theatre scholar Brander Matthews, the relevant excerpts from which appear here. The original forward of the co-authors appears as well.

The Yellow Jacket

It is with pleasure that I accept the invitation of the authors of *The Yellow Jacket* to say a few words by way of prologue to their play. In more than forty years of play-going, I have seen few performances as interesting as that to which they invited me. And the interest of this performance is twofold. It is due, first of all, to the charm of the Oriental tale they have transplanted to our Occidental stage and to the delicate art with which they have brought before us the manners and customs of a race strangely unlike ourselves. Secondly, the play is presented, not in accord with the methods familiar nowadays in our own theatres, but in accord with the methods characteristic of the Chinese theater and therefore unfamiliar to us . . . The Chinese story is set in action in the Chinese fashion, a fashion very unlike that which now obtains on the English-speaking stage -- although not altogether unlike that which prevailed in the playhouses of our island ancestors in the spacious days of Elizabeth . . . The Chinese theater, in its turn, has its own conventions and traditions, acceptable to the Oriental because he is so accustomed to them that they seem to him "natural." But some of these departures from fact appear very strange, not because they are violations of nature, but because they are wholly unlike the departures from fact which we accept because we are accustomed to them. Very wisely have the authors of *The Yellow Jacket* set their story on the stage according to the conventions and traditions of the theater where its several episodes were originally exhibited. They give us a Chinese drama, dealing with Chinese motives, and presented in the Chinese manner. With a firm reliance on our appreciation of the exotic, they invite us to smile at conventions which seem to us ludicrous in the extreme -- and then, a moment later, they summon us to use our imagination to curb our laughter, and to let ourselves be taken captive by the sad plight of the human beings who people their play. Their drama derives its double charm from the tact and the taste with which they have wooed us to enjoy an exotic theme frankly put before us in an exotic fashion.

-- Brander Matthews

CHARACTERS

PROPERTY MAN

CHORUS

WU SIN YIN (GREAT SOUND LANGUAGE),
Governor of the Province

DUE JUNG FAH (FUSCHIA FLOWER), *second
wife of* WU SIN YIN

TSO (FANCY BEAUTY), *maid to* DUE JUNG
FAH

CHEE MOO (KIND MOTHER), *first wife of* WU
SIN YIN

TAI FAH MIN (GREAT PAINTED FACE), *father
of* DUE JUNG FAH

ASSISTANT PROPERTY MEN

SUEY SIN FAH (LILY FLOWER), *wife of* LEE
SIN *and maid of the first wife,* CHEE MOO

LEE SIN (FIRST FARMER)

LING WONG (SPIRIT)

WU FAH DIN (DAFFODIL)

YIN SUEY GONG (PURVEYOR OF HEARTS)

WU HOO GIT (YOUNG HERO OF THE WU
FAMILY), *destined for the Yellow Jacket*

SEE QUOE FAH (FOUR-SEASON FLOWER)

MOW DAN FAH (PEONY)

YONG SOO KOW (HYDRANGEA)

CHOW WAN (AUTUMN CLOUD)

MOY FAH LOY (PLUM BLOSSOM), *daughter of*
TAI CHAR SHOONG

TAI CHAR SHOONG (PURVEYOR OF TEA TO
THE EMPEROR)

THE WIDOW CHING

MAID

GIT HOK GAR (PHILOSOPHER AND SCHOLAR)

KOM LOI (SPIDER)

LOY GONG (GOD OF THUNDER)

FORWARD

The purpose of the creators of this play is to string on a thread of universal philosophy, love and laughter the jade beads of Chinese theatrical convention. Their effort has been to reflect the spirit rather than the substance. To do this, the property man had to be overwrought; the Chorus had to be introduced. Signs usually indicate the scenes on the Oriental stage; the Chorus voices them for us.

While the story of *The Yellow Jacket* is not taken from any direct source, it is hoped that it may convey an imaginative suggestion of all sources and reflect the childhood of drama.

It might be said in a Chinese way that scenery is as big as your imagination.

Primitive people the world over begin to build their drama like the make-believe of children, and the closer they remain to the make-believe of children the more significant and convincing is the growth of their drama.

The Authors.

ACT I.

At the rise of the theater curtain, blue silk draperies are disclosed, embroidered with gold dragons, forming a tableau curtain. These draperies are arranged to part in the center. When drawn, they hang in graceful folds on each side of the stage. The PROPERTY MAN *enters indifferently from the opening at center of curtain, strikes thrice on a gong and exits. The* CHORUS *then enters, bows right, left and center. His costume is that of rich Chinese scholar, the dominant note being red. His manner is most dignified. His actions are ceremonious.*

Chorus. Most honorable neighbors, the bows, which I so humbly and solemnly divest myself of, are given in reverence to the three powers -- Heaven -- Earth -- Man. I have been appointed by my humble brothers of the Pear Tree Garden to conduct you through a story of our celestial land to be played upon our most unworthy stage. Permit me to thank that vice of curiosity which beckoned you hither that we might paint before your august eyes our humble fancy. I bow. (*Bows three times.*)

Let me intrude a slight history of our most unworthy theater and the reason that we refer to our players as brother of the Pear Tree Garden. A most curious tale -- our beginning! It had its birth in the dynasty of the most wholesome one, the great Ming Wang. In reverence for so glorious a beginning we have kept our stage ever the same. For this antiquity, august and honorable, we ask indulgence. The good and honored Ming Wang, son of Heaven and of glorious memory, was visited by an enchanted dream -- full of strange beauty. In sleep he rambled over the moon. When the morning lifted his eyelids, he wished his wife to behold the dream-painted beauties which had joyed his sleep. The Court, at his command, clothed in the glory of his dream, played the story of his moon-colored fancy beneath the pear trees of his summer palace-yard for her he loved. While I fill up time with many words, my brothers are burning costly incense before the God of the Theater who, they hope, will bountifully answer their prayer and make them worthy to win your approval. Much of our acting will be strange. Our play deals with mother's love, the love of youth, and the hate of men, which makes them do unhappy things. Spirits of those who once walked flowery or pestilent paths in this world will reach out their hands to sufferers in our history. We hope out of our imperfect efforts there may come to you some pleasure. I fear I have intruded too long upon your welcome and that you are in haste for my brothers to begin. They, too, are impatient, for the perfume of their sacrifice even now floats upon the august air.

Men will speak fair words with blackened minds.. That you may not be carried away by their wiles, we have enmasked them with paint, red, white, and black, that you may know them; but they will never know that you know that their souls are mirrored in their faces, for men look many times to see themselves, as they are pleased to see themselves. It is mostly so with villains. As prompter for my brothers, I will be ever before you to help you to an understanding of our doings. For so much kind patience as you have shown, I give you thanks and shall tell my brothers. (*Bows three times.*)

Observe well with your eyes and listen well with your ears. Be as one family, exceedingly happy and content. Heaven has no mouth. It makes men speak for it. (*Bells.*) The gusts of Heaven breathe on the bells and they tinkle with joy on the eaves of the pagoda.

Ere departing my footsteps hence, let me impress upon you that my property man is to your eyes intensely invisible. (PROPERTY MAN *now comes before curtain again. Strikes gong and exits.*)

I bow.

(*Claps his hands three times; curtains part, revealing a set in dull orange with green and gold trimmings. There are two doors, one stage left for entrance and one stage right for exit. In the center at the back is an oval opening surrounded by a grill, within which the musicians sit. Above this opening is another, square in form, which represents Heaven. About the walls of the scene are Chinese banners and signs of good cheer. Huge lanterns hang from above. At the left is a large property box, and above it are chairs, tables, cushions, etc., in fact all properties used in the play.* CHORUS *takes his seat up center. Music.*)

'Tis the palace of Wu Sin Yin, the Great, a most unhappy man, for he possesses two wives. He comes, Wu Sin Yin, the Great.

(*The gong sounds and the cymbals crash; the curtain on door left is pulled aside. Enter* WU SIN YIN. *He comes down stage, then walks to right, then to center, turns twice round, and seats himself. The* PROPERTY MAN *assists him to arrange his costume, then smokes complacently.* WU SIN YIN *gazes solemnly before him; his*

whole action on entrance is consciously done to display his costume;
when seated, he spreads his legs and turns out his toes, displays his
fingernails on his left hand, two of which are very long, one being
gilded and the other colored green; he fans himself; during this
business, the orchestra plays, the cymbals crash, the drum rolls, and
the wooden block is struck. The cymbals are struck also, when he
mentions the name of the Emperor.)

Wu Sin Yin. I am the most important personage in this play.
Therefore, I address you first. By your gracious leave, with many
apologies, I will state in all modesty, for your edification only, for of
course I know who I am and how great and august I am, while you are
not so favored, that I am Wu Sin Yin, the Great. I have the third eye of
wisdom here. I shape the destiny with my finger-tips of the people on
the Yangtsekiang. (*Sits in great state fanned by attendant.*)

I would bow to you, but it is beneath my dignity. My wives
kowtow to me in abject slavery, which is as it should be with wives.
This is my sun-kissed palace on the purple hill. Here by seal and by
the red pencil on a yellow silken banner, I hold my court and issue my
edicts. Here the abject subjects of my province crawl to bring me the
harvest of their labors, for it is decreed by the Son of Heaven, our
Celestial Emperor, of the Eighth Dynasty (*Rises and bows three
times.*) that they bring me the fruits of their slavish menial toil. With
all this felicity of personal importance, I am still augustly unhappy, for
I possess two wives -- a first wife and a second wife. Chee Moo, the
first wife, has a child crab-like and spider-formed. It was her mistake,
not mine. I have a right divine to like or dislike my wives at pleasure.
Happiness is necessary to a great governor in order that his menials
may be happy by reflection, as I am in the presence of my second wife,
Due Jung Fah, who shines in the light of my favor. I must, in august
sympathy for my situation, delicately dispose of the first wife and
crooked child -- very delicately -- for Chee Moo's family is powerful;
and if I beheaded her uncouthly, they might be annoyed. I must
contrive a secret and respectful and courteous departure for her honorable
soul. Then I may pass my hours in celestial bliss with Due Jung Fah,
my beautiful second one. How shall I accomplish it? I am admonished
of the approach of my honored father-in-law, Tai Fah Min, who is
wisely virtuous and will advise me. (*On exit, curtain at right door is
lifted and the orchestra plays until curtain falls. The* PROPERTY

MAN *removes the chair and places it left among other properties.*)

Chorus. 'Tis the garden of Due Jung Fah, the second wife of Wu Sin Yin, the Great. (*Enter* DUE JUNG FAH, *followed by her maid,* TSO, *door left. Both hold their fans before their faces and walk with mincing steps to center, during music.* DUE JUNG FAH *keeps always a little in advance of* TSO.)

Due Jung Fah. Gentle listeners, here in my garden, with ceremonial bow, I tell you, I am Due Jung Fah, most unhappy of ladies. I am the second wife of Wu Sin Yin, the Great. There would be music in my heart if it were not for the first wife. The butterflies and bees and the humming-birds do not come to my garden. They fly to make hers beautiful. (*To* TSO.) Interrupt me not. The gold-fish die in my lily ponds and swim sun-kissed in Chee Moo's across the wall. Where she walks with her monkey-faced child, the hyacinths bloom, the purple wisteria and the white jasmine fill the air with fragrance for her painted nostrils. I breathe and breathe, and the air is heavy with death of flowers. Oh, oh, even the lanterns in her evening walk brighten her path, while mine fade and I stumble. (*Stops* TSO, *who would speak.*) Tell me not. I marvel that any one should do her homage. My mind is crowded with thoughts of her cripple monster-child, for my soul has not given forth a child-seed. The air is filled with the approach of some one. Let us depart. (*As* DUE JUNG FAH *exits door right, music.*)

Tso. No one comes. The opportunity was not permitted me to tell you truly that I am Tso, the maid of Due Jung Fah. When I met you, my mistress wanted to unburden her august soul to you. Though I was filled with sky words, I am too adroit to talk when she wishes to. I am the dust in the sunbeam. I am one of the darkest shadows of our play. It is the modest little maid whose manner is filled with sunlight that throws the prettiest little shadows of the dark. Innocence makes the best play-shadow. The night shadow has no danger, for you see it as you pass. Sweet little flitting shadows like mine trip you in your path. I threw a tiny rainbow shadow across Due Jung Fah's eyes which looked like the first wife in her richest jewels and prettiest gown; and then a big thunder-cloud shadow across the eyes of Wu Sin Yin, and the cloud took on the image of his twisted child. If Chee Moo is gently disposed of, Due Jung Fah becomes the first wife and I become the first maid. The first maid, Suey Sin Far, faints at the incense of some flowers. Lee Sin, her husband, deserves a wife more brave. Why not a gentle little shadow? (*Exits. Music.*)

Chorus. 'Tis a road leading to the palace of Wu Sin Yin, the Great. He comes, Tai Fah Min! mounted on his milk-white steed!

Loud crash of cymbals: curtain on door left is lifted and TAI FAH MIN *enters followed by two men; he carries a whip and does pantomime of riding and driving a horse; one of the men who follow him carries a banner inscribed with Chinese characters; this banner is red; the other carries a large fan on a stick; he comes down to left, then crosses right, then to center; goes through business of dismounting his horse, throwing his leg high in the air; the* PROPERTY MAN *assists him and helps his man hold his supposed horse; he lays his whip on the ground behind him; during all this, music.*

The supernumeraries retire up stage with supposed horse. TAI FAH MIN *pivots on one foot, takes out his fan, which is carried at the back of his neck, and bows to audience. Gongs.*

Tai Fah Min. My horse! Remove him! He must not hear the secret thoughts of his master. Tai Fah Min is my name. I come from the Southland, where the sun kisses the hilltops. I rule a province there as rich as the one of him I come to visit. I bow to you, (*Bows three times.*) risking my dignity in doing so. A father's love hastens me hither, for I am the parent of the most wretched of ladies, the second wife of the celestial governor of this province, Wu Sin Yin, the Great. Chee Moo, the first wife, and her monster-born child stand between my beautiful daughter, Due Jung Fah, and her husband. No one will envy her dead. Whatever pathway a father finds to give happiness to a daughter is not offensive to the gods. This province is too crowded with august wives, and the honorable Chee Moo, the first wife, and her dragon-eyed child, should be generous to others who need the celestial air they breathe. Due Jung Fah, my daughter, will then be all and I will be all. This is the road to the palace. (*To attendants.*) Bring back my sublime horse! Attend me on foot.

PROPERTY MAN *brings forward the supposed horse and he goes through the pantomime of mounting; they assist him.* PROPERTY MAN *picks up whip and hands it to him; he beats the supposed horse. Exit* TAI FAH MIN *and attendants; door right.*

The PROPERTY MAN *now places a table center, which he*

carries from left, places a red cover on it; then two chairs on either side, which he also covers with a red cloth, and puts a small stool on each.

Chorus. 'Tis a room in the palace of Wu Sin Yin, the Great.

Enter door left, WU SIN YIN. *Attended by a man with a fan, he seats himself in chair right of table; his dress is arranged as before by* PROPERTY MAN, *etc.; during this, music. Enter attendant with* TAI FAH MIN'S *card and kneels. After* WU SIN YIN *is seated, enter* TAI FAH MIN, *attended by a man with a fan;* WU SIN YIN *rises, pivots on right foot once, then clasps his hands, opens his fan, which he takes from back of neck, and seats himself.* TAI FAH MIN *does the same business and seats himself left of table.*

Wu Sin Yin. Tai Fah Min, my exalted second father-in-law, I receive you into my palace and presence with exuberance of fancy. My beloved second father-in-law may assume that Wu Sin Yin, the Great, has bowed to him with filial obeisance.

Tai Fah Min. And my celestial son-in-law may felicitate himself with the glorious fancy that his second father-in-law also has bowed. The palace of the great Wu Sin Yin breathes incense of happiness. The gods smiled and it rose like a flower from the earth for the habitation of our master. The teak-wood was carved by moon-rays dancing on its surface, the rugs were woven by humming-bird beaks as they played hide-and-seek with their love-mates among the silken threads on the loom. The gods --

Wu Sin Yin. Ah, Tai Fah Min, my Tai Fah Min, you exaggerate the magnificence of my palace by compliments of great length. It is most humble. The beauties of my mind are enmeshed by the threads of evil woven there by the spider's art, else why should I, Wu Sin Yin, the Great, be the most unhappy of men? (PROPERTY MAN *here comes forward with tray on which are two cups; he places them on the table.*)

Tai Fah Min. The most radiantly happy!

Wu Sin Yin. Ah, if your daughter were only my first wife -- *not* my second, my Tai Fah Min.

Tai Fah Min. My daughter dare not look so high. She has not yet reached that great state -- motherhood.

Wu Sin Yin. I must have advice that brings unclouded to my arms and lips, the rosy lotus lips and arms of Due Jung Fah. Advise me my way, Tai Fah Min.

Tai Fah Min. My brain speaks, but my heart stands still.

Wu Sin Yin. Who could guide me better than my second father-in-law, who has such interest in my affairs?

Tai Fah Min. (*Anxiously.*) I speak. The first wife, Chee Moo, stands in the hate of your subjects, because the child she bore was cramped, crab-like, monstrous and unwise in its likeness of evil. The devils damned it at its birth with -- the monstrosities of the --

Wu Sin Yin. (*Interrupting.*) Mother's soul. Forget not that.

Tai Fah Min. That will save us with your subjects. If it had inherited the noble godlike spirit of the father, Wu Sin Yin, the common hordes would have demanded it for the next ruler. They dare to loathe the fruits of your body. Your scholars would advise as I do, Wu Sin Yin.

Wu Sin Yin. And that is --

Tai Fah Min. Hush! Let us pass into another room where none may listen. (*They walk three times about the stage and stop each in the other's place.* PROPERTY MAN *changes chairs. Music.*) We are safer here in this isolated spot. This palatial room is more fragrant than that we have passed from.

Wu Sin Yin. Use up no more air in compliment.

Tai Fah Min. We must whisper. No matter how safe you hide the egg the chicken will hatch. A sweet passing heavenward for the first mother and the child.

Wu Sin Yin. (*Gleefully.*) And Due Jung Fah will come to me with no shadows between us. But my conscience constrains me.

Tai Fah Min. (*Soothingly.*) Think on the gorgeous munificence of her funeral! To die the wife of Wu Sin Yin, the Great, is like breathing zephyrs of the south as against living in a typhoon. Think how proud her family should be of the ceremonies as we lay the first wife with her ancestors! Her death will be most glorious.

Wu Sin Yin. Can we make her family believe it?

Tai Fah Min. It would be deplorably bad taste if her family did not appreciate the magnificence of the funeral that your dignity will afford her.

Wu Sin Yin. A blind cat catches only a dead rat. Have I among my servants one in dignity becoming to the deed, for we could not leave it to the public executioner?

Tai Fah Min. Lee Sin, the farmer -- worthy, god-favored and properly menial.

Wu Sin Yin. (*Thoughtfully.*) The farmer is strong.

Tai Fah Min. He will gently plough a furrow with his sword in Chee Moo's neck, and the gods will smile upon such husbandry.

Wu Sin Yin. Send for him! (*Enter* TSO *door left, with short strain of music.*)

Tso. Most august and greatest of men, representative of the Son of Heaven; I kneel, bow and ask that my mistress, Due Jung Fah, your devoted second wife, may speak with her august lord and husband.

Wu Sin Yin. (*Condescendingly.*) My wife may speak to her husband-master. (*Exit* TSO, *after bowing to both men.*)

Tai Fah Min. See how humbly my daughter approaches you. (*Enter* DUE JUNG FAH, *followed by* TSO; *kneels and bows to* WU SIN YIN; *music.*)

Due Jung Fah. Most wonderful and only husband in the world, of whom even as the second wife, I, Due Jung Fah, am most unworthy. (*Bows.*)

Wu Sin Yin. Luscious one, I greet you. Rise and greet your worthy and far-seeing father, Tai Fah Min!

Due Jung Fah. I could not bow to my ancestors' tablets, much less to my noble father, before I had bowed my head in the dust three times to my gracious husband. (DUE JUNG FAH *here kneels and bows to* TAI FAH MIN. *All rise and bow.*)

Tai Fah Min. My daughter has the modesty that Confucius praises. Her voice is low and gentle. Gracious and celestial one, pardon the emotions of the greetings of a father in your presence.

Wu Sin Yin. How would you fancy, my Due Jung Fah, as first wife, to languish unclouded in the lavish smiles of Wu Sin Yin, the Great?

Due Jung Fah. But Chee Moo, my sister, the glorious first wife, lives. (*Pretending to be startled, looking from one to the other.*) Not dead! I should faint of grief.

Tai Fah Min. (*Aside to her.*) Remember it is your duty to fill your husband's eyes with happiness and obedience, that wifehood in you may be glorious to the end that such a child as Chee Moo bore shall not live to rule in the Flowery Kingdom. Wu Sin Yin and your father ask it.

Due Jung Fah. I love the province of the august Wu Sin Yin.

Who does the deed?

Tai Fah Min. Lee Sin, the farmer.

Due Jung Fah. I am resigned, if it can not be done more gently with the dream-giving opiates.

Wu Sin Yin. I had the flowers about her filled with the softest poison perfume that she might breathe their august exhalations and pass gently to the honorable and desirable land of dreams. I went as the morning broke to weep over her departed soul, but is was she who was in tears over the honorable departure of the bees and butterflies and humming-birds who for love of their mistress had sucked the poison honey of the flowers and laid themselves to rest for her they loved. Their selfishness in robbing their mistress of her eternal sleep was inexcusable.

Due Jung Fah. I will retire and pray seven days at the tablets of my ancestors for the soul of Chee Moo and her child.

Wu Sin Yin. Your prayers shall cover but the space of one day.

Due Jung Fah. Wu Sin Yin, the Great! I dwell in the unhappiness of my sister-wife. Fan me! (*Exit* DUE JUNG FAH *door right, after bowing three times, followed by* TSO. *Music.*)

Wu Sin Yin. Send for the executioner! I shake hands with myself, Tai Fah Min, and leave you. (WU SIN YIN *clasps his hands, bows, opens his fan and exits door right, followed by* TAI FAH MIN; *cymbal and gong.* PROPERTY MAN *now removes chairs and table.*)

Chorus. 'Tis the garden of Chee Moo, the unhappy first wife of Wu Sin Yin, the Great.

Enter CHEE MOO *door left, with child, which is represented by a stick with pieces of cloth wrapped around it and hanging down. Comes down and crosses right. During following speech soft wails from orchestra.*

Chee Moo. Oh, woe is me! Murder is in the air. The evil spirits build walls about me whichever way I go. Now you know that I am Chee Moo and this the child, Wu Hoo Git. The devils put toads in our path to croak and awake him that he might cry out and reveal us; bats in the air follow us by night and hang their great withered wings from the rafters of Heaven, like a dead forest, to impede us by day. My boy, my pretty boy! whom evil plotters call cripple and monster-formed but who, as you see, is celestially beautiful. Let your baby dreams be a silent prayer to your ancestors for help. I will cry out to them from a mother's heart for your protection. We will fly to the mountains, the place of the issuing clouds, where your mother will weave fabrics of silk to cradle you in and care for you until your baby arm can wield a sword to confound your enemies. The lantern of my love hangs in the temple of my mind, and I pray you, my ancestors, let no unkind wind spirit or water sprite quench the flame of my child-love. (*Exits door right.*)

Chorus. 'Tis a courtyard in the palace of Wu Sin Yin, the Great. (*Music. Enter* LEE SIN. *Comes down left, crosses right and bows.*)

Lee Sin. I am Lee Sin, the child of the rice fields. The chopsticks of the poor and the chopsticks of the rich await my harvest. I feed them as the golden pheasant feeds its young. Where I labor the god of the soil smiles on my ox and me, for we are sacred. (*Bows; prostrates himself before* TAI FAH MIN, *who enters door left; loud crash on cymbals and gong.*)

Tai Fah Min. Rise, Lee Sin, I would speak.

Lee Sin. Father of the second wife, I bring you greetings.

Tai Fah Min. Son of the soil, I realize the dignity of your greetings.

Lee Sin. Wu Sin Yin bade me come. I left my ox to feed and dusted my feet and came.

Tai Fah Min. You labor too hard. I would help you.

Lee Sin. If you took me from my labor you would rob me of the joy of living -- which is my all.

Tai Fah Min. Would you add to the gold in your purse, Lee Sin?

Lee Sin. An avaricious man is like a snake trying to swallow an elephant. I have enough -- and that is all I need.

Tai Fah Min. You have a wife who may think more wisely, Lee Sin.

Lee Sin. Suey Sin Fah is my wife, and maid to the beautiful Chee Moo, first wife of Wu Sin Yin, the Great. She, too, is happy and content, for she is good.

Tai Fah Min. What do you love best in all the world, Lee Sin?

Lee Sin. My parents and my wife, the little Suey Sin Fah.

Tai Fah Min. And have you no love for your master, Wu Sin Yin, the Great?

Lee Sin. I bow in the dust three times to him. He stands in the place for me of the Emperor, the Son of Heaven. (*Gongs, both bowing.*)

Tai Fah Min. You would not refuse then to do his bidding?

Lee Sin. To refuse would mean my death, and that I would give him for the asking.

Tai Fah Min. And if he asks you to kill for him?

Lee Sin. He would not ask it.

Tai Fah Min. (*Hands him death order, represented by tiger's head on a scroll.*) It is the command of the Son of Heaven. (*Gongs and both bow.*)

Lee Sin. The tiger's head! What criminal name is penciled on the gaping mouth? My eyes are like swords danced upon by evil spirits. I can not see. Chee Moo, my wife's dearest mistress, and the child! I can not kill them. I will go to my ancestors first. (*Drops scroll.*)

Tai Fah Min. Then Suey Sin Fah will go with you.

Lee Sin. Why does not the public executioner wreak his master's impatience on the head of Chee Moo? He is skilled in killing first wives.

Tai Fah Min. It must be a quiet and merciful affair, otherwise it might become a scandal. Her family should congratulate her on the release of her suffering soul, for those beheaded or strangled are free from suffering, but wives' families are strangely inconsiderate.

Lee Sin. He that rids his house of an evil had better suffer the evil than tell the world.

Tai Fah Min. I am going to Wu Sin Yin to drink delicious tea. Bring us the head of Chee Moo. (*Exit TAI FAH MIN door right, fanning himself. Screeching sound played on instruments.*)

Lee Sin. The tiger's head! (*Picks up scroll.*) Ancestors, save me. An hour ago my ox and I were happy. The soft breeze on the rice fields brought us the music of Heaven. An instant, and the typhoon comes with a word, and the land is bleak, and death hovers where the sun-rays played. This is the evil moon wrought by man's mischief. He is not content and will not suffer his poorest neighbors to be content. The tiger's head! I must do the murder to save my wife, little Suey Sin Fah. (*Enter SUEY SIN FAH, door left. Music. Comes down left, bows three times.*)

Suey Sin Fah. May I be permitted to tell this august worthy audience -- to whom I bow, for it is my business to be humble -- being both a maid and a wife -- for I am the maid of the august gracious Chee

Moo, the first wife, and the wife of the god-loved farmer, Lee Sin.

Lee Sin. (*Back to her.*) And like to be the widow of that same Lee Sin, for the evil spirits encircle him.

Suey Sin Fah. I pray my ancestors that I may not be maid and widow at one time. Your eyes roll. What demon spirits clutch your heart, my husband, Lee Sin? The veins in your forehead burst, your hands twitch with the wrenchings of the evil one. (*Violent beating on gong and crash of cymbals.*)

Lee Sin. (*Shows her scroll.*) The tiger's head with a name upon its tongue.

Suey Sin Fah. Not yours, Lee Sin, my love, not yours!

Lee Sin. Chee Moo! I must be her executioner.

Suey Sin Fah. Chee Moo, my august mistress in the tiger's mouth! Let us die together and save Chee Moo and the boy, who are even now enchained prisoners within the walls of her flowery garden at the displeasure of her unkind husband.

Lee Sin. I can not. The tiger! The mother dies by the sword; the child deserted in the wolf land.

Suey Sin Fah. Is this the husband of my breast, is this distorted demon the one to whom I gave a wife-heart?

Lee Sin. I bow to the gods to tear all tender feelings from me that I may work myself into an unkindness to do Chee Moo's murder.

Suey Sin Fah. I love the august Chee Moo and her beautiful child. She is suffering from the machinations of Due Jung Fah, who is the human spider in the world-box. We must save Chee Moo.

Lee Sin. If I obey not the mandate of Wu Sin Yin, the Great, your life and mine will answer for it.

Suey Sin Fah. Death with our ancestors will be just as sweet in our love. The good of the people demands that Chee Moo live to raise her boy.

Lee Sin. But if I fail, Chee Moo will die the same by the hand of another found to do the work, as others will come to plough the rice fields when I and my ox are dead. Where is the honorable Chee Moo?

Suey Sin Fah. Praying in her prison to the great-eyed god for the soul of her boy, Wu Hoo Git.

Lee Sin. What am I to do?

Suey Sin Fah. Kill little Tso, and pass her off for the august Chee Moo.

Lee Sin. (*Suspiciously.*) You are jealous of little Tso.

Suey Sin Fah. Tso is a fox and makes mischief for us all. She dreams black plots at night and whispers them in the willing ears of Due Jung Fah. The gods smile when a bad being is killed, for it is so rare. The good do the dying. That makes them good.

Lee Sin. But Tso does not look like Chee Moo. We should fail.

Suey Sin Fah. (*Business.*) The sword that takes this from this can slash this out of semblance. (*Business taking pin from her hair.*) Pin this in her hair. I took it from my mistress' head-dress. Where are you going?

Lee Sin. After my august sword. (*Exeunt* LEE SIN *and* SUEY SIN FAH, *door right. Enter door left,* TSO. *Music.*)

Tso. A moonbeam fell where the murder was contrived. I know all, for I listened. I was behind it and heard Wu Sin Yin and Tai Fah Min plan it all. There must be moonbeams somewhere when great passions are working. If it had been a sunbeam there never could have been a murder. (LEE SIN *enters, takes sword from* PROPERTY MAN. TSO *does not see him at first. He stands and looks at her. She finally sees him and begins to flirt.*) I knew you were here, Lee Sin.

Lee Sin. How could you know?

Tso. A butterfly lit on my heart and said, "Beware -- there is a heart-thief here."

Lee Sin. The butterfly lied. I am married.

Tso. That is the whole trouble in the honorable august world. All the fascinating men are married.

Lee Sin. Work not your wiles on me, for I am rough, honest and not fascinating.

Tso. It is the honest husband that falls first, for he is foolish, and doesn't know or doesn't mean to, or doesn't know that he wants to mean to. I pray my ancestors *not* to give me too honest a husband.

Lee Sin. (*Aside, as he crosses to right.*) She is the evil thing. Her fox soul should be released. I must do it.

Tso. You will find the honorable Chee Moo and her august monster-child yonder. The light from the jewel in the forehead of her god-image will fall upon the mortal spot and lead the sword.

Lee Sin. How knew you of my purpose?

Tso. A tortoise by the pool told me. He was so slow he overheard the plot in passing. Is your honorable sword very sharp?

Lee Sin. As sharp as the east wind.

Tso. Will you hack her one blow?

Lee Sin. No more.

Tso. How long will it take?

Lee Sin. The time it takes a lark to swallow a grasshopper. (TSO *shows glee.*)

Tso. Where will the sword cut? (*He walks up stage and shows her at neck. She shudders.*) Will it be very hard on your hands?

Lee Sin. It will be.

Tso. When will you do the deed?

Lee Sin. Now. (*Business.* LEE SIN *strikes at her neck with sword.* PROPERTY MAN *comes forward and holds a red flag before her face.*) I am blind with august blood. Where is the head? (PROPERTY MAN *throws a red sack on the stage.* TSO *exits door right.* LEE SIN *picks up red sack and talks to it.*) The remnant of a soul that lived! I will clip the ears. I will chop off the honorable nose. I will slit the precious eyes -- that drooped to my humble eyes once. Without eyes, ears, lips, and nose, you, as the first wife, Chee Moo, are as good as any.

Suey Sin Fah. (*Enters door left.*) Where is the head? Show me the head? Oh, woe is me; it is my august mistress, Chee Moo!

Lee Sin. The fox maid, little Tso!

Suey Sin Fah. It is Chee Moo, my mistress, Chee Moo!

Lee Sin. My sword worked the magic. I carved her to look like Chee Moo. There is the eye that drooped in love to your humble husband's.

Suey Sin Fah. She drooped her eye to you? I recognize it now. She should be dead! Look to your exalted sword! Oxheaded devils cling to its blade.

Lee Sin. The evil ones upon my blade mock her -- not me, and they shall mock at Wu Sin Yin, for I shall present him with the sword together with her head. (SUEY SIN FAH *pins jewel on the bag.*) Bid Chee Moo flee with her child. (SUEY SIN FAH *exits door right.*) The world is fire-lined. To my work -- I drag away the body, for without its head it is sweeter to fertilize a field of poppies.

LEE SIN *goes through business of picking up supposed body and exits door right; music;* PROPERTY MAN *now places table center, covered with red cloth; also chairs on either side, which are also covered with red cloth, with stools on their seats.*

Chorus. 'Tis the palace of Wu Sin Yin, the Great.

Enter WU SIN YIN, *door left; roll of drum; seats himself at right of table. Enter* TAI FAH MIN, *takes seat on left of table; music stops.* PROPERTY MAN *brings tray on which are two cups and places the same on table.*

Wu Sin Yin. It is accomplished, my Tai Fah Min? Does your daughter sit in the coveted place she longed for?

Tai Fah Min. (*Complacently.*) Let us drink tea.

Wu Sin Yin. Bring tea, and cups of honeysuckle flowers and rose petals.

Tai Fah Min. It is glorious when the bad die and the good live.

Wu Sin Yin. Glorious! A rose petal for my tea.

PROPERTY MAN *pretends to deliver one with chopsticks. Enter* LEE SIN *door left, kneels and bows three times to* WU SIN YIN, *rises and puts basket which he has carried with him on table, laying his sword on top.*

Lee Sin. Most celestial master, I fall upon my knees, for they hold me not. Her head has been removed and quietness reigns. In the basket, my honorable master. The august sword is there, too, most honorable master. Forget not the august sword.

Wu Sin Yin. (*Removes sword and peeks into basket.*) Burn perfumed incense as I peep at it. You have chopped off the lips that I have kissed!

Lee Sin. They lied, great master.

Wu Sin Yin. You have slit the eyes that blinked to me!

Lee Sin. And to others, great master.

Wu Sin Yin. You have chopped off the ears that have listened to my love!

Lee Sin. They have heard too much, great master.

Tai Fah Min. Her head to the pigs! Another honeysuckle leaf for my tea.

Wu Sin Yin. She *was* my first wife. I'll bury the trunk with august honor. Inform Due Jung Fah that I come. She need pray no longer. My arms ache for her, Tai Fah Min. (*Music; exit* WU SIN YIN, *followed by* TAI FAH MIN, *door right.*)

Lee Sin. (*With head.*) To the pigs! To the pigs with the head, but the demon sword for the girdle of Wu Sin Yin. (*Exit* LEE SIN, *music, door right.* PROPERTY MAN *removes table and chairs, placing them on stage left. Music, plaintive theme.*)

Chee Moo. (*Enters left with child, as before. Down center.*) To the mountains, where the evil eye grows blind in the pure air of Heaven. (*Enter spirit,* LING WON, *with roll of drum at upper opening. Music.*)

Ling Won. And the eye of Heaven sees all.

Chee Moo. Who are you that floats upon a fleecy cloud? Are you an executioner who bears a sword?

Ling Won. Fear not, I am the spirit of Wu Hoo Git's great-grandfather, the first Wu Hoo Git.

Chee Moo. Then the breath of this child is your own life breeze, still playing on this earth. And this is the little Wu Hoo Git, who inherits your to-day and your to-morrow.

Ling Won. As I inherit his yesterday and his yesterdays before it. I am the spirit-self of his great-grandmother, too; we of yesterday are two in one.

Chee Moo. How mean you?

Ling Won. The land of the dead is so crowded that married souls become as one in space and the silkworms of the dead land weave us into one cocoon that we may not crowd our neighbors.

Chee Moo. Why does not his great-grandmother speak?

Ling Won. It is not so ordained. She, being the woman, offended the ears of the gods -- and her husband -- with many words when alive, so the just gods suffer me only to speak now that we are dead.

Chee Moo. Can she hear and see us, too?

Ling Won. She can hear and see all. There, too, the gods are just, for in life the nights enamored me from home to listen to the moon-birds in the shadows of the trees, while I sucked the honey of the night-blooming cereus along the way, and too often the morning dawned while I still drank in the songs of the women on the flower boats.

Chee Moo. And will little Wu Hoo Git live as you do in death?

Ling Won. Too soon if you obey me not. I come to warn and save him.

Chee Moo. Who would harm my little Wu Hoo Git?

Ling Won. The august Wu Sin Yin, his father, even now

sharpens a sword to cut the thread that holds him to this life.

Chee Moo. I dreamed it and so I fled.

Ling Won. I sent that dream; little Wu Hoo Git would have passed to us had it not been that his great-grandmother, the other half of my spirit-self, sewed a stitch in the brain of Lee Sin, the farmer, so that he could not pick up the thread of thought woven there by Wu Sin Yin, your husband, who had ordered the murder of the little Wu Hoo Git.

Chee Moo. (*Horrified.*) Too terrible! Oh, oh, I could fill a crystal vase with a mother's tears.

Ling Won. I come to break the crystal vase of a mother's tears that would drown her boy.

Chee Moo. What shall I do?

Ling Won. Send the august Wu Hoo Git on his world journey alone.

Chee Moo. You would not take the little Wu Hoo Git, for you have a woman's heart within your breast and know a mother's meaning.

Ling Won. You must come to us that Wu Hoo Git may live to the glory of the Emperor.

Chee Moo. But he will lose his way without a mother's care and love.

Ling Won. The future is for the gods; we are spirits and know only the path back to the moon whence he came. His steps are toward the sun, whither he goes.

Chee Moo. Let me go with him.

Ling Won. Not so. Wu Sin Yin would know you, for you are grown. He is so little that he looks like other babes and may escape.

Chee Moo. But he needs a mother to feed and look after him.

Ling Won. The ravens will feed him; the eagles will show him the mountain peaks; the humming-birds will tell him the names of the flowers along his path; the goldfish will show him whither the streams flow straight. And a maiden will arise to teach him the story of love. Fear not. The Gods of Mercy and of Love will hold his hands.

Chee Moo. My Wu Hoo Git -- my little Wu Hoo Git. Your mother's heart melts for you.

Ling Won. He will go up and up and up, till he wears the sun-hued garment.

Chee Moo. The sun-hued garment! My Wu Hoo Git. (*To* SPIRIT.) Leave me not. My heaven-descended son of the morning fades in my arms as you fade. He goes from me into the glory of paleness, while I cry out for his peaceful rest.

Ling Won. The evil lines only wrought by demon cunning fade from his cheeks before the light of a new soul day. The cramped and evil thoughts born of his father's life flee before the sword thrusts of good thoughts which a mother marshals to cradle him.

Chee Moo. You go from me!

Ling Won. Write Wu Hoo Git's name and history on his coat and come to us. Farewell -- we must depart into the shadows.

Chee Moo. Leave me not -- oh, leave me not! (*Laughing and crying.*) Wu Hoo Git, my Wu Hoo Git. I am a willow weeping over the stream of my own life-blood. I will write your name on your garment in a mother's blood, that the life of the mother's veins from which you sprang may enter into and become a part of your soul. (CHEE MOO *here bites the second finger of her left hand until the blood comes, which she allows to drop into the palm of her hand; then dips the finger-nail of her right hand into the blood and writes on the white under-garment of the child, sobbing during the speech.*) My baby -- my boy! (*Writes:*) This is Wu Hoo Git, pure and perfect, now, decreed to live ten thousand years. A mother's tears, falling as rain from heaven, will fill the valleys across his path that his life-boat may float from mountain peak to mountain peak and confound his enemies who follow after. More words in the mother's blood -- I grow weak.

> Ancestor guard you,
> Love embrace you.

(*Stops. To* SPIRIT, *who is gone:*)

Will I hear this baby cry and not be able to come to him? Must I see the tears in his baby eyes and not be able to wipe them away?

Ling Won. (*Outside.*) Yes. Yes.

Chee Moo. The mother who would give all and does give all -- the ink in my veins runs out. Every drop must go to the boy. (*Writes:*) Be kind to her who gives you love. Hope, pray, fight, live to make others happy. The last drop -- the last drop in my veins to tell the story of my boy and put a prayer on his garment. All -- my baby boy -- all! A mother's love! I can not let you go. Your baby hands cling about my heart. The light grows gentle as the light of dreams. Wu Hoo Git -- my baby -- my Wu Hoo Git.

Tableau Curtain.

She now becomes faint with loss of blood and sinks to the stage.
PROPERTY MAN *and his assistant bring ladder and place it at center of upper opening.* CHEE MOO *rises and climbs up four rungs of the ladder.* PROPERTY MAN *holds ladder.*

Chorus. She climbs to Heaven. (*Music. Enter door left,* SUEY SIN FAH, *followed by* LEE SIN; *come center, see child, but take no notice of ladder or* CHEE MOO.)

Suey Sin Fah. What babe is this? I see not the mother.

Lee Sin. His name is writ in blood upon his garment. 'Tis Wu Hoo Git! We will fly with him. (*Exeunt with child, door right.*)

Chee Moo. (*On Heaven ladder, climbing farther up.*) My Wu Hoo Git! Your mother will never see you wear the sun-hued garment, but she will know.

NOTE: *At end of act, in place of curtain calls, the* CHORUS *comes before the blue curtain and offers thanks in the name of the company.*

Chorus. (*Appearing.*) I bow and thank you in the name of my brothers of the Pear Tree Garden for the kindness you have shown. I ask indulgence. I would permit them to appear and voice their thanks, did not tradition forbid. I shall tell them; it will put joy in their hearts. At the close of our story, if they still stand in the light of your favor, it will please me to permit them to come before you, if you do not adulate them too much for their good. I bow. (*Exits.*)

Curtain.

ACT II.

After the house curtain is taken up, the tableau curtains are slightly parted and the PROPERTY MAN *enters. He walks to extreme right, then to extreme left and back to center, striking large gong; then exits through opening in tableau curtains. Orchestra on stage plays short overture. At crash of cymbals,* CHORUS *appears before the curtains and bows to right, left, and center.*

Chorus. I come again because I promised. I bow again. (*Bows three times*.) You may rely on my august word, for I deal in facts alone uncolored by fancy. My brothers of the Pear Tree Garden are not accountable to truth, as they speak what the author of our play -- I will advise you later of him -- has set down for them to speak. Authors and poets color the truth by the prettiness of their fancy. I bow to them, however, telling you to beware of them, for I derive my opportunity from the soaring of their imagination to present my august self to you. To this extent authors are magnificently worthy. Wu Sin Yin, the evil father, was unable to kill his august son, Wu Hoo Git. This celestial young prince had dwelt twelve moons, when last you heard his baby cry of parting with his honorable and august mother, Chee Moo, who took her passage heavenward in your glorious presence. But time has honorably pursued its venerable way. Wu Hoo Git has grown into youthful manhood, and stands at the portal of flowery life. He must pluck the azaleas of youth and observe them wither at the touch of his golden finger-nails. He must know the temple of the body before his body knows the temple of his mind. (*Bell sounds off*.)

The great bell calls me -- as it calls him. The bell-maker cast it of pure gold and silver, but its note proved brazen. The Son of Heaven was supremely annoyed. The bell-maker recast it. When the metal was molten, to save her father's life, for fear its note might again carry base tones, his daughter disposed of her body by springing into the mass of white heat; so her soul became of the bell wrought by her father. The metals welded with her spirit and its tone was then one of virtuous harmony and love. Wu Hoo Git, too, must pass through molten life, that the fires may purify his soul and weld it into the purest strain. I augustly bow; you honorably listen.

CHORUS *turns his back to audience, makes gesture with his fan. At crash of cymbals, tableau curtains are drawn.* CHORUS *now goes up to table, center.* PROPERTY MAN *discovered seated on stool in center of stage. When music stops,* PROPERTY MAN *arises, indicates to* CHORUS *that scene is set and crosses to left.* CHORUS *then speaks.*

Chorus. 'Tis the home of Lee Sin, the farmer; though humble in appearance, it is crowded with riches. (*Music. Enter* SUEY SIN FAH, *left. She comes down left, opens imaginary door, steps over the door-sill, closes door, crosses to center and stands in front of stool before speaking.*)

Suey Sin Fah. It is the twentieth anniversary of the birth of Wu Hoo Git, who has grown into beautiful manhood. The Goddess of Mercy, Kuan Yin -- she who hears prayers and is the giver of children -- has given me no baby of my own to care for, but in secret mercy has given me Wu Hoo Git to foster-mother. When I thought I held a babe and the breath of childhood was sweet, I looked and the flower had bloomed. Youth sprang from my arm-petals to laugh and run and play the first games of life. A few days give the first farewell to the mother's arms, a few months and the babe is a babe no more, a few years and our mother journey is done. We look in the mirror of the past with the gray upon our temples, and we find strong arms to protect us where we had protected the helpless babe. The boy runs away. He promises to return. He thinks he will return to the mother's breast. You may think that all is well with Wu Hoo Git, but it is not so. Due Jung Fah's son, the Daffodil, grows to man, bars the way to Wu Hoo Git and his world-place. Like all adolescent boys, Wu Hoo Git longs for the world and its dangers. If he leaves our sheltering care, he will never return to the mother breast except in memory. I worship my soul alone.

Sits on stool, center. Music. Enter LEE SIN, *door left. Carries hoe over shoulder, wears a beard. Comes down left, opens imaginary door, steps over sill, closes the door, crosses to right.*

Lee Sin. Prosperity is mine. My ox ploughs the field and it grows pearly with rice. You touch the loom and it weaves rich fabrics. We dwell in the glory of our beautiful foster-child. (SUEY SIN FAH, *going to him, puts one arm about his neck and covers her face with the other hand.*)

Suey Sin Fah. The august Wu Hoo Git has gone forever.

Lee Sin. Not so. Tell me not so. I murdered for him. Could a father do more?

Suey Sin Fah. The string of our kite is broken and the kite drops down from its heaven-kissed place past the horizon. He is grown, and longs for the paths of pleasure where the way is piled with hungry evil gods. He demands the shadows of his past. He cries for his ancestors and we dare not give them to him. We must put him from his purpose or the evil-born son of the second wife, Due Jung Fah, will pursue and slay him.

Lee Sin. Fear not! He is not of the common horde whose palm is dulled to pleasure by hard toil. He is august and needs the luxury of the joy of living. The gods rain favors of grace and beauty and perfumed paths on such as he. Remember whence he sprang. His treasure chest is full of gold which the gods gave to feed his glorious appetite. Soon the man's life journey to match his exalted station must call him.

Suey Sin Fah. Still I fear. I must wait by the hearthstone, where he will never play again. Never again will he make my knees his ancestral tablets and coo his baby prayer to them.

Lee Sin. Neither spirits nor Due Jung Fah's son can harm him now. (*Crosses to left. Opens imaginary door.*) Look! He comes like the sun over the eastern hill. He brings a new day to us. (*Crosses to right again. Music. Enter door left,* WU HOO GIT.)

Wu Hoo Git. (*Strikes picture in doorway. Comes down left. Leaps over imaginary door-sill and crosses to center.*) I am Wu Hoo Git! I am tired of classics. I long for the free air of life.

Lee Sin. You will not find contentment there.

Wu Hoo Git. Then where shall I find contentment?

Lee Sin. In hard work and pure love.

Wu Hoo Git. And where will I find pure love?

Suey Sin Fah. In a mother's arms.

Lee Sin. In a wife's embrace.

Wu Hoo Git. The woman answers one way, the man another. In the world there are many answers. I must hear them all to judge.

Lee Sin. Go not from us. Be counseled by a father.

Suey Sin Fah. And by a mother's love.

Wu Hoo Git. Where is my real mother waiting? Where does my real father reside?

Lee Sin. (*Confused.*) Our love withholds much that you will know in time.

Wu Hoo Git. In time -- always in time. I have played hide-and-seek with the sun-rays and moon-rays, I have laughed from the mountain peak at the typhoon sweeping the valley below. But when I ask you for my ancestral tablets you tell me to wait.

Suey Sin Fah. Till wisdom comes.

Wu Hoo Git. Why should I be denied? A babe knows its mother. I demand my parents. I feel the blood of eagles in my veins. I demand,

I say!

Lee Sin. I can not.

Suey Sin Fah. I will not yet.

Wu Hoo Git. Then I go to find them. (*Goes up right to door.*) Even at the portals of high Heaven. My purse is full, but without my ancestors, I dwell not in honor.

Lee Sin. The world is large and you know not the dangers that will cross your stumbling way.

Wu Hoo Git. I fear not. I am grown to be an august man. (*Large gong. Music. Exit door right.*)

Suey Sin Fah. (*Going up toward door right.*) Wu Hoo Git, my Wu Hoo Git! Come back to me! Oh, go not away, my boy! Rest here cradled in my love. Permit me to rock you to sleep to the song of gentle breezes and the tune of tiny bells.

Lee Sin. (*Goes to* SUEY SIN FAH. *Puts arm around her.*) He has the call of the world now and must answer.

They exeunt door right. PROPERTY MAN'S *assistants place four stools in a row across stage with spaces between them. Take two stools from left and place them right of stool which is at center; take one stool from wall left and place it left of stool center.* PROPERTY MAN *then makes gesture to* CHORUS *and crosses to left.*

Chorus. (*Rises.*) 'Tis the flowery way of pleasant evenings. He comes! Wu Hoo Git's rival, the Daffodil, coddling his brain with dark thoughts. (*Sits.*)

Music. Enter DAFFODIL *preceded by two attendants; one carries large red banner, the other, large fan. They stand either side of door left. He strikes attitude in doorway with fan, turns around slowly. As he faces front again,* PROPERTY MAN *drops sword on bottom of property box. Expression of pain crosses* DAFFODIL'S *face. He crosses to center.* PROPERTY MAN *brings bouquet of flowers for him to smell, standing left of him.*

Wu Fah Din. I advise this honorable audience that I am a man, though I possess a daffodil nature. I go to view delightful embroideries, but retard my footsteps, that you may observe my charm. I was born great. Wu Sin Yin was my father, and Due Jung Fah, the second wife, my mother. A wonderful alliance, as I am the superb result. (PROPERTY MAN *holds flowers for him to smell again.*)

I am, therefore, the rival of Wu Hoo Git, who dwells, it is whispered, in an humble mountain home, whence he will go forth to seek his world-place. I am not happy while he dwells anywhere -- so he must not dwell. He is simply vulgarly manly, while I possess feminine qualities of great luxuriance.

Smells flowers again. PROPERTY MAN *draws them away from him and puts them in box left.* PROPERTY MAN *then sits and reads Chinese paper.*

I would contend with him, man to Daffodil, but it might break my finger-nails and establish a bad precedent. You may think the match unequal, because of my delicacy in a contest with brawn; but I assure you that it is not so. Craft, guided by cruelty, outweighs vulgar manliness. I must contrive to destroy his honesty and cleanness of life. (*Attendant fans him with large fan.*)

I will call to my aid Yin Suey Gong, whom you will meet and know, by the hump on his back. I will have him present his porcelains to the unsuspecting Wu Hoo Git. He deals deliciously in porcelains. He will drop flowers of pleasure in Wu Hoo Git's path that my rival may inhale their odors of vice. Observe how I contend with brawn. (*Music. Attendants go up right and exit.* DAFFODIL *goes up toward door as he speaks.*) Cut the flowers in my path that I may walk.

Exits door right. Music changes. Enter door left, YIN SUEY GONG. *Carries staff. Music continues during speech.*

Yin Suey Gong. (*Coming down to center bowing.*) I am Yin Suey Gong of the monkey form. The air was lukewarm when I came, ghost clouds were racing the wind. I was dusted by butterfly wings along my path. Bringing pleasure to the owners of gold is my business. A dragon yawned and belched me forth. A tooth caught me and I was born cramped of back. I give those who were born straight (*Chuckles.*) and august of face the world's pleasures. Then to avenge myself on mother nature, who distorted me, I pluck down their star and delight in its fall. (*Chuckles.*) I watch the flower lanterns of their vanity burn till the ribs stick out like skeletons. Then I laugh, for they are crooked in purse and without love. I flatter them till I have them in my grasp, then I mock at them, for they are fools. I deal with the fair and they become crooked-brained. I juggle hearts. I toss them in the air and cross them and dance them on my finger-tips and catch them on my upturned nose. Sometimes one falls and leaves a blood spot where it fell. Then I gurgle and juggle on, for hearts are my currency and a few marred and broken ones are easily replaced.

Wu Fah Din. (*Enters, comes down left and crosses to right, dropping folded red paper, which represents a Chinese check. Back up stage to door right as he speaks.*) Wu Hoo Git approaches. Enmesh him. Tarnish him. It must be done with perfume, and gently. (*Exits.*)

Yin Suey Gong. (*Center.*) I shall approach with my arms full of presents for the adolescent Wu Hoo Git. (*Music. Enter* WU HOO GIT *door left.*)

Wu Hoo Git. (*Coming down left.*) Where do I find myself?

Yin Suey Gong. In the land where the honey is sweet and the bees have lost their sting.

Wu Hoo Git. What is this land?

Yin Suey Gong. (*Bows going up to him.*) This is the land of perfumed pleasure. Where the cups are filled with silver rice-wine and the lips of love are heavy with greetings and your every desire is answered.

Wu Hoo Git. Its story has been traced on a sweet-meat jar. But it is not the land I seek, for it tells not of my ancestors. (*Moves a little right. Turns back to audience.*)

Yin Suey Gong. You are augustly wise. You are old and learned. I bow to the august magnificence of your dress, the delicacy of the golden guards to your honorable finger-nails, your wonderful jewelry of amber -- your astute wisdom -- (WU HOO GIT *shuts eyes in delight at flattery.*)

Wu Hoo Git. I am transcendentally wise.

Yin Suey Gong. Your boots will surely decorate a city's gates when you have passed to your ancestors. You are old for your age. The world and life will make you older. Dreams await you. I greet you and lay the world at your feet.

Wu Hoo Git. I would put you in a seat of friendship beside me.

Yin Suey Gong. There are only two things to please the taste of an august man like you. (*Bowing.*) Some will tell you in deceit that there are many things to please, but there are only two.

Wu Hoo Git. Only two in the broad world, to people my pleasure?

Yin Suey Gong. Only two. You may travel, you may study, and you may know, but pearly wine and luscious women are all that you will find. Some far countries boast of the dance, but it is a part of woman. Our august land oft speaks in song, but that, too, is sweet from the lips of woman only. It is not the note or string. It is the lips that sing. To know wine and women is rarer far than to know classics. The great scholars know this, (*Bows.*) but praise not my honesty. (*Turns away right.*)

Wu Hoo Git. You make me wonder. I have learned philosophy. But it concerns me not in my search for my ancestors. (*Starts toward door right.*)

Yin Suey Gong. Be tutored by glorious woman, the rims of whose rice wine-cups are crystallized with kisses. (*Moves away a little.*)

Wu Hoo Git. What are kisses?

Yin Suey Gong. The meeting of the pollen of two flowers that float to each other on a heaven-sent breeze.

Wu Hoo Git. Such an august meeting must make the sweetest incense for the gods.

Yin Suey Gong. It does -- only the evil one more often catches the breath.

Wu Hoo Git. And why?

Yin Suey Gong. The gods have others taste the sweets first for fear of poison.

Wu Hoo Git. But there can be no poison in the meeting of flowers.

Yin Suey Gong. There may be birth and birth leads to death. (*Music, during which* WU HOO GIT *crosses to left, listening.* YIN SUEY GONG *watches the effect on him.*) Love birds, flowers of happiness, come to garden your pleasure. They will teach you life, rarer than philosophy, richer than classics.

Enter door left four Flower-girls at music cue. Strike picture in doorway, bow forward, then to left. They cross and stand above stools.

To your sale thrones, my princesses fair!

Girls come to below stools, backs to audience. They mount at music cue, with the help of the assistant property men. Girls then turn front, fans still before their faces.

Wu Hoo Git. (*When music stops, crosses to center.*) How modest they are! Fans before their rose faces! (*Looks at girls, delighted.*) I am glad I came to this world. It makes smiling in my heart.

Yin Suey Gong. It has pleased many.

Wu Hoo Git. By what charm do women hold us enchained?

Yin Suey Gong. Wise men have wondered. (*Laughs, moves right.*)

Wu Hoo Git. May I approach them with my voice?

Yin Suey Gong. And get strange answers!

Wu Hoo Git. How many moons have passed since you graced the earth?

See Quoe Fah. (*Dropping fan.*) Sixteen years of moons.

Wu Hoo Git. Put up your fan! Who are *you*?

Mow Dan Fah. A peony flower.

Wu Hoo Git. Then you will fade.

Mow Dan Fah. Pick me while my perfume lasts.

Wu Hoo Git. You are as dainty as the embroidery on an Empress's gown. (*Frightened, she puts fan over her face.* WU HOO GIT *moves to* YIN SUEY GONG.) May I speak to the next one?

Yin Suey Gong. The gods painted many that man might choose one!

Wu Hoo Git. (*Starts to go up right.*) Let me go back to philosophy and my ancestors.

Yin Suey Gong. (*Stopping him.*) And never know life?

Wu Hoo Git. (*To third girl, who lowers fan.*) She tipped her fan to me. I saw her eyes. I will wait and talk to her. Her hands are like penciled porcelain. She has the color of plum-tree buds. Are you -- just like the other?

Yong Soo Kow. I was kissed by a more southern sun.

Wu Hoo Git. Then two flowers met and a -- a child was born?

Yong Soo Kow. You were not one of the flowers!

Wu Hoo Git. What means she?

Yin Suey Gong. A sunbeam played upon her hydrangea lip.

Wu Hoo Git. (*Excited.*) And danced in her eye and painted her cheek?

Yin Suey Gong. You should have been the sunbeam. She invites you.

Wu Hoo Git. This was never taught me in philosophy. How much there is to learn. (*Indicating fourth girl.*) That one coughed. (*Sighs.*) Send her to the Drug Hall of Propitious Munificence for the Great Blessing Pill, or the Double Mystery Pill, or the Thousand Gold Pill for maidens. I suffer to see her suffer.

Yin Suey Gong. Her cough is a gentle salutation. She fears you may go astray if you talk too long to her august sisters.

Wu Hoo Git. (*Delighted, whispering.*) Does she think so much of me? I like her. She has a mother's heart.

Yin Suey Gong. They all have mother-hearts.

Wu Hoo Git. I never had a mother. (*Crosses down center. Turns back to audience, looking at girls.*) Now I have four.

Music. Girls sing. At end of song, short dance. The girls turn around on stools and face front again. During song, WU HOO GIT *crosses to left. At end of dance he speaks:*

She sings with lips that part like opening roses. My foster-mother never sang like that. The blood runs faster in my veins. (*Crosses to Yin Suey Gong.*) I feel something here that beats.

Yin Suey Gong. That is your heart. Philosophy knows nothing of it.

Wu Hoo Git. I like her. She is so sweetly made -- round and soft and delicate -- like a vase we would embrace for fear it might fall and shatter its loveliness.

Yin Suey Gong. You may hold her and embrace her beauties.

Wu Hoo Git. I might let her fall and shatter her dainty roundness.

Yin Suey Gong. You will learn in time.

Wu Hoo Git. (*Tries.*) But my arms may not be strong enough.

Yin Suey Gong. Hers were made to help you.

Wu Hoo Git. (*Crosses to* CHOW WAN, *left; awkwardly embraces her. Other girls lower fans and look at him. He then crosses back to* YIN SUEY GONG.) It is easier than I thought. She grows more delicately beautiful. She is sweeter than the rarest vase. I like the holding of her. Her breath is incense.

Yin Suey Gong. You may taste her lips. (*He crosses to* CHOW WAN *again, ingenuously kisses her and crosses back to* YIN SUEY GONG.)

Wu Hoo Git. Sweetmeats rare. (*Starts to kiss* CHOW WAN *again, stopped by* YIN SUEY GONG.)

Yin Suey Gong. I will sell her to you.

Wu Hoo Git. (*Astonished.*) Is she for sale?

Yin Suey Gong. Everything I possess is for sale.

Wu Hoo Git. Would you keep none for yourself?

Yin Suey Gong. I would be selfish to retain such delicate wares. All perfumed flowers may be cut by a golden knife. They wait upon the market for your desire. (*Bowing.*)

Wu Hoo Git. I will buy them all.

Yin Suey Gong. Like most men you would have them all, but, if you purchase four maids, you would sell three, or present them to your friends.

Wu Hoo Git. (*With inspiration. Moves left.*) Then I will buy her who coughs. (*Girls drop fans and put them up quickly.*) They dropped their fans and looked at me. I never felt such a delicate shock. It is like reading the classics at one glance by the light of ray-tailed comets. May they do it again?

Yin Suey Gong. Not till you purchase.

Wu Hoo Git. And what must I pay?

Yin Suey Gong. All you have in your chased gold purse.

Wu Hoo Git. (*Crosses to* YIN SUEY GONG, *right.*) But I have nine thousand taels! What shall I do when I give them all to you?

Yin Suey Gong. Send home for more, like every august son who would see the world.

Wu Hoo Git. (*Turns left looking at purse.*) Nine thousand taels for a mother!

Chow Wan. I am worth more. (*He looks up at her.*) You will find it so.

Wu Hoo Git. (*Drops purse.*) Take my purse, most gracious Yin Suey Gong. (*Goes to* CHOW WAN, *left.*) Lee Sin will send more. She would suffer so alone.

Music. Three girls turn on stools with backs to audience and descend, assisted by the PROPERTY MAN, *and exeunt door right.*

YIN SUEY GONG *follows them up to door and turns, looking at* WU HOO GIT. WU HOO GIT *helps* CHOW WAN *off of stool.*

Wu Hoo Git. They do not smile on me.

Yin Suey Gong. The evil one fans them with jealousy. You did not buy them, too.

Wu Hoo Git. Are they angry?

Yin Suey Gong. They are filled with humility. Farewell! (*Aside.*) He drowns in the vase of pleasure. The Daffodil will smile.

Exit right, laughing. PROPERTY MAN'S *assistants push four stools together, then bring four chairs and place them back of stools, touching them. An assistant exits right but returns immediately with two bamboo poles to be used as oars. Hands one to another assistant and they stand a little above and to the right of the chairs.* PROPERTY MAN *gets drapery and places it over back of chairs. Then he places two cushions on the stools which he gets from left near property box. Music stops when* WU HOO GIT *speaks.*

Wu Hoo Git. By what sweet name are you called? (*Taking her hand.*)

Chow Wan. Chow Wan, Autumn Cloud.

Wu Hoo Git. (*Dropping her hand, backing away.*) That's augustly pretty. What shall I do with you now that I have bought you?

Chow Wan. (*Goes to him, places head on his shoulder.*) I will teach you.

Wu Hoo Git. Your voice is like an honorable zephyr. Bring it closer! (*Puts arm about her.*)

Chow Wan. You are learning.

Wu Hoo Git. But you have not taught me a thing that I could behold.

Chow Wan. The gods have taught you many things that you can feel yet know not of.

Wu Hoo Git. I do not understand, but I like you better than philosophy.

Chow Wan. When you have said farewell to me, you will be a wiser philosopher.

Wu Hoo Git. (*Backs away from her.*) Must we part? (*Starts to embrace her, she evades him, crosses to center below.*)

Chow Wan. Not for many perfumed days. (PROPERTY MAN *makes gesture to* CHORUS, *who rises.*)

Chorus. 'Tis a flower boat which floats upon a silver river of love. (CHOW WAN *seats herself on cushion of boat and invites* WU HOO GIT *to enter.*)

Chow Wan. Come with me in the flower boat and float among the lotus plants while the night birds perch on the moon-rays and sing to us, and I answer their song. (*He gets into the boat. After he is settled, two assistants pretend to row the boat. Musician rubs two pieces of sandpaper together in time with the strokes.*)

Wu Hoo Git. You think of such sweet ways to wander from the minutes of the third day of the third moon to the fourth day of the third moon.

Chow Wan. In my arms you will wander ten thousand years.

Wu Hoo Git. (*His arm about her.*) I wish your three sisters had stayed with us. It would have warmed their hearts to see us thus. (*She drops her fan.*)

Chow Wan. You are so worldly wise. (*Fans herself slowly.*) They would have purred with delight.

Wu Hoo Git. (*Song offstage.*) The silver sails fill with the summer breeze. Wild bells tinkle in my august veins. I never heard them before.

Chow Wan. (*Turns away from him.*) See the lotus lanterns on the water wafting their candle-light to us!

Wu Hoo Git. (*Starts up.*) This is the night of love. Let not the morning come.

Chow Wan. A love boat passes us in the moonlight.

Wu Hoo Git. (*Looking. She follows imaginary boat from left to right with her hand.*) It holds a woman and a man in sweet embrace. It is the lotus-lipped fan girl I met with you.

Chow Wan. Yin Suey Gong has sold her to him. (*They follow the imaginary boat with their eyes.* WU HOO GIT *with his hand around to right holds picture until song offstage stops.*)

Wu Hoo Git. I should have bought her and saved her from him.

Chow Wan. Your gold is not enough for one. (*She puts head on his shoulder.*) Let us land for more.

Wu Hoo Git. Wait until the night is passed.

Chow Wan. No! We will find it sweeter in my home. You fill the purse for the fruits, cakes, and candies. I will shadow the lanterns and draw the silken curtains to await your coming. (*He starts to embrace her. She stops him.*) I have more to teach you.

At gesture from WU HOO GIT *the assistants stop rowing. They get out of boat. Music stops. Assistants with bamboo poles exeunt right.* PROPERTY MAN *takes drapery away. Assistants remove chairs. The fourth stool is left in center of the stage with red cushion on it.* PROPERTY MAN, *after gesture to* CHORUS, *sits left. Assistants now exeunt left.*

    Chow Wan. Fill your purse.
    Wu Hoo Git. It takes so much money to love, my Autumn Cloud. (*Music; he exits right.* CHOW WAN *watches him exit.*)
    Chow Wan. He has flown on wings of swiftness for a second purse full. (*She crosses at back to left.*)
    Chorus. (*Rising.*) 'Tis a love nest.

    CHOW WAN *opens imaginary door, steps over sill, closes door, and sits on stool center. Music continues.*

    Chow Wan. He has flown on wings of swiftness for a second purse full. I must wait at home alone. I will change my gown to one of softer silk; dress my head like a princess for my Wu Hoo Git. Bring me lanterns of blue and pink that their light may tint the eye glance of him who comes. Crowd my abode with almond flowers and open the lattice so that the moon-rays dancing on my goldfish pond may make love to the lantern's light within. Fill the air with perfumes of sandal-wood. Bring me my handkerchief of pale blue embroidered with purple wisteria. I must weep at my Wu Hoo Git's long delay. Bring my Yeuh Chin that I may be playing when his footfall tinkles on the path. Place carved wood screens about me that no one may behold my beauty but him I wait for. He comes! He comes! My lover returns with his purse of gold.
    Yin Suey Gong. (*Enters door left, comes down, opens imaginary door, steps over sill, closes door and goes to* CHOW WAN. *Music stops.*) What do you here alone?
    Chow Wan. Waiting as becomes me. Wu Hoo Git is filling his purse with gold drops.
    Yin Suey Gong. It is not enough. I can sell you to an emperor.

Chow Wan. An emperor! (*Rises. Moves down right a little and stands with back to audience.*) Lead me to his fascinations.

Yin Suey Gong. A chair of lacquered gold awaits you. You must approach him as becomes his rank.

Chow Wan. (*Music on moon-guitar. She goes up to door right and turns.*) I will approach him freely. (*Exits door right.* PROPERTY MAN *removes stool and cushion to left.*)

Yin Suey Gong. This is my lucky day. I've sold all my porcelains but I must have Wu Hoo Git's second purse full to line my treasure sack. I must flatter him into another purchase, or my head will smile from a bamboo pole at my crooked trunk. My head against his purse of gold.

Wu Hoo Git. (*Music. Entering door left, running to left center.*) Chow Wan -- my Autumn Cloud! I bring the mountain's gold to you.

Yin Suey Gong. Your purse is welcome.

Wu Hoo Git. Where dwells my honorable Autumn Cloud -- Chow Wan?

Yin Suey Gong. Drifting in the azure sky after a butterfly's perch. I will find you a spring cloud that is warmer.

Wu Hoo Git. I understand not your speech.

Yin Suey Gong. The august Wu Hoo Git has grown so old in an hour of pleasure that he has come to man's estate and should now follow the pleasures of an august man.

Wu Hoo Git. I want my Autumn Cloud.

Yin Suey Gong. Kite flying is more for the education of a man who has seen the world and grown weary, as you have.

Wu Hoo Git. But I am not weary. Where is my Chow Wan? I have a purse of jewels for her.

Yin Suey Gong. You should be augustly happy, for most men who have seen the pleasure path have lost their purse. Chow Wan has flown to a daintier nest, silk woven.

Wu Hoo Git. Flown, as the morning light comes to greet our love!

Yin Suey Gong. I will sell you a more comforting mate.

Wu Hoo Git. But I own her heart, for I bought my august Autumn Cloud with my gold.

Yin Suey Gong. I sold her for the gold of another whose purse was deeper.

Wu Hoo Git. But she is completely mine. The crevices of her heart are mine to nestle in. She told me so herself. You are a thief.

Yin Suey Gong. I should not else be supremely wise.

Wu Hoo Git. Bring back my august other self to me. You opened Heaven's doors of love to me, gave me the sweets of life -- the perfumed breath of the ages of love. Then you close the doors, and tell me to find that joy-light again in other eyes.

Yin Suey Gong. You had your hour of fleeting pleasure. Do you expect with your small glint of gold to buy a lifetime of happiness?

Wu Hoo Git. I am grown to man and I can wreak the vengeance of my might on him who steals my blessings.

Yin Suey Gong. Be augustly calm. Woman is merely a matter of gold. Give me more than he gave and I will buy her back.

Wu Hoo Git. From the arms of another? The gods themselves can never make her the same Autumn Cloud you stole.

Yin Suey Gong. Another will do as well, if you close your exalted eyes.

Wu Hoo Git. You shall change, as she has changed, so that all the gods of yesterday and the gods of tomorrow can not right you into what you were. I will carve your august hump.

Yin Suey Gong. I will give you back your gold for mercy.

Wu Hoo Git. I am not for sale. Bring me your august hump that I may chop it into the likeness of my Autumn Cloud. (*Crosses to left.*)

Yin Suey Gong. I will defend my august hump.

He drops his staff. They stand in attitude of fighting. WU HOO GIT *left,* YIN SUEY GONG *right.* PROPERTY MAN *takes short double sword in scabbard and one short single sword in scabbard out of property box, crosses to center, hands double sword to* YIN SUEY GONG, *single sword to* WU HOO GIT, *and retires to left. During fight, musician comes down to center below* CHORUS' *table and works cymbals. Cymbals crash with the striking of swords. The whole fight is conducted in a slow methodical manner, with much turning.* WU HOO GIT *finally cuts off the hump of* YIN SUEY GONG, *taking red bag from under his coat, and he sinks to the stage in a sitting position back toward the left.* PROPERTY MAN *places pillow for* YIN SUEY GONG *in a wrong position. He motions him to bring it closer, which* PROPERTY MAN *does with his foot.*

YIN SUEY GONG *now lies down, making himself quite*

comfortable. WU HOO GIT *stands over him, and as he holds the bag up at arm's length, a loud crash of cymbals.* WU HOO GIT *then crosses to left and victoriously gives his sword to* PROPERTY MAN.

CHOW WAN *enters left, stands near doorway.*

Wu Hoo Git. (*Going up to her left center near door.*) Enfold me in your arms. Taste my lips again, Chow Wan, my Autumn Cloud. (*Embracing her.*)

Chow Wan. (*Bitterly; goes down, kneels and leans over body of* YIN SUEY GONG.) You have killed my Yin Suey Gong. Who will sell me now? Evil spirits clutch at you. Depths of night enfold you. (*Falls over body weeping.*)

Wu Hoo Git. I departed his hump for selling you from me.

Chow Wan. He got more adorable gold than you could give.

Wu Hoo Git. (*Crossing right at back.*) Gold is not the measure of the heart.

Chow Wan. Go into the pleasure world and see. My monkey, my Yin Suey Gong, my beautiful Yin Suey Gong.

Wu Hoo Git. Console yourself. (CHOW WAN *looks at him.*) I am not going to kill him again. (*Girls enter left and cross down to body of* YIN SUEY GONG.)

Chow Wan. He has killed our master!

Girls. Killed him! (*All kneel.* SEE QUOE FAH, *left of* CHOW WAN, MOW DAN FAH, *right of* CHOW WAN, YONG SOO KOW *left of* SEE QUOE FAH.) Our poor Yin Suey Gong!

Chow Wan. (*Pathetically.*) Who will traffic in our love now?

Wu Hoo Git. Gold *is* the measure of your affection. Your hearts are outbalanced in the scales by a grain of yellow dust in the heart traffic of him I slew. I repent his death, for in an evil way he was a tutor who taught me pleasure; though a traffic not smiled upon by the gods, it must have some purpose for good or it would not be. May he glory in his ancestors!

Chow Wan. You have no ancestors.

The Girls. No ancestors?

Wu Hoo Git. I have tarried too long in the way of pleasure. I go to seek my ancestors. I give him back his hump. (*Throws red bag on stage. Exits door right.*)

Chow Wan. He is monkey-shaped and can walk upon the clouds.

(*Girls hold hands up.*) He is above human. Put back his hump and he will live again to traffic in our hearts. His superb breath returns. His honorable eyes roll to us. We will be sold again. (MOW FAH DAN *gives red bag to* CHOW WAN.)

Yin Suey Gong. (*Coming to life. During scene when* YIN SUEY GONG *comes to life, music effects.*) Restore my honorable hump -- (CHOW WAN *places it under his coat.*) that I may breathe delicious breath. (*Sighs.*) He cut it off.

Chow Wan. Wu Hoo Git. He will perish for his deed. He has no ancestors to pray to.

Yin Suey Gong. No ancestors! No ancestors! (*He rises, picking up staff. Girls rise and back away right.*) I am augustly avenged. To the market place for hearts. (*Girls exeunt right followed by* YIN SUEY GONG *to door.* PROPERTY MAN *kicks death pillow to assistant left, then picks up two swords. Puts them in scabbards in box left.*)

Chorus. (*Rises.*) The Daffodil, tired of waiting for results, visits Yin Suey Gong.

Wu Fah Din. (*Enters left, followed by attendant, who carries red silk cord and stands up center.*) Where is the pleasure you promised me? Where are the delightful tintinnabulations of joy at his undoing? Feast my eyes.

Yin Suey Gong. He has gone.

Wu Fah Din. Lead me to his destruction.

Yin Suey Gong. He has gone to seek his ancestors.

Wu Fah Din. A cord about his neck. (*Attendant comes down, places cord around* YIN SUEY GONG'S *neck.*) Twist it, that I may see his lying tongue swell from his mouth.

Yin Suey Gong. Time, give me time. When the arrow misses you do not throw the bow away, but send another shaft on truer lines. I will contrive his ruin.

Wu Fah Din. Give me the cord. (*Takes end of cord.*) Follow to the palace. (*Starts up for door right.*)

Yin Suey Gong. The scarf chafes my neck.

Wu Fah Din. It remains a gentle reminder, while we contrive again. (*Exeunt right.* PROPERTY MAN'S *assistants place table with cover center. Chair with cover and small stool on it right of table. They exeunt left.*)

Chorus. (*Rises.*) 'Tis the house of Tai Char Shoong, the

illustrious, father of Plum Blossom, the adored heroine of this play. (*Enter* PLUM BLOSSOM (MOY FAH LOY) *and* SEE NOI *left and hold picture in doorway.*)

Moy Fah Loy. Come quickly. (*They move down left.* PROPERTY MAN *stands down left with bamboo pole in horizontal position across stage.*) From the window of this room we can see him pass. (WU HOO GIT *enters, comes down left, crosses below* PROPERTY MAN *to right and exits up right.*)

See Noi. What, what, what!

Moy Fah Loy. Saw you not the youth of the kite hill? To the window! Open the lattice that I may peep. (SEE NOI *opens imaginary shutters.*)

See Noi. 'Tis Wu Hoo Git! Be careful lest he see you. (*Pulling her upstage.*) Remember your maiden modesty.

Moy Fah Loy. (*Looking at* WU HOO GIT *through imaginary windows.*) Saw you ever one who walks like him with godlike mien? He stands so straight the clouds separate to form a pathway for his brain. (*Turns, looks at* SEE NOI.) He looks not back. His eyes are not for woman, but eternities. (MOY FAH LOY *closes imaginary shutters and crosses to below table.* PROPERTY MAN *retires left with pole.*) Oh! A madness of dejection enters my fancy and chills my heart.

Enter TAI CHAR SHOONG *left. Strikes picture in doorway. Wood block and small gong. Coming down left between* SEE NOI *and* MOY FAH LOY.

Tai Char Shoong. See Noi! Let my Plum Blossom be robed in richness becoming the birth of my daughter. (MOY FAH LOY *crosses to* SEE NOI *who goes to door with her as she exits left.*)

Tai Char Shoong. (*Crosses and sits right of table.*) See Noi, I am about to give my daughter in betrothal. (SEE NOI *comes down left.*)

See Noi. I feared it, illustrious master.

Tai Char Shoong. How dare you fear what I command! You have loosed your tongue to my daughter.

See Noi. (*Frightened.*) No more than she has heard herself; gossip, breeze carried through each window lattice.

Tai Char Shoong. And of what do busy tongues complain?

See Noi. Of the future mother-in-law you would give in marriage.

Tai Char Shoong. A perfect woman, filled with knowledge of what a wife should be.

See Noi. 'Tis whispered her son's first wife died of his mother's accomplishments.

Tai Char Shoong. What more could she have done for my daughter's sake?

See Noi. If it must be so, may she possess a hundred children and a thousand grandchildren.

Tai Char Shoong. It is too few to wish her. (*Music.*)

Moy Fah Loy. (*Enters left, richly gowned, comes down to below table center. Bows.*) Honorable father, I have done your bidding.

Tai Char Shoong. (*He holds out his hand. She comes to him.*) Let a smile of joy dwell upon your lips and behave in your most graceful manner, for the Widow of Ching comes to negotiate for the marriage of her son.

Moy Fah Loy. (*Turns front. Eyes down, head turned away.*) I smile in the house of my father, I might weep in the home of his friend.

Tai Char Shoong. A wife must take what the gods bestow upon her. (*Rises.*) Now approach the august mother-in-law. Forget not the courtesies of such a meeting.

Music. The WIDOW *and Maid enter on a wheelbarrow trundled by assistant, followed by another with green card. They cross down left, then to right and up. Assistant presents card to* TAI CHAR SHOONG, *who crosses to left, then assists them to alight from wheelbarrow and exits right. Assistant with wheelbarrow exits right.*

Widow. Tai Char Shoong, I bestow upon this house a bow. (*Bows. Maid takes small stool off chair and as* WIDOW *sits, places it under feet and retires back of her.*)

Tai Char Shoong. And I bestow upon the Widow of our great mandarin, departed to his ancestors, and the mother of our youthful mandarin, a bow. (*All bow again.*) Bring jade cups of tea and pipe. (PROPERTY MAN *brings tray with two tea bowls and two cups and*

Chinese pipe. Places tray on table center. Then lights pipe, crosses to left, and sits.)

Widow. Is this Moy Fah Loy?

Moy Fah Loy. I am Moy Fah Loy. (*Below table, bowing to her.*)

Widow. Let me observe you. Turn about with graceful composure. (*She does so.*) Your hair is arranged complacently; your feet are large.

Tai Char Shoong. (*Down left.*) That she may walk the easier to attend upon her mother-in-law.

Widow. Let me observe the nails of your fingers. There is a hair left in one eyebrow. It shows carelessness in preparing for my observation. Your lips should be painted thinner. Can you embroider? (SEE NOI *gives lighted pipe to Maid.*)

Moy Fah Loy. Kingfishers and storks.

Widow. Good birds, both. (*Maid gives pipe to* WIDOW.) Can you prepare with daintiness sweetmeats, watermelon seeds, rice wine? (*She puffs pipe. Returns it to Maid who then hands it to* SEE NOI, *who places it on table.*)

Tai Char Shoong. (*Sadly.*) Her august mother, divinely departed, instructed her in the virtues of the home.

Widow. Permit me, Tai Char Shoong, to examine into your daughter's virtues, as I am augustly versed in virtues. You should wait upon me, your mother-in-law, with modest obeisance.

Tai Char Shoong. Could she be other than a worshipful slave to such an honorable mother-in-law?

Moy Fah Loy. There are thirty-six kinds of mother-in-law, and she is every kind.

Widow. I will bestow upon you because of the excellence of this house, ten thousand taels.

Tai Char Shoong. My house and daughter are illustriously honored.

Widow. (*Rises. Maid picks up stool as* WIDOW *rises and places it on chair.*) We will gracefully take the daughter of Tai Char Shoong into our hearts and home.

Tai Char Shoong. The splendor of the honor of bestowing such a mother-in-law upon my daughter dazzles my modest eyes.

Widow. I take my departure. You are augustly blessed, my Plum Blossom, in having me to guide your way, in my illustrious son's house.

Moy Fah Loy. Augustly blessed!

Widow. (*Crossing up to door.* TAI CHAR SHOONG *goes to above table.*) Prepare your gracious self for the six ceremonies within three days, for I need your worthy service in my home. (*Bows and exits, preceded by Maid.* TAI CHAR SHOONG *bows and exits up right.* PROPERTY MAN *crosses to table, takes tea tray and pipe. Smokes pipe as he crosses to left. Places them in box left and sits.*)

Moy Fah Loy. (*Going to* SEE NOI *up right, who holds her in her arms.*) My mother-in-law! (*Looking up.*) Bring me poison!

See Noi. Say not so, honorable one. Think on the family.

Moy Fah Loy. Lead me to the tablets of my mother that I may pray to her and know.

Music. They exeunt right. PROPERTY MAN *and assistants arrange four chairs across stage with backs to audience and a stool center.* PROPERTY MAN *crosses to center and superintends placing of chairs. Over the backs of chairs, beginning from the right,* PROPERTY MAN *places white cloth tablets on which are painted in Chinese characters the following names: Chum Shou, Moy Kwai Fah Loy, Moy Fah Loy. He gets the two tablets mixed on the chairs left of stool center, and after reading the names, changes them. After so placing the tablets,* PROPERTY MAN *sits on stool left, and starts to read paper. An assistant enters with bowl of rice. Gives it to* PROPERTY MAN, *who smiles and takes it. Assistant exits.* PROPERTY MAN *then bows to* CHORUS, *who has become annoyed at delay, and then sits and begins eating rice with chopsticks. Music during this business.*

Chorus. 'Tis the resting place of the bodies of the departed.

Wu Hoo Git. (*Enters left, comes right of stool center. Music forte until he gets to center, then stops. Looks at tablets.*) Here in the city of the dead I will find my impressive ancestors. I will pray at the tombs for the gods to give me an honorable mother. I must have had an august father once, for every one, they say, has had at least one august father. I will pray at the tombs for the gods to give me an honorable mother, with a delicate name -- one that drops like a sweet song from the lips. (*Reads, chair first right.*) Chum Shou, "Graceful Long Life." I like not her name. (*Crosses right.*) I will not pray to her. Here is a tomb that is deep in the ashes of burned paper money. I will dust away the ashes with my solemn breath. (*Blows on tablet, then reads tablet number two right.*) Moy Kwai Fah Loy, "Rose Bud." I care not for roses. With my solemn breath I cover her again with ashes. (*Blows breath on tablet, moves to left.*) Here is a quiet ancestral tablet. From within issues precious light. (*Reads number one left.*) Moy Fah Loy, "Plum Blossom." I like plums and I have scented the perfume of their blossoms. I will take Plum Blossom for motherhood. (PROPERTY MAN *puts down bowl of rice and places cushion before chair left center, holding chopsticks in other hand.*) I kneel, (*Does so.*) for I have found an exemplary tablet that conforms to my adorable self. (*Music.*) Plum Blossom mother, to you whom I find late in life, my speech choked with tears, my heart weary with long suffering, I kneel. (PROPERTY MAN *takes bamboo pole from wall left, crosses to right of* CHORUS' *table and stands with back to the audience -- holding pole in perpendicular position.*)

Chorus. 'Tis a celestial weeping-willow tree.

PLUM BLOSSOM *enters left, crosses to center at back and stands just below pole, with fan over her face.*

Chorus. The maiden peeps from the shadow of the tree at the youth of her fancy. (*Music stops.*)

Moy Fah Loy. Who kneels at the tablets of my Plum Blossom mother?

Wu Hoo Git. An august child just born to her. What fairy of beauty crosses my prayer! A princess in dress and carriage, a lily foot. Light radiates from her person and shines through her garments. Raise your fan to me.

Moy Fah Loy. (*In surprise does so. Then covers her face again.*) I did not mean to do it. (*To audience.*) 'Tis he of the kite hill.

Wu Hoo Git. Painted banner of love! You fill the pockets of my eyes with graciousness. I like you. I wish that you were buried here that I might take you to motherhood.

Moy Fah Loy. It is my mother that lies there, and I came to burn incense at her tablets.

Wu Hoo Git. (*Rises, goes up to her.*) I will assist your honorable hands.

Moy Fah Loy. It is most unholy to speak to a man --

Wu Hoo Git. At the grave of our exalted mother?

Moy Fah Loy. I like your voice. It is sweet. (*She sits stool center.* PROPERTY MAN *crosses left and places pole against wall left and then sits.*) I will be unholy while See Noi, my maid, yonder in the flowery path prays to her mother's ashes and sees me not.

Wu Hoo Git. I selected the right mother.

Moy Fah Loy. Then she is not your real honorable mother?

Wu Hoo Git. I liked her name and thought she would be an honorable mother. I needed one.

Moy Fah Loy. I am glad you chose her. I couldn't have spoken to you if you had not been one of our sublime family. (*Peeps at him through fan.*)

Wu Hoo Git. I can behold with my eyes your celestial heart through the lattice of your fan.

Moy Fah Loy. How wonderful you are! The openings are so small for you to peep through and my heart is so augustly large.

Wu Hoo Git. I know the august woman heart. I have traveled the road of pleasure. I have sailed on the flowery sea of sin. (*Crosses to right.*)

Moy Fah Loy. How enchanting! You walk like an emperor. (*He stops walking.*) Walk for me.

Wu Hoo Git. I walk. (*Moves several steps toward her.*) How old are you? You must be forty, you are so beautiful and wise.

Moy Fah Loy. (*Tapping her fan.*) Walk.

Wu Hoo Git. I walk. (*Crosses to left.*)

Moy Fah Loy. Walk with your venerable footsteps nearer, that I may see you through my fan. (*He turns toward her.*) Not with your eyes fixed upon me, but your head held high in majesty.

Wu Hoo Git. I should walk into your eyes and lips.

Moy Fah Loy. Then I could not use them.

Wu Hoo Git. There is a way. (*Kneeling left of her.*) I have learned it.

Moy Fah Loy. From another maiden? (*Turns her back on him.*) I do not know augustly why, but I do not like that.

Wu Hoo Git. I will teach you.

Moy Fah Loy. Then I shall have traveled the flowery paths just as far as you. (*Turns to him again.*)

Wu Hoo Git. Augustly deign to place your eyes this way. I would have celestially sworn that I had measured the depths and heights of joy; I only stood on the rim of the false jade cup till I looked into your eyes.

Moy Fah Loy. (*Drawing away from him slowly.*) We are forgetting our mother.

Wu Hoo Git. I have a thought. (*Rises.*) If you are my sister and I am your brother, I had better adopt another mother.

Moy Fah Loy. Tell me why?

Wu Hoo Git. We can not love unless you will be my mother-wife.

Moy Fah Loy. What shall we do? I am on the threshold of betrothal.

Wu Hoo Git. Then I renounce our mother and will contend with him who seeks your hand.

Moy Fah Loy. (*Rises. Smiles.*) Let us augustly kneel and burn incense and pray to find a way. (*They kneel before chair number one, left.*)

See Noi. (*Enters door left, crosses to right at back and down right.*) Moy Fah Loy, Plum Blossom; do my eyes deceive me! On her knees with a man, and she was left in my exalted care!

Moy Fah Loy. Is that you, See Noi? I was engrossed in prayer.

See Noi. (*Crosses to* MOY FAH LOY.) All the prayers of all the gods and all the world burned up in an incense pot could not save you now. (*Takes her by the arm. Pulls her to right center.*) You are ruined. You have spoken to a man!

Moy Fah Loy. He is my brother.

See Noi. Impossible! I knew your mother.

Moy Fah Loy. He has adopted my mother. He had none, so I gave him half of mine. You taught me charities.

Assistant removes two tablets from chair left of stool center, rolls them and wakes PROPERTY MAN *to give them to him. Then takes second chair left and places it up left, back to audience. The other chair left of stool he removes to wall left.*

Moy Fah Loy. Half my mother was all I had to give.

See Noi. Evil spirits have you. Your maiden modesty has flown. You have talked with a man!

Wu Hoo Git. I will marry her, for she is good.

See Noi. Plum Blossom, daughter of Tai Char Shoong, marry a man without a mother! The maiden bloom of her cheek you have brushed away. You have blighted the fruit of her usefulness. Her father will behead me for this dishonor.

Wu Hoo Git. I will make her happier than a father could.

See Noi. Your doors are not opposite. Your wealth can not match hers. You have no mother and are unequal. Home, I say! (*Takes* MOY FAH LOY *up to door right, sobbing.*) And see my gray head pay the price your shamed virtue brings upon your father's house.

Moy Fah Loy. I must be very wicked. (*They exeunt.* SEE NOI *crying.* PROPERTY MAN *picks up red cushion and places it left, near property box.*)

Wu Hoo Git. (*Follows up to door and turns.*) If I am to believe my eyes, I have lost true love. Shadows encircle me. Who are you, the rapping of whose bamboo stick, tapping its way hither in measured tread, encroaches on my silence?

Enter door left, MAUN GUNG, *blind fortune-teller, accompanied by rapping on wood block in orchestra. Down left, crosses and up right before speaking. Carries long bamboo stick, which he raps on stage, still accompanied by wood block in the orchestra.*

Maun Gung. The blinds of darkness have been drawn across the windows of my head. I see not. I am a beggar; the past, the present and the future parade before me. I know all.

Wu Hoo Git. How can you know when you can not see?

Maun Gung. Let your kindness loose its purse-string to help me on my stumbling way and I will tell.

Wu Hoo Git. (*Gives money.*) How know you life with holes for eyes?

Maun Gung. I look within. There lies all there is to know.

Wu Hoo Git. Then you are not a prophet of the days to come?

Maun Gung. I read the days to come by the light of the days that have gone. My brain sights travel the ghostly ways of memory. What a man was, he is; and what he is, he will be. A fool can prophesy.

Wu Hoo Git. Know you the year and moon of my birth?

Maun Gung. Not so, for your birthday was the death day of what you were before.

Wu Hoo Git. Was I born rich or poor?

Maun Gung. You were born rich, for your mind is rich and that is all.

Wu Hoo Git. Whom seek I?

Maun Gung. You have a youthful voice, therefore warm blood is in your veins. You seek your love-mate.

Wu Hoo Git. And will she come to me?

Maun Gung. If you pray to your venerated ancestors to guide her right.

Wu Hoo Git. (*Fearfully.*) And if I have no ancestors?

Maun Gung. (*Raising stick.*) Even my bamboo has its celestial shadow and, if you have no ancestors, you are an unwanted soul cast back on the shores of earth to starve of joy.

Wu Hoo Git. Speak not so! I will not hear it.

Maun Gung. You like not the truth.

Wu Hoo Git. (*Angrily.*) I will send you to your ancestors to plead for me.

Maun Gung. I can not plead to them. I will live forever there, but will not know my neighbors. Learn for yourself, as I have. (*Exits, tapping cane, door right.*)

Wu Hoo Git. Stay, tell me more! He goes from me as all have done in the world. Everything I touch turns to blackness in my hand. (PROPERTY MAN *stands on chair up left with bamboo pole and silk cord with noose.*) I behold a weeping willow. I shall die on its branch, then my love will be sorry. I will find my ancestors. (*Stands on stool center.* PROPERTY MAN *lowers pole. He puts noose around his neck, then jumps off stool.*)

Chorus. He hangs himself, but fear not, the spirit of his mother watches over him, and will send a wayfarer who will cut him down.

Enter GIT HOK GAR *left, crosses down left. Sees* WU HOO GIT *and backs away to left. Large gong. He then turns to* PROPERTY MAN *who holds out sword to him. He takes it and cuts at cord.*

Wu Hoo Git. Who are you that would take from me the joy of compelling the world to miss me?

Git Hok Gar. The world laughs when there is one less mouth to feed. If you would make the world respect you, stay and fight it.

Wu Hoo Git. (*Takes off noose, rubs throat.*) I prefer my celestial breath.

Git Hok Gar. Dying hurts unnecessarily.

PROPERTY MAN *grabs sword from him and puts it in box, then places pole against wall left.* GIT HOK GAR *turns and looks at him. Assistant crosses to right and removes tablets from chairs and places them in box left. Turning to* WU HOO GIT.

You are too young to seek death. What leads you to this making off?

Wu Hoo Git. The loss of a love that encircles my life like a star light-ringed.

Git Hok Gar. To enjoy love you must enjoy life.

Wu Hoo Git. I am a worldless man. Even at the threshold of my days -- I am shameful. I have no shadows, no ancestors to bring a blessing to my love.

Git Hok Gar. Have you no home?

Wu Hoo Git. My father and mother are foster.

Git Hok Gar. Then you owe them more than those who, in giving you life, had a duty toward you. Home! You are rich in mind, which is all. (*Crosses up right.*)

Wu Hoo Git. But the circle about my heart! My love ring!

Git Hok Gar. Make yourself great in right living and your ancestors will find you. Cheerful, my boy, I will lead you to your home and my gray head will find you life and love, which I missed for want of guiding. Come! To your home! (*They exeunt right.*)

PROPERTY MAN'S *assistant removes one chair to wall right. The other he places against* CHORUS' *table and another assistant take stool from center and places it against the chair and below it.* PROPERTY MAN *then places sword on it, dusting it first.*

Chorus. 'Tis again the house of Lee Sin, the farmer. (*Music.*)

Suey Sin Fah. (*Enter left, followed by* LEE SIN. *They come down left, open imaginary door, step over the sill.* LEE SIN *closes the door.*) Will he never come, Lee Sin?

Lee Sin. When he has learned the world.

Suey Sin Fah. He has forgotten us.

Lee Sin. My majestic ox does not forget the stall where he is fed. (*Crosses to right. Music.*)

Wu Hoo Git. (*Enters with* GIT HOK GAR.) My home, the door.

Git Hok Gar. (*Left of him.*) Enter bravely and make amends.

Wu Hoo Git. I am ashamed. You go first.

Git Hok Gar. (*Raps on imaginary door. Opens door. Enters.*) I am Git Hok Gar, philosopher. Have you a son?

Suey Sin Fah. Not dead!

Git Hok Gar. He is at your threshold seeking forgiveness.

Wu Hoo Git. (*Enters imaginary door.*) May I enter?

Suey Sin Fah. Wu Hoo Git, my boy, my Wu Hoo Git! (*Embraces him, weeping.* GIT HOK GAR *moves up right.*)

Wu Hoo Git. I choke! (*Crosses to center.*) How are the august rice fields, the loom and the ox?

Suey Sin Fah. You have not forgotten them?

Wu Hoo Git. I am learning to remember, for memory comes with love, and I have met one who lit the enchanting candle in my heart. Her lips are flower buds that open with delight at the warmth of my superb kisses, but even as my day broke with a roseate dawn, a despair cloud crossed the sky, and death hovered in my path. I have no ancestors.

Suey Sin Fah. My poor boy!

Wu Hoo Git. Pity me not. Manliness sneers at pity. Open the door of knowledge to me. Who are my ancestors?

Lee Sin. They are --

Suey Sin Fah. No! No!

Lee Sin. I will tell!

Suey Sin Fah. It will cost us his life and yours.

Lee Sin. I care not. (*Crosses to* WU HOO GIT. TAI CHAR SHOONG *enters dragging* MOY FAH LOY *by the hand.*) I murdered for love of you. What must our boy suffer for love! Your father was --

Tai Char Shoong. (*Who has come down left.*) Dwells Wu Hoo Git here?

Wu Hoo Git. I am the august Wu Hoo Git. Who are you that break upon us like an angry sea?

Tai Char Shoong. Father of the glorious Plum Blossom, whom you betrayed.

Wu Hoo Git. I found your celestial daughter at the tablets of her mother. She was pure and beautiful and I loved her.

Moy Fah Loy. And I him.

Tai Char Shoong. (*To* WU HOO GIT.)   Your days are numbered.

Wu Hoo Git. Not by the count of man.

Tai Char Shoong. But by a father's count.

Wu Hoo Git. I will marry her, and make her mine.

Tai Char Shoong. You, without ancestors!

Suey Sin Fah. Season your anger while I speak! To your knees, Wu Hoo Git, and receive your sacred heritage. (*He kneels, back to audience.*) Raise your eyes heavenward. (*She takes out baby jacket with Chinese letters on it.*) Your mother now speaks.

Wu Hoo Git. My mother!

Suey Sin Fah. (*Showing him the baby jacket.*) Each blood-stain from this baby jacket is the history of your being and breathes a mother's blessing.

Wu Hoo Git. My soul -- my mother!

Suey Sin Fah. These lines are too sacred for me to voice. Your lips alone must form the words.

Wu Hoo Git. My eyes are choked with tears.   Breathe my mother's name.

Suey Sin Fah. Chee Moo, the beautiful!

Wu Hoo Git. Chee Moo! I feel her a little above my head.

Lee Sin. And your father --

Wu Hoo Git. My father! The highway of too much joy opens to my famished soul.

Lee Sin. Wu Sin Yin, the Great.

Wu Hoo Git. The Great!

Tai Char Shoong. If this were true, Wu Hoo Git would rule this province where the Daffodil, son of Wu Sin Yin, the Great, now sits in splendor.

Wu Hoo Git. My mother crowns me with a truth cloud. I will prove her air message for her I love.

Tai Char Shoong. I believe you not! Make your boasting words realities and Plum Blossom is yours.

Wu Hoo Git. And so I will. But what have I to guard the way of life?

Lee Sin. (*Who has taken sword from chair up center, now comes down.*) This sword of courage. (*Gives sword to* WU HOO GIT *and steps back a little.*)

Suey Sin Fah. (*Gives baby jacket.*) And this guiding star of a mother's love to guide him.

Wu Hoo Git. A mother's love!

Moy Fah Loy. (*Crossing to center.*) Make a prayer each day big enough to match it and I will do so, too. (SUEY SIN FAH *and* LEE SIN *retire upstage right.*)

Wu Hoo Git. I will write your name on my hand-palms that everything I touch and feel will be Plum Blossom. I may never clasp my home and heart again. Let me mingle my breath with yours.

Git Hok Gar. (*Crossing to left.*) You are already breathing the harshness of the world. You must fulfill the life for which your mother died. (*Two assistant property men with chariot banners enter door left and stand each side of it.*) A stern way is licking your feet. Come! Your glorious chariot awaits you.

Wu Hoo Git. (*Rising. Crosses to* GIT HOK GAR *left.*) Carry I naught away with me but honorable memories and leave all behind me at this doorway of farewells?

Moy Fah Loy. (*Crosses to center.*) Yes, one part of me you take. My way shall be crippled till your return, then restore it to me.

Wu Hoo Git. Speak the joy you have in store for me.

Moy Fah Loy. (*Takes off slipper.*) My slipper! Let it bide next your heart on your weary way. In the hour of frightful necessity, shake it and I will come to you. (*Gives it to him.*)

Wu Hoo Git. What do you meantime without your august slipper?

Moy Fah Loy. Stand on one leg like a bird.

Wu Hoo Git. On one leg like an august bird! (*Kisses her.*)

Suey Sin Fah. Wu Hoo Git! (*Music.*)

Git Hok Gar. Come! Mount! (GIT HOK GAR *goes up and stands between the chariot banners.* MOY FAH LOY *hops on one foot and stand on chair up center, waving farewell.*)

Wu Hoo Git. I go to seek my heritage. (*They start across the stage, accompanied by the chariot banners.* MOY FAH LOY *hops on one foot and stands on chair up center, waving farewell.*)

Lee Sin. Courage, my boy! Courage! (*They go to right, then upstage and turn near door.*)

Wu Hoo Git. Farewell! (*Holding slipper up in the air.*)

Tableau curtain.

Chorus. (*Appearing through opening in tableau curtain and bowing.*) I bow in personal appreciation of your approval, if truly manifest, of my Wu Hoo Git, upon whom my fancy will now bestow the Yellow Jacket and the Peacock Feather. I speak in the first person, for I am accustomed to adulation, and it does not in the least discompose me. My brothers of the Pear Tree Garden are far otherwise; a little flattery upsets their modest equipoise. While there may be those who desire to secure the credit or discredit, I will say -- your generosity forces me to admit it -- I wrote this play -- a mere trifle. I composed the music, too. I taught them the story of my grandiloquent imagination. I showed them where to walk, how to talk. In my august fancy I painted the scenes. My menial, the property man, at my august celestial suggestion, will now give them thunder-clouds and snow-storms to assist their meager interpretation. The play is mine, the acting virtually mine. Such remuneration as you have bestowed upon us by your gracious patronage, I accept. Such sums as I may deem necessary I shall pass on to my brothers. At the end of the play you may call them before you if you like. It will please me, and praise them sparingly, but of course, I shall know that you know that the celestial thought was wholly and modestly mine. I bow. (*Exits.*)

Curtain.

ACT III.

After house curtain is raised, PROPERTY MAN *comes before tableau curtains, walks back and forth across stage, beating large gong. As he exits behind the curtains, orchestra on stage begins to play. At crash of cymbals,* CHORUS *comes before tableau curtains.*

Chorus. I still observe my honorable way and come to you, making my words brief and less august at each superb presentation of myself, for the more my brothers have to say, the less need I. The second father-in-law, Tai Fah Min, though dead, still lives in spirit to retard Wu Hoo Git's august progress. But, forget not that our hero is older and augustly wiser. Having wearied of rice wine and song girls, he now approaches the portals of august philosophy. All man approach the god-like realms of thoughtful sufficiency after the bodily attainments wane. I bow.

Turns back to audience and at gesture with his fan, tableau curtains are drawn. Walks to his table, center, as music is played before speaking. Four stools have been placed across stage center, spaces between them. PROPERTY MAN *discovered sitting on stool right center. When* CHORUS *gets to table he rises and indicates the scene.*

Chorus. The Daffodil takes his steps among his mulberry bushes, watching the silkworms spin while he threads his brain with evil.

Music continues. DAFFODIL *enters, comes to stool left center, does business of smelling imaginary bushes, then goes to center.* PROPERTY MAN *brings flowers for him to smell, which he waves aside scornfully.* PROPERTY MAN *returns flowers to box left and then crosses to right at back and stands at upper end of drapery, which is hung to form a screen about a chair placed upon a table against wall right and represents the* DAFFODIL'S *palace. Piano during speech.*

Wu Fah Din. I apologize for the apparent inadequacy of my brain against Wu Hoo Git's brawn. I am as disappointed as you are that I have not been able to kill this young Wu Hoo Git. Bear with me, however, for I will eventually do so. Wu Hoo Git not only lives, but starts on a journey to take my place in life and dispatch me. Such a result would be deplorable, as you know. I had with my kindness of nature planned for him a gently lingering death. I must now unkindly kill him outright, for your entertainment. I must be most careful in so doing, for, if I kill him, despising brute force as I do, my subjects, who should be his subjects, would immortalize him and the truth would come out. I have discovered some truths also about myself which I prefer not to have known. I shall retire to my palace (*Indicates it and moves up right.* PROPERTY MAN *dusts drapery.*) and on my cushioned throne, watch from its battlements. (*Ascends throne. Screened by drapery.*) I invoke all the subtle forces of my brain against Wu Hoo Git's brawn. I will impede his journey toward my person and my throne. I will throw death evils in his pathway. I will place before him a lofty mountain peak, that he may exhaust himself in climbing over it. I direct the battle with my fan. (*Disappears behind drapery.* PROPERTY MAN'S *assistants move two tables from left. Place them center, touching each other, and put two stools which are now underneath the tables on top of them.* PROPERTY MAN *crosses right, below tables, and stands at upper end of them.)*

Chorus. 'Tis a lofty mountain peak. (PROPERTY MAN *rests elbow on upper stool and puts head in his hands. Enter* WU HOO GIT *and* GIT HOK GAR. *Music.)*

Wu Hoo Git. (*Crosses to center, below table.)* Show me the battle-ground. Must I contend here, or shall I wander farther?

Git Hok Gar. (*Left.)* No man can foresee his battle-ground. Every shadow or darkening cloud may bring him peril. The way grows long. Think, my boy.

Wu Hoo Git. (*Crossing to* GIT HOK GAR.) I can think when I am dead. Love quickens my desire for triumphant vengeance, that I may conquer all, secure my throne, and place Plum Blossom on a seat of love beside me.

Git Hok Gar. (*Turning, looks at imaginary mountain, center.)* What! Must we drag ourselves over another mountain, with its ragged roof?

Wu Hoo Git. I shall o'ertop them all, for nothing shall stay my progress. (*Climbs to top of stools on table, center, assisting himself by holding imaginary branches. Then helps* GIT HOK GAR *to mount table.)* From the o'ertopping view I see the tiled roof where bides Plum Blossom. I see my home, too, and peacefulness behind me.

Git Hok Gar. And before you monsters, terrors and murder to overcome.

Wu Hoo Git. I care not, for all my tasks now are born of love. Come on! (*Starts to descend from table. As he places foot on stool right of table, cymbals crash.)* I feel a hand of ice encircling my sublime leg.

Git Hok Gar. It is an evil stream spirit that would drag you in. Cleave it with your fiery sword.

Wu Hoo Git. I would desperately cleave, (*Starts to draw sword.)* but it is gone. (*Turning to* GIT HOK GAR, *smiling.)* It overheard my solemn thought. You can crush enemies and friends with the weight of the tongue. (*Descends to stage, assists* GIT HOK GAR *to descend and they exeunt right. Music.* PROPERTY MAN'S *assistant takes one table and stool and moves it left. Another removes the far table and stool to left.)*

Wu Fah Din. (*Appears above drapery.)* He is such an impetuous youth, is he not? See how madly he is rushing into the dangers I am preparing for him. His climbing of that mountain was a mere exhibition of brawn. I will confront him with the raging torrent.

Retires behind drapery. PROPERTY MAN *crosses to right, picks up end of plank which lies between two stools. Assistant picks up left end of plank. As they place it on stools,* PROPERTY MAN *pretends to have hurt his finger. Another assistant looks at it sympathetically.* PROPERTY MAN *indicates scene and they retire to left.*

Chorus. 'Tis a wayward river and a bridge.

Wu Fah Din. (*Rises behind drapery.*) Bridge! Bridge! I had hopes of this river, but my gentle mind overlooked the bridge. However, it may be a weak bridge. (*Retires behind drapery.* WU HOO GIT *and* GIT HOK GAR *enter door left. Music for entrance. They come to left center.*)

Git Hok Gar. Water confronts us.

Wu Hoo Git. But see, a span of thoughtful kindness awaits us.

Git Hok Gar. The chasm is so deep and chill and the way across so narrow. Let us go about and find a safer crossing. (*He crosses down to extreme left.*)

Wu Hoo Git. Come on! It has been left us by brave souls who have passed before.

Git Hok Gar. So in all journeys in life, bridges have been built by those who left their deeds behind them.

Wu Hoo Git. Armored with courage, I draw my sword of progress! The end will never be seen if my first footfall weakens. (*Steps on bridge from left. Falls to his knee*) I stumble to my knee.

Git Hok Gar. The gods would make you humble at starting.

Wu Hoo Git. A silent prayer to the baby-mother message. (*He prayerfully kisses garment.*) Behold! The spirits are satisfied. They rock us not. (GIT HOK GAR *mounts bridge from left.*) In the water, mirrored below, I see a face like my own. It has lines of evil in it.

Git Hok Gar. The serpent lines of your father's face crawl in yours by reflection.

Wu Hoo Git. Is my face a serpent's nest? What must I do to cleanse it?

Git Hok Gar. Bathe it in the sunshine of virtue.

Wu Hoo Git. Behold! Over my father's shoulder grins the fox's face again that molests my sight.

Git Hok Gar. It is Tai Fah Min, who gloats at your struggle to be free from the curse of a father's crime.

Wu Hoo Git. What shall I do?

Git Hok Gar. Purify your soul and he will flee with the snake face.

Wu Hoo Git. In the mirror of the sublime water I now behold precipices, depths, valleys, snow-encircled peaks! Birds swim in the pearly air beneath the clouds like fishes in the clear stream beneath. The fox face again molests my sight! I will consult my garment of direction. (*Observing garment again.*) The lines trickle toward the eastern path at the bridge's end, with mother blood-drops larger to indicate the way. Come on! For Plum Blossom I conquer on earth and in Heaven. (*Gets off bridge to right.*)

Git Hok Gar. (*Following him.*) My brave boy. We step upon a tiny peak of yellow rock. (*Music. They exeunt right.* PROPERTY MAN *and assistant remove stools and plank, leaving stage clear.*)

Wu Fah Din. (*Appears.*) It is useless for me to tell you of the fear in his heart as he crossed that bridge. He was continually calling out for a woman. I will throw an inky darkness in his path, that it may affright him. (*Retires behind drapery.*)

Chorus. 'Tis a thunder-cloud. (*Music.* LOY GONG *enters door right, stamps around in a circle just inside door, finishing right center.*)

Wu Hoo Git. (*Enters door left with* GIT HOK GAR. *Comes to left center.*) Who are you that impedes my way with clamorous noise?

Loy Gong. I am Loy Gong, the God of Thunder, requested by a world power to o'ershadow you. I keep mortal aspirations down for the other gods through bellowing fear. (*Hits standard with hammer. Cymbals.*)

Wu Hoo Git. But I fear you not. My wisdom buds with courage, impregnable to gods and man, and teaches me that every word-might or heavenly power has one still higher before whom it quails -- called love.

Loy Gong. And what is love?

Wu Hoo Git. For me, Plum Blossom.

Loy Gong. And what flower fear I when the floor of Heaven bends beneath my tread?

Wu Hoo Git. The sky-flower -- the august rainbow of good thoughts and deeds! (LOY GONG *drops hammer*.) Before its seven light-rays you crouch in silence.

Loy Gong. (*Fearfully.*) I would fill your purse, to keep my secret, for if my weakness were known to man, I should lose my solemn fearfulness.

Wu Hoo Git. (*With contempt.*) My wisdom cannot be purchased.

Loy Gong. I will welcome you on my icy peaks and whisper music to you.

Wu Hoo Git. When I arrive on your august peaks, I care not what tones you take, for I shall have within my veins the warmth of Plum Blossom's love.

Loy Gong. (*Goes toward door right.*) I withdraw my august self in fearfulness of wisdom. (*Exits door right. Music.*)

Git Hok Gar. (*Crosses to* WU HOO GIT, *center.*) You have met the most fearful of the gods and vanquished him.

Wu Hoo Git. Give me the earth to conquer, that the earth may no longer deny me my heritage and my Plum Blossom's love. (*End of speech in doorway. Exeunt right.*)

Wu Fah Din. (*Appears.*) This makes me decidedly uncomfortable. What tripping potency has he to overcome a god? Can it be that he is coupling brain with brawn? My seat of dignity rocks in fearfulness. Let Kom Loi ensnare and slay him. (PROPERTY MAN *brings a large web made of gold string which is tied on a framework of wood with thread and sets it up, right, leaning sleepily against it. Enter* KOM LOI, *as* SPIDER, *and takes position back of web, right.*)

Chorus. 'Tis a golden spider-web.

Wu Hoo Git. (*Entering left with* GIT HOK GAR, *crosses to right, stops in front of web.*) What is this tangled mesh that stretches from earth to Heaven and pretends to bar my way with petty entanglements? My celestial curiosity leads me to inquire.

Kom Loi. I beckon your sublime presence.

Wu Hoo Git. It invites me with a gentle voice. I am led to desire a closer view.

Kom Loi. Let me encircle you with the beauties and love-knots of friendship.

Wu Hoo Git. Its voice is as gentle as Plum Blossom's. It must be my friend. (*Peeps.*) I see but indistinctly through the fluttering weave of rainbow lights the faces of Wu Sin Yin and Tai Fah Min directing malice. I will observe more closely. (*Wets finger and makes slit in web.*)

Kom Loi. (*Enraged voice.*) Beware! I asked you to enter my abode as a friend. You stick your finger in the eye of my hospitality. Beware!

Wu Hoo Git. (*Looking up.*)   An august Spider and his enchanting web! (*Frightened.*)

Git Hok Gar. The thing is dangerous and I am a man of peace. I will depart my footsteps to the other side of the mountain. (*Picks up chair, crosses left, sits facing left.*)

Wu Hoo Git. (*To* SPIDER.) I repent my fault.

Kom Loi. Repentance may help your soul, but will not reweave the strands in which I catch human flies that would know my lair. You shall die. (SPIDER *bursts forth and throws silken strands.*)

Wu Hoo Git. (*Frightened.*) It is an evil thing that has entangled me for vice of curiosity.

Kom Loi. Beware!

Wu Hoo Git. I am in the Spider's eyes -- a web of light dances 'twixt his demon seeing-sockets and mine. It is an august new power that holds me fast. I must use my sublime brain, for the spider has not my sublime brain. I possess a celestial thought. I will cut with my sword the eye-chain that binds me to the monster. I cut with my impressive sword. (*Starts back.*) I am free to meet him now -- man to Spider! (SPIDER *throws out silk ribbon rolls from web.*) He spits witch daggers at me, to destroy my love and life. I augustly sever them. I observe I am celestially his unequal match. (SPIDER *throws more silk strands at him, furnished by* PROPERTY MAN. *He cuts them at first. Finally he becomes tied up in many strands and falls.*) I am woven in the web of evil. My sword hacks but cuts not. The web dulls its fiery edge. I am being tied to the earth-rocks! I have a thought. I will call Plum Blossom. I will shake the slipper. (*Shakes slipper.*) Moy Fah Loy, Moy Fah Loy, save me!

Moy Fah Loy. (*Enters door to Heaven, center, above as a disembodied spirit.* KOM LOI *attempts to throw more ribbons, but is stopped by* MOY FAH LOY'S *voice.*) The slipper shook. The earth stood still. The winds blew me here. I command the demon Spider to depart.

Kom Loi. (Makes another attempt to throw ribbons -- stops with arm in mid-air.) My web spins not. My joints crinkle in the light of purity. I seek the dark. *(Exits door right, stepping through web. Music.* PROPERTY MAN *removes frame, gathers up silk strands, takes them off, door right.)*

Wu Hoo Git. (Proudly. Down left.) The strands about me melt in celestial light. The Spider withers before my exalted gaze. I feel in my expanding soul the power to o'ercome all monsters wild. I would that Plum Blossom might see my unaided triumph. She would adore my fiery bravery.

Moy Fah Loy. Moy Fah Loy sees all and knows all. *(Music.)*

Wu Hoo Git. (Crosses to center, listening.) Plum Blossom's rippling voice, yet I behold her not.

Moy Fah Loy. I am the disembodied soul of her you loved so constantly, permitted for a moment only with heavenly vision to behold you.

Wu Hoo Git. (Sees her.) Wherefore do you approach me on the steps of Heaven? Why does a dazzling halo of light gloriously encircle you like dew-drops on a star? What evil one has snatched you from the flower paths of earth, while you were sublimely mine, to place you beyond my human ecstasy? I shall know; and, if it be one of earth, my sword shall avenge our parting; if it be one who has passed beyond, my pursuing spirit shall follow him and knife him with the blasts of anguish. *(Crosses up to right center.)*

Moy Fah Loy. You shook the slipper and I came in your hour of need.

Wu Hoo Git. I shook it that you might behold my hour of august victory. Alone, I vanquished the beast of the fields. (PROPERTY MAN *and assistant bring table on which are two stools to center.* WU HOO GIT *takes one stool, places it right, at table, the other stool remaining on table.)* I will build a mountain that shall kiss high Heaven, and on the top of it I will cone ten thousand peaks till, topping the highest with my dainty foot, you palpitate within my august arms.

Moy Fah Loy. We palpitate not in Heaven.

Wu Hoo Git. Despite the terror of your thoughts, I ascend. *(Climbs on table impulsively.)*

Moy Fah Loy. Ascend not, for all men who strive to build a Heaven ladder and know the secrets of the gods have met with defeat and punishment.

Wu Hoo Git. But my ladder is love-woven and each rung is a love strand upon which the humblest may tiptoe to Heaven.

Moy Fah Loy. But it must be born of love you know not of. My prayers alone must guide you, not myself.

Wu Hoo Git. (*Climbs to top of chair on table, back to audience. Music.*) I would place the kiss of august victory upon your painted lips.

Moy Fah Loy. I have no lips.

Wu Hoo Git. I would take you in my glorious arms that your heart might impress your hero's heart.

Moy Fah Loy. I have no heart.

Wu Hoo Git. But stand you not on venerable legs?

Moy Fah Loy. I stand on thinnest air. I have no legs.

Wu Hoo Git. No legs in Heaven! Then you are false to me and unworthy of my glorious victory.

Moy Fah Loy. I know not arms, nor legs, nor kisses. I left my body at home for my celestial father, Tai Char Shoong, to guard till your return.

Wu Hoo Git. (*Turns on stool facing audience.*) It was an august oversight. You should have brought your impressive body with you. I descend from Heaven. (*Climbs down right of table.*)

Moy Fah Loy. I go and leave you to your august way.

Wu Hoo Git. Stay but a little. Give me some exchange of sweetness, my rose of Heaven. (PROPERTY MAN *takes stool off table and places it left. Music stops.*)

Moy Fah Loy. The small space of time I have to encourage you is spent. I can tarry but a breath time, then breathe myself away.

Wu Hoo Git. Then float guiding on, in your cloud-like boat to inspire my aching heart, and I will follow, till the world is mine and nothing left to conquer.

Moy Fah Loy. I can but leave the promise of fragrance to come, for the petals of my love are not yet full blown to answer you. The zephyr-wagon blows homeward and I must ride with it or lose my way. Farewell!

Wu Hoo Git. Stay! Stay! Love is never lost for heroism is born of it.

Moy Fah Loy. Love is in the heart when far away.

Wu Hoo Git. Love is in the heart, always. When next you

come, forget not to bring your exalted lips.

Moy Fah Loy. I shall augustly remember, for I observe man knows not woman without her lips. I depart for my body.

She exits upper door center. Music. WU HOO GIT *mounts stool right of table, holds out his arms toward* MOY FAH LOY, *then turns to* GIT HOK GAR *who has crossed to upper left-hand corner of table.*

Git Hok Gar. I observe your eyes roll with unfalling tears, your lips are heavy with undelivered kisses of farewell.

Wu Hoo Git. There is no place to remove them. (*Crosses down center.*) Give me back my Moy Fah Loy, even in spirit.

Moy Fah Loy. (*Left center.*) Experience and years only can know spirit love.

Wu Hoo Git. We must climb still higher into the golden way. I would fear to meet more elements, if it were not that I had embraced disembodied Plum Blossom and know that nothing can harm me now. (*Exeunt door right. Assistant property man removes table and stool to left.*)

Wu Fah Din. (*Appears above drapery. Watches them off.*) I surmised not he had a slipper. It is a most dangerous potency to overcome. It upsets my plans frightfully. I must contrive a way to get it. What barks? (*Terror.*) I summoned nothing of this nature. Can it be Wu Hoo Git has sent this monster after me while I was cogitating his destruction? (*To* ATTENDANT *below:*) Ask who it is. Speak to it boldly or I will toss you at it bodily.

Attendant. (*Hesitates.*) Who are you?

Tai Fah Min. (*With a fox head on.*) You may not know me in this guise, but I am a fox spirit, and being a fox, I have changed my form, so fear not. My brain is the brain of Tai Fah Min, the second father-in-law of Wu Sin Yin, and so your grandfather. I come to help you to wreak mischief on Wu Hoo Git. I might have accomplished all of my iniquity but death came along and took me. The gods were kind, however, and on my path to the spirit world I stumbled on a fox body, unused some days by the departed fox, and sublimely climbed into it. So I was released from an abode in the depths to prowl and help you in your mischief on Wu Hoo Git. I shall hinder him of success; if my tail be not cut off in the bloody encounter which must ensue, I shall do him murder. He shall perish and then you rule unmolested. (*He struts upstage.*) I will take on frightful shape. I can swim, I can run. He shall not escape me. I have a reason; I have a tail. (*Exits right.*)

    Wu Fah Din. (*Exultantly.*) I have cause to be proud of my ancestors. I banish trembling fear and all kindness from my heart. The traditions of my family attend upon my wisdom. My grandfather is here to aid me. With such mighty strength, my bloody contention is no longer wit against wit, brawn against brawn; for I meet him with all the venom of my heritage. I have him now.

    Wu Hoo Git. (*Enters with* GIT HOK GAR *left.*) But tell me. When you trod this path in youth did such things impede your way?

    Git Hok Gar. No, I had none to envy me, but you are born to opposition because of the rights you seek. (*Down left. Messenger enters to* DAFFODIL *with red papers up right.*)

    Wu Fah Din. Now for the slipper and his death! My message is from my grandfather, who you know is Tai Fah Min. You will see what a terrible shape he will assume. Prepare your flowery handkerchiefs for the flood of tears which you will shed at the death of Wu Hoo Git.

    Horrible monster tiger enters down right, assisted by PROPERTY MAN, *who lights fuse in nostrils and dusts head, which conceals* TAI FAH MIN. *Its body is supported by an assistant inside.*

    Wu Hoo Git. What monster approaches me -- with lightning orbs, thunder voice, and meandering gait of horror? Bring him nearer that I may pierce his armor with my flashing eyes!

    Git Hok Gar. (*Fearfully crosses Center to tiger.*) It is the tiger-father of all tigers! Its claws dig graves. (*Roar from tiger.*)

    Wu Hoo Git. What language speaks it? I understand it not.

    Git Hok Gar. It is the language of death. (*Urges* WU HOO GIT *back.*) I am old and must perish soon. You are young, so run!

    Wu Hoo Git. Not I. (*Crosses to center.*) I shall augustly sever it to crown my love with victory. (*Tiger roars.*)

    Git Hok Gar. It thunders answer. Flee!

    Wu Hoo Git. Not I. (*Moves down front and around tiger, which crosses to center. Dismembers body with sword. Assistant runs.*) The head runs without legs. I like it not.

    Tai Fah Min. (*Within tiger's head.*) I have you now. Crumble before my bark; shriek at my snap; die at my bite. I am Tai Fah Min.

Wu Hoo Git. Who conspired with my father, Wu Sin Yin, to depart my beloved mother, Chee Moo.

Tai Fah Min. I assault you with my teeth. I would gloriously chew you and honorably digest you, for, while you live, you menace the glorious future of my daughter's child. (*They fight. Cymbals, drums, etc.*)

Wu Hoo Git. I chop your throat. I cut it with fiery blade from ear to ear.

Tai Fah Min. I mind it not.

Git Hok Gar. It is invulnerable. It is a fox.

Wu Hoo Git. I augustly neglected the thought. I will sever its tail. (*Cuts off tail and stamps on it.*)

Tai Fah Min. (*Falls.*) I am undone without my brush. 'Tis murder most unkind.

Wu Hoo Git. (*Proudly.*) Kind or unkind, I contemptuously tread upon it with my sublime foot. (*Music.* PROPERTY MAN *places ladder center.*)

Git Hok Gar. (*Crosses to above fox, lying on floor center in tiger skin.*) Know, unhappy fox spirit, this glorious boy, seeking vengeance for a mother, places you in a clean soul dress at Heaven's threshold in return for your unwonted crimes. You should die in thankfulness. (*Moves left again.*)

Wu Hoo Git. What! I would repent my graciousness.

Git Hok Gar. You can not; you must be noble now. The lantern of his life is flickering.

Tai Fah Min. (*Comes out of head and dress.*) I humbly repent everything for a sight of Heaven. I prayerfully and peacefully die. (PROPERTY MAN *places pillow under his head.*)

Wu Hoo Git. Be augustly leisurely about it then. I do not wish to be impatient.

Wu Fah Din. He trades me and my important office for Heaven. (TAI FAH MIN *dies, crawls out of tiger skin, and afterwards gets up and walks to ladder center.* PROPERTY MAN *stops him and looks at* WU HOO GIT.)

Wu Hoo Git. (*Going up to ladder.*) Stay! You can not yet aspire to the celestial bliss where dwells my mother whose blood is on your hands. Depart below.

Tai Fah Min. (*Crosses to door right. Snarls.*) May Plum

Blossom never sweeten your presence again. (*Exits door right.*)

Wu Hoo Git. (*Moves to door with sword, then turns front.*) Like all dying men he would trade with Heaven.

Git Hok Gar. Philosophy is ever victorious in warfare.

Wu Hoo Git. Not philosophy, love. The body of the tiger which I severed now bars my august path.

Git Hok Gar. I would triumphantly mount over it. (PROPERTY MAN *removes tiger and pillow, folding up pillow.*)

Wu Hoo Git. (*Observing.*) It mounts for itself. It departs before me. (*Grandly.*) I notice such things not. (*Exeunt right.*)

Wu Fah Din. If I triumph I will come out and view him. If I fail I wish not to view my failure. I will part him from his friend. I will freeze him into nothingness. (*Disappears.*)

Chorus. (*Rises.*) 'Tis a snow-storm.

Music. PROPERTY MAN'S *assistants enter doors right and left with white flags rolled with cut paper, which they shake out. They come downstage, cross and exeunt opposite doors from which they enter.* PROPERTY MAN *walks to center with tray of cut paper which he throws into the air, over his shoulders, then crosses to left again.*

Wu Hoo Git. (*Entering left with* GIT HOK GAR, *crosses to right center.*) What is this blast which confronts us? What is this that freezes up the warmth of your kindness?

Git Hok Gar. It is my welcome shroud for which I long have waited. You have grown so fat in wisdom you need me not. Bow me a farewell. I am approaching my robe of wood. Take my august covering to warm your worth. I need it not on my journey. (*Having taken off coat, offers it to* WU HOO GIT.)

Wu Hoo Git. Nay, you must. (*Pushing away coat.*)

Git Hok Gar. I need it not. Put goodness in yourself, to shut out cold. The mountain's peak of life is now in view for you. From its bleak nose you can see the riches of the world and your path beyond. If the wisdom you have purchased on your journey abides with you, it will be as gloriously fanciful as a summer's sea.

Wu Hoo Git. (*Putting coat around shoulders of* GIT HOK GAR.) Is it decreed that I must mount alone?

Git Hok Gar. Every man must look into the garden of his soul alone. My journey is done. My life is spent. Yours is only begun. I die. (*Falls to stage.* PROPERTY MAN *puts pillow under his head, kneeling above him; spreads white cloth over him, then pulls out his beard, spreading it on white sheet. Music.*)

Wu Hoo Git. Die not so easily! Snow crowns your gray hair with the peace of death. I am blinded, too, in white crystals that sparkle upon me. (*Covers his face with his hands.* GIT HOK GAR *throws off white sheet. Rises, goes up center, turns -- looks at* WU HOO GIT, *smiling and with gesture of blessing. Climbs ladder to Heaven. Center opening above. Leaves his coat in snow, where he died.*)

Chorus. He ascends to Heaven!

Wu Hoo Git. (*Places hands over coat of* GIT HOK GAR.) I put the warmth of my youthful hands upon you to give you life. You are dead and gone from me.

Git Hok Gar. (*Above.*) I live above the coldness of the world. (*Exits off right. Music stops.*)

Wu Hoo Git. (*Holding white sheet over* GIT HOK GAR'S *coat on floor.*) I build an icy tablet to his memory. I sink, I freeze. (*Falls to stage.*) I would shake the slipper, but it is a block of august ice. Moy Fah Loy! Plum Blossom! You, too, desert me in my hour of death. (PROPERTY MAN *crosses with tray of snow in one hand. Places pillow under his head. Puts tray of snow on ladder center.*) I augustly pronounce myself passed to my ancestors. (PROPERTY MAN *covers him with white sheet. Dumps tray of cut paper on sheet and crosses to left and sits.*)

Chee Moo. (*Enters above as spirit from right.*) I am Chee Moo, your honorable mother, who wrote your story in my blood. May the sweetness of my Heaven-prayer bring warmth into your world-body.

Nung Fu. (*Enters door left with hoe.*) Here is a man snow-bound and chill. I dig him out with my farm hoe.

Wu Hoo Git. Moy Fah Loy? My words are frozen. She hears me not.

Nung Fu. He must be august to have climbed so high. An icicle kiss melts upon his lips. He is thinking of some one. Then there still is life.

Wu Hoo Git. Lead me to the mountain top one august step above that I may see the world of love and my inner self.

Chow Wan. (*Above, not seen.*) It is yours, my child, my Wu Hoo Git!

Wu Hoo Git. What voice was that?

Nung Fu. I heard naught.

Wu Hoo Git. I dream in iciness. Lead on, for it is not in grandeur that we learn to know, but guided by the simplicity of nature's guardian of the soil we see with child eyes again all the loveliness of the world from the mountain peak of progress. How bright and glorious the sun shines! Its imperial golden liquid light dazzles my eyes. The sky becomes one huge brass bowl save for that one little gray cloud out yonder. (*Pointing above audience front.*)

Nung Fu. (*Screening eyes with hands.*) I see no cloud there, but here the sky has a gray cloud -- my mother's soul cloud.

Wu Hoo Git. Then the one I see is my mother soul cloud. So with every golden shower of happiness there is a touch of grey -- for one must pause in happiness to shed a tear for a mother heavenward passed. (*Sitting up.*) The jacket burns into my soul and conquers the freezing chill. Courage enwraps me. I shake off the numbing iciness that congealed my veins. Am I deceived again or are my eyes at last open to the circling vision of realities which were only dreams? (*Rises, goes to door right.*) I'll toss my naked self against the palace gates. (*Exeunt.* CHEE MOO *exits above. Music.*)

Wu Fah Din. You have heard his almost indelicate threat. I'll retire to the inner chamber of my palace and gracefully lock myself in. I will swing tighter the gate bars, wall myself about and send a crippling force against him. (*Descends from throne. Comes from behind drapery. Stands in doorway right.*) I will await him where my walls are strongest and from their top I will pelt his ambitious head with tiles.

Music. Assistant property man removes ladder, placing it up left. Assistants move the drapery on standards right and place it across stage at back up center showing reverse side. An assistant then gets table and stool from left. Another gets table and chair from right. They place the tables center near drapery, one below the other with the chair on the upstage table and stool on floor below the downstage table. Assistant exits right. Another assistant exits left. PROPERTY MAN *brings red cushion and places it on chair on table center and also places the Yellow Jacket folded in green handkerchief on right-hand corner of lower table. He goes to right of drapery and motions for* CHORUS *to come out.*

Chorus. (*Coming out from behind drapery, goes to right center. Music.*) It is the throne-room of the palace of Wu Sin Yin, the Great, from which our hero has been deprived so long. (*Retires behind drapery center. Music forte.*)

Wu Fah Din. (*Enters left. Comes down center. Ascends throne.* PROPERTY MAN *assists him. Cymbals.* PROPERTY MAN *crosses to left, then places stool up left center and sits on it, back to audience. Music stops.*) I am deserted by all, but my self-importance still remains. I feel an august valor born of my inability to get away, for I am not yet undone. Deserted as I am, I can not be vanquished. He may break down my door bolts. He may trample my flower-beds, but when he meets me face to face upon my throne, he will tremble before the encircling power that crowns me with the wealth of ages and my family's vanquishment. (*Music for* WU HOO GIT'S *entrance. As* WU HOO GIT *enters,* PROPERTY MAN *rises facing left and holds stool in his hands.*)

Wu Hoo Git. (*Enters door left with sword. Beats upon the stool held by* PROPERTY MAN *four times with his sword. Cymbal crash for each stroke.* PROPERTY MAN *drops stool, then* WU HOO GIT *enters imaginary gate.*) Where is the throne I seek by right? Who sits upon it?

Wu Fah Din. (*Looking down at him contemptuously.*) If courage stands high in you, I, too, have some in my veins, for the blood of the same father enriches us both.

Wu Hoo Git. (*Brandishing sword.*) Usurper! Think you to stop my way, when I have met the battling heavens? When I have conquered the peaks and held their snow-crowns until they melted before the warmth of my hand? (*Places one foot on stool center.*) Descend, bow deeply and trade your place for mine.

Wu Fah Din. (*Seated on throne chair.*) If you will trade in gentleness, I will surrender gently. A throne is most uncomfortable. (*Rises. Descends throne to center.*)

Wu Hoo Git. The sun-hued garment! I demand it!

Wu Fah Din. (*Goes to right of table. Pushes Yellow Jacket in handkerchief across table toward* WU HOO GIT.) I extend to you the badge of office. I have always disliked the color, it is so cold. (WU FAH DIN *crosses to right center.* WU HOO GIT *takes off his own jacket and hands it to* PROPERTY MAN *who puts it in box left.* WU HOO GIT *then takes Yellow Jacket out of handkerchief.*

PROPERTY MAN *assists him to put it on.*

Wu Hoo Git. Bump your head to me. (DAFFODIL *kneels right center.*)

Wu Fah Din. My head! I am glad I have a head to bump. (*Bumps head twice. Wood block.*) May I still retain it?

Wu Hoo Git. My first act in assuming my power shall be one of mercy. Choose your prison.

Wu Fah Din. (*Looking up.*) A garden! A garden filled with smiling flowers. (WU HOO GIT *makes a gesture of assent.*) Then I retire to its fragrance. (*Backs upstage. Exits right.*)

Wu Hoo Git. (*Crosses to center, back to audience.*) Victorious at last! I ascend the throne of my ancestors. (*Music. He mounts throne. Turns front standing.*) I shake the slipper for my Plum Blossom. (*Shakes slipper. Cymbals crash. General entrance.*) My Plum Blossom! (*Music changes. Play piano.*)

Moy Fah Loy. (*Crossing to him center on one foot.*) I guided them to you.

Wu Hoo Git. Have you brought your impressive body with you?

Moy Fah Loy. Yes.

Wu Hoo Git. Ascend my throne. (*She ascends. Sits on chair.*) Your slipper shall be my scepter. (*Puts it on her foot, standing right of table center.*)

Moy Fah Loy. My love!

Wu Hoo Git. My Plum Blossom! (*All kneel and bow low.*)

Chee Moo. (*In upper opening center.*) The world and wisdom are his. (*Music.*)

Tableau curtain.

CHORUS *comes out before tableau curtains.*

Chorus. And now, most august and honorable neighbors, you may bestow your kindly recognition upon my brothers as I nominate them each in turn and they will personally augustly thank you.

Tableau curtains are drawn. Company lines up across stage. CHORUS *now points out each member of the company in turn, beginning with* CHEE MOO, *then* WU HOO GIT, MOY FAH LOY, *etc., indicating character first one side of the stage then the other,* PROPERTY MAN *last.*

Chorus. Chee Moo, the mother!

My hero! (*Indicating* WU HOO GIT.)

My little heroine! (*Indicating* MOY FAH LOY.)

The philosopher! (*Indicating* GIT HOK GAR.)

The nurse! (*Indicating* SEE NOI.)

The temptress of the flower boat! (*Indicating* CHOW WAN.)

The purveyor of hearts! (*Indicating* YIN SUEY GONG.)

The daffodil! (*Indicating* WU FAH DIN.)

The farmer and his wife! (*Indicating* LEE SIN *and* SUEY SIN FAH.)

The Widow! (*Indicating her.*)

Tai Char Shoong! (*Indicating him.*)

The second wife! (*Indicating* DUE JUNG FAH.)

A siren! (*Indicating* SEE QUOE FAH.)

And yet another siren! (*Indicating* YONG SOO KOW.)

And now quite visible to your eyes, our property man. (PROPERTY MAN *who has been seated on box left, smoking, rises, crosses to* CHORUS *center, shakes hands in the Chinese manner, bows to audience, crosses to right.*)

Curtain.

1915 -- Paul Carus -- *K'ung Fu Tze*

The decades just before and after the turn of the century were a confusing period spiritually. Many Euroamericans who in an earlier generation would have accepted Christianity uncritically now found it unsatisfactory. As a result, they began to turn to the genuine religions of the East and to Western imitations such as Theosophy.

Although nearly completely forgotten today, Paul Carus was an important popularizer of Eastern religion and philosophy during this time. He did not formally follow any religion, but found much to admire in Buddhism. When he chose to write a play, however, he selected not Buddha but Confucius as his protagonist. The publishing company which he founded (the Open Court Press, still in existence today) provided a ready outlet for his thoughts and works.

Unlike most previous writers, Carus showed his respect for the Chinese by doing thorough research into Confucius' life and circumstances. He used the actual names and characteristics of his disciples, included extracts translated from the Chinese classics, and did not tamper with the general outline of Confucius' biography. However, he tended not to be properly critical of his sources. For example, he presents the meeting of Confucius and his rival Lao Tze; this story was almost certainly invented by a later disciple of Lao Tze for the express purpose of discrediting Confucius.

Despite (or because of) Carus' appreciation of the Chinese, their image in this play conforms more to Western expectations than to reality, in no small part due to the form of the piece. Carus subtitled his work a "dramatic poem," and quite clearly, the poetic elements dominate the dramatic. All the characters are extremely courteous and refined, overly so by Western standards. Even those who transgress against the rigid and repressive rules of their society acknowledge their wrong-doing. As previous plays had misrepresented the Chinese by insulting them, K'ung Fu Tze misrepresents them by idealizing them.

K'ung Fu Tze

CAST OF CHARACTERS

K'UNG FU TZE (*Confucius*)

LADY CH'IEN KWAN, *Wife of Confucius*

NIECE OF CONFUCIUS

TZE KUNG, *the faithful disciple*

MANG-I, *a prince of aristocratic appearance*

TZE LU, *the courageous*

MIN SUN, *orator and diplomat*

YEN HUI, *"Continuator of the Sage," the favorite disciple, much younger than the others*

K'UNG LI, *the son of Confucius*

K'UNG CHI, *the grandson of Confucius, a boy of twelve years, later on famous as the author of* The Doctrine of the Mean

TZE KAO, *a hunchback, of unusual brightness*

LAO TZE, *the old philosopher opposed to Confucius*

LAO TZE'S ATTENDANT, *a boy or half-grown youth*

DUKE TING, *of the state of Lu*

A NATIVE OF LO, *the capital of the state Chow*

AN OLD MAN, *displeased with his son*

A YOUNG MAN, *sued by his father*

LIU PANG, *Emperor Kao Ti, founder of the Han Dynasty and institutor of Confucian worship; ascended the throne B.C. 202. Appears in* TZE KUNG'S *vision*

Bridesmaids, groomsmen, musicians, and singing damsels

ACT I.
Scene 1.

The Reception Room of Confucius in the year 518 B.C. In the background an entrance wide enough to show two persons outside. The door opens and two men, TZE KUNG *and* MANG-I, *are seen outside bowing to each other.*

Tze Kung.
　　Please enter, sir!
Mang-I.　　　　　I shall not be so rude
　　As to take precedence before my betters.
Tze Kung.
　　I am a simple man and your inferior;
　　E'en your deportment proves your higher rank.
　　Apparently you are of noble birth.
　　'Tis not your dress alone; I see quite plainly
　　You are accustomed to court etiquette,
　　While I am but a modest commoner.
Mang-I.
　　Pray do not estimate my birth too high.
　　You are a gentleman of great distinction,
　　Of polished manners and accomplishments.
Tze Kung.
　　You are too kind in over-estimating
　　My worth. O, pray shame not your humble servant
　　By greater courtesy. Please enter first!
Mang-I.
　　Let us step o'er the threshold both at once.
Tze Kung.
　　That would behoove me not. So please walk in,
　　And I will follow you. You are too kind.
Mang-I.
　　With your permission I will enter, then.
Tze Kung.
　　Pray do so, sir.
(MANG-I *enters and* TZE KUNG *follows.*)
　　　　　　　　And I will call the Master;
　　But kindly tell me sir, what kind of business,

Brings you to him. You are --------?
Mang-I.

                                    I am Ho Chi,
Son of his Excellency, the late Mang Hsi,
State Minister of Lu, and commonly
Am called Mang-I.
Tze Kung.

(*Bows low.*) Mang-I! I'm greatly honored!
I'm Twan Mu Tze and am addressed Tze Kung.
I come from Wei and I take pride in being
A pupil of the Master, K'ung Fu Tze.
I know your honorable father died
But a few weeks ago, and all the people
Sincerely mourn his premature demise.
He was a truly good and honest man,
Rare in this troubled and degenerate age.
Mang-I.

(*Bows.*) My father simply tried to do his duty;
'Tis all that he accomplished since Duke Chao
Appointed him his Minister of State.
He knew, he said, that he was unprepared
For his high duties. When he came to die
He charged me to do better and to learn.
"There is K'ung Ch'iu," he said, "a master sage
Who's commonly addressed as K'ung Fu Tze.
He dwelleth in this state of Lu, and he
Knows more about our ancient institutions,
About propriety and right and wrong,
Than any living mortal, near or far.
Go thou," my father said, "and learn from him."
Tze Kung.

Blest be the memory of your dear father,
For truly he was right in what he thought
Of Master K'ung. Indeed K'ung is a sage.
Some time ago I heard his knowledge praised
And went to him ambitious, proud and eager
To join at once our learned noble Master.
Mang-I.

How do you rank our K'ung Fu Tze as sage?

Tze Kung.

    I do not know, nor can I well describe it.
    I've had the heavens all through my life o'er head,
    But do not know their height. I've had the earth
    Beneath my feet, but do not know its depth.
    I serve the Master, learn from him; his wisdom
    Is infinite and inexhaustible!
    I'm like a thirsty man who, with a pitcher,
    Goes to the river's brink. I draw the water
    And drink my fill -- pure water -- yet know not
    The river's depth and breadth and its supply.

Mang-I.

    I envy thee, Tze Kung! I fain would follow
    This same good, noble Master, K'ung Fu Tze!

Tze Kung.

    And thee I welcome as a worthy comrade!
    Thou art descended from a noble race,
    And kin thou art to my own ducal house.

Mang-I.

    Thou speakest truly, friend; my family
    Is old and powerful, but princely birth
    Does not confer a merit to be proud of.
    It is the merit of mine ancestors;
    Not of mine own, and I must live to earn it.
    I only shall deserve my noble birth,
    If I in thoughts and words and deeds prove noble,
    If I excel in wisdom, truth and faith,
    And if my soul be worthy of my rank.

Tze Kung.

    Such is the man I love! Such is my Master;
    For you may know perchance that K'ung Fu Tze
    Traces descent from the imperial house
    Of Yin. His ancestor was Fu Fu Ho,
    Best by his title known as the Duke Li,
    The elder brother of Fang Sze; and Fu
    Resigned the throne in favor of Fang Sze.

Mang-I.

    I heard of it before but was not certain.

Tze Kung.

> Oh, if I were of noble family
> Like unto K'ung or, sir, like unto you,
> I would with all my power aspire to grow
> Worthy the honor thus inherited.

Mang-I.

> You are my friend, and, verily, he whom
> His deeds have knighted is alone a knight.
> Those who by noble birth are noble, are
> But promises; they never shall be noble
> Until they have redeemed their obligations.

(*Enter* CHENG YU *and* MIN SUN, *both bowing to* MANG-I.
TZE KUNG *addresses the latter with dignity, by way of introduction.*)

Tze Kung.

> Ho Chi, son of His Honor, the late Mang Hsi,
> And styled Mang-I, here are the two disciples
> Of our great master K'ung, whom I regard
> As being most distinguished in our ranks.
> You will be pleased to meet them, and the more
> You know them both, the better you will like them.
> Here is Min Sun, a dear good fellow student;
> He is addressed Tze Ch'ien. And here's Chung Yu,
> Known as Tze Lu and also called Chi-Lu.

Mang-I. (*Addressing* MIN SUN, *standing nearest.*)

> Were you attracted by the Master's fame,
> And did you come to profit by his wisdom?

Min Sun.

> An awkward country lad I hither came.

Tze Kung.

> But see, Mang-I, what K'ung Tze made of him.
> He is an orator, a diplomat,
> A man who has command of choicest speech;
> Endowed he is with talent for persuasion.
> Oh, it is wonderful how much he's changed!

Min Sun.

> Indeed it is, and all is K'ung Tze's work.

Tze Kung.

> Excuse me, sir, I'll go and call the Master.
> I'll tell him of your presence and describe

The merits of his noble visitor.
Mang-I.

    Pray, friend Tze Kung, do not exaggerate
    The small accomplishments which I possess.
   (*Exit* TZE KUNG, *bowing to* MANG-I. *To* MIN:)
    Your home is in the rural districts, sir?
Min Sun.

    I came here from the midst of reeds and sedges
    And joined the school of our revered great Master;
    He trained my mind to filial piety,
    Taught me the examples of the ancient kings --
    And how I loved to be instructed! How
    I loved to learn the wisdom of our sages!
    But then another picture lured me on;
    I saw the people in authority,
    With all their pomp, their banners and umbrellas,
    In gorgeous dress, surrounded by retainers.
    I liked these shows, and yet I felt distressed,
    Because the spectacles did not agree
    With all that I had learned of justice, virtue
    And of propriety. The Master's lessons,
    However, have sunk deeply in my heart,
    And the examples of my fellow students
    Have also set my mind at rest.
    I see the emptiness of all the pomp,
    And I regard it now no more than dust.
    I value virtue now, virtue alone.
    This solves for me all problems, and my mind
    At last has found completest satisfaction.
Mang-I.

    I know you follow the right master, sir.
    The master that impressed you certainly
    A paragon of wisdom is and virtue.
    And what is your experience, Tze Lu?
     (*Turning to* TZE LU.)
Tze Lu.

    I sought the Master's good advice, and asked,
    "What can you do for me? And how may I
    Profit by you, your wisdom and your learning?"

Quoth he: "What love you best?" and I replied
"I love my sword, my sharp and shining sword."
"Well," said the sage, "your stature and deportment
Bode courage. If you add a higher training
To your activities, you can become
Superior, and a man of sterling worth."
That has from boyhood e'er been my ambition.
Thought I, superior men are born, not raised;
And so I ventured to object; "There grow
Some bamboo stalks here on the southern slope,
So straight that culture could not make them straighter;
Their fibers are so strong they pierce the hide
Of a rhinoceros." And he, the Master,
Replied with calm composure: "It is true,
Superior men are born, yet even they
Need training. Aye! Your well-grown bamboo stalk
Can do far greater things if it be armed
With iron point and winged with feathers. Yea,
The arrow-maker chooses stalks both strong
And straight to make good arrows. So the sage
Needeth disciples of good character."
That day I joined our learned, noble Master
And am convinced that I have found the man,
The only man who leadeth the right way.

Mang-I.

You are the man for me; let us be friends!

(*The door opens. Enter* K'UNG FU TZE *with* TZE KUNG.)

Tze Kung.

This is Mang-I, son of His Excellency,
The late Prime Minister of State.

K'ung Fu Tze.   Be seated,
My noble sir, be seated. Let me hear
What I can do for you.

Mang-I.

                              My father, sir,
In due appreciation of your wisdom,
Charged me in his last will and testament
To ask you for advice and kindly guidance,
And bade me learn from you the principles

Of government, the standard and the rules
Both of good conduct and propriety.
But above all, I need a thorough knowledge
Of ancient ceremonies and of rites
Sorely neglected in our present day.

K'ung Fu Tze.

I shall do all I can for you, dear sir,
The principles are easy -- application,
The details and the practice difficult.

Mang-I.

I humbly beg your pardon, honored sir;
I am no scholar, nor a sage like you.
I find the practice frequently quite easy.
I know how to conduct and bear myself;
It seems to come to me like second nature.
The principle alone 'tis puzzles me.

K'ung Fu Tze.

Nature has made this world relational.
There are two opposites, the Yang and Yin,
Which show themselves in their peculiar mixtures
Throughout creation: be it as sun and moon,
As earth and heaven, as female and a male,
As light and darkness, or as day and night,
As positive and negative; and man,
You know it well, is mixed of earth and heaven.
All is relational in human life,
And there are five relations all ordained
In laws of nature between Yang and Yin.
Yang is the strong and lordly part, the mover;
Yin, being womanly and meek, endureth.
There's the relation between prince and subject,
Between a father and his son; and thirdly,
Between the elder and the younger brother;
Fourthly, between the husband and his wife;
And fifth and lastly, between a friend and friend.

Mang-I.

Blest be this lucky day on which I met you;
But pray, dear Master, how must I proceed
To profit, to advance, to learn from you?

K'ung Fu Tze.

> I see that you are vigorous and manly,
> Your gait and stature bode both strength and courage.

Tze Lu.

> Sir, he reminds me of our former talk,
> He's like the bamboo on the southern hill
> Which grows up straight and has no nick or bent,
> So straight that culture could not make it straighter.

K'ung Fu Tze.

> But culture can improve on nature's work.

Mang-I.

> Your words indeed are true, and I will learn
> The lessons that you teach. You'll find me ready
> To accept instruction with due reverence.
> Before I leave, sir, may I be permitted
> To ask a special favor?

K'ung Fu Tze.

>   Speak, and I
> Will do whatever lies within my power.

Mang-I.

> The ancient capital of our great empire
> Is many-peopled Lo. The customs there
> And rites are still observed in purest form.
> The ruler, being of the house of Chow,
> Is emperor at least in name, and there
> The archives are; there is the library
> Which holds the choicest lore of former ages,
> The temple services are there retained
> Now as in olden times, and there at court
> The ceremonies are most dignified.
> Would you, great Master, undertake a journey
> To Lo, the seat of deepest thought and learning,
> And introduce me to its wondrous treasures?

K'ung Fu Tze.

> I will, dear sir; and thou shalt be to me
> As mine own son, to whom I shall bequeath
> The deepest words of wisdom I have found.

Mang-I.

> Our gracious overlord, the Duke of Lu,

Is well acquainted with my father's wish;
He has approved of it, and biddeth me
To send his royal greetings to your Honor.
He says that he will speed the voyage by
Equipping you with carriage and good horses.
He'll give you letters to His Majesty
The Emperor; which will prepare for you
A dignified reception, and will open
To you the temples and the archives.

K'ung Fu Tze.

                           Welcome,
Most welcome, is this offer, friend Mang-I,
And most auspicious shall this journey prove.
In Lo there lives Li Erh, a famous sage
Called Lao Kuen, also Lao Tan
Or Lao Tze, the old philosopher,
The venerable keeper of the archives.
He sees the urgent need of a reform
And he will help us in our enterprise.
He'll smooth our paths, and his authority
Will be of greatest service to our cause.

Scene 2.

Courtyard in the House of K'UNG FU TZE. *From the door on the right, the* NIECE *of* K'UNG FU TZE *peeps out, looking expectantly toward the door in the center. She withdraws quickly. The door in the center opens and* TZE LU *leads out* MANG-I. *The two walk out toward the right when the lady comes out and passes them.* MANG-I, *stepping aside to make room for her, bows low and reverently; she acknowledges the salutation by a slight but dignified motion of her head and disappears in the house.*

Mang-I.
    Pray tell me, my friend Lu, who is this lady?
Tze Lu.
    She is the niece of our great Master, K'ung.
Mang-I.
    I might have thought she is some kin to him --

So stately and superior, a true lady.
Forsooth, it can be seen that K'ung Fu Tze
A scion is of an imperial line;
Whatever is connected with the sage
Beareth the stamp of royalty.

Tze Lu.

                       You know
He has descended from the house of Yin
That held the empire for six centuries
And more, until Chow Sin, the unworthy tyrant
The last one of his race upon the throne,
Was vanquished by Wu Wang, the war king, Fa,
The founder of the present dynasty,
The house of Chow which now the empire holds.

Mang-I.

This house rules but in name. It has no power,
For every prince does as it pleases him.
The barons are no better; nor are they
In turn submissive to the dukes, their princes,
And the result is chaos -- needing reform.

Tze Lu.

Yea, from the chaos suffers all the world.
Our wise and able Master tries reform,
And a reform he surely will achieve.

Scene 3.

The Women's Apartment in the house of K'UNG FU TZE.
LADY CH'IEN KWAN, *the wife of* K'UNG FU TZE, *and his* NIECE
are seen engaged in sewing.

Niece. Auntie, Auntie Ch'ien, is it wrong to look at a man?

Lady Ch'ien. What do you mean, dearie? You didn't look at a
man, did you? (*Looking at the girl with a serious expression of
reproof.* NIECE *nods with a roguish smile of admission.*) And who
was it?

Niece. I don't know. He was a stranger. He must have been
visiting uncle. Oh, he was a man! A real man.

Lady Ch'ien. You met him? (NIECE *nods again.*) I hope it was by accident?

Niece. Certainly, it was the sheerest accident. He came through the gate when I looked up from my embroidery and gazed through the window. He couldn't see me. He was hardly like a man.

Lady Ch'ien. You called him just now a real man.

Niece. Oh, yes, a real man. He is manly but he looked more than a man.

Lady Ch'ien. Like a gentleman?

Niece. Oh, much more! There was something superior about him. (*Musing.*) You know, auntie, if I were a sculptor I would carve Kwang Ti, the great God, the war lord, like him. I wonder who he was. Really auntie, I am not curious, but perhaps you could ask uncle who his visitor was?

Lady Ch'ien. What an improper suggestion! Uncle would be indignant to learn of your inquisitiveness.

Niece. Would he? Oh, I don't mean anything improper, I only wished to know something about him. You see, he might inquire about me.

Lady Ch'ien. How could he, child? He didn't see you.

Niece. Oh, yes he did. (*After a pause.*) You see, while I looked out of the window, Tze Lu met him. The two walked together and went to the house to uncle. I watched the door because -- well, because I wondered -- because he stayed so long.

Lady Ch'ien. My child, I am alarmed. I have never noticed in your behavior a lack of propriety, and I must say that this is -- to say the least -- not becoming in a girl of good family. How can you take any interest in a strange man?

Niece. I took no interest in the stranger. I was only interested in uncle, and wondered what the stranger had to say to him and what uncle might think of the stranger. Can't I be interested in uncle?

Lady Ch'ien. Oh, certainly, in uncle, but you say the stranger saw you. How did that happen?

Niece. Well, auntie, that was another accident. You see, I needed some more silk skeins. I have enough red and pink silk, but I need orange. The stranger wore a scarf of deep orange and I wanted a skein of that color, and it must be exactly that color, for no other will do. So I went to call the nurse to send her to the merchant, but she had to see the scarf. I called the nurse and couldn't find her; and then I went out into the courtyard, thinking that I would find the girl over there in the kitchen. I was a little afraid that the stranger would cross the yard and so I waited a little and watched the door. Well, I don't say exactly that I was afraid of meeting the stranger but I tried to avoid him; but just when I crossed the courtyard the door opened and he saw me. That is why I wanted to ask you if it is wrong to look at a man. I was in an awful position. You can't realize, auntie, how awful it was.

Lady Ch'ien. You poor child, you should not have ventured into the yard.

Niece. Now you see; he looked at me and stood still only for a moment, gazing at me as if in a dream, then he bowed low and passed out of the gate.

Lady Ch'ien. I hope you didn't look at him?

Niece. Oh, no, I only took a quick peep at him, but he looked at me.

Lady Ch'ien. You should not have raised your eyes even for a second.

Niece. How could I help it? He was so courteous and so respectful -- and he was so manly! You should have seen him. I had scarcely time to note the color of his scarf. That scarf was fine, and only for the sake of the scarf I should like to know who he was.

Lady Ch'ien. My dear child, I must reprove you for your behavior; and I expect of you most decidedly that such scenes shall not occur again.

Niece. But, auntie, it was all an accident. I couldn't help it.

Lady Ch'ien. My dear, that is all very well, but I have the impression that you stand in need of advice. You are no longer a child. The time has come when you must be watchful and guarded in your conduct. Let virtue and honor be always your first consideration. Avoid even the mere semblance of impropriety. Even the thought of a man must never rise in your mind. You have made a series of mistakes. First, you should not have looked up from your embroidery; second, you should not have looked out of the window; third, if a man entered the gate you should not have beheld him at all. Then you should not have thought of him as being a man. Oh, and how dreadful it was to go out where you could meet him!

Niece. But, auntie, he didn't look dangerous. I am sure he is a gentleman and he looked like a prince. He must have been a nobleman. His dress, his gait, his carriage were distinguished and he was as beautiful as a young god. I loved the very sight of him. Oh, auntie, I wish you had seen him, you would have liked him, too. I'm sure there is no one in all the Middle Kingdom so manly and so lordlike as this mysterious stranger.

Lady Ch'ien. Child, my wayward child! What is the matter with you? You speak as if you were in love. Calm yourself. You are infatuated with a vision.

Niece. In love? Is that possible?

Lady Ch'ien. Forget the stranger and learn the rules of modesty and propriety. A young girl like you must not allow her heart to be carried away. You are young and inexperienced, and do not know the dangers of the world.

Niece. Teach me, auntie, I will be glad to learn.

Lady Ch'ien. Look here, my good niece, this is the picture of your grandmother. She was Lady K'ung, the mother of your uncle K'ung Fu Tze, and she indeed was worthy to become the mother of a great sage. Grandfather K'ung was a mighty man and a general of renown. He had been married to a lady who bore him nine daughters and no son. How he longed for an heir who could perform the proper ritual sacrifices at his tomb! So he went to his friend, the honorable Yen, a man of distinction, and asked him for one of his daughters in marriage. The Honorable Mr. Yen addressed his three daughters and said: "Is there one of you who will marry General K'ung? He has been a courageous soldier and stood the brunt of many a fight in the service of the Duke of Lu. In his best years he was strong and tall. He still stands over ten shoes in height, but he has grown old and counts now eighty years." Mr. Yen then asked his oldest daughter, "Would you take him for a husband?" But she cherished in her heart the image of another man who was fair to look upon, and said: "I feel myself honored by General K'ung's proposal but I prefer to have my own choice." The second daughter answered: "If I marry General K'ung I shall have to be a nurse all my wedded life. Instead of having a husband I should have a patient on my hands. Pray let the general take some one else for wife, someone who would like to become a young widow." When Mr. Chen turned to his youngest daughter, she replied, "Father, do with me as thou thinkest best. I will be thy obedient child." And the father rejoiced, saying: "Thou art a fit bride for the general. Mayst thou bear him a son worthy of the noble K'ung family." Her son is K'ung Tze! A woman must be humble and submissive, and especially before her marriage she should be demure and modest.

Niece. That is very good. And really I will be modest and humble; I admire all the virtues, but I care little for obedience. I will be obedient and marry anybody whom you or uncle wish, provided it is the man I love, and I want to look up to my husband as my lord. But he must be lordlike and of course *(In a peevish tone.)* he must treat me as his lady. You do not mean a wife to be the slave of her husband? If the rules of propriety mean complete submission to some old shaky invalid, I would rather not marry at all.

Lady Ch'ien. What do you say, my child? You speak not as it behooves the granddaughter of the noble General K'ung. I must reprimand you most severely.

Niece. Oh, dearest aunt, do not blame me. Consider yourself and the sad fate of all women. We are not allowed to be ourselves. We have no choice. Our lot is to be obedient. First, we must obey our parents, then our husbands. We have no rights ourselves, and happy is our lot if our husbands are half-way worthy of our attention and accept our services with kindly recognition. You know, auntie, what I wish? I want a husband whom I love, and he must love me -- or I would not care for him.

Lady Ch'ien. You wayward child. You do not know enough of life, and you dream too much. I fear there are sad disappointments in store for you.

Niece. Then let me have my dreams as long as cruel reality has not yet destroyed them. *(Enter* K'UNG FU TZE. LADY CH'IEN *kneels down; so does his* NIECE, *the latter with some hesitation.)*

Lady Ch'ien. My husband and my lord!
K'ung Fu Tze.

                              Rise, my good wife.
Rise to your feet and hear the important news!
In company with Lu, Kung, and Mang-I,
The son of the late Minister of State,
I go to visit Lo, the ancient city
And whilom capital of our great country,
The venerable center of our culture,
Where lives the greatest of philosophers,
The noble, venerable Lao Tan.
And there I shall imbibe at its first source
Hoary traditions of our history
And knowledge of the great men of the past.

All shall be utilized for a reform
Of this decadent nation, and the future
Will be as bright and glorious as great Yu
And Shao and Wu Wang could ever make it.
I will revive the virtue of the ancients
And I shall be the leader in reform!
My star is rising, nevermore to set.

Curtain.

ACT II.
Scene 1.

The Hall of Light in the City of Lo, in the year 518 B.C. The imperial throne-room of the house of Chow decorated in a gorgeous old Chinese style. Behind the elevated throne a picture of the Duke of Chow with his infant nephew. Enter K'UNG FU TZE *with his disciples.*

Mang-I.
    This is a place which I have longed to see.
    How beautiful it is and full of relics,
    Of sacred symbols, ancient art and pictures.
K'ung Fu Tze.
    It is the Hall of Light, the venerable
    Old throne-room of the imperial house of Chow.
    Here is a lesson. We cannot understand
    The present age unless we know the past!
    The last one of the house of Yin, Chow Sin,
    Is known as tyrant and his crimes are many.
    We owe our father love and reverence,
    We owe allegiance to our sovereign, but
    Such rights imply great duties, and if duties
    Are heedlessly neglected, Heaven will punish
    The trespassers! So Heaven dealt with Yin.
    A sovereign's, as a father's, rights depend
    Upon his goodness; if he lacks true goodness,
    He surely forfeits his authority.
    Si Peh, named Ch'ang, Chief of the West, Wen Wang,

Had suffered much abuse, was cast in prison
By Sin, the tyrant, and in tribulation
Found comfort only in the Book of Yih,
The sacred permutations which divined
For him a glorious triumph of his cause,
And truly, he regained his liberty.
Then after him, his valiant son Wu Wang,
With the assistance of some other princes,
O'erthrew the debauched tyrant in pitched battle.
And thereupon the tyrant lost his realm.
Wu Wang ascended the imperial throne
As founder of the dynasty of Chow.
See here above the royal seat portrayed
The Duke of Chow, a brother of Wu Wang,
Holding aloft the infant emperor,
Named Ch'ang, the heir apparent to the realm.
Wu Wang had died and left a minor son,
Ward of his faithful brother, Duke of Chow.
The Duke might easily have set himself
Upon his much-lamented brother's throne,
But he would not deprive his orphaned nephew
Of his inheritance. He kept the trust,
And here you see this noble, honest man!
The vassals of the empire swear allegiance
To their child emperor whose rights he shielded.
See here the secret basis of Chow's greatness!
Justice alone can make an empire strong;
When justice lacks, decay is not far off.

Mang-I.

Sir, wonderful is this, and history
Is full of lessons! You expound them well.
And from the past we learn the principles
By which the future should be guided.

K'ung Fu Tze.

                                        Friends,

Our culture is much older than the Yin.
Here are the first five rulers of our realm;
Here is Fu Hi, the oldest of them all
Who lived more than two thousand years ago

In ages of remote antiquity.
Here are his diagrams, eight combinations
Of whole and broken lines, of Yang and Yin,
Of positive and negative, developed
From the primordial unit, T'ai Chih,
The absolute containing in itself
Duality. Here is Fu Hi's successor,
Shen Nung She, inventor of the plow.
Hwang Ti, the Yellow Emperor, gave us
The calendar and built the first great temple
Wherein to worship God, the Lord on High.
He was a master in philosophy,
Extending the eight trigrams of Fu Hi
Into the four and sixty hexagrams.
His wife, Si Ling, taught us to rear the silkworm.
Yao the Great and Shun laid the foundation
Of great prosperity; they regulated
The river courses, thus preventing floods,
And it was Yu the Great who built the dykes.
Shao did not appoint his son successor,
He did not deem him worthy of the honor;
He chose the humble Shun of lowly birth,
Distinguished by his filial piety.
And filial piety is bottom rock,
The bottom rock on which we build our culture
Whose application lies in five relations,
And five ideals stand out paramount;
Humaneness, uprightness, propriety,
Enlightenment, and, last not least, good faith.
Here we have seen the treasures of the past,
But higher still than art and precious relics
We deem the learning of the sage, for he
Can teach us wisdom, truth, and also virtue.
The greatest mind that now our country holds
Is Lao Tan, the old philosopher;
And you and I shall see him face to face.

Scene 2.

The Archives of Chow in the city Lo. LAO TAN, *a man of advanced years with a flowing white beard, is seated at a table with a lute before him.*

Lao Tan. The reason that can be reasoned is not the eternal reason. The word that can be spoken is not the eternal word. The reason that can be reasoned is man's reason. Man's reason is vain and subject to error. I long for the eternal reason, the reason of Heaven. Heaven's reason is unnameable. It is the mother of the world, the mother of the ten thousand things. We call it Tao. Man's reason is but a faint echo of the Tao. Man imagines, however, that his human and all too human reason is unfailing. The genuine human reason and the heavenly reason are truly one and the same. I long for the eternal reason, the Tao. She is my mother, I am her child. But to be the son of the eternal reason, I must have no reason of my own; no reason in contradiction to the Tao, the heavenly reason. I must empty my heart of desire.

(*He begins to play the lute and sings in a melodramatic strain:*)

> He who desireless is found
> The spiritual of the world will sound;
> But he who by desire is bound
> Sees the mere shell of things around.

(BOY *enters and makes a bow. He waits respectfully until* LAO TAN *stops playing, then bows again.* LAO TAN *looks up expectantly.*)

Boy. K'ung Chin of the state of Lu, attended by Tze Lu, Tze Kung, and Mang-I, the son of His Excellence Mang Hsi, late Minister of Lu, are here to pay you their respects.

Lao Tan. Who is K'ung Chin? Is it K'ung Tze, the modern sage of Lu, who would fain reform the whole world by reviving the past? (BOY *hands him a slip of paper bearing the name of* K'UNG FU TZE. LAO TAN *reads it.*) Indeed, that is the man. It is K'ung Tze with some of his disciples. Let him enter. (BOY *bows and goes out.*)

Lao Tan. (Speaking to himself.) He is gaining fame and people praise him; yet it seems to me that he clings to externalities. (*Lets his fingers run over his lute again.*) He preaches virtue; he proclaims justice; he insists on ceremonial, the ceremonial of the past, the old dead past. The great reason, the ineffable, inexpressible reason is not so complicated. Does K'ung know its simplicity? I fear he is far from it. What we need is singleness of heart.

(*Accompanying himself on the lute,* LAO TAN *sings again:*)

> The simplicity of the unexpressed
> Will purify the heart of lust.
> When there's no lust, there will be rest,
> And all the world will thus be blest.

The great Tao, the eternal reason, is as if non-existent. It is as empty as the expanse of heaven but its use is inexhaustible.

(K'UNG FU TZE *and his disciples enter with conspicuous dignity.*)

K'ung Fu Tze.

> Blest be our entrance here where holy scrolls
> Greet us from all the shelves. These curious writings
> Come from the hands of our ancestral sages.
> The hoary past is speaking unto us
> Here in the archives of old emperors.
> Yea, enviable is thy fate, great Lao Tan,
> Curator of the holy scriptures here!

(LAO TAN *has risen and the two sages bow repeatedly.*)

Lao Tan.

> If I can help thee, worthy guest, command me.

K'ung Fu Tze.

> O noble Lao Tan, thy wisdom is
> Well known through all the empire. Kindly, sir,
> Let us reap benefits from thy great knowledge.
> Most wondrous the resources thou hast here
> In these famed archives of the House of Chow,
> Which since the day of Wu has ruled the country.
> There may be documents in thy possession
> That date as far back as the house of Yin;

Yea, traces may be here among thy treasures
Of the primordial founders of our land,
Of the five ancient rulers; of Fu Hi,
Inventor of our script; of Sheng Nung She,
The godly husbandman who taught the people
To fashion plows from wood; further Hwang Ti
The Yellow Emperor, or one of his
Six ministers; perhaps some other sages
Have left some record of their ancient rites.

Lao Tan.

The men of whom you speak, sir, are all dead,
And now are moldering in their graves. Their words
Alone are extant still. 'Tis of no use
To see the places where they lived, to handle
The manuscripts they wrote with their own hands
Simply for us to make a show of learning.

K'ung Fu Tze.

Allow me to insist that all the rulers
Should make a show of their authority,
And their authority is based upon
The wisdom of tradition, of the past.
The people ought to see that they are governed.

Lao Tan.

No, sir. I differ from you on this point.
The people scarcely knew of the existence
Of our great rulers. Lesser ones they liked
And praised. Still lesser ones they feared, and then
The least, the meanest, smallest they despised.

K'ung Fu Tze.

No, sir, oh no!

Lao Tan.

     Yes, sir, they still despise them.

K'ung Fu Tze.

Rulers must seek advice from noble sages,
Must recognize their worth. Should not the sage
Stand high exalted? He should be distinguished,
And monarchs should surround themselves with sages.

Lao Tan.

The sage should imitate the eternal reason,

The great Tao which makes all things arise.
What would you do if you were called to rule?
K'ung Fu Tze.

    I would establish righteousness and justice,
    Would make the ruler truly be a ruler,
    The subject be a subject, would reform
    The empire, would convert the world to virtue,
    And I would do, in short, what should be done.

Lao Tan. (After a short pause, ironically.)

    You would, indeed, make much ado. You would
    Make a great show of virtue and assert
    Your principle.

K'ung Fu Tze.

               Sir, what else should I do?

Lao Tan.

    What should you do, you ask? Do no ado!
    Do not assert yourself. Does heaven e'er
    Assert itself? But heaven for aye endures;
    Your person put behind, for only thus
    Cometh your person to the fore. The sage
    Will never boast of his own worth. He quickens
    But does not own; he works but does not claim;
    Merit he gains, but does not dwell on it.

K'ung Fu Tze.

    The sage should set the people an example
    Of justice, of benevolence, and virtue.

Lao Tan.

    Of virtue? Sir, it seems you mean the sage
    To make a show of virtue; 'twere but a sham.
    True virtue knoweth naught of show or sham.
    True virtue is unvirtue, not ado.
    If goodness makes a show of goodness, sir,
    It is sheer badness and hypocrisy.
    Further, if beauty makes display of beauty,
    It is sheer ugliness, to be despised.
    When people lose the Tao, virtue comes;
    Then they begin to talk and preach of virtue.
    If they lose virtue, then benevolence
    Comes in its place. They lose benevolence

And justice comes. When they lose justice, too,
They preach propriety. Propriety
Is but a semblance of true loyalty,
Of goodness, virtue, faith. This hankering
After traditions old, this reverence
Of virtue, justice, and benevolence
Is but mere empty show which but conceals
The lack of reason and of genuine virtue.
It is the flower of reason, not its fruit.

K'ung Fu Tze.

You undervalue what the sage can do
If he but find the place which he deserves.

Lao Tan.

A noble man who finds his time, will rise;
But if he does not find his time, he drifts,
And like a roving plant he'll have to wander.
Let go, sir, your ambitious affectation,
Your haughty airs. All this is of no use.

K'ung Fu Tze.

Sir, you are frank!

Lao Tan.

                   Truthful you'd have me be.
True words, sir, are not pleasant; pleasant words
Are scarcely true.

K'ung Fu Tze.

                 You are discouraging.

Lao Tan.

Do I discourage when I would correct?
I'd but discourage him who seeketh self;
Not him who seeketh Tao and would find it.
I seek the Tao, and the Tao, sir,
Serves me as guide. It is the middle path
Between extremes and leads us to the goal.
The Tao teaches virtue, teaches goodness,
And all we need is goodness.

K'ung Fu Tze.

                Goodness only?

Lao Tan.

Meet all with goodness; meet the good with goodness

And likewise, too, meet evil ones with goodness.
K'ung Fu Tze.

> My principle is justice. Do not to others
> What thou wouldst not have done to thee. Indeed
> The good ones we should meet with goodness, truly!
> But bad ones I would meet as they deserve.
> For why should we the bad ones also treat
> With goodness, say? The words which thou hast spoken,
> Are hard to understand.
> (*As if speaking to himself:*)
> > > > Oh, I had hoped
> To learn from thee of ancient rituals,
> Of ceremonials and propriety!

Lao Tan.

> For all of which I care so little, sir!
> So let that go. I have no more to say.

K'ung Fu Tze.

> Then we will part, and I for one regret
> That from thy wisdom I could learn no more.

(*Both rise and bow, and* LAO TAN *accompanies* K'UNG FU TZE *to the door. Exit* K'UNG FU TZE, *accompanied by* MANG-I, TZE LU, *and* TZE KUNG.)

Lao Tan.

> So that was K'ung Fu Tze, the great reformer:
> Is he the herald of a sterile future?
> Will he build up our nation? Woe to us!
> Or am I so mistaken in the truth?
> There is a gulf 'twixt us cannot be bridged.
> Would he might find the Tao, but its light
> Shineth in vain; he comprehends it not.
> (*He begins to muse.*)
> How few there are who understand the Tao!
> We look at it and yet we see it not;
> We listen for its voice but hear no sound;
> We grope for it but cannot touch its form;
> Yet it exists, it molds this whole grand world.
> It is a being wondrous and complete;
> Ere heaven and earth, IT was. How calm it is!
> Alone it standeth and it suffereth not,

Therefore it is the mother of the world.
I do not know its name -- I call it Tao.
K'ung meaneth well, but will with failure meet;
He cannot find his time and he will drift
From place to place in idle quest. And I?
And I? I am forlorn, Oh, so forlorn!
I am a stranger here; I long for home.
My days are numbered and I will depart.
Yes, Yes! Abroad in life and home in death!

Scene 3.

A street in Lo, the capital of Chow. Enter a native of Lo, LO.
K'UNG FU TZE *passes by. He appears disconcerted and agitated, as if
he had lost his way. Exit* K'UNG FU TZE. *Native of Lo looks back
after* K'UNG FU TZE, *shakes his head and expresses astonishment.*

Lo. A remarkable man! I wonder who he is? A striking figure!
(*Enter* MANG-I, TZE LU, *and* TZE KUNG.)

Tze Lu. Sir, have you seen a stranger here?

Lo. Yes, sir, I have.

Tze Lu. Perhaps it was the Master, K'ung Fu Tze. Did he appear
to you extraordinary?

Lo. Indeed he did, sir. The man I saw had a forehead like Yao,
the wise emperor; a neck like Kao Yao, the great minister of Shun;
shoulders much like Ts'ze-Ch'an, who governed Cheng so well in times
of great disorder! He wanted a little below the waist of the height of Yu
the Great, the builder of our dykes. Indeed, an extraordinary man, but
his general demeanor was that of a stray dog.

Tze Lu. That is our Master; we have found him.

Tze Kung. Whither did he go?

Lo. There he comes now.

(*Enter* K'UNG FU TZE.)

Tze Kung.

O Master, venerable Master! At last we found you.

Mang-I.

We were much worried and have searched for you.

K'ung Fu Tze.

O friends, I'm disconcerted, and I feel

Defeated and dejected since I met
The ancient sage, the famous Lao Tan.

Mang-I.

You have no reason to be thus downcast.
With all due reverence for Lao Tan,
I think that he but failed to understand;
Maybe that he at bottom means the same.

K'ung Fu Tze.

I know the birds can fly, and fishes swim;
I know wild beasts can run. But man devises
Snares for the runner, nets to catch the swimmer
And with his arrows brings the flyers down.
I know it, but the dragon I know not.
The dragon is mysterious and grand;
The dragon can bestride the wind and clouds
When rising heavenward. I know him not.
This Lao Tan, methinks, is like the dragon.

Mang-I.

Be not discomfited, my dear, good Master,
E'en though your views do not agree with Tan's
You have an aim, a noble aim. You will
Accomplish something in this world. And I
Will stand by you.

Tze Kung.

      Pursue your aim, dear Master.
We will stand by you, and we shall not flinch.

Mang-I.

We will be faithful to the very end.

K'ung Fu Tze.

I thank you from the bottom of my heart.
You both are faithful, and you both are manly.
Since you've been with me, Kung, I have no longer
Seen sneers in faces of unfriendly people
Who would not countenance my thought. But here
Against the great philosopher Lao Tan
You are of no avail. Mang-I, you, too,
Have proved a help, but all your influence
Will not win the support of this lone thinker
For our great, noble cause.

Mang-I.
                              My dear good Master
    I have such faith in you I cannot see
    How you can feel so grievously dejected
    Merely because one dreamy simpleton
    As old as he is singular and hazy
    And odd, differs from you. Leave him alone.
    If he or any one of his admirers
    Would venture to oppose us, let them do so.
    We need opponents and we'll meet them squarely.
    Your mission 'tis to rear the eternal pillars
    Of good doctrine, of propriety,
    The golden rule, the five relationships.

K'ung Fu Tze.
    I thank you, my good friends, most cordially.

Tze Kung.
    Not for ourselves alone, we speak for all
    Your followers and your true disciples.

Mang-I.
    We will convert the world to you. And, Master,
    (*With some hesitation.*) I wish to be allied to you and to
    Your family. Kindly allow me, sir,
    To send to you as soon as we reach home,
    A go-between who would arrange my marriage
    To your fair niece.

K'ung Fu Tze.
                              My niece?

Mang-I.
                              Yea, to your niece.

K'ung Fu Tze.
    My niece to me is like unto a daughter,
    And no one, friend Mang-I, would be more welcome
    As son-in-law than you. Your cheering word,
    Most noble sir, shall be a prophecy
    Of the great future which before me lies.

ACT III.

Scene: *Home of* K'UNG FU TZE *in the year 517 B.C.* NIECE *of* K'UNG FU TZE *is seen in festive bridal attire, attended by maids.*

Niece.

> The day is come, and here I wait for him;
> And oh, to look upon him -- to behold
> His manly figure and his kindly face.
> Hand me the lute and I will sing the song
> My uncle taught me, the old bridal song
> That has come down to us from hoary ages
> And which exactly fits my present mood.

(*A* MAID *hands her a lute. She plays and sings:*)

> At the gate awaits me now,
>   Screened from sight, hi-ho!
> One with tassels o'er his brow
>   All of white, hi-ho!
> Gems beam bright!
> What a sight! Hi-ho!

> Through the courtyard now he goes
>   Past the screen. Hi-ho!
> Jewels which his headgear shows
>   Are of green, hi-ho!
> Such a sheen
> Is rarely seen. Hi-ho!

> He approaches now the hall,
>   I am told; Hi-ho!
> 'Tis my bridegroom, among all
>   Fair to behold, hi-ho!
> Decked with gold,
> Fair to behold. Hi-ho!

(*Enter* K'UNG FU TZE *and his wife.*)

K'ung Fu Tze.

> My dearest niece, no fault has yet been made.
> The go-between has come and we've transacted
> All details as prescribed by ancient custom.
> Your names and ages have been stated; presents
> Have been exchanged and our consent is given;
> The day of marriage has been duly fixed.
> And we await the bridegroom, now to take thee
> Home to his parents' house, yea, to their palace,
> For they are wealthy and of royal blood.
> Thy mother-in-law expects thee, with desire
> To have thee with her, for she loves thee dearly,
> The bride of her beloved and favorite son.

Maid.

> The groom is coming; the procession neareth;
> Mang-I is as gorgeous as Kwang Ti himself,
> Surrounded by his relatives and friends.

K'ung Fu Tze.

> (*To the servant.*) Show the musicians in, and call the maids.

(*Enter musicians and a group of girls. The former with their instruments take seats on the right; the latter surround the bride. The table with the lute is removed and a palanquin is brought.*)

K'ung Fu Tze.

> Is the trousseau in readiness?

Lady Ch'ien.

> It is.
>
> Here are the boxes packed with proper care.

(*Turning to her* NIECE.)

> O, my dear niece, how happy is your lot,
> That just the man to whom your heart went out
> Asked you in marriage. This is rare, my child.

(*The door opens. Enter* MANG-I, *followed by a procession. The music plays.* MANG-I *bows to* K'UNG FU TZE, *his wife and the bride.*)

K'ung Fu Tze.

> (*To* MANG-I)
> My friend, this is a day of purest joy.
> Thou wilt the husband be of this my niece,
> A maiden pure and undefiled, a treasure

In education and accomplishments
As well as noble in descent. She will
Obedient and submissive prove to thee
As it behooves a wife; and thou, my friend,
Wilt prove her lord, her husband, her protector.
This day is most auspicious. 'Tis to be
The luckiest of the lucky days of life.
With this my wish, friend Mang-I, take her home.
Be happy with her; do thou make her happy;
Be happy both, according to your love.

(The music begins; the groomsmen and bridesmaids lead the bridegroom to the bride, whom he conducts with ceremonious courtesy to the palanquin. All the attendants join in singing the ditty on "The Locusts" from the Shi King I, I, 5. Our translation is by William Jennings.)

How do the locusts crowd --
     A fluttering throng!
May thy descendants be
     Thus vast, thus strong!

How do the locusts' wings
     In motion sound!
May thy descendants show
     Like them, no bound!

How do the locusts all
     Together cluster!
May thy descendants, too,
     In such wise muster!

(While the bride is carried out in the palanquin, they sing the "Bridal Song," from the Shi King, I, I, 6: translated by William Jennings.)

Ho, graceful little peach-tree,
     Brightly thy blossoms bloom!
The maid goes to her husband;
     Adorns his hall, his room.

Ho, graceful little peach-tree,
    Thy fruit abundant fall!
The maid goes to her husband;
    Adorns his room, his hall.

Ho, graceful little peach-tree,
    With foliage far and wide!
The maid goes to her husband;
    His household well to guide.

(*Exeunt all except* K'UNG FU TZE *and* LADY CH'IEN.)

K'ung Fu Tze.
    A happy day this is for me. The marriage
    Of Mang-I to our good niece can only serve
    To make him even more attached to me
    Than ever; and I prize his friendship high.
    This morning only have I summoned been
    To call on our most gracious lord, Duke Ting,
    Who seeks my service. I am called upon
    To govern first a district, then the state.
    Here is my chance; I shall make use of it.
Lady Ch'ien.
    Our lord Duke Ting is young and pleasure-loving;
    He is not constant, and success is doubtful.
    I do not trust the honor beckoning thee.
K'ung Fu Tze.
    Wife, have no doubt, for in my inmost soul
    I feel that Providence selected me
    To carry out the great plan of reform.
    There is no one on earth except myself
    Who knows the needs of mankind, who can teach
    The rules of conduct, who can regulate
    The five relations, and I feel convinced
    The Lord on High will speed me with success.
    When I was young I was in office twice.
    First I was keeper of the stores of grain,
    Then I had charge of public fields and land.
    Both offices were humble, certainly,

But I was faithful in these smaller duties.
My calculations balanced and the cattle
Under my care did prosper. Madam, then
Do you remember when our son was born
The Duke sent me a present of two carp --
It was the father of the young Duke Ting --
In friendly recognition of my work.
I shall be just as faithful now in this,
My new position, with its wider range.
It is the cause of heaven I advocate,
The cause of heaven cannot be doomed to failure.

ACT IV.
Scene 1.

Twenty years later. Court of the State of Lu, in 497 B.C. In the background, the judgment seat with a screen behind. In the foreground, YEN HUI, TZE KUNG, *and* TZE LU.

Tze Lu.

(*To* YEN) There was a time when I was jealous, sir,
Jealous of you for our great Master's love.
But you have overcome all my ill-feeling.
For, to be frank, I love you too.

Tze Kung.

      And you
Are worthy to be cherished by us all.
You are so thoughtful, gentle, lovable.
The Master loves you, and who loves you not?

Yen Hui.

O, do not praise me, I do not deserve it.
I love the Master and I cannot help it.
I loved him as a child. My father loved him.
My father, being one of his disciples
Looked up to him with deepest reverence.
And I was born to this my father's spirit,
In deepest reverence for the Master, K'ung.
I have imbibed it with my mother's milk
And was brought up in this same atmosphere.

When I grew older and began to think,
I saw good reason for admiring him
Who is the safest guide for all the world.

(*Unnoticed by the others*, K'UNG LI, *the son of* K'UNG FU TZE,
enters and listens.)

Tze Lu.

And you are right, my friend, my dear Yen Hui.
The Master showed for me consideration;
He often followed my advice, and I
Was near to him, nearer than all the others;
But since you came and joined our company
You have become nearest of all, and he
Looketh to you to carry on his work.
'Tis you whom he regards as his successor.

Tze Kung.

He loves you more than his own son, and I
Gladly confess that you deserve his favor.

K'ung Li.

(*Aside.*) 'Tis true, my father loves him more than me.

Yen Hui.

I still am young and lack experience;
You both are older and know more than I.
I've much to learn, and how can I be fit
To be allowed to carry on the work
Of our great Master's wisdom? No, dear sir,
I feel my great unworthiness too much
To stir in you a cause for jealousy.
It is enough for me if I can serve him;
That is high honor and great privilege.

Tze Lu.

I have no grudge, Yen Hui, and if I had
I would suppress it, for you are too dear
To mine own heart.

K'ung Li.

(*Aside.*)   Why waste this sympathy
On yonder gosling?

Tze Kung.

                    And now especially
Since our great Master has been called to office

We must not split but firmly stand together.
Yen Hui.

> I am so glad the Master did not deign
> To serve the state when called on by Yang Ho.
> Yang Ho was a usurper. He it was
> Who had Duke Chao expelled, and then deprived
> Him of his throne, and caused all the confusion
> In our state Lu. He wanted but the name
> Of K'ung Fu Tze -- K'ung's fair untarnished name,
> To shield and justify his unjust rule.

(*Exit* K'UNG LI, *whose departure is observed by the others.*)
Tze Kung.

> Who was that?

Tze Lu.

> Was't not the Master's son?

Yen Hui.

> It was indeed K'ung Li.

Tze Lu.

>   He seems to have
> No tittle of his father's noble spirit.

Yen Hui.

> Oh, he's not bad; he's but indifferent.
> He does not know the worth of his great father.
> He would have liked the Master to accept
> The offer of Yang Ho. And for a while
> K'ung wavered, for he deemed it possible
> To change the man, to make him do the right.
> He hoped he might convert the unscrupulous
> By acting as his mentor and adviser.
> Once slyly said Yang Ho to K'ung Fu Tze:
> "Can he be called benevolent who leaves
> His jewels in his bosom and his country
> In worse confusion?" "No," our Master said.
> Yang Ho continued: "And you want employment
> But waste your opportunity. Our years
> Slip quickly and the months pass by -- accept!"
> The Master then replied: "Your words seem true,
> Perhaps I ought to enter into office."

Tze Kung.

> The Master wavered; yea, he was inclined

To accept the tempting offer of Yang Ho.
But I prevented it. I pointed out
The vicious character of Yang and that
The cause of a usurper should not be
Encouraged or supported. But since then
The righteous heir, Duke Ting, is reinstated.
And happily Duke Ting has found employment
For K'ung Fu Tze in this our state of Lu.

Yen Hui.

When K'ung Fu Tze first served as governor
Of the small district at Chung-Tu of Lu,
What great reform was then at once accomplished!
Things dropped in streets were not picked up or stolen;
The strong did not make evil use of power,
The merchants used right weight, the old were honored,
And womanhood respected. Above all,
All funeral observances were strictly
And piously observed.

Tze Kung.

                      Yea, that was good,
But better still was the establishment
Of our young duke's authority. The barons
Had grown too powerful. But K'ung Tze broke
Some of their castles where they bade defiance
And humbled them. Thus spread our Master's fame
And now K'ung Tze commands the confidence
Of our good duke, His Royal Highness Ting,
Holding the place of Minister of Justice.
The other princes now begin to fear
That Lu, our little country, will outshine
In glory all the others. Yea, our neighbor,
The Duke of Ch'i, would gladly conquer Lu.

Yen Hui.

He won't succeed.

Tze Lu.

                 He may. We cannot tell.

Yen Hui.

I see no danger, friend.

Tze Kung.

                The Duke of Ch'i

Is filled with hate against Duke Ting of Lu.
And do you still remember how our Master
Defeated Ch'i's intrigues at Chia-Ku,
The meeting place of the two sovereigns?
The Duke of Ch'i would have imprisoned Ting,
Had not our Master with his innate wisdom
Defended justice to protect our cause.
Since then, Duke Ting has confidence in K'ung.

Tze Kung.

The danger is not past, for our Duke Ting
Is like the rest.

Yen Hui.

What do you mean, friend Kung?

Tze Kung.

Beauty to Ting goes always before duty.
I learn the Duke of Ch'i will send a present
Of thirty spans of steeds -- you know the Duke
Loves racing horses; and of eighty damsels.
With song and dance they will so entertain
The Duke as greatly to distract his soul
And make him hate the very name of virtue.

Mang-I.

The Duke has heard of it, but is determined
Not to receive the present. If he did
Our Master could not stay. Here comes K'ung Tze.

(*They bow low. Enter* K'UNG FU TZE.)

K'ung Fu Tze.

I greet you, friends, and above all Yen Hui,
The most affectionate, best of my students.
At last my time has come; at last I have
An opportunity to prove my doctrine.
His Royal Highness Ting, our noble ruler
The Duke of Lu, lends me his ear and listens
To the advice I give.

Tze Lu.

We know it, sir.
The fame of Lu is growing since Duke Ting
Has made thee counselor of state.

K'ung Fu Tze.

I see

Great vistas open now and I shall need
Assistance. Dear Tze Lu, the Duke of Wei
Wants an advisor and he needs a man
Of strength; wilt thou be able to keep order?
Tze Lu.
   I certainly will try to do my best.
K'ung Fu Tze.
   Not every man is fit to do the same,
   And different tasks require quite different men.
   Thou wilt be in thy proper place, Tze Lu.
   So go to Wei, and when thou exercisest
   Authority, remember that what thou
   Dislik'st in thy superiors, do not
   Thyself display to those in thy command.
Tze Lu.
   My aim shall be to do thee credit, Master.
K'ung Fu Tze.
   I wish to know what every one of you
   Would do to realize his highest aim
   If he were given full authority.
   Tze Lu, do thou speak first.
Tze Lu.
                              My honored Master,
   I would induce the people to be strong,
   Would make them self-reliant, energetic
   And brave to stand up for the right.
K'ung Fu Tze.
                              And thou,
   Tze Kung, what are the methods thou wouldst use?
Tze Kung.
   With your permission, I would guide the people,
   And I would teach them the right way.
K'ung Fu Tze.
                              Yen Hui,
   Wouldst thou approve the methods of thy friends
   And fellow students? Both are men of talent.
   Tze Lu is full of courage, and Tze Kung
   Persuasive in his manner as a teacher.
Yen Hui.
   My Master, I would like to find a sage

Upon the throne, whose counselor I'd be;
And I would help him to diffuse instruction
Among the people on the five relations
And on the lessons they imply. I would
Teach every one within my realm the rules
Of music and propriety, would spread
The love of harmony, that they no longer
Would care to have their cities fortified
By wall and moat, but fuse their heavy spears
And swords into the tools for tilling land.
Their flocks would graze unharmed without protection
In open fields. No war would widow wives
And orphan children, and there'd be no chance
For Lu Tze to display his bravery
Nor for Tze Kung to be an orator.
K'ung Fu Tze.

Yen Hui, I prize thy view as the most lofty.
I see that thou hast sounded all the depths
Of wisdom; thou art fittest to become
The true "Continuator" of my doctrine.
I need disciples, men of different type;
I need men of literary taste
And diplomats, and men of strength and valor;
I need instructors and philosophers,
They all shall be enlisted in the cause --
Our cherished cause, the cause of all mankind;
But thou, Yen Hui, art nearest to my heart;
And 'tis thy love which comprehendeth all,
All wisdom and all courage and all learning,
All oratory and all diplomacy.

(K'UNG FU TZE *walks toward the door, his disciples standing on either side bowing, when* LI, *his son, comes from one side upon the stage and passing over in the center, reaches the door first.*)
K'ung Fu Tze.

Li, son, my only son, how does it happen
That thou tak'st precedence before thy father?
Hast thou not read the Books of Odes wherein

(LI *returns, shakes his head and bows with a contrite expression.*)

Thou canst become acquainted with the spirit

> Of ancient sages, emperors and nobles?
> They were distinguished by propriety
> And strictly courteous behavior, son.
> They never would have taken precedence
> Before their betters, nor before their parents.
> Remember, son, and read the Book of Odes.

(LI *steps aside and allows his father and the disciples to enter. He stays behind. Shaking his head.*)

K'ung Li.

> He is a sage, I doubt not; he's a scholar;
> But he is always preaching, moralizing
> And talking wisely. I am sick of it.
> It bores me, it annoys me. How shall I
> Find time to read the Book of Odes? I must
> Be filial, must behave decorously;
> I must observe rules of propriety --
> Their is no leisure left for anything.

(*Enter an* OLD MAN *with his* SON.)

Old Man. Pray, sir, is here the court where I can find his high honor, the Lord Minister of Justice?

K'ung Li. Do you refer to K'ung Fu Tze?

Old Man. Indeed I do.

K'ung Li. If so, this is the place. Here K'ung Fu Tze makes his decisions.

Son. Father, let us go hence. If you will only be reasonable, I will do what I can to satisfy you.

Old Man. What you can? No, no, I know what that means. You shall do what you must. You are my son, and you must obey. K'ung Fu Tze teaches filial piety and he will punish you severely if he hears my case. You must surrender completely. It is not sufficient to do what you can.

Son. Father, let us go back, I am afraid.

Old Man. I will not go back. I will complain of you, and His Honor will deal with you as you deserve. He will probably put you in the stocks; your feet and your hands will be locked and you will carry a placard, "Punished for lack of respect to his father," or something like that. I will send your friends to the marketplace to gaze at you and you will become a public example for the whole town. All your neighbors will gather around you and mock you.

Son. Father, let us go home.

Old Man. No, no! I will have judgment. K'ung Fu Tze is a wise judge. He will teach you filial piety. He can punish, you know; he had to have but one criminal executed, and crime almost disappeared. But he had to have one man, a real criminal, executed. Maybe he will have you executed, too. Think of it. There are so many different kinds of criminal punishment. I do not know what manner he would select. There are five kinds of capital punishment.

Son. O father, let us go. I am not so bad as you make me out. I have the best intentions. I will do all I can.

Old Man. No, no. You must stay and hear judgment.

K'ung Li. I will call my father, the judge. (*To the* OLD MAN) He knows of your case, does he not? You were here before?

Old Man. Yes! Oh yes! He has heard us, but he did not give judgment. He said we should consider our case and come again. So we have come again and here we are.

K'ung Li. I will call His Honor. (*Exits.*)

Son. Father, let us go home.

Old Man. Oh, no, sir; you must stay and hear your doom. His Honor, the judge, will teach you a lesson. Maybe he will simply give you a flogging.

Son. Oh, father, what wrong have I done to deserve any punishment at all?

Old Man. Oh, son, son! Do you not know that it is very wrong to contradict your father and to quarrel with him? Think of it! That is what you've done. You have quarreled with your father, with me, with your own father!

(*Enter* K'UNG FU TZE, *followed by magistrates and his disciples. Seats himself before the screen. The old man and his son prostrate themselves.*)

K'ung Fu Tze.

You have come back, you two, to hear my judgment,
But I am loathe to give it. I will wait
Till ye among yourselves have peaceably
Arranged your quarrels.

Old Man.

              But, sir, he is my son,
I am the father of this obstreperous boy.

K'ung Fu Tze.

> (*Slowly.*) I see you are! -- I understand that you
> Have educated this wayward child.
> He may be bad. But, say, who bears the guilt
> If not the father who has failed to teach
> His son the rules of filial piety?
> My judgment is to send you both to jail
> And keep you there until you have made peace.

Old Man.

> What do you say, your Honor? Hear I right?
> Do you regard me guilty, me the father,
> Of this my son's great faults?

K'ung Fu Tze.

> Indeed I do
> And I shall punish you e'en as severely
> As him.

Old Man.

> Me? Me the father?

K'ung Fu Tze.

> Yes, indeed,
> And, as it seems to me, this is but fair.

Old Man.

> Let us go home, your Honor: I believe
> I can persuade my son to better living.

K'ung Fu Tze.

> Go home, and do not dare to come again
> Without a good and real cause. The judges
> Are not installed to hear paltry complaints.
> Where fathers are true fathers and where sons
> Are sons, there is no need of courts and judges.

(*Exeunt* OLD MAN *and his* SON. *Music in the distance.*)

K'ung Fu Tze. What do these sounds portend?

Tze Lu. I'll see, my lord. (*Going to the door and looking out.*) There is a festive procession coming, lord. It seems to me the music they have intoned is frivolous.

K'ung Fu Tze. Indeed the tune is frivolous. Who is this company of female minstrels?

Tze Lu. My lord, I know. I see it now. These ladies are the singing damsels which the Duke of Ch'i has sent to our Lord Ting, the Duke of Lu. There are the thirty span of horses, too. Oh, how they prance! And here appears Duke Ting himself.

K'ung Fu Tze.

> I fear my hour has come, I must withdraw.
> The Duke is sick of virtue, sick of me,
> Sick of good government. Here is no longer
> A place for me. I'd better leave the field
> To sport and to frivolities, to vice,
> To flatterers and to these singing damsels.

(K'UNG FU TZE *retires slowly to a corner of the stage, followed by his disciples. The armed bailiff of the court steps aside. The music continues. Enter* DUKE TING *with retinue and singing* DAMSELS.)

Chorus of Damsels.

> Taste the sweets
> Life can give;
> Laugh and love
> While you live;
> Taste the joys
> Which we bring,
> While in glee,
> Merrily,
> Songs we sing.
> Join us in our wanton play! Hi ho!
> And enjoy life while you may. Hi ho!

(K'UNG FU TZE *and retinue exeunt.* TZE KUNG *remains on the stage, and approaches the* DUKE.)

Tze Kung.

> Duke Ting, most Royal Highness, hear me speak.
> I have for you some news of great importance.

Duke Ting.

> What can be more important than the beauty
> That now surrounds us? But speak on, Tze Kung.

Tze Kung.

> Your councilor, your Highness, K'ung Fu Tze,
> Who has done glorious service in your state
> Will take his leave unless these damsels go.

Duke Ting.

  Indeed! Think you that K'ung Fu Tze will go?
  I shall be glad to be so rid of him.
  He acts as my bad conscience and he grudges
  Me every joy in life; and me he blames
  For every mishap, every accident.
  When our ancestral temple burned, he claimed
  That my ancestors were enraged at me
  And would refuse me further help. They were
  No better than I am. And all my neighbors,
  The Dukes of Ch'i and Wei, the Emperor
  At Lo and all the princes, enjoy themselves,
  Why should not I? And you, my friend, Tze Kung,
  You should be wise enough to understand
  That drinking vinegar instead of wine
  Is not a sign of virtue but of folly.
  Come, Kung, and join me in my gaity;
  Be my companion in the place of K'ung.

Tze Kung.

  No, sir, I cannot. I would rather starve
  With K'ung the sage than live in opulence
  On royal bounties here amid these pleasures.
  So fare you well! We leave you to your pastimes.

(*The* DAMSELS *again dance.*)

Chorus of Damsels.

  Taste the sweets
  Life can give;
  Laugh and love
  While you live;
  Taste the joys
  Which we bring,
  While in glee,
  Merrily,
  Songs we sing.
  Join us in our wanton play! Hi ho!
  And enjoy life while you may. Hi ho!

Scene 2.

A scene on the road, in 497 B.C. K'UNG FU TZE *is seen on his travels.*

Tze Kung.

How grand this scenery of Tai San,
The mountain range which separates me from Lu.

K'ung Fu Tze.

How beautiful those cliffs, but difficult
They are to travel though, impervious to the foot.
Hand me my lute, friend Kung.

Tze Kung.

Here 'tis, dear Master.

K'ung Fu Tze.

(Plays lute and in a melodramatic voice recites the poem of Tai San.)

Would rise to the lofty peak;
Ravines and cliffs debar.
So truth though ever near
Is to the seeker far.
How wearisome to me
Those tangling mazes are.
I sigh and look around,
The summit is in full view:
With woodlands it is crowned
And sandy patches, too.
And there stretch all around
The highlands of Lian Fu.
Thickets of thorns prevent
Any ascent.
No axe is here
A path to clear;
The higher we are going
The worse the briars are growing.
I chant and I cry,
And while I sigh
My tears are freely flowing.

Tze Kung.

My Master, do not yield to gloomy thoughts.
Perhaps the crazy man of Tsu was right,
That you had best the bygones left unmended.

K'ung Fu Tze.

What did he say?

Tze Kung. He spoke of you in a little verse, in tone humorous, almost satirical, but there was much truth in his words. He sang:

"O Phoenix, oh Phoenix, thy virtue is pinched!
The bygone is ended and cannot be mended:
But truly the future can still be clinched.
Cease, ah! continue not!
For statesmen today are a dangerous lot."

You took a deep interest in him at the time.

K'ung Fu Tze.

I did, indeed, and his queer rhyme is true.
Virtue is pinched and statesmen verily
Are dangerous.

Tze Kung.

And Master, let me add
Truly the future can and must be clinched.
You stand up for the right, and I believe
The right must finally be recognized.

K'ung Fu Tze.

Tze Kung, see here. These fragrant orchids
Grow by the wayside mixed with common grass.
Flowers they are of royal worth, but here
They stand unheeded. Such is the sage's fate.

(*He takes his lute and plays. He sings.*)

So gently blow the valley breezes
With drizzling mist and rain,
And homeward bound a stranger tarries
With friends in a desert domain.
Blue heaven above! for all his worth
Is there no place for him on earth?

Through all the countries did he roam
    Yet found he no enduring home.
Worldlings are stupid and low,
    They naught of sages know.
So swiftly years and days pass by,
And soon old age is drawing nigh.
              (*Analects*, III, xxiv.)

ACT V.
Scene 1.

The garden of K'UNG FU TZE *in 479 B.C. A table with a lute and two chairs. In the background a house from which* K'UNG FU TZE *is coming. He looks feeble and carries a staff. Dragging his staff, he approaches the table and sits down. His appearance is worried and he lets his fingers run over the lute. Enter* TZE KUNG.

Tze Kung.
    My Master, oh, my good, beloved Master,
    How did you pass the night?
K'ung Fu Tze.
                  Tze Kung, my friend,
    Why do you come so late?
Tze Kung.
                 Master, I thought
    You needed sleep; but you have risen early.
K'ung Fu Tze.
    I dreamt ill-boding dreams.
Tze Kung.
               You are not well,
    And you were restless in your sleep last night.
K'ung Fu Tze.
    I dreamt that I was sitting in the hall,
    Between the central pillars, offerings
    Before me, as was custom of the Yin.
    According to the ancient ritual
    The dead was treated as a guest and placed
    Above the eastern stairs, but then the Yin
    Regarded him as host and guest at once,

And so they coffined him between the pillars,
Down in the hall. The Chow treat him as guest,
So now he's placed on top of the western stairs.
I am a man of Yin and I belong,
Between the pillars in the hall. That dream
Portends the truth. My time has come to die.
Tze Kung.
    Not yet, my Master.
K'ung Fu Tze.

                              Life has been a failure;
My son is dead and he accomplished naught.
But worse was the bereavement which I suffered
Through the demise of my beloved Yen Hui.
He was too gentle for this world of trouble;
Too kind, too noble, and too wise. His hair
Bleached early, ere he reached his thirty years,
And when but thirty-one he passed away,
He who should have succeeded me. 'Tis he
Who was my best disciple. Since he died
I feel that Heaven has rejected me.
Tze Kung.
    My dear old Master, do not speak in gloom.
K'ung Fu Tze.
    I speak but as I feel. In better days
    I used to see, when seated at the table
    At dinner time, before me at my place
    The noble countenance of Yao Ti;
    And when I raised my eyes I plainly saw
    The great Shun on the wall. I have not seen
    The Duke of Chow in dream as formerly.
    He was a blessing in my life, a source
    Of comfort, but I am as if abandoned
    By all the spirits of the past, the heroes
    Of our antiquity, our ancient culture.
Tze Kung.
    You are discouraged by disease, good Master.
    Remember, you are one of our great men.
    You are a sage, yea truly, the Great Sage
    As great as any one among the ancients.

K'ung Fu Tze.

    I dare not rank myself among the sages
    Nor with the men of perfect virtue, Kung.
    I simply strive to be a teacher, patient
    And diligent. I love the ancients dearly.
    And am but a transmitter, not a maker.
    The best of me is but a composition
    Of greater ones that have preceded me.

Tze Kung.

    Your declaration proves your modesty,
    For certainly the greatness of the past.
    Has taken its abode in you.

K'ung Fu Tze.

                    Yea, Kung,
    This much is true, that after great Wen Wang
    Heaven revealed the truth in me: and Heaven
    Will not allow the cause of truth to perish.

Tze Kung.

    The glory of the past will never die!
    Have you not left us treasures everlasting?
    You have collected the five sacred scriptures
    And also the four books; you have instructed
    In your great doctrines many worthy men.

(*Enter* K'UNG CHI, *the grandson of* K'UNG FU TZE.)

K'ung Chi.

    Do I intrude?

Tze Kung.

                Your grandfather's not well.

K'ung Fu Tze.

    K'ung Chi, my grandchild, you are welcome, boy.

K'ung Chi.

    Grandfather, can you spare me a few moments?

K'ung Fu Tze.

    I'm listening, my boy, what is your wish?

K'ung Chi.

    I want to have instruction in your doctrines.
    It is but proper that a child should learn
    His father's trade, his business or profession,
    Why should I be excluded? Your life's aim

       Is so much grander, nobler, so much higher,
       Than that of others. All the more I should
       Become proficient in the work you do.
K'ung Fu Tze.
       You are still young, my boy, but I consent,
       For I feel confident that you will take
       The place of my deceased disciple Yen,
       My much beloved, greatly lamented friend,
       Tze Yuan.
Tze Kung.
             Take here some of grandfather's books
       And read them, boy. You may not care for this,
       The Book of Rites, nor for the Odes, but here
       The Book of History will please you surely.
K'ung Chi.
       Thank you, dear sir. (*Turning to* K'UNG FU TZE.)
       Thank you, grandfather, thank you very much.
       But I should also like to have the Odes. E'en in the
       Book of Rites I'm interested.
(*Goes off with the books.*)
Tze Kung.
       Posterity will yet hear of K'ung Chi,
       The grandson of the greatest sage of China,
       And thou, dear Master, with such a descendant
       As Chi shouldst not complain. Do not expect
       That thou canst be successful during life,
       For while thou livest, jealousies will be,
       There will be puny minds who grudge thee honors
       And influence and power. But do not be
       Discouraged. Thine ideals are eternal
       And they will live when thou hast passed away.
       When all the mortal part of thee is gone
       Thy truer self will gain due recognition.
       Thou wilt be greater after death, dear Master,
       Than thou hast been in life, and emperors
       Will bow before the grand, divine, deep truth
       Which thou hast taught.
(TZE KAO *enters hurriedly, and bows to* K'UNG FU TZE.)
K'ung Fu Tze.
               Tze Kao! So unexpected!

Tze Kung.

    We thought you and Tze Lu were still in Wei!

Tze Kao.

    Indeed I was, but managed to escape.

Tze Kung.

    And where is Lu? Has he remained in Wei?

K'ung Fu Tze.

    I fear the worst. Tze Lu is brave and faithful.
    I always said that he was not to die
    A natural death. I know the state of Wei
    Is in rebellion. Tell me all you know.

Tze Kao.

    The rebels gained, and I advised the Duke
    To leave the capital, but he thought little
    Of my incompetent advice. He stayed
    And with him Lu. To tell the story briefly,
    The palace was surrounded by a mob
    To kill the Duke; and Tze Lu stayed with him.
    He charged his enemies with fearless courage
    Felled some, but finally was overcome.
    Thereafter fell the Duke himself.

K'ung Fu Tze.

                      Alas!
    Tze Lu! My noble, brave Tze Lu! But you,
    Tze Kao, you escaped the rebels.

Tze Kao.

                    Perhaps
    The mob spared me because I was too ugly;
    They did not deem me worthy of their steel.
    I am too insignificant and dwarfish.
    I am a puny fellow, and against me
    E'en criminals are generous and kind
    And noble-hearted. Some most envious fellow
    Who, having done great wrong, was led before me
    While I still served as magistrate in Wei,
    And I as judge condemned him by the law
    To lose his leg. Now think! I on my flight
    Was suddenly confronted with that man.
    Yea, then I thought I had escaped in vain,

This one-legged scoundrel would surrender me
And make me die a martyr for the cause
Of law and order. But that he did not do.
He recognized me, greeted me right kindly,
And pointed out to me a safe escape.
Said I to him: "And don't you hate me, then,
Because I had you punished?" "No," said he,
"For you were judge and had to do your duty.
I noticed then," he said, the one-legged villain,
"That you were not ill-willed, as judge in court,
That you were loath to have the law enforced.
You are in trouble now and might be slain,
It would not help me to deliver you
Into the hands of these bloodthirsty rebels.
Flee, then, and save yourself and when you come
To Lu, greet K'ung Fu Tze, your worthy Master.
May the time come when he, the sage, will bring
Peace upon earth and make men well disposed."

K'ung Fu Tze.

Thou art my good disciple, Kao Tze,
And provest true my doctrines. I am grateful.

Tze Kao.

The one-legged man deserves your thanks, not I.
He is a thinker, and he argued thus:
"The age is rotten." That is what he said,
"Rotten," he said. "The princes live for pleasure,
The magistrates and judges are appointed
For flattery and they take bribes; and truly
There is no law or order in the world.
Honesty does not pay, and criminals
Remain unpunished. That's the rule," he said.
"And you alone," addressing me he said it,
"And you alone made an exception, sir.
Whenever such a state of things prevails
There is no use in striving to be honest,
And so I went astray. Yes, I did wrong
And I deserved the punishment you gave me.
You told me at the time -- and I remember
The lesson which you taught -- 'Let villains know

That there is law and order in the world,
That they can make with honesty a living,
That justice will reward the good and punish
The evil-doer, then they will reform.'
If I had lived in orderly conditions,
Nor seen that villains triumph and the good
Were suffering only for their meekness' sake,
I would not have transgressed the middle path."
That is the reason, venerable Master,
Why he believed in you.

K'ung Fu Tze.

              And, I will add,
You see, my friends, that man is good by nature;
'Tis bad example only that perverts him.
The people would be good if but their princes
Would models prove themselves to be of virtue.
(Turning to KAO.)
You are of stunted growth, but you are wise;
Your mind is well developed and your wit --
It does me good to see you ere I die.

Tze Kung.

We hope to have you with us, and enjoy
Your wisdom still for many years.

K'ung Fu Tze.

                No, no,
My course is run. 'Tis but a short time since
A *lin* was captured by the ducal hunters.
I went to see the noble animal
And truly 'twas a *lin*. For, as you know,
That noble animal appears whene'er
A sage superior lives upon the earth.
A *lin* arrived, 'tis said, the very day
When I was born; and now the *lin* is dead.

Tze Kung.

Sir, do not take that fact so seriously.

K'ung Fu Tze.

What other explanation can there be?

(He takes the lute and plays.)

Huge mountains wear away, Alas!
The strongest beams decay, Alas!
And the sage like grass
Withers, Alas!

Tze Kung.

You make me despondent, Master. If you lose courage
What shall become of me!

(He sits down, takes the lute and sings.)

If the huge mountain crumble, say
Whither mine eyes shall wend?
If the strong beams will rot away
On what shall I depend?
If sages wither like the grass
From whom shall I then learn, alas?

K'ung Fu Tze.

My course is run, and death is near at hand.
I have grown old and feeble. There's no prince
Will offer me the place of his advisor.
My doctrine now is finished.

Tze Kung.

Yea, finished, sir!
It is completed, but it has not ended;
It but begins. The world will come to you,
Sit at your feet and follow your advice.
I see as in a vision the whole nation
Worship the sage of sages. Emperors
Will build you temples and bring offerings.

K'ung Fu Tze.

Thou art a comfort to me, Kung, my friend.

(TZE KUNG takes the lute again and sings.)

If all would go away
I would not leave my Master;
With him I mean to stay
Through sickness and disaster --
Aye, aye, forsooth.

Will stay unto the end
Till death the cord has torn,
And as his nearest friend
Will at the tomb still mourn --
    Aye, aye, forsooth.

The rest of all my life shall be
Devoted to his memory --
    Aye, aye, forsooth.

Head of K'UNG FU TZE *sinks gradually upon the table as if falling asleep. The background opens and, surrounded by clouds, the Confucian temple at Ku Fu appears with the sage's image. The emperor* KAO TZU, *the founder of the Han Dynasty, is seen with retinue. He is offering incense. While the ceremonies are in preparation and the celebrant mandarins are marching up,* TZE KUNG *addresses* K'UNG FU TZE.

Tze Kung.
    O Master, listen to my prophecy
    As in a vision I behold the future!
    Thy doctrine will take root in human hearts,
    The people flock to thee, and emperors
    Will honor thee with holy sacrifice.
    A dynasty, a great new dynasty,
    Will actualize thy thought, and it will rise
    Out of the midst of sturdy commoners.
(Turning to the scene that has opened, TZE KUNG *continues.)*
    There is a peasant youth; 'tis Liu Pang,
    Good-natured, affable, and much beloved
    Among the villagers of P'ei. Liu Pang
    Is destined to accomplish deeds of greatness.
    He leads his men to victory, for great
    Prince Hwai, whose cause he has espoused, but Heaven
    Reserved the throne for the great commoner
    Known to the world as Emperor Kao Ti.
    I see thee now before me. Praise to thee
    For exercising clemency, for stopping
    The fury of the troops, and teaching victors

Stern discipline and mastery of self.
Great Kao, praise to thee, for abrogating
The old barbaric penal code; for being
Humane upon the throne! Thou comest to teach
The people culture. Thou hast wisdom learned
From K'ung Fu Tze. It is the Master's spirit
That moves in thee and guides thy government.
I see thee now approach the sacred spot
Where on the grave of the great saint a temple
Has been erected. Hail Kao Ti! Hail! Hail!

(*Here follows performance of ritual.*)

Tze Kung.

(*Turning to* K'UNG FU TZE.)

O K'ung Fu Tze, this is thine after-life.
See here the honor given unto thee,
And listen how an emperor of worth,
The emperor of better generations,
The victor, strong in arms and kind in peace,
The founder of a broad and glorious culture,
Devout and pious, will address thy spirit:

Kao Ti.

O, K'ung, illustrious and all complete;
Thou ancient Teacher and thou perfect Sage!
Full is thy virtue, absolute thy doctrine.
Among all humankind there's none thine equal.
All kings, rulers, and princes do thee honor.
Statues of justice thou hast handed down.
A pattern art thou unto all of us.
We worship thee in humble reverence,
And filled with awe we sound our drums and bells.

Curtain.

1920 -- Jean H. Brown -- *The Honorable Mrs. Ling's Conversion*

European and American missionaries had been active in China in substantial numbers since the middle of the nineteenth century. In the early years of this undertaking, the more sanguine of them had hoped to convert not only the Emperor and the mandarins to Christianity, but through them, the whole of Chinese society. Despite their zeal, however, their efforts did not lead to success. They had not reckoned on the conservatism of the Chinese peasantry, and the long Chinese tradition of religious syncretism. As a result, their converts were always a small minority, and the steadfastness of these few remained questionable.

This play, originally printed and distributed by a missionary organization, was probably never meant to be performed. It represents the by-then faded but still persistent hope of Western proselytizers that China would eventually embrace Christianity. Despite a somewhat heavy-handed presentation of its message and an unconvincing ending, the play does contain three-dimensional characters. It also has some accurate observations of Chinese culture, and of the cross-cultural misunderstandings that made the missionaries' task so difficult. In particular, the observations on the Chinese language are sound. The play is almost certainly based on the personal experiences of the author, who is otherwise obscure.

Along with the text, excerpts from the author's comments on costumes and properties appear as well, as they also contribute to the image of the Chinese portrayed.

Reprinted by the generous permission of the Brown University Library.

The Honorable Mrs. Ling's Conversion

Costumes

MRS. LING *wears the dress of a wealthy Chinese lady. In the first scene, when the curtain rises, she has on a handsomely embroidered silk skirt. Her kimono* [sic] *is bright-colored but not elaborate. The one which* GOLDEN LILY *brings to her from the trunk is more elegant, and this she puts over the one she already has on. Her hair, which is parted in the middle, is brought very smoothly over the ears and is coiled low on the neck. She wears a flower in the side of the coil in addition to the headdress which she is adjusting when the curtain rises. To give the appearance of the tiny feet of a Chinese woman, her toes are bound into a pair of small Chinese shoes. The binding, which is a strip of cotton two or three inches wide, winds around the foot to the ankle and is so adjusted as to keep the shoe in place. Her make-up should be very white with very bright rouge on the cheeks and lips, and eyebrows very black and sloping.*

GOLDEN LILY *wears plain dark blue cotton kimono and trousers. The trousers are loose and reach half-way between the knees and the ankles. She also wears a small square apron of the same material which hangs without gathers from a cord around the waist, straw sandals, and no stockings. Her hair, drawn very straight back from her face, is worn high in a Psyche knot from the top and sides of which project long silver ornaments. Three narrow flat strips of shining metal seven or eight inches long, half an inch wide, and pointed somewhat at the ends will answer as substitutes for these hair ornaments. Large loops of heavy steel wire will do for the silver earrings which she wears. Her make-up should be a yellow-brown with no red in it. In the third and fifth scenes she wears a light blue cotton kimono and flowers in her hair.*

SOOTHSAYER *wears a long loose coat nearly to the ankles. It has ample sleeves which cover his hands. His trousers are tied closely about the ankle. He wears a red flannel hood which extends down the back to the waist forming a long narrow cape. The edge of the hood is bordered with a strip of velvet or other black material two inches wide. He also wears large spectacles. His make-up should be yellow-brown.*

CHILDREN *wear bright colored trousers and kimonos. The girls wear either a narrow band decorated with flowers, or a hood which may be made from large bandana handkerchief, one corner of which is folded back from the face, the opposite corner hanging down the back to form a cape.*

OLD RAG *wears a small black skull cap with a red knob on top.*

HEAVENLY WISDOM *wears a loose white cotton coat extending a little below the hips, and loose light blue cotton trousers which are tied neatly at the ankle. He wears a black skull cap with a red knob on top. His make-up should be dark brown.*

COOLIE *wears plain dark blue or black cotton coat and trousers. The coat is loose and extends a little below the hips. The trousers come half-way between the knees and the ankles and hang loose and straight. His hat is made of bamboo and grass and is broad-brimmed, extending almost to the edge of his shoulders. The small crown comes sharply to a peak. The hat may be constructed from cardboard and covered with raffia. He wears grass sandals on his bare feet. Make-up should be dark brown.*

BIG SISTER *and* SISTER NUMBER THREE *wear plain light blue cotton kimonos and trousers. Their hair is worn parted and combed very smoothly over the ears and coiled low on the neck. They also wear a flower in the coil The make-up should be rather light.*

MR. LING *wears the elegant costume of a Chinese official, consisting of a long silk coat and sleeveless overcoat, and trousers and leggings of contrasting colors. The leggings are tied neatly at the ankles. His hat is a round turban with upturned brim. It has a tassel of red silk that spreads itself all over the crown and the hat is worn tied under his chin. He wears a long string of large glass beads around his neck. He also wears large spectacles. His make-up should be yellow-brown.*

DR. WOODBY *is dressed in plain white.*

MISS WOODBY *is dressed in simple street costume.*

If Chinese shoes cannot be obtained, wear plain black slippers. Chinese characters should all wear white stockings except with sandals, when no stockings are worn.

Properties

It adds greatly to the interest of the play to have the properties genuine articles from China: idols, ancestral tablets, scrolls, and curios may often be obtained from missionary boards at a small rental charge.

. . .Charms: The SOOTHSAYER'S *charms are two oval pieces of wood 3 inches in length, rounded on one side and flat on the other and tied together with a string four or five inches long. Fortunes are good or bad according to the manner in which these fall when they are tossed up. Two flat sides or two rounded sides or a flat side and a round side all have their special significance. . .*

Chinese cups are without handles. They may often be obtained from Chinese restaurants. . .

Scrolls for wall decorations. Anyone with artistic taste can design these. They may be made of red paper decorated with Chinese inscriptions in black, or of white paper with colored floral or landscape designs. . .

ACT I.

Scene: *A room in* MRS. LING'S *house. In the back and center of the stage is an altar decorated elaborately in gold and black, on which are ancestral tablets and Chinese idols. Placed at back and center of altar and somewhat elevated is the Goddess of Mercy, the divine Kuan-Yin. A brass incense burner filled with smoking incense sticks is before the goddess. On either side of the brass burner is a tall red candle in a brass candlestick. The wall back of the altar is decorated with a large red banner elaborately designed in embroidery and Chinese characters. On each side of the red banner are scrolls depicting scenes from Chinese life. The other walls of the stage are also hung with scrolls. A small wooden box or leather trunk stands on a bench at the right of the stage. A small table is placed on the left of the stage and a chair stands at the right of the altar. Potted plants and palms are placed about the room.*

As the curtain rises, MRS. LING *is seen in the center front of the stage seated before a small table which holds a Chinese lacquer dressing-case, adjusting a head-dress.*

Mrs. Ling. (*Looking into the mirror.*) There, that is better. A little more rouge on my lips and more black on my eyebrows and I shall do very well. Better than my sister-in-law, anyway. She's a fright, her feet are so big -- not small and dainty like mine. The book of etiquette says that a woman's feet should be bound short, so that she can walk with mincing steps and sway like a willow tree (*Sways backward and forward as she speaks.*), and that suits me exactly. There's nothing so vulgar as big feet! My golden lilies have been the envy of all my neighbors. But where is my hair-oil? Where is my daughter-in-law? Sweep House, come here quickly! Stupid, where is my hair-oil? (*Enter* GOLDEN LILY, *who searches in the drawer of the dressing-case.*) I look like one of those white-faced barbarian women with my hair all frowzled up like this. Come, stupid, help me comb my hair. And find my hair ornaments and earrings.

Golden Lily. (*Meekly.*) Yes, honorable Mother-in-law, I'll find them for you. Here they are in this drawer. (*Puts flowers in* MRS. LING'S *hair and helps her to adjust her headdress.*)

Mrs. Ling. The sage says, "In powdering the face, remember that the heart should be kept pure and white; in arranging the head-dress, consider that the heart needs to be carefully regulated; in oiling the hair, resolve to make the heart pliable and docile." That's very good advice for you, stupid; you need to be made docile. A young wife should be an echo in the house. Now, stupid, go and call the soothsayer; I want to go calling if today is propitious. Go quickly, I tell you, and bring him here. I must find out if the wind and the water are good. You are so slow, stupid!

Golden Lily. (Dejectedly.)   Yes, honorable Mother-in-law. *(She goes out.)*

Mrs. Ling. (To herself as she looks in the glass.) Now if the soothsayer says the day is lucky for crossing the threshold, I'll dress up and go and see some of my neighbors. I'll put on my best -- no, my second-best clothes are good enough -- better than theirs, anyway. Won't I make them envious!

Enter GOLDEN LILY *and* SOOTHSAYER.

Golden Lily. The soothsayer has come, Mother-in-law.
(SOOTHSAYER *bows Chinese fashion with hands clasped.* MRS. LING, *overawed, rises and bows in the same manner.*)

Mrs. Ling. Stupid, give him a chair and table. (GOLDEN LILY *brings chair and table.*)   Be seated, venerable soothsayer. (SOOTHSAYER *seats himself before the table, clears his throat, casts his eyes up to the ceiling, clears his throat again.*)

Soothsayer. Madam, the all-wise is before you. He can tell your fate written in the pathway of the stars and can unfold the will of the gods. He can see far into the future and knows all that affects your fortune, both the great and the small.

Mrs. Ling. (Greatly impressed.) Venerable soothsayer, I tremble at the thought of your wisdom. You who know the great and the small of my life, tell me, now, if this is a lucky day for me to journey forth from my threshold. Are the wind and the water favorable?

Soothsayer. (Casting his eyes upward and looking wise.) I will consult the book of the all-wise, the infallible guide for daily life. You were born (*Looking in book he has drawn from his sleeve.*) --

Mrs. Ling. (Eagerly.) In the eleventh moon.

Soothsayer. You need not say -- the all-wise knows everything. The eleventh moon, of course, and hem--hem--hem--the--sun--

Mrs. Ling. (With still greater eagerness.) On the third sun.

Soothsayer. (*Severely.*) Do not interrupt. Certainly it was on the third sun. (*Fumbles at his book, scrutinizing the pages closely.*) We will see if the charms agree with the infallible guide. (*While* MRS. LING *and* GOLDEN LILY *look on with keen interest, the* SOOTHSAYER *dives down into the other sleeve and produces the charms, tosses them on the table three times. He clears his throat, casts his eyes up, looks solemn, then says oracularly.*) The charms agree.

Mrs. Ling. And shall I meet any unlucky person?

Soothsayer. (*Dives down into his sleeve and produces a mirror.*) I will look into the mirror of fate where the image of all those whom you shall meet is reflected. (*Looks wisely into the mirror.*) Madam, if you ride through the street of Singular Good Fortune, you will meet no unlucky person.

Mrs. Ling. And shall I say any unlucky word?

Soothsayer. (*Oracularly.*) Madam, keep a silent tongue and you will utter no unlucky word.

Mrs. Ling. I am a woman of few words. That will be easy for me. (SOOTHSAYER *shrugs his shoulders and pulls a face, sceptically.*) And I shall travel in safety?

Soothsayer. Madam, follow my instructions and you will travel in safety.

Mrs. Ling. Sweep House, go get a string of cash. Since the forecast is good, give him a long string. (GOLDEN LILY *goes to the chest and produces a string of cash, which she presents to the* SOOTHSAYER, *who takes it solemnly and hangs it about his neck.*)

Soothsayer. (*Rising.*) But beware of the evil eye, madam; beware!

Mrs. Ling. (*Rising.*) That I will, but I beg you to leave me a charm, venerable master, which shall protect my house from its malign influences.

Soothsayer. (*Taking a strip of colored paper from his sleeve.*) Hang this on your door, madam. Do not fail.

Mrs. Ling. Sweep House shall do so at once.

Soothsayer. (*Bowing Chinese fashion.*) Sit! Sit!

Mrs. Ling. (*Bowing in same manner.*) Slowly, slowly walk. (SOOTHSAYER *goes out.* MRS. LING, *forgetting to give the charm to* GOLDEN LILY, *puts it on the table beside her dressing-case.*) Now, stupid, take away the chair and the table. The wind and the water are good, so help me to dress. Get my gown out of my chest. No, not that one, the other one. You are so slow and so stupid! Why do you suppose I paid so much money for you when you were a baby! Bah, my son is to be pitied with such a wife as you! Come now, be smart. Fill my pipe. I haven't eaten smoke since I got up, and my stomach is faint. (GOLDEN LILY *takes the pipe from the altar and prepares to fill it.*) Put more water in and pound the tobacco down well, stupid one.

Golden Lily. (*Dejectedly hands the pipe to* MRS. LING.) Yes, honorable Mother-in-law. (*Sniffles and wipes her eyes.*)

Mrs. Ling. (*Smoking.*) Come now, get my foot-warmer. See that there are fresh coals in it. (GOLDEN LILY *does so.*) Well, put my feet on it. Oh, it's not half warm! Sniffling again, eh? Ungrateful creature! There is my sister-in-law, she beats her slave nearly every day, and you know I don't beat you unless I have to.

Golden Lily. (*In a muffled voice.*) Yes -- yes -- honorable Mother-in-law.

Mrs. Ling. Come now, help me with these clothes. Fix my kimono, stupid one. You are so awkward! I shall certainly beat you if you are so clumsy. Well, how do I look? Can't you look up, foolish one? Are you blind?

Golden Lily. Oh, honorable Mother-in-law, you are very handsome. You are like the Kuan-Yin.

Mrs. Ling. (*Pleased.*) Ha, ha, the Kuan-Yin indeed! Not so bad from such a foolish creature as you are. When I was young I was called a jade stone, I was so beautiful; but then, as the saying goes, three-tenths of beauty is beauty, and seven-tenths is dress. (*Preening herself.*) But you, stupid, no matter how much fine dress you wore, could never be a Kuan-Yin. Kuan-Yin, indeed! Go and worship her, Daughter-in-law. Beg her to send you a son who will carry on the honorable name of Ling and will do reverence to my name -- not a stupid girl like you. I shall curse you, remember, if you do not have a son, and you shall be despised and worthless in our family. So far only two worthless girls like yourself! Here I live on the street of Ten Thousand Grandsons and have only one grandson to my name, thanks to you. (GOLDEN LILY *at the altar has lighted the candles and incense and now bows three times.*) Put up the papers and drive the evil spirits away, for I feel them about. (*She continues to smoke.*) See that they do not intercept your prayers. (GOLDEN LILY *pins the idol papers on the altar. Enter* PRECIOUS GOLD, BEAUTIFUL PEARL, *and* OLD RAG, *running breathless and frightened.*)

Children. (Together.) Oh, Mother! Mother! MOTHER!

Mrs. Ling and Golden Lily: (Together.) What's the matter? What's the matter?

Precious Gold. (Pointing to the door.) Hi ya! There's a foreign woman coming down the street. We were standing at the outer door of the court, and we saw the foreign woman coming.

Mrs. Ling. (Sternly.) You should not stand at the outer door. Haven't I told you many times that it is very shameful for girls to appear out of doors? There will be a scandal among the neighbors if you do so, and worse still, you will displease the spirit of your great-great-great-grandmother, who was famous because of her virtue. For twelve years she never looked outside of her door.

Precious Gold. It must have been very dull, Grandmother.

Mrs. Ling. Dull! It was very virtuous. You children stay in the house in future or I shall punish you. Those foreign people will steal you and shut you up in their dark cellars. Daughter-in-law, go and see if the foreign devil is coming. (GOLDEN LILY *goes to the door and peers out. The children follow, clinging to her.*) Well, stupid, what do you see?

Golden Lily. She is coming here. She is knocking. Shall I let her in?

Mrs. Ling. (Hesitates.) No--well--yes--yes--let her come. I have never invited one of those foreign barbarians into my house, but it is the fashion nowadays to let them come and see the house. I despise them, but let her come. Children, come here. Stay beside me. I have heard they make medicine out of children's eyes and do horrible things.

Enter GOLDEN LILY *with* MISS WOODBY. MRS. LING *rises and both women bow ceremoniously in Chinese fashion.*

Miss Woodby. Peace, honorable madam.

Mrs. Ling. (Stiffly.) I invite you to sit.

Miss Woodby. You sit first, honorable madam.

Mrs. Ling. You sit first. (*They press each other to sit. Finally both sit at once.*) Have you eaten rice?

Miss Woodby. I have eaten. Have you eaten rice?

Mrs. Ling. Not yet eaten. Daughter-in-law, pass the pipe.

(GOLDEN LILY *brings the pipe which is on the corner of the altar and offers it with both hands to* MISS WOODBY.)

Miss Woodby. No thank you. (*Waves it aside with a motion of her hand.*)

Mrs. Ling. (*Surprised.*) Don't you eat smoke?

Miss Woodby. No thank you

Mrs. Ling. Now that is strange. I have very little strength if I do not eat smoke. Daughter-in-law, pass the tea. (*From the altar,* GOLDEN LILY *brings cups of tea and with both hands presents them, one at a time, to* MISS WOODBY *and* MRS. LING) Will the honorable lady have some of this bad-tasting tea? It's not fit to drink.

Miss Woodby. You drink first, honorable madam.

Mrs. Ling. No, you drink first.

Miss Woodby. No, you drink first. (*Both urge each other to drink in this manner, but finally both drink together.*)

Mrs. Ling. You speak our language very well.

Miss Woodby. Oh, very little and very poorly. My brogue is very heavy.

Mrs. Ling. You must be very clever to speak our language so well. How long have you been in our country?

Miss Woodby. Five years.

Mrs. Ling. (*In exaggerated astonishment.*) Five years! Hi, ya! But you are clever! Wonderful! You speak just like a native, so plainly! (*Turning to* GOLDEN LILY, *aside.*) Her brogue is so heavy, I can't understand half she says.

Golden Lily. (*Aside.*) Oh hush, Mother-in-law; she will hear you. (*To* MISS WOODBY.) You speak our language very plainly, teacher.

Mrs. Ling. How old are you, teacher?

Miss Woodby. Thirty-five, nearly.

Mrs. Ling. From your venerable appearance, I would have taken you for much older. (MISS WOODBY *laughs.* MRS. LING *feels* MISS WOODBY'S *dress.*) You have very pretty clothes. How many tiers of clothing have you on? Aren't you very cold?

Miss Woodby. Oh, no. See! I have two tiers of clothing on. (*Showing her skirt and underskirt.*) How many tiers have you?

Mrs. Ling. Oh, I have four tiers. (*Shows two or three kimonos.*)

Golden Lily. (*Looking closely at* MISS WOODBY'S *hair.*)

Teacher, do you comb your hair?

Miss Woodby. (*Laughing.*) Oh, yes indeed, several times a day!

Golden Lily. (*Aside to* MRS. LING.) It's so frowzy, Mother-in-law!

Miss Woodby. (*Turning to* GOLDEN LILY.) But whose are these children? Are they yours?

Golden Lily. The girls are mine, the boy is their cousin.

Miss Woodby. They are very pretty children.

Mrs. Ling. Oh, very homely, very homely. Not smart.

Miss Woodby. What are your names, children? (CHILDREN *hide behind their mother and grandmother.*) You need not be afraid of me. I love children. Come, tell me your name. (*Speaking coaxingly to* PRECIOUS GOLD.)

Mrs. Ling. Her name (*Pointing to* PRECIOUS GOLD.) is Precious Gold, and second sister's name is Beautiful Pearl. Boy's name is Old Rag. That's his milk name. When he goes to school to have the darkness lifted, he will be called Ink Grinder.

Miss Woodby. I understand you give these names to the boy to protect him from the evil spirits.

Mrs. Ling. To be sure -- for no other reason.

Miss Woodby. And do you think the evil spirits will not touch your little girls?

Mrs. Ling. Oh, no, they are only girls. Spirits do not think it worth while to harm them.

Miss Woodby. And what is that the little boy wears about his neck?

Mrs. Ling. That is a charm to keep the evil spirits away. Boys are our greatest treasure, and we Chinese take good care of them. We say, "One deformed son is worth more that eighteen daughters as wise as the apostles of Buddha."

Miss Woodby. But why do you not consider your girls precious also?

Mrs. Ling. Girls! -- Girls are as dangerous as smuggled salt. You always lose your money on girls. Besides, girls have no brains. They are stupid and worthless creatures. Look at my daughter-in-law, see how stupid and ignorant she is.

Miss Woodby. But she could be taught. If she had a chance, she could learn. Has she ever been to school?

Mrs. Ling. To school! No, indeed! What would she go to school for? She couldn't learn. Could you, stupid one?

Golden Lily. (With eyes cast down and very meekly.) No, honorable Mother-in-law.

Mrs. Ling. You haven't any brains, have you?

Golden Lily. No, honorable Mother-in-law.

Mrs. Ling. You're only a poor stupid girl, aren't you?

Golden Lily. Yes, honorable Mother-in-law.

Mrs. Ling. My son, now, is very clever. His stomach is full of wisdom. He knows all the wise sayings of the sages.

Miss Woodby. But if you would allow his wife to go to school, she would become wise too. I came to China to teach women like your daughter-in-law, and little children like these. I have a school where they may learn. Do let them come to me. You love this great country of yours. We missionaries love China too, and desire her good. You Chinese women have many burdens, many sorrows. We American women have come to help you. We have come to tell you the Jesus way, that you may know the joy and happiness of it.

Mrs. Ling. (As they both rise.) Honorable teacher, I cannot offend my ancestors by listening to you. They would punish me if I did so and send plague and disease upon me. I do not like the way you foreigners come to our country and upset our customs. We are very well as we are, and we do not wish you here.

Miss Woodby. (Smiling.) But perhaps you will come and call on me. Come and see my house some day, and look around our school. And let the children and your daughter-in-law come too. (MRS. LING *bows stiffly.*)

Golden Lily. I greatly thank you, honorable teacher. (*All bow ceremoniously, Chinese fashion,* MISS WOODBY *still bowing as she backs to the door.*)

Miss Woodby. Peace, peace to you all. (*She goes out.*)

Mrs. Ling. (Turning to GOLDEN LILY *and speaking sharply.*) Stupid one, never allow a foreigner to come into my house again. Do you hear? I hate and despise them. And I forbid you going near them -- you or the children. I will have none of their religion. (*In sudden recollection.*) Ah, the soothsayer! What did he say? Beware of the evil eye. What have you done with his charm, lazy one? (*Shrilly.*) You did not hang it on the door and this is the result. The evil eye of that foreign woman is upon us. No telling what disaster will come to us now. Where is the charm? What have you done with it?

Golden Lily. (*Taking it up from the table.*) Here it is, Mother-in-law.

Mrs. Ling. Well, what did you put it there for? Go fasten it to the door and drive away the influences of the evil eye of that foreign woman. (*GOLDEN LILY fastens the charm on the door.*) Now you and the children go and worship the Kuan-Yin. (*Outside, the sound of a gong is heard.*) It is the hour of prayer. (*Gong sounds again.*) The priests are chanting. (GOLDEN LILY *and the three* CHILDREN *stand before the altar, bowing in unison three times while the gong-beating continues. The priests are heard chanting the Buddhist rites "Ah-me-doh-ah-me-doh-ah-me-doh-ah-me-doh" in a prolonged, chanting tone. Curtain is drawn, and the priests sing:*)

Dzao T'ien dzao di iu dzao zen
Da yiu zen nai dz pe zen
Nyun pen T'ien dang da Tso-tsai
Tzao van dzen sin you chin pai.

(*Curtain opens, the gong sounds, and the chanting is continued while the* CHILDREN *and* GOLDEN LILY *stand in tableau before the altar.*)

Curtain.

ACT II.

Scene: Sitting room in a missionary home. The furniture is willow; matting on floor; in the center and front a table, on each side of which is a rocking chair; at the back and center a bookcase; on the left of table a small desk partly facing the audience; pictures on the walls, and flowers and ferns suitably arranged about the room.

DR. WOODBY *sits at the desk writing, tears up sheets of paper, throws them in wastebasket, folds others, puts them in envelopes, stamps envelopes, seals them. A clock on the book-shelf strikes nine. She glances up at it, then turns to her work again. School bell sounds from without. Singing is heard in the distance. She rises and listens at the door. Smiles as she turns to the desk again. Enter* MISS WOODBY *hurriedly with books and reports in her hand. She places them on the table and sits in the chair to the right.*

Miss Woodby. Good morning, Lucy.

Dr. Woodby. Good morning, Frances.

Miss Woodby. Where did you go so early this morning that I did not see you at breakfast?

Dr. Woodby. (*Takes up her letters and moves to the gable, seating herself in the left chair.*) I was called out to see a patient and could not get back in time for breakfast. When I returned, Heavenly Wisdom said you had already gone to school.

Miss Woodby. Yes, we are just through chapel services. Did you hear us singing?

Dr. Woodby. Indeed I did. It always thrills me when I hear those dear girls singing. Your chapel services are one of the most inspiring features of our life here. I can think of no greater work than this that you are doing among the girls in China.

Miss Woodby. Unless it is yours, my dear. Doors that are closed to me are opened eagerly for you. You are sought for the gift of healing.

Dr. Woodby. That is true. Though I should not be satisfied unless I could also give spiritual comfort together with healing. (*Takes up one of her letters.*) I am writing to our society at home telling them of your work and mine.

Miss Woodby. Oh, then do not forget to tell them how unspeakably happy we are in doing it; how crammed full of interest our days are. I fancy sometimes the folks at home pity us for living out here alone; but if they could see the girls in school, if they could see their bright, eager faces, and if they could see you as you go to the hospital and clinics making life better for thousands, surely they would envy rather than pity us. Of course, they must know we do have our hardships and disappointments, many of them; but the joy of the work far outweighs these.

Dr. Woodby. Let me read you what I have written. (*Reading from her letter.*) "I cannot find words to express the joy and satisfaction of this work. We are busy every minute of the day and sometimes of the night too, but happy -- oh, so happy! You must come and see for yourselves if you would be convinced. Do come, all of you." (*Puts the letter in an envelope and seals it.*)

Miss Woodby. It surely would be exciting if all those dear ladies should suddenly descend upon us.

Dr. Woodby. Yes, wouldn't it? Fancy some of those good

immaculate housekeepers over there in the little old United States being obliged to sleep in some of the places we sleep in when we are touring the field. Wouldn't they shiver with horror!

Miss Woodby. However, I think most of them would settle down just as we do and think it a great life.

Dr. Woodby. Probably they would. I hope so, anyway. (*Rings the bell.*) We could put them all to work, certainly, if they were here. (*Enter* HEAVENLY WISDOM. *Whisks in briskly.*) Heavenly Wisdom, take these letters to the postman at once. You must hurry, for I want them to go on the next steamer.

Heavenly Wisdom. (*Smiles broadly and bows.*) Yes, missy. My catchee him all the samee, chop chop. My catchee him number one plopper. (*Whisks out, putting the letter in the top of his cap and placing his cap on his head.*)

Miss Woodby. Dear old Heavenly Wisdom! His name is among the faithful; but what a whirlwind he is. He upsets all our traditional beliefs in respect to Oriental leisure and repose. When he says he will do a thing "chop chop," we know he will do it with electric speed.

Dr. Woodby. But, oh, if he did not use that awful pidjin English on us. Why will he not speak in Chinese? He evidently distrusts our ability to do justice to his native tongue.

Miss Woodby. And for that I confess he has some justification. Doubtless we do murder the celestial language horridly. It was only yesterday, you remember, you ordered fruit for dinner, and because you gave the wrong tone, you got sheep's tails.

Dr. Woodby. (*Laughs.*) Funny, wasn't it? I am afraid I make many a slip in tone. I haven't forgotten the time the cook put a cup of sugar in the gravy instead of hot water because I made a mistake between the first and fifth tone. (*Both laugh.*)

Miss Woodby. Oh, this language! Its difficulties are not to be numbered. (*She takes up some of her reports, begins folding them, slipping some of them into envelopes.*)

Dr. Woodby. Here, I'll help you. (*She takes a few and folds them also. They both work a moment in silence, then* MISS WOODBY *sighs.*) Why the sigh, my dear?

Miss Woodby. Oh -- you remember -- I told you about the family I called upon the other day, Mrs. Ling and her daughter-in-law?

Dr. Woodby. Yes, I remember. You were all used up about it when you reached home.

Miss Woodby. Well, I am worried about them. I can't get them out of my mind for some reason. The girl's face haunts me. It was absolutely woebegone. She was so crushed and pitiful, clearly so unhappy. (*Rising and walking back and forth behind the table.*) Oh, I tell you, Lucy, I feel desperate sometimes when I see girls like Golden Lily ground to dust, trampled upon, the drudge and slave of the whole family! I feel as though I must help her. But how am I to reach her! The doors are closed against me, and I feel powerless.

Dr. Woodby. However, Mrs. Ling did receive you. That's something. I didn't suppose she would even do that much.

Miss Woodby. No, I scarcely expected that myself; but she was only coldly civil. Mrs. Greatheart, the Bible woman, says she is a regular vixen. At present Mrs. Ling's son, Golden Lily's husband, is away on business in the North, and during his absence Mrs. Ling is even more tyrannical than usual towards his wife. Mrs. Greatheart says Golden Lily would like to attend our services at Eastgate but she does not dare to because her mother-in-law is so bitterly opposed to foreigners. (*Seating herself.*) Mrs. Greatheart is tremendously stirred up about it, but feels as helpless to act as I do. Curiously enough, although I feel this burning indignation towards Mrs. Ling, I pity her, too, and I long as much to help her as to emancipate Golden Lily from her clutches. There is something about her that attracts me powerfully. You know how some of these Chinese women have that characteristic.

Dr. Woodby. (*Rising.*) Yes, I have seen them dominate the whole family -- husband and all.

Miss Woodby. From what Mrs. Greatheart tells me, I judge Mr. Ling is of the henpecked variety.

Dr. Woodby. I shouldn't wonder if he were. But it is just that sort of woman who can be of immense power for good if one can reach her.

Miss Woodby. Oh, Mrs. Ling must be won! But how?

Dr. Woodby. (*Going over to her sister and placing her hand on her shoulder.*) My dear, it can only be done by the power of the still, small voice.

Miss Woodby. (*Taking her hand.*) You dear old Saw-bones! I am so impatient -- I forget so often! But you are my blessed reminder.

Dr. Woodby. There is nothing, Frances, nothing so potent in all the world as the still, small voice of the spirit.

Miss Woodby. I know it, Lucy. Help me to remember!

Dr. Woodby. (As she walks to the door.) My dear, we will help each other to remember. *(She goes out at left.* MISS WOODBY *takes up reports, slips some into envelopes and seals them. Enter* HEAVENLY WISDOM *from the right.)*

Heavenly Wisdom. Missy, teacher, one little missy wanche comee look see. Coolie man him talkee, talkee alle time, talkee too much.

Miss Woodby. Oh, very well. Bring her in here, Heavenly Wisdom. *(Continues her work.* HEAVENLY WISDOM *goes out right. (Loud voices are heard without.)*

Coolie. (From outside.) I tell you I will come in.

Heavenly Wisdom (Just outside the door.) No can do, no can do. Too dirty.

Coolie. Dirty, nothing! She won't go less I go too, and the baggage goes where I go, you old paper tiger.

Miss Woodby. (Going to door.) Why, what is the matter, Heavenly Wisdom?

Heavenly Wisdom. To much blobbery. Hem make too much blobbery.

Miss Woodby. Well, Heavenly Wisdom, you seem to be making a good deal of noise yourself.

Heavenly Wisdom. Him alle samee, wanche come with leetle sister. No can do. No plopper.

Miss Woodby. Oh, it's proper enough. Let him come, if he must, and the baggage too.

Enter PLUM BLOSSOM, *very shy and timid, with umbrella, bundle, and teapot. Enter* COOLIE *carrying a pole on his shoulder, from one end of which hangs a small trunk or basket and from the other, a roll of bedding. He puts the baggage down.*

Coolie. Hi, ya! *(Wipes his face with his sleeve.)* Hi, ya! That 'ere's a heavy load for one man. That 'ere paper tiger *(Pointing with his lips toward the door.)* didn't want to let me in, but said I, I ain't going to let that leetle sister part from me nor that baggage neither 'till I put them in your hands. That's her bed and that's her clothes. *(Pointing with his foot.)* Hi, ya! *(Wiping his face again.)* It's a long mile we've come.

Miss Woodby. Where have you come from?

Coolie. (*Pointing with his lips.*) Small Horse Village, up there in Bamboo Mountains. (*Seats himself in a chair to the right.*) It's a long way for the leetle one. Twenty miles. (*Indicating with his ten fingers outspread.*) Understand? Her and me come down with some of the neighbors that was bringin' down tea and rice from up there. Hi, ya! Had to get up at cock-crowing. We are mighty tired and hungry. Just had a bite over there on the Street of Refreshing Breezes. (*Slight pause.*) When we was drinkin' our tea over there, a woman come along and wanted to know where the foreign devil's school was. She was cryin' like. Looked as if she felt pretty bad, and I said "Just come right along with us. We're goin' to the foreign devil's school ourselves." So she come along.

Miss Woodby. And where is she now?

Coolie. (*Pointing with his lips.*) Out there. She was cryin' all the time. Wanted to see the teacher woman.

Miss Woodby. We will see her presently. Now tell me, little sister, what's your name? (*Little girl moves nearer to* COOLIE, *hangs her head lower but does not speak.*)

Coolie. Plum Blossom, that's her name.

Miss Woodby. How old are you, Plum Blossom? Can't you speak the language?

Coolie. She's afraid. She can talk fast a-plenty at home. Tongue claps all day like a water-wheel when she ain't afeard.

Miss Woodby. Don't be afraid, Plum Blossom. Come tell me how old you are. (PLUM BLOSSOM *hangs her head still lower.*)

Coolie. (*Indicating with his fingers.*) Ten and two. Understand? Plenty old enough to be a little stay-at-home, but her father's got some of those new-fangled ideas. He wants her to be a learned book woman, wants her to stuff her stomach full of words just like a man's. Can't be done. Now there's my wife, Old Broom and Dustpan, she's number one good when it comes to hoein' rice and plowin' and carryin' tea -- just as good as me, but when it comes to learnin' (*Laughs.*), she's as stupid as a pig. Don't think much of these new foreign idees anyhow.

Miss Woodby. (*Smiling.*) Oh, don't you? Why not? (*Slipping reports into envelopes.*)

Coolie. Why, a man told me these foreign devil schools say the world is round. Round! (*Laughs.*) Any fool can see it's flat, flat as my hand, 'cept where there're mountains like Bamboo Mountains. (MISS WOODBY, *laughing, seals one of her envelopes with her tongue. The* COOLIE *looks on, his eyes widening in amazement.* When MISS WOODBY *takes up a second report and seals it, his astonishment bursts into words.*)

Coolie. Hi, ya! There! What -- you doin'? Leetle sister, look, look at her! Hi, ya! There! (*He brushes past little sister and peers into the face of* MISS WOODBY, *then takes up an envelope, looking at it curiously.*)

Miss Woodby. Well, what's the matter?

Coolie. Say, what kind of glue have you got on your tongue? We Chinese haven't any glue like that on our tongues.

Miss Woodby. (*Puzzled.*) Glue! On my tongue?

Coolie. Yes, what you stuck the letter with.

Miss Woodby. (*Gradually understanding.*) Oh! (*Laughing.*) The glue is not on my tongue. It is on the envelope, see? (*She shows him an envelope.*) Now you try it. (*The* COOLIE *takes the envelope and rubs his tongue over it and presses it between his hands.*)

Coolie. Hi, ya, leetle sister, look at that! Ain't that queer? Everything is queer about these foreigners. (*Looks around the room.*) Now ain't this a queer lookin' house, Plum Blossom? (PLUM BLOSSOM *whispers to him.*) Clean, did you say? Yes, but it has a queer foreign smell, hasn't it? (*Sniffing the air.* MISS WOODBY *rings the bell. Enter* HEAVENLY WISDOM.)

Miss Woodby. Call one of the teachers, Heavenly Wisdom. Call Big Sister. Now, Plum Blossom, don't be afraid. You will be happy when you get used to us.

Coolie. She cried her eyes out to come, and I swear she'll cry her eyes out to get home. Contrary, just like a woman.

Miss Woodby. (*Patting her shoulder.*) Oh no, she is going to be very happy with the girls. (PLUM BLOSSOM *looks up and smiles. Enter* BIG SISTER.) Big Sister, here's a new girl. Take her to the junior department and give her something to eat and show the carrier where to take the bedding.

Big Sister. Yes, teacher, I will go at once. (COOLIE *takes up his load, and* PLUM BLOSSOM *and he follow* BIG SISTER *to the door. After they pass out,* BIG SISTER *turns at the door.*) Oh teacher, there's a woman in the courtyard who wants to see you. She came with these people.

Miss Woodby. Oh, yes, the load bearer spoke of someone he met on the road. Show her the way here. (MISS WOODBY *seats herself at the table and is looking over her reports when* GOLDEN LILY *enters and stands timidly at the door*.)

Golden Lily. (*Hesitatingly*.) Teacher!

Miss Woodby. (*Looking up*.) Why! -- Why! You, Golden Lily! (*Rises and meets her*.) It's you? How did you get here? Come, sit, sit.

Golden Lily. (*Beginning to cry*.) I -- I -- I!

Miss Woodby. Why, there now, don't cry. Tell me about it.

Golden Lily. (*Sobbing*.) I -- I --

Miss Woodby. There! There! Don't cry. Tell me what the trouble is.

Golden Lily. I ran -- I ran away.

Miss Woodby. You ran away? Couldn't stand it any longer?

Golden Lily. No -- no. She -- she -- burned -- my -- arm. She was so angry.

Miss Woodby. (*Horrified*.) What! You mean she has burned you?

Golden Lily. Yes, with incense burners. (*Pulls up her sleeve and shows a scarred arm*.)

Miss Woodby. Oh, dear, dear! Horrible. I must call the doctor. (*Rings the bell and writes a note. Enter* HEAVENLY WISDOM.) Heavenly Wisdom, take this note to the hospital.

Heavenly Wisdom. Yes missy. (*He goes out*.)

Miss Woodby. (*Bending over* GOLDEN LILY.) Oh, this is dreadful. You poor child.

Golden Lily. The pain was terrible. It is not so bad now. She said she would burn the other arm today, so I ran away. Oh, she will be very, very angry when she finds it out. (*Enter* SISTER NUMBER THREE.)

Miss Woodby. Oh, Sister Number Three, the doctor could not come?

Sister Number Three. No, but she told me to take the patient to the hospital. (*Looks at the arm*.) What a pity! It's a bad burn, but we can help you.

Golden Lily. And you will let me stay with you? Oh, please do not send me back there!

Miss Woodby. (*As they all move to the door*.) Yes, you may stay -- for the present at least. (GOLDEN LILY *goes out*. SISTER NUMBER THREE *turns back to speak to* MISS WOODBY.)

Sister Number Three. (*With alarmed face*.) But teacher, won't they send for her?

Miss Woodby. (*Sighing.*) I suppose so, Sister Number Three; but in the meantime we can hope, and best of all, we can pray for the still small voice to enter the mother-in-law's heart.

Sister Number Three. (*Rolls her eyes up incredulously, as she exclaims.*) The heart of the honorable Mrs. Ling!

Curtain.

ACT III.

Missionary sitting room. HEAVENLY WISDOM *bustling about dusting and sweeping. He sweeps the dust under the book-shelves. Enter* MISS WOODBY, *looking about the room.*

Miss Woodby. Oh, Heavenly Wisdom, my sister has not come in yet, has she?

Heavenly Wisdom. No, miss, him no samee. Him do big pidjin.

Miss Woodby. Yes, I know she is busy. (*Sits down at the table. Works a moment.*) Oh, Heavenly Wisdom, did you buy that food I spoke of for the school?

Heavenly Wisdom. Less, miss my buy heapee chow chow.

Miss Woodby. Rice?

Heavenly Wisdom. (*Counting on fingers.*) Less, lice.

Miss Woodby. And fruit?

Heavenly Wisdom. Less, flute.

Miss Woodby. And fish?

Heavenly Wisdom. Less, fliss. My buy velly good chow chow. Number one ploppa chow chow. My no likee buy bad chow chow.

Miss Woodby. Very well. That will do. (*Turns to her work again.*)

Heavenly Wisdom. (*Hesitating.*) Missy.

Miss Woodby. Yes, what is it, Heavenly Wisdom?

Heavenly Wisdom. Me wantche go 'way. Go play leetle bit.

Miss Woodby. You mean you want a day off?

Heavenly Wisdom. Less, Missy. My wantche go catchee one piecee wifo.

Miss Woodby. Oh, I see. You want to get married?

Heavenly Wisdom. Less. Number one good wifo.

Miss Woodby. She has big feet, I suppose.

Heavenly Wisdom. No, him no have big feet. Him have leetle feet. (*Indicating the size with finger and thumb.*) Nice leetle feet. Leetle feet more better.

Miss Woodby. More better! Why are little feet more better?

Heavenly Wisdom. Him no can walkee too muchee, then him no can talkee too muchee. Him more quiet, more better.

Miss Woodby. Well, we won't discuss that now. You may go tomorrow if you wish.

Heavenly Wisdom. Tankee, missy. (*Goes out, turns, puts his head through the door into the room again.*) Oh, missy, you wantche stewed Irish for dinna?

Miss Woodby. (*Puzzled.*) Stewed Irish for dinner? Oh, yes, certainly. Irish stew. (*Exit* HEAVENLY WISDOM *on the left. Enter* DR. WOODBY *on the right.*) Well, I am glad you're here, Lucy. I have been waiting for you, hoping you would come in. I need your advice about Golden Lily.

Dr. Woodby. Yes, what is it?

Miss Woodby. Her arm is better, is it not?

Dr. Woodby. Quite well, now. It was a bad burn, though. Imagine the cruelty of such a thing! She must have suffered terribly. But how happy she seems to be now, going to school here with the other girls.

Miss Woodby. That's just it, she is happy. And the girls in the school love her so, they will do anything for her. Have you noticed the new clothes she is wearing? Those belong to different girls in the school. They have lent them to her. But oh dear, I am afraid every day someone will come and take her away.

Dr. Woodby. Well, we did the only thing there was to do. We took the girl in and cared for her.

Miss Woodby. And I want to keep her here. I feel as though we must save her from the tyranny of that mother-in-law. (*Loud knocking from outside.*)

Voice Shouting. Open the door there, gatekeeper! Hi, ya! Open the door there. (*Gong beats.*)

Miss Woodby. (*Rising and looking into the distance.*) What is the matter, I wonder. Someone must be coming into the compound.

Dr. Woodby. Someone of importance, too, evidently. (*Rises.*) Such a commotion is not made over an ordinary person. (*Goes to the door and looks out.*) It must be an official, to judge by the size of his retinue -- four chair-bearers, a heralder -- and here comes the runner with the official card. What can it mean!

Miss Woodby. Well, we shall soon know. Here comes Heavenly Wisdom. (*Enter* HEAVENLY WISDOM *with a large red envelope.*)

Heavenly Wisdom. (*Excitedly.*) One big pidjin man! Him comee -- look, see!

Miss Woodby. Very well, bring him here. (*Exit* HEAVENLY WISDOM.) Dear, dear, what shall we do! (*Both take the card from the envelope and look at it.*) Yes, see, the Honorable Ling, the husband himself has come.

Dr. Woodby. A most unusual proceeding. A matter of this kind is usually taken up through a go-between; but if the Honorable Ling wishes to converse with you personally, all the better. The go-between is always an obstruction to a straightforward understanding. Let's see the head of the Ling family, by all means.

Miss Woodby. The head in name only. I fancy he is an underling compared to the honorable Mrs. Ling.

Dr. Woodby. Sorry I can't stay and see the proceedings through, but I must go.

Miss Woodby. Oh, Lucy, can't you stay and help me? How can I ever get through the round and square of Chinese etiquette without your prompting -- to say nothing of more important matters?

Dr. Woodby. I really can't. I have an important operation this morning and I must be off now. As for the round and square, no foreigner can know that fully; do be as brief as decency will allow. As for knowing what to do about Golden Lily, I am sure you will have wisdom. Goodbye, my dear. (*She goes toward the door.*) Here comes the Honorable Ling. (*Exit* DR. WOODBY *on the left.* HEAVENLY WISDOM *opens the door at right.* HONORABLE LING *enters. He bows profoundly, Chinese fashion.* MISS WOODBY *also bows in the same manner.*)

Miss Woodby. Sit, honorable gentleman. Be seated, Honorable Ling.

Honorable Ling. I am too contemptible to sit in your honorable chair.

Miss Woodby. I beg you to sit in my humble chair.

Honorable Ling. I am not worthy to come under your honorable roof.

Miss Woodby. My humble roof is honored to receive your most distinguished person. I invite you to sit.

Honorable Ling. I will sit, but 'tis shameful for me to place my contemptible person before your honorable self.

They both sit at the same time. The HONORABLE LING *removes his large spectacles as a mark of respect. Seats himself with knees spread and feet placed squarely before him. He looks around rather embarrassed as though troubled to find words.*

Honorable Ling. Honorable madam, I have left my dirty and disreputable home and have come to your honorable and distinguished roof to talk with your honorable self on important business.

Miss Woodby. (*Bows.*) Important business?

Honorable Ling. It is about my unworthy son's Stay-at-Home.

Miss Woodby. Your son's Stay-at-Home?

Honorable Ling. Yes, your honorable self. She ran away, and my Dull Thorn has had people looking everywhere for her -- has had all the wells searched -- thought she had drowned herself. Only today we heard that she was under your honorable roof.

Miss Woodby. Yes, your daughter-in-law is here.

Honorable Ling. My Dull Thorn sends word to your honorable self that my son's Stay-at-Home must return at once. My Dull Thorn is a very determined woman. All the people of my humble roof must obey her. She is very angry with my son's Stay-at-Home. I am not angry; I am sorry for her. I do not make her return to my house; but my Dull Thorn would be very angry if she comes not.

Miss Woodby. Madam Ling does not like foreigners.

Honorable Ling. No, she does not like. I like them. I want my children to come to your foreign schools. I dare not say one word. My Dull Thorn gets so angry when I speak so. I go to foreign worship house sometimes. My Dull Thorn, she does not know I go there. She would curse me, if she knew. She would take opium to revenge me, if she knew. I tell my Dull Thorn that missionaries come to help my people, but she will not listen.

Miss Woodby. I am very glad that you feel as you do, and some day I am sure Mrs. Ling will change her opinion of us. Now about Golden Lily, your daughter-in-law. You think she cannot stay here with us and go to school?

Honorable Ling. No -- No. It will not do. My Dull Thorn is unwilling. I dare not defy her. She must go home.

Miss Woodby. I am sorry, very sorry, for we could help your daughter-in-law and give her a happy life; but we will see that she gets home today. You will try to protect her, will you not? Do not let Madam Ling abuse her. I beg you will restrain her from doing further harm.

Honorable Ling. It is hard; but I will try, honorable madam. (*Gets up and bows ceremoniously.*) Be seated, honorable madam.

Miss Woodby. (*Also bowing.*) Slowly, slowly walk.

Honorable Ling. (*Retiring to the door.*) Sit, sit, honorable madam. (*Exit* HONORABLE LING. MISS WOODBY *sits down.*)

Miss Woodby. Well, that's over! Poor Golden Lily! I can't bear to tell her, but I must. (*Rings the bell. Enter* HEAVENLY WISDOM.) Heavenly Wisdom, tell Golden Lily to come to me. (*As* HEAVENLY WISDOM *turns,* GOLDEN LILY *rushes in and flings herself down beside* MISS WOODBY, *burying her face in her lap. Exit* HEAVENLY WISDOM.)

Golden Lily. Oh, teacher, I know, I know! I have heard. She has sent for me. Oh, how can I bear it?

Miss Woodby. Poor child! I am so sorry! Yes, Mrs. Ling says you must go back. There is no help for it. You must go home. It is very hard for you, I know (*Strokes her head.*), but you will try to be brave and patient; and afterwards you will try to remember all that you have learned here. You will remember the words of the Great Teacher that we have been reading about.

Golden Lily. (*Sobbing.*) Yes, yes. I -- will try -- to remember.

Miss Woodby. (*Both rising.*) And you will pray for your mother-in-law. You will win her by love and kindness, and she will come to see that the Christian teaching is a great and good thing and not an evil, as she supposes.

Golden Lily. I -- will -- remember.

Miss Woodby. And, Golden Lily, remember I am always your friend. I will pray for you and I will help you, if I can.

Golden Lily. (*Backing slowly to the door, her face partly buried in her arm.*) Goodbye, dear teacher, goodbye.

Miss Woodby. (*Waving her hand sadly.*) Goodbye, Golden Lily.

Curtain.

ACT IV.

In MRS. LING'S *courtyard.* GOLDEN LILY *is seen washing at a tub in the center front of stage. At the back extending from right to left is a long pole filled with Chinese clothes hung out to dry. On empty poles* GOLDEN LILY *hangs up the clothes that she rinses from the tub. As she does so, she sings a hymn to an old Chinese melody. She continues humming the melody as she hangs up the clothes and smooths out the creases of those already hung out, then returns to the tub.*

Golden Lily. (To herself.) Hi, ya! Sometimes it seems as if I couldn't bear the load any longer. Mother-in-law gets harder to please every day. Nothing suits her, and I slave from morning to night, washing, cooking, running here and there for her. She flies into a temper over the least thing. She hates me more than ever since I ran away to the missionary school. How she did beat me for it when I got home!

Precious Gold. (*Running in.*) Mother!

Golden Lily. (*Startled.*) Oh! Precious Gold, you frightened me so.

Precious Gold. I'm sorry, Mother, but what were you singing just now? It's very good to hear.

Golden Lily. That is a Christian hymn. You must not tell Grandmother that you heard me singing it.

Precious Gold. (*Nodding her head understandingly.*) No, I won't tell her. Did you learn to sing it at that wicked foreign school?

Golden Lily. Hush, child, do not say that.

Precious Gold. But Grandmother says they take children's eyes out and make medicine of them.

Golden Lily. Oh! That is not true, Precious Gold. The children in the foreign school are very happy there learning many beautiful things, and everybody loves them.

Precious Gold. What did you learn there, Mother? Did you sing all the time?

Golden Lily. Oh -- no - child. We sang a great deal, but they taught me to read, too, and to write, and -- and (*She hesitates with a thoughtful, far-away look.*) --

Precious Gold. (*Impatiently.*) And what else, Mother?

Golden Lily. It was so -- so wonderful! They -- taught me about -- the -- Jesus way.

Precious Gold. The Jesus way, Mother. What is that?

Golden Lily. (*Still slowly.*) I can't -- explain very well, Precious Gold. I am so stupid, and I was there such a -- little while. (*Wistfully.*) I don't understand it, myself. Teacher said that the Jesus way was to love the people that hated you and -- to be kind to those who ill-treated you and -- if anyone strikes you -- on one cheek (*Indicating right cheek with her right hand.*) you must turn the other also. (*Indicating the left cheek.*)

Precious Gold. (*Decidedly.*) I don't. I scratch! I bite!

Golden Lily. (*Shaking her head.*) But that is not the Jesus way. Oh! -- It's hard. Oh -- very -- very -- hard.

Mrs. Ling. (*Offstage.*) Precious Gold! Precious Gold! Where is that good-for-nothing child?

Precious Gold. (*In loud whisper.*) It's Grandmother.

Golden Lily. Go, child, and remember you must not say a word.

Precious Gold. No -- no -- I won't, Mother. (*Runs off stage calling loudly.*) Coming, Grandmother.

Golden Lily. (*Begins washing listlessly, then pauses.*) If anyone strikes you on one cheek (*Indicating with her hand the right cheek.*), you must turn -- the other one also. (*Indicating the left cheek.*) Oh -- can I do that? It's hard, oh, very -- very -- hard, but I'll try. And teacher says I must pray for Mother-in-law. I will do that now (*Kneels by the bench.*) Oh, Jesus, bless Mother-in-law, soften her heart and help her to know God and the Jesus way. And oh, Jesus, forgive my sins and bless Mother-in-law. (*Enter MRS. LING.*)

Mrs. Ling. Come here, daughter-in-law, come here. What are you doing on the floor? Why aren't you at your washing, lazy one? What are you doing kneeling there? Tell me at once. (GOLDEN LILY *helps her across the stage to a chair on the right.*)

Golden Lily. Honorable Mother-in-law, I was praying.

Mrs. Ling. Praying! To what? Not to the divine Kuan-Yin, for here you were at the wash tub, and the divine Kuan-Yin is in the house on the shelf. You are lying to me.

Golden Lily. No, honorable Mother-in-law, I tell you the truth. I was praying.

Mrs. Ling. Praying for what, huzzy? For a son, I hope.

Golden Lily. No, Mother-in-law, I was praying to the Christian

God, to the Great Spirit who cannot be seen, and to Jesus Christ, his son.

Mrs. Ling. (*Wrathfully.*) What! Do you mean to say that you have been praying to the foreign devils' God? Ah, I see you have disobeyed me. Did I not command you to forget all that you have learned at the foreign devils' school? Did I not command you never to think of that place again?

Golden Lily. Yes, honorable Mother-in-law, but I cannot forget, for I found peace and happiness there. And, oh, Mother-in-law, I desire that you should be happy also, and peaceful; for you know, Mother-in-law, that the idols do not make you happy, and that you are living in daily fear of evil spirits. When you came in I was praying to Jesus that you would come to understand the Christian truth and learn to obey it.

Mrs. Ling. (*Rising in a fury.*) Praying for me to be converted to the Christian teaching! How dare you, impudent one! I forbid you to go to the Jesus Doctrine temple again; do you hear me? You shall be punished for this. Our ancestors will be very angry at you. Go now and appease the divine Kuan-Yin for the insult you have given her. Make a food offering to our ancestors and burn incense to the kitchen god.

Golden Lily. No, honorable Mother-in-law, I am sorry to anger you, but I cannot worship the Kuan-Yin any longer, nor the ancestral tablets.

Mrs. Ling. (*With increasing anger.*) What! Do you mean to disobey me, impudent one? We will see who rules in this house. Take that, huzzy. (*Slaps her cheek sharply.*)

Golden Lily. (*Putting her hands to her cheek, moaning as she recoils to the door.*) Oh -- oh -- oh! (*Turning, she advances steadily.*) Mother-in-law -- Mother-in-law! Strike -- this cheek also. (*Turning the other cheek.*)

Mrs. Ling. (*Impulsively raises her hand to strike, then gasps and stares at* GOLDEN LILY *in astonishment.*) What? What do you mean?

Golden Lily. That is part of the Jesus way, Mother-in-law.

Mrs. Ling. The Jesus way! What do you mean?

Golden Lily. Teacher said that the Jesus way was to love the people that hate you, to be kind to those who ill-treat you, and -- if anyone strikes you on one cheek you must turn the other also. So strike this cheek, Mother-in-law, strike this cheek!

Mrs. Ling. (*Looks at* GOLDEN LILY *incredulously, then sinks into her chair, bewildered and subdued.*) She asks me to strike the other cheek! She is kind to me even though I ill-treat her! The Jesus way! Go! Go! Leave me! Leave me!

Golden Lily. (*Retires to the door, looks back smiling.*) Mother-in-law, I bless you. I love you. (*She goes out.*)

Mrs. Ling. She even loves me! (*Remains with head bowed on back of chair.*)

Curtain.

ACT V.

Scene: Same as Act I, except that the dressing-case has been removed from the table and a small paper-covered Chinese Testament is in its place. When the curtain rises, MRS. LING *is seen standing before the altar. She is disheveled in appearance and is without paint or powder. She has the look of one who has passed through a great emotional experience. Standing before the altar, she slowly blows out the candle on the left, muttering to herself.*

Mrs. Ling. Strange, strange! In three short days what strange things have happened to me! (*She takes up the ancestral tablet and gazes long and searchingly on it, shaking her head slowly. Then in a hoarse whisper.*) I dare not! (*She takes up several of the idol papers that are fastened to the altar. Some of them slip through her fingers to the floor. She looks at the others closely.*) I never doubted them before! (*The rest of the papers fall to the floor. Hesitatingly, she takes down the Kuan-Yin and gazes earnestly upon it.*) Can it be, Kuan-Yin, can it be that my belief has been shaken? Oh, will you be angry, will you punish me? (*She slowly places it on the table and sits down by it, not moving her eyes from it and looking very much troubled.*) Do not strike me dead, Kuan-Yin. (*She sees the book on the table and picks it up in a half-frightened way. She turns the pages slowly, her brows contracted in deep and troubled thought. Then in a whisper, reading very slowly.*) "The Jesus way, the Jesus way," she said. "Bless them that curse you -- do -- good -- despitefully -- use you -- persecute you -- if -- anyone -- strikes you -- on one cheek -- Ah! (*She leans her elbow on the table and bows her head on her hand, murmuring*.) The Jesus way! The Jesus way! (*After a prolonged pause*, GOLDEN LILY *enters timidly. She looks about, not seeing* MRS. LING *at first. Then discovering her, she starts and turns to leave the room.* MRS. LING *hearing her, looks up, and, with something of her old domineering way:*) Golden Lily, don't go! Stay!

Golden Lily. (*Frightened.*) I -- I was looking for something. (*Seeing the book in* MRS. LING'S *hands.*) Oh -- Mother-in-law, you have it -- my book.

Mrs. Ling. Yes, I found it where you had hidden it in your red bridal chest.

Golden Lily. Oh, please let me have it -- my precious book!

Mrs. Ling. (*In something of her old sharp tone.*) But I want it. I am going to --

Golden Lily. (*Interrupting her.*) Oh -- please don't burn it. They gave it to me at the school -- my precious book!

Mrs. Ling. I want the book -- to read -- not to burn it.

Golden Lily. (*Greatly astonished.*) Mother-in-law! To -- read it!

Mrs. Ling. Yes, Golden Lily, to read it. Strange things have happened to me while I have refused to see you or anyone these last three days.

Golden Lily. Oh, yes, Mother-in-law, the honorable Great Man and I have been greatly troubled about you.

Mrs. Ling. I wished to be alone.

Golden Lily. Tell me about it, Mother-in-law.

Mrs. Ling. Golden Lily, the other day, when you turned the other cheek, my anger flew away suddenly, and I saw the truth. I have sinned heavily against you, but your love and patience have shown me that I have been a very wicked woman. Forgive me for my cruel treatment. (*Outstretching her hands.*)

Golden Lily. (*Grasping her hands.*) It is the Jesus way to forgive, Mother-in-law.

Mrs. Ling. The Jesus way! The Jesus way! For three days those words have rung in my head, and I have been afraid, oh, greatly afraid.

Golden Lily. Afraid! Of what, Mother-in-law?

Mrs. Ling. Of the Kuan-Yin, of our ancestors. Oh, they will be angry with me, I know. They will punish me for thinking of the Jesus way.

Golden Lily. No, no, Mother-in-law. They cannot harm you. I am only a poor, stupid girl, and I know the Jesus way just a little, but I know that it takes away all these fears and gives us joy and peace.

Mrs. Ling. Oh, that is what I want -- peace -- for I am tormented.

Golden Lily. And the Kuan-Yin cannot give you peace.

Mrs. Ling. No! No! Not peace.

Golden Lily. Nor happiness.

Mrs. Ling. I am a very unhappy woman. (*She buries her face in her hands.* MR. LING *enters and* GOLDEN LILY *goes eagerly to meet him.*)

Golden Lily. Honorable Great Man, come and tell Mother-in-law about the Jesus way.

Mrs. Ling. (*Amazed.*) Can it be -- ?

Golden Lily. Yes -- yes, she wants to know. (MRS. LING *has looked up when* MR. LING *entered. It is her turn to be surprised.*)

Mrs. Ling. Honorable Great Man, you, too, have been learning the Jesus way?

Mr. Ling. Yes, and though I know but little, I am convinced that it is a great and good religion.

Mrs. Ling. It -- must be. But Kuan-Yin and our ancestors will surely send disaster to our family if we renounce the worship of them.

Mr. Ling. For more than a year I have been thinking of these things, and I am persuaded that the worship of our ancestors and of the idols is a great evil to us and to our country. These superstitions have filled us with fear and made us slaves.

Mrs. Ling. (*Slowly and thoughtfully.*) Perhaps -- you are right.

Mr. Ling. (*With growing earnestness.*) New times have come to our country -- great times, such as have never been seen before. Our people must be freed from these deadly superstitions and rise to new liberty and greatness. The Jesus teachings are great and noble. I am convinced that if we follow these, we shall be a great people.

Mrs. Ling. Almost you persuade me. But what will our son say if we embrace the new religion? He, of all others, is most zealous in observing the rites.

Mr. Ling. Our son? He, too, has been thinking of these things. Only a few days ago he wrote me that he is no longer satisfied with the old religion, and that he has already become a learner in one of the foreign temples in Peking. He says that he is convinced that he and we need this new and vital religion.

Mrs. Ling. Can it be that he has accepted the new faith! (*Pausing, then resolutely.*) It is enough; I hesitate no longer. (*She rises from her chair, and in a commanding tone:*) Golden Lily, take the Kuan-Yin away and the tablets and all the idols in the house and command that they be burned at once. (GOLDEN LILY *takes the tablet and the idol and goes out.*) Honorable Great Man, take the idol papers and cast them to the flames also.

Mr. Ling. It is better so. (*He gathers up the idol papers from the floor and from the altar -- all but the* SOOTHSAYER'S *charm on the door.* GOLDEN LILY *enters and sees the charm still there.*)

Golden Lily. One more piece, Honorable Great Man. (*Pointing to the charm on the door.*)

Mrs. Ling. It is the charm the soothsayer gave me to protect the house from the influence of the evil eye. Let it remain.

Golden Lily. We need not fear the evil eye if we follow the Jesus way.

Mr. Ling. The soothsayer, I believe, is an old humbug.

Mrs. Ling. Humbug? Surely not. For years he has been my infallible guide. Remember how only a short time ago he was able to tell us by means of his magic mirror that Golden Lily had run away to the foreign school.

Golden Lily. Oh, Mother-in-law, he deceived you. He saw me in the inn where I rested, and he heard me ask the way of one of the travelers.

Mr. Ling. Ha! I see! And then when you sent for him, he pretended that he saw Golden Lily going there in his magic mirror.

Mrs. Ling. (*Indignantly.*) Imposter! Bring me the charm. (GOLDEN LILY *brings it, and* MRS. LING *tears it in pieces and throws it on the floor.*) No longer shall my gold fill his knavish pockets.

Mr. Ling. Good! Very good!

The children rush in, PRECIOUS GOLD *first, followed by* BEAUTIFUL PEARL, *and then by* OLD RAG. *They are very much excited. Their voices are shrill, their eyes almost pop out of their heads.*

Precious Gold. (*Breathlessly.*) Grandmother! Grandmother! They are burning the idols, and the smoke is going way up high! Oo -- oo -- way up high! (*Gestures with her arms with an upward movement.*)

Beautiful Pearl. (*Imitating her.*) Oo -- oo -- way up high!

Old Rag. Oo -- oo -- up high!

Mrs. Ling. Come here, children. Old Rag, sit on my knee. Let me tell you. We are not going to have any more idols in this house.

Precious Gold. That's good. They made me afraid. I am glad.

Beautiful Pearl. I am glad, too.

Old Rag. I glad!

Mr. Ling. And we are going to learn the Jesus way.

Precious Gold. Oh, I know about that -- Mother told me. And may we go to the foreign school? The children have such good times there.

Mrs. Ling. Yes, yes. I make no more objections.

Mr. Ling. Old Rag need not wear the charm any longer. We are not afraid of evil spirits taking him away. (*He takes the charm from off the boy's neck.*)

Golden Lily. And I think we ought to give him a new name. Old Rag is so ugly.

Mr. Ling. Good idea. What shall it be?

Mrs. Ling. Everlasting Virtue. How is that for a name? Would you like it? (*Speaking to* OLD RAG.)

Old Rag. Good! (*Knocking is heard off stage. They all listen intently.*)

Mrs. Ling. Someone is coming. Golden Lily, go -- see who it is.

Golden Lily. (*Goes to the door, peers out, exclaims joyfully.*) Oh! It's teacher! It's teacher! (*She beckons with her hand.*) Come in, teacher, this way. (MISS WOODBY *enters.* GOLDEN LILY *whispers excitedly to her at the door.* MISS WOODBY *starts and glances hastily at* MRS. LING, *then at the empty altar.*)

Miss Woodby. Why -- ! (*She starts forward with outstretched hands toward* MRS. LING *who has risen to meet her.*) I am so glad -- so very glad and thankful.

Mrs. Ling. And I, honorable teacher -- I, too, am glad. I do not understand how it all came.

Miss Woodby. (*Wonderingly.*) It was the still small voice of the spirit speaking in your heart, honorable madam.

Mrs. Ling. (*Placing her hand on* GOLDEN LILY'S *shoulder.*) And it spoke through Golden Lily!

Curtain.

1921 -- Shen Hung -- *The Wedded Husband*

Practically since arriving in the US in the 1850s, the Chinese had enjoyed dramatic performances here in their own language. As they later spread throughout the United States, they built Chinese-language theatres in many American cities. These theatres, modeled exactly on those in their homeland, regularly imported actors and scripts from China. This type of drama flourished especially in San Francisco, and somewhat later, in New York.

For a remarkably long time, however, no Chinese playwright so much as attempted a play in English. Except for one previous title registered with the Copyright Office in the late 1890s, this text is the earliest specimen of its type. The author had attended George Pierce Baker's famous playwriting workshop at Harvard in 1919, and submitted this play to *Poet Lore* magazine, which published it in 1921. Two other plays written in English by Chinese authors appeared in the magazine within the next two years. Taken together, the three texts represent a new step in both the assimilation and the literary productivity of Americans of Chinese descent. Shen Hung later returned to China, where he continued to write and direct. He was later given a high post in dramatic administration by the government of the People's Republic.

One might expect that the first play to break decades of silence would attempt to refute the image of the Chinese generated by and for the consumption of the dominant Euroamerican culture. This is not the case, as *The Wedded Husband* instead adopts this image uncritically. Its Chinese are deferential, conservative, and more or less willing slaves to ancient customs. Not until an angrier generation of Asian-American playwrights emerged in the 1970s would this image be challenged. Still, the text presented here is a pioneering one.

The Wedded Husband
A Realistic Chinese play

CHARACTERS:

LORD WANG, *An old man about fifty-five. Rich, responsible, experienced, determined -- sometimes to the point of obstinacy.*

MISS WANG, *A beautiful lady about twenty-four. Very quiet. A dutiful daughter who strictly observes the ethical teachings of Old China.*

SIR CHEN, *A kind gentleman, but weak; he never could hold his own ground.*

MASTER CHEN, *his son, the insane boy, about twenty. A simple, true, open-hearted man.*

DOCTOR, *A warm-hearted man; perhaps a little too frank.*

MR. YANG, *A young man about twenty-five, educated in the new school. Independent and daring. However, he still observes the manners and ceremonies of the aristocrats.*

MAID, *Very devoted to her master and mistress.*

PLACE: *Tientsin, China.*

TIME: *Just after the Revolution when nobles were still addressed by their titles and the people in general hesitated to break the old Chinese traditions.*

ACT I.
The Betrothal.

PLACE: LORD WANG'S *second reception room. (In the houses of aristocrats there are generally three reception rooms: the big reception room, for polite guests, the second reception room, for intimate friends; and the Ladies' Reception Room, where the mistress of the house receives her friends.)*

TIME: *Afternoon of a very hot summer day; the betrothal was announced that morning.*

LORD WANG, SIR CHEN, MASTER CHEN, DOCTOR, *and* MR. YANG; *all seated at the banquet table. Two servants fanning their masters with big fans. The banquet is about over.*

Two jugglers are exhibiting their stunts to amuse the men at the table; this is finished in two minutes. One servant lays his fan on a chair, takes up a bag of silver coins, and throws one handful after another to the jugglers. Each time he throws it, he calls out "This, the reward from LORD WANG," "From DOCTOR," *etc. The jugglers salute by half-kneeling on one leg. They pick up the coins and go out by left door.*

All stand up and salute each other by a "gentleman bow." The servants are busy arranging the table; they remove the tea cups to the tea tables.

Mr. Yang. Your Lordship, certainly a beautiful banquet. Thank you.

Lord Wang. Please don't say thanks; our friendship is beyond that.

Boy. When will the concert start?

Lord Wang. About two o'clock. My son-in-law is here for the first time. Mr. Yang, will you show him my house and my garden?

Mr. Yang. Yes, your Lordship, let's take a walk in the garden.

Boy. Father, let's go.

Sir Chen. Perhaps Doctor would care to join us.

Doctor. No, I prefer to sit down and have a smoke. It's too hot outside.

Mr. Yang. Come along, Doctor, I have something to tell you. *(All go out by the left door except the servants.)*

First Servant. Hot.

Second Servant. Yes, very hot.

First Servant. Hope it won't be so hot on wedding day.

Second Servant. (*Hesitating.*) Dreadful to think about -- such hot weather!

First Servant. What is the trouble?

Second Servant. Nothing.

First Servant. (*With suspicion.*) -- Are -- are you well?

Second Servant. I am all right.

First Servant. Then make sure of it. The plague is raging in the city. You cannot be too careful.

Second Servant. Exactly. You know Wang-far and Li-lien-sung. Are they not healthy and strong? Did they not talk and laugh with us just three days ago? Hm, the plague, that worries me.

First Servant. But you must not worry. His Lordship, our master and guests are happy today because of the betrothal ceremony, so we servants should also be cheerful.

Second Servant. I wish I could be happy. But the plague -- you know, there will be a big ceremony on the wedding day -- suppose you or I --

First Servant. Stop. The saying is "If you think of misfortune, misfortune befalls you."

Second Servant. But I am not afraid of anything.

First Servant. I am not either. But if anything happens to me on the wedding day, it's -- it's because you think of it.

Second Servant. No, I am all right, don't blame me for anything. Look how you yourself are scared by the plague. I am quite cheerful, why shouldn't we be? We had the betrothal ceremony this morning. (FIRST SERVANT *does not answer.*) Well, it's hot. (*Taking up a fan and fanning himself.*) Whose pipe?

First Servant. Belongs to Doctor.

Second Servant. Shall I send it?

First Servant. Lay it on the tea-table. (SECOND SERVANT *does so while the* MAID *enters on the right.*)

Maid. Ha, ha, the banquet is over.

Second Servant. Ah, congratulations, the bride-maid.

Maid. Yes, thank you. I am happy, happy, happy. I shall be with my Koo Niang for three more years.

Second Servant. Her Ladyship did not come to see the betrothal gifts.

Maid. Of course not. You ought to know our customs. She can't come, if the groom is here. She is coming now.

Second Servant. Don't let her come. The party may return; the concert hasn't started yet.

Maid. Then I better tell her. (*Goes out. During the above conversation the* FIRST SERVANT *has practically finished the table. He pus the fruit dishes on the teatable.*)

Second Servant. Seems to me the maid is the happiest about the wedding.

First Servant. She ought to be. Though she is only a maid, she is a great friend of our lady. She has been with her for ten years, and now three years more.

Second Servant. A good, clever maid.

First Servant. Yes, she is very warm-hearted. Well, are we through here now?

Second Servant. Yes, we want to hear the concert too. (*The* DOCTOR *enters on the left, followed by* LORD WANG. *The* DOCTOR *takes his pipe which* SECOND SERVANT *lights for him. Both servants take the fans and begin to fan them.*)

Lord Wang. You may go now. (*The* SERVANTS *leave.*)

Doctor. This room is the best; quiet and cool.

Lord Wang. You like to smoke; smoking is your duty.

Doctor. Not necessarily a duty. But smoking prevents the plague and does many other good things.

Lord Wang. What are the health conditions in the city now?

Doctor. You mean the plague? Furious.

Lord Wang. Too bad.

Doctor. The hot dry weather causes it. All gatherings are dangerous, including the concert today.

Lord Wang. It's our custom to have some sort of entertainment for a happy occasion. If not the betrothal ceremony --

Doctor. Betrothal ceremony! (*Puffing.*)

Lord Wang. Yes, why?

Doctor. Well, old friend, you see yourself the boy is insane.

Lord Wang. Only a little bit abnormal.

Doctor. Even a little bit. I cannot see why you insist on marrying your daughter to him. It can't be for money. Sir Chen is not so well off as your Lordship, if you permit me to say that.

Lord Wang. Doctor! (*Trying to stop the* DOCTOR *and talk himself.*)

    Doctor. I cannot see any reason at all. It is a crazy idea. Insane!

    Lord Wang. Doctor!

    Doctor. I beg your pardon. I confess it's all useless now, since the betrothal was announced this morning.

    Lord Wang. Doctor!

    Doctor. Your Lordship, let's talk of something else.

    Lord Wang. No, Doctor. I wish to talk it over with you.

    Doctor. Well?

    Lord Wang. What do you think of me as a friend -- as a man?

    Doctor. You are a faithful, responsible friend. Good, kind-hearted, though sometimes obstinate.

    Lord Wang. What do you think of me as a father?

    Doctor. Well! It's very hard for me to understand your insistence on this marriage.

    Lord Wang. Do you still remember how I was about twenty years ago?

    Doctor. The old time memory is not very pleasant, your Lordship.

    Lord Wang. Exactly, twenty years ago, I was a poor student.

    Doctor. Yes.

    Lord Wang. Sir Chen is a mighty good man, but a little too kind, too weak. And his son is also too weak, mentally.

    Doctor. Yes, I agree with you perfectly.

    Lord Wang. During the years I have prospered, Sir Chen has met one misfortune after another. The old family is near ruin now.

    Doctor. Yes, you mean financially.

    Lord Wang. Yes, and that's due to his kindness, or rather, weakness.

    Doctor. Then is it your purpose in this marriage to save Chen's house?

    Lord Wang. Exactly, my daughter can save it. She is like me, responsible and dutiful. (*Short pause.*) And don't you think it is proper for me to do this? I who owed everything to him.

    Doctor. To give your gratitude?

    Lord Wang. It is also a friend's duty.

    Doctor. In that case -- (*Looking for his tea cup.*) I understand --

    Lord Wang. Here is your cup -- your name is on it.

    Doctor. Thank you. In that case -- of course you are less to blame. However, what does your daughter say?

Lord Wang. She promised me. (*Music is heard.*) My knowledge -- er -- I know -- I thought there was another -- let's join them in the hall; the concert has started. (*Both go out. The* MAID *enters at the right.*)

Maid. Come along, nobody is here. The concert has started.

Miss Wang. (*Entering by the right door. She is not particularly joyful today, nor very sad. In fact, she has practically no expression on her face.*) They had their banquet in this room.

Maid. Yes, and on the table are your betrothal gifts. Here is a golden hair-pin, wishing you every satisfaction in your marriage. Here are a pair of silver buckles, which will bring good fortune to both of you. Here are embroidered silk bags, for the prosperity of your family, filled with peanuts that greet you with joyful long life. And tea. Happiness in your marriage. Eggs, painted red, you shall be much happier when you have a baby. Sugar, ah, yes, very sweet, very sweet. So beautiful, so graceful.

Miss Wang. (*During the previous speech, she is only nodding. Ordinarily a Chinese girl would be very happy and very proud of the gifts. Pointing to something on the table.*) What is that?

Maid. A thumb ring.

Miss Wang. A thumb ring for a betrothal gift! That means -- from whom?

Maid. Why so surprised? What does that mean?

Miss Wang. That means good-bye forever. From whom?

Maid. From Mr. Yang.

Miss Wang. Yes, of course.

Maid. Ah, miss, you have not smiled for the last five days. Are you happy now? You used to tell me everything. Tell me, are you happy now?

Miss Wang. Of course.

Maid. (*Sighing.*) Then Mr. Yang is mistaken this time.

Miss Wang. Mr Yang?

Maid. Yes, he is here to join the ceremony and (*Swallowing.*)-- you are not angry with Mr. Yang? You were both so fond of each other before.

Miss Wang. No, I am not angry.

Maid. Mr. Yang guessed that you were very unhappy, because of this betrothal.

Miss Wang. (*Pretending to be angry*.) How dare you tell me such a thing?

Maid. Pardon, miss, I only tell what Mr. Yang said. Mr. Yang said you are going to marry a man whom you don't care for.

Miss Wang. I know he will never forgive me.

Maid. Miss, are you going to marry a man whom you don't love? (*No answer*.)

Maid. Ah, Koo Niang, remember, remember the tradition. You can never marry again, if you are once wedded to a man. Never -- anything may happen; but you, never again.

Miss Wang. I cannot think of this; I won't.

Maid. Ah, Koo Niang, think. (*In a low voice*.) Now it is not yet too late.

Miss Wang. It is my father's wish.

Maid. But his Lordship would not force you to this marriage if you refused?

Miss Wang. He is my father.

Maid. But your happiness in the future?

Miss Wang. I have something more to consider than my own happiness.

Maid. Something more?

Miss Wang. Yes, it is a daughter's duty to obey her father. Our ethics teaches us so. If I should refuse him -- the people -- what would they say?

Maid. What would they say?

Miss Wang. They would call it a scandal; my father's reputation and family's reputation would then be ruined by me.

Maid. (*Sighing*.) So the family --

Miss Wang. No, not that, but -- but my father's happiness. My refusal would break his heart.

Maid. Miss, pardon, Mr. Yang is going to Mongolia tomorrow.

Miss Wang. (*Slightly surprised*.) Going to Mongolia!

Maid. Yes, to the great north, the great desert. He came here purposely to say farewell to you. Will you see him -- in this room?

Miss Wang. No, I cannot see him.

Maid. Miss, you must. He will not understand if you don't explain to him. (*Laughter is heard outside*.) Here he comes. (*She runs to the left door but suddenly turns back*.) Gracious! The groom is with him. Let's get away, quick. (*Both go out*. MR. YANG *enters by left door, followed by* MASTER CHEN.)

Boy. Mr. Yang, wait for me a minute. Wait for me a minute.

Mr. Yang. (Shaking his head.) You are certainly fond of me, aren't you?

Boy. Surely. It is too hot, lend me your fan. *(Takes it and salutes by half-kneeling.)* Thanks. *(Fans himself with two fans.)* Like a butterfly!

Mr. Yang. Well.

Boy. (Looking around.) Say, don't tell anybody. I want to ask you a question.

Mr. Yang. A question?

Boy. Yes, is my wife pretty?

Mr. Yang. Your wife?

Boy. I mean her -- Miss Wang. Once betrothed to me, always my wife.

Mr. Yang. (Shaking his head.) Is that so?

Boy. That's tradition. My father told me that. Now tell me, is she pretty? I love her.

Mr. Yang. Why, have you met her before?

Boy. Not yet.

Mr. Yang. And you say you love her?

Boy. Yes.

Mr. Yang. How could it be possible? It's the greatest joke I ever heard. "Love at first sight," you go beyond that.

Boy. If I want to love, I need no sight.

Mr. Yang. Tell me, why do you love her?

Boy. Because, because she is my wife.

Mr. Yang. Your wife, to love her is your duty. *(He pauses.)* Now let us drop the subject. It is too ungentlemanly to joke about such a sacred thing as love.

Boy. I mean it seriously. I love her.

Mr. Yang. (Shaking his head.) Well?

Boy. Another question, do you think she will love me?

Mr. Yang. (Thinking hard, then desperately.) She hardly will.

Boy. Not?

Mr. Yang. No.

Boy. Never mind, I love her all the same. I can wait.

Mr. Yang. (Looking at BOY.) Wait?

Boy. If she does not love me today, I will wait till tomorrow;

then day after tomorrow.

Mr. Yang. Love is a matter of heart and not a matter of waiting.

Boy. All the same to me. I wait, and wait, and wait till some day when my hair is white --

Mr. Yang. Nonsense!

Boy. And if she does not love me then, perhaps she will love me after my death.

Mr. Yang. Stop, stop. My friend (*Moved.*). My friend, I am sorry. I -- misjudged you.

Boy. You like me now, do you?

Mr. Yang. Yes.

Boy. Take a walk with me in the garden.

Mr. Yang. No, we cannot go again. The ladies --

Boy. It's too hot here; I am going alone. (MR. YANG *catches him by the coat.*)

Mr. Yang. No, you cannot go, because you are the groom.

Boy. Too many things a groom can not do. Let me go. (*Attempting to run away.*)

Mr. Yang. A groom is not supposed to meet his bride before the wedding day.

Boy. Why shouldn't he?

Mr. Yang. Oh, just a matter of tradition.

Boy. (*Unbuttoning his coat.*) I see, I see, but I am going. (*Slipping out of his coat, he runs away. At the door, he turns back and laughs heartily, pointing at* MR. YANG.) Now, a walk in the garden. You cannot stop me, you get my coat.

Mr. Yang. Here, here, get your coat. It is very impolite to go without your coat. Take it, I'll let you go.

Boy. Throw it to me.

Mr. Yang. (*Looking at him, smiling.*) A lovable fool, isn't he?

Maid. (*Entering by right.*) Mr. Yang.

Mr. Yang. Oh! How is the messenger?

Maid. I have done the best I can.

Mr. Yang. I am very grateful to you.

Maid. My Mistress is here.

Mr. Yang. Is she? (*Turning, he sees* MISS WANG. *There is silence between them.* THE MAID *withdraws quietly. The two salute each other by half-kneeling.*)

Miss Wang. (*Very slowly.*) Very glad to see you, Mr. Yang.

Mr. Yang. Very glad to see your Ladyship. Are you well?

Miss Wang. Yes, thank you. (*Deep silence.*) I heard that you are going away.

Mr. Yang. To Mongolia, the great North, the great desert, the land of hopes. I shall start tomorrow morning.

Miss Wang. Tomorrow, that's three days before my wedding. Why in such a hurry?

Mr. Yang. I don't mean to get away before your wedding. But, you know a broken-hearted man is no decoration for a happy occasion.

Miss Wang. Do you call it a happy occasion?

Mr. Yang. Yes, well, he isn't so bad as people think he is. A mighty good man; surely a devoted husband. I begin to like him.

Miss Wang. Mr. Yang, please understand, please forgive me.

Mr. Yang. Yes?

Miss Wang. It is not I who am untrue to you.

Mr. Yang. Please don't say that. I shall not blame you. (*He pauses.*) Doctor has told me everything.

Miss Wang. Then no word is necessary from me. (*After a pause.*) Shall this be our last meeting?

Mr. Yang. Well, I am going to Mongolia tomorrow. Remember me as your friend. I shall always be at your service. Farewell to you.

Miss Wang. Good-bye. (*It is as if they have a thousand words to speak to each other, but don't know where to begin.*)

Maid. (*Outside.*) Beg pardon. (*Enters.*)

Mr. Yang. What is it?

Maid. Let's get away quick. They are coming; the concert is over.

Mr. Yang. Get away? I beg you pardon!

Maid. No, no, we are not afraid of them, but the groom, he is coming with them. (*Laughter is heard.* MR. YANG *and* MISS WANG *salute each other by half-kneeling.* MISS WANG *goes out by the right door with the* MAID. MR. YANG *follows several steps behind her, staring at her. They are half-way down the stage when the others enter.*)

Boy. Doctor, what is the secret, the point of your story?

Doctor. The point of the story is they all regret it, after they have done it.

Mr. Yang. They regret it?

Sir Chen. Doctor is telling us the legend on which the opera is based.

Mr. Yang. I see. (*Feels relieved.*)

Doctor. This is called the legend of "Guitar." She was the most beautiful daughter of the emperor. Her marriage to the Mongolian king was an arranged marriage -- you know, to strengthen the alliance of the two nations.

Mr. Yang. Why did they regret it?

Doctor. She was very unhappy.

Lord Wang. That's her sacrifice, admirable!

Doctor. Two nations went into war all the same and she died. (*Glancing at* LORD WANG.) Friends, sometimes sacrifice is worse than no sacrifice.

Lord Wang. Well. (MAID *runs in; saluting.*)

Maid. Your Lordship, my miss -- she has fainted.

Lord Wang. Fainted? Doctor, come with me.

Mr. Yang. Hm. (*The* BOY *tries to slip out but is caught by* MR. YANG.)

Boy. I want to see here, to find out what is the matter.

Mr. Yang. You stay here. I told you before; groom and bride should not meet before the wedding.

Sir Chen. I am afraid that the weather is too hot. What do you think of a postponement of the wedding?

Mr. Yang. That is the right way to do.

Sir Chen. I hope his Lordship will consent to do so.

Lord Wang. (*Entering.*) I was frightened, but Doctor wants me to tell you it is not serious.

Sir Chen. Good! Lord Wang, I fear it is too hot.

Lord Wang. Yes, it is.

Sir Chen. Mr. Yang and I are talking about a postponement of the wedding.

Lord Wang. Because of the hot weather?

Mr. Yang. Yes, and the plague.

Lord Wang. No, we cannot do it.

Mr. Yang. But my Lord, the plague is a serious matter.

Lord Wang. No, I asked the fortune-teller to select a date for the wedding. He said four days from today we shall be under the best star.

Mr. Yang. Pardon me, your Lordship, that's superstition.

Lord Wang. I know it, but that's tradition; and my duty is to observe the tradition.

Doctor. (*Entering.*) Very fortunate.

Mr. Yang. How is she now?

Doctor. Overcome by heat.

Mr. Yang. Nothing serious?

Doctor. (*Shaking his head.*) No, at present nothing serious. However, she is very weak. Your Lordship, I wish to see the wedding postponed.

Mr. Yang. We just decided not to so so on account of the star.

Lord Wang. (*Looking at* MR. YANG.) No.

Doctor. (*Appealingly.*) She is very weak and liable to be attacked by the plague.

Lord Wang. (*Walking away.*) No.

Doctor. Please give me the pipe. Thank you. My advice was never followed, was it? (*He smokes.*)

ACT II.
The Wedding.

TIME: *Four days after the First Act.*

PLACE: SIR CHEN'S *Reception Hall.*

A Chinese Marriage Ceremony:

The walls are decorated with red silk; red carpets are on the floor. A table at center with four chairs. Candles are burning.

1. Ushering in the guests.

2. The master of ceremony takes his position.

3. Reading of greetings.

4. Introducing the groom; music.

5. Introducing the bride; music.

6. Solemnizing.

7. Bride introduced to groom.

8. They are introduced to father-in-law; to guests.

During the above ceremony, the groom does all the bowing and the bride stands still with the bride-maids. Servants fan the guests.

Lord Wang. The weather is so hot. If the guests will excuse the bride.

A Guest. Certainly, let us all be introduced together.

The GROOM *bows. The* BRIDE *is given a mirror. The*

BRIDE *is also given one end of the red and green "happy-silk"; the*
GROOM, *the other end. The* GROOM, *helped by his best man,*
walks backward to the "wedding apartment." They walk on red cloth
or red carpets which two SERVANTS *are busy in arranging. They*
are preceded by a happy young couple, each carrying one candle stand.
The musicians and the lantern-carriers precede the candle-carriers.

Suddenly the BRIDE *drops her mirror. A shiver runs through the*
guests.

A Guest. She dropped it! (*The* BRIDE *throws away the silk.*)

A Guest. She throws away the silk! (*The music stopped by*
LORD WANG, *abruptly.* LORD WANG *shows surprise and*
indignance on his face. He starts to speak.)

The Bride. Help me, help me.

Guest. She speaks! (*The music starts again, while the* MAID
helps her to walk.)

Lord Wang. What is the matter?

Maid. Her Ladyship is, her Ladyship is very --, she is
unconscious now.

Doctor. Sick? (*Running to the* BRIDE.) What is the matter?
Stop the music. Lord Wang, if you will entertain the guests in the
other room --

Lord Wang. But the wedding ceremony is not complete.

Doctor. (*To the* MAID.) Let me help you. (*They go out*
through the left door.)

Lord Wang. Friends, kindly pardon me a minute, I must -- (*He*
follows the DOCTOR *and* MAID.)

Sir Chen. I feel very sorry that the ceremony should be
interrupted like this. But you will excuse my daughter-in-law.

A Guest. Certainly, certainly. It is an accident. An accident very
often happens. We do not mind the impoliteness; because it's an
accident.

Sir Chen. Perhaps it is the heat.

A Guest. Perhaps, perhaps. Since it is the heat, she perhaps will
soon recover.

Sir Chen. And we may resume the ceremony.

(LORD WANG *is heard saying "I will take your advice this*
time." "I understand.")

Lord Wang. Our honored friends, I feel very sad because the ceremony cannot be continued today.

Guests. We are very sorry, your Lordship.

Sir Chen. Serious?

Lord Wang. Doctor thinks it is not serious unless it is the plague. Friends, if you will allow me to entertain you in the other room --

A Guest. Certainly, certainly, your Lordship. Since the important part of the ceremony has already taken place, your humble -- er -- friends beg to ask leave. (*He glances at the other guests.*) Your permission.

Lord Wang. I really do not know what I was saying. I don't mean to ask you to part from us.

A Guest. No, not at all. Please don't let this matter worry your Lordship too greatly. May we greet you with good day? (*Saluting.*)

Lord Wang. Thank you. (SIR CHEN and LORD WANG *usher the guests out. All the guests salute the* GROOM *before they leave the room. The* GROOM *picks up the "happy-silk" and piles it on a chair. The* MAID *enters.*)

Boy. (*Brightening up.*) Ah, how is she now?

Maid. Very ill, sir.

Boy. (*As if the lady's illness does not concern him.*) Maid, do you know where Mr. Yang is?

Maid. (*Very much surprised.*) Mr. Yang?

Boy. Yes, I want to ask him something; I don't know what to do now. (*Sighing.*) I am so lonely.

Maid. (*Very angry, controlling herself with difficulty.*) Mr. Yang is now in Mongolia. Your humble maid wishes he were here.

Boy. I wish so too. I want to ask him something; but too far away now. (*Sighing.*) So many things the groom cannot do! (LORD WANG *and* SIR CHEN *enter at the right.*)

Lord Wang. We have dismissed our guests. It is too bad to have an interruption like this upon a wedding ceremony. But they are gone now.

Sir Chen. It is too hot, your Lordship.

Lord Wang. (*To* MAID.) How is my daughter now?

Maid. She is still unconscious, your Lordship.

Lord Wang. What did Doctor say?

Maid. He sent me to wait upon your Lordship.

Sir Chen. I hope it is not the plague.

Lord Wang. No, I think not. She was weak.

Sir Chen. Perhaps not yet recovered from the fever she had a few days ago.

Lord Wang. Maybe. I am disappointed. We old men cannot always take care of the young; and arrange all things for them. They ought to know their own duty, their own responsibility. Such an interruption! Just because of illness!

Doctor. Have you followed my advice?

Lord Wang. Yes, I have dismissed all polite guests. Yet I don't see the necessity of doing so.

Doctor. Well. (*A pause.*)

Lord Wang. What about my daughter?

Doctor. Too bad, too bad.

Lord Wang. How, tell me!

Doctor. (*Looking at him.*) You can guess it, can't you?

Lord Wang. What do you mean by that?

Doctor. (*In a low voice.*) The plague. (*Then very loudly and with force.*) The plague!

Lord Wang. The plague, is it true? (*Looking at the* DOCTOR'S *face.*) Yes, it is. (*Pacing the floor.*) No, I cannot believe it.

Doctor. The plague is raging in the city. It spreads like fire. What a hot day it is, and a trying ceremony!

Lord Wang. Doctor, are you sure of that?

Doctor. Sorry to tell you I am only too sure.

Lord Wang. (*Exceeding grief makes him give way like a woman.*) My fault, my fault. She was very ill; I insisted on the wedding to take place today. My fault!

Doctor. To regret what has been carries us nowhere. The present is more important; the present demands more of our attention.

Lord Wang. But how could I help regretting the has-been? Since the other day you told me the true state of things -- if anything should happen.

Boy. Hm. (*He is playing with the silk during the preceding speeches.*)

Lord Wang. I killed her, I killed -- (*Completely losing control.*)

Doctor. (*Trying his best.*) But she might recover.

Lord Wang. Let us hope so, let us hope so. Then I shall do my best to make her happy, to make up my mistake.

Boy. Father, she may recover.

Doctor. (*Interrupting* BOY.) Very good, very good, now I want to say something.

Lord Wang. Yes.

Doctor. Advise you again. This time whether you like it or not, it must be carried out.

Lord Wang. Doctor, your advice is always right. If I had ever listened to you before --

Doctor. All right. Now listen to me. The plague is very contagious and very dangerous. As a matter of safety, I want to quarantine this house. Do you all understand me?

Lord Wang and Sir Chen. (*Showing disapproval.*) Quarantine! Impossible!

Doctor. It is absolutely necessary -- a matter of life and death. I order you to leave here at once.

Lord Wang. What about my daughter?

Doctor. I will get nurses to take care of her.

Lord Wang. But she will need some --

Doctor. Now my friend, and Sir Chen, I have been a friend of your families for years and I am a doctor. I know what I am talking about. You never followed any of my advice before, and I don't care. But this time, my duty as a doctor demands me to make you follow my advice. All of you must leave here. Now, are you going to cooperate or are you not?

Lord Wang. To send away the maid and the servants too?

Doctor. Unless you want to risk their lives.

Lord Wang. (*Glancing at* SIR CHEN.) Perhaps this is the wisest way.

Sir Chen. But your Lordship, this is not our custom.

Doctor. Every tradition has been broken down during the revolution, Sir Chen. Quarantine is a common practice of the West and surely a wise one.

Lord Wang. We have to talk it over, Sir Chen. Let's go to your library. (*To* DOCTOR.) We have some preparations to make. (*Both go out.*)

Boy. Doctor, I want to ask you a question.

Doctor. What do you want to know?

Boy. Do you want all of us to go away?

Doctor. Yes.

Boy. How about me?

Doctor. You too.

Boy. How about my wife?

Doctor. (*A little surprised.*) Of course she can not go.

Boy. Is she going to be all alone in this house?

Doctor. The nurses will be here shortly.

Boy. Why do you take away all her beloved ones?

Doctor. It is for your safety, and for the community's safety. I can do nothing else.

Boy. Suppose I stay here?

Doctor. What is that?

Boy. I stay here and nurse my wife.

Doctor. (*Looking at* BOY, *cannot help laughing.*) Ha, ha, no, you cannot.

Boy. Why not?

Doctor. The reason is apparent. My friend, (*Short pause.*) this must be a great shock to you, quiet yourself.

Boy. Doctor, I am not nervous. I want to stay because I love her.

Doctor. Sir Chen and Lord Wang, they are all going. They all love her.

Boy. Let them go; but I am not going.

Doctor. The plague is very contagious. (*To himself, frowning.*) What is the trouble; what idea is getting into his head?

Boy. No, I won't desert her.

Doctor. (*Appealingly.*) Now, my dear friend, you are not deserting her -- nothing of that kind. The plague is very contagious and exceedingly dangerous. It means your safety, your life --

Boy. (*Shaking her head.*) Because I am her husband.

Doctor. The idea of deserting her. It's foolish. Quarantine is a universal practice of the West.

Maid. (*Interrupting.*) Pardon my master, let your maid stay for you.

Doctor. What's the idea?

Maid. I am a maid. But my master -- he cannot take chances.

Boy. But why, why, you are only a maid.

Maid. I am, sir. My mistress, her Ladyship -- would be very sad if you -- if anything happens to you.

Boy. I thank you, but you won't do. I am going to her right away. (DOCTOR *catches him.*)

Doctor. Here, here! Where are you going?

Boy. To my wife!

Doctor. (*Stares at him fiercely.*) You fool! (LORD WANG *and* SIR CHEN *enter by the right door.*)

Lord Wang. (*Startled by the word "fool."*) What is the matter?

Doctor. You are his superior; you understand; you are sane. Why don't you explain to him? He wants to be with his wife.

Lord Wang. Impossible!

Boy. Doctor, I want to ask you -- er -- another -- philosophical question.

Doctor. Huh, philosophical! (*Shaking his head.*)

Boy. People call me insane, a fool. So if my question is not right, please don't --

Doctor. (*Impatiently.*) What is it?

Boy. Why should a man love his his wife?

Doctor. Why should a man love? I give it up. I say, I give it up.

Sir Chen. The plague is a serious matter. I have only one boy, that is you.

Boy. Father, the plague is everywhere. This is as safe as any place.

Doctor. Now tell me, what good can you do by staying here?

Boy. Nurse my wife; perhaps she is not so hopeless after all. She might recover.

Doctor. Of course she might. But I warn you, if you stay, you will get it yourself.

Boy. Doctor, Doctor, I want to ask you another question.

Doctor. (*Almost losing his temper.*) Yes, sir.

Boy. What is your profession?

Doctor. I am a physician, a medical man.

Boy. What will a physician do?

Doctor. I am trying my best to take care of the sick; cure them and save their --

Boy. No, Doctor, you don't do that. (*Pause.*) You don't cure the sick; you give them up. And now, now, now (*Unbuttoning his coat.*), you talk about my safety, the community's safety, you want to save your own life. (*Runs away, slips out of his coat; stands at the door; laughs, turns back and points at the* DOCTOR.) At last, to my wife. Doctor, you cannot stop me, you get my coat.

Doctor. (*Roaring.*) Hu-er, hopeless now, hopeless now. (SIR

CHEN *drops into a chair,* LORD WANG *helping him.*)

Maid. If your Lordship permits, I want to stay with my master and mistress. (*She walks in.*)

Doctor. (*Sorrowing.*) Huh, three victims of the plague. My advice was never followed.

First Servant. (*Entering by right.*) Sir, the nurses are here, waiting for your Lordship's order. (LORD WANG *nods. The* SERVANT *goes out.*)

ACT III.
Love.

TIME: *Eight weeks after the Second Act.*

PLACE: *Ladies' reception room in* SIR CHEN'S *house.*
MADAME CHEN *is playing a flute. The music is very soft and low; and the incense is burning.*

Maid. (*Dancing in slowly; in a low voice.*) Beautiful, beautiful. (*Her* LADY *nods and continues to play till finishing the piece.*) Ah, madam; that's beautiful. It makes me so happy. You must be very happy yourself, aren't you?

Madame Chen. I am. I gave up this for a long time because it tires the player so much. But today -- I don't mind it at all.

Maid. Ah, Madame Chen.

Madame Chen. Shall I play you "The Birds Welcome the Spring?" That's Mr. Yang's favorite.

Maid. Madam, won't you have a little nap and rest yourself?

Madame Chen. No, thank you.

Maid. You exert yourself too much today; remember, you have just recovered from your illness. Seven weeks! Just think.

Madame Chen. It seems to be a long time, doesn't it?

Maid. Seven weeks, terrible. Such a long time. It must have been awfully tiresome to you.

Madame Chen. No, I don't think so. You know a very ill person is not conscious of time. He forgets everything.

Maid. (*After a moment's reflection.*) Is that really so?

Madame Chen. Yes, it is so to me. I don't know what happened when I was ill. I can't remember a thing. (*Shaking her head.*) It must seem terribly tiresome to other people.

Maid. Madam, the plague is a bad thing; it is contagious. Even doctors could not do much.

Madame Chen. Was it you who nursed me during those seven long weeks?

Maid. I am lucky, I came out unhurt.

Madame Chen. We should be thankful that it is all over.

Maid. (*Sighs.*) But the dead can never come to life again.

Madame Chen. It is our duty to think more of the living. (*During the above scene, the* MAID *is adding more incense to the burner.* LORD WANG *enters.*)

Lord Wang. I have some good news for you. His telegram says he will arrive this afternoon. We expect him every minute.

Madame Chen. So soon?

Lord Wang. Yes, because he is quite anxious to see you.

Madame Chen. (*Embarrassed.*) Yes, father.

Lord Wang. I want you to meet Mr. Yang in your ceremonial dress. This color is too dull -- looks like half mourning. Why don't you dress in red? That is the traditional color for happy occasions.

Madame Chen. But my father-in-law would --

Lord Wang. No, he will not object. The mourning period for your husband was over last week. Now I am going to order the servants to decorate the house. I don't want to see any white, I want everything in red. You do what I tell you.

Madame Chen. Yes, I will. (LORD WANG *goes out.*)

Maid. Madam, Lord Wang ordered us to change our mourning dress; all white things are put away. They said Mr. Yang is coming today.

Madame Chen. He is coming back. I am going to appear in my ceremonial dress to receive him.

Maid. He was in Mongolia.

Madame Chen. He was called back by my father.

Maid. Did his Lordship --

Madame Chen. And Mr. Yang shall be the future master of the house.

Maid. Future master?

Madame Chen. Are you surprised? You didn't think so before, did you? From now on, I shall be the happiest woman on the earth!

Maid. Why, madam, (*Smiles.*) haven't you been happy before?

Madame Chen. Yes, I am happy when my father is. I am his

daughter. But poor father -- my father changed his mind.

Maid. Changed his mind for what?

Madame Chen. (*Grasping the* MAID'S *hands.*) Can't you understand, can't you? Mr. Yang is coming back. How delighted -- oh, how happy I am. Ah, why do you look at me? Am I blushing? -- if you were in love!

Maid. After all this, his Lordship changed his mind.

Madame Chen. Of course, my father-in-law also consented.

Maid. (*Thinking a moment as if seeking light.*) Do you still?

Madame Chen. Yes.

Maid. You are not going to marry him?

Madame Chen. Yes.

Maid. (*Surprised.*) You are?

Madame Chen. It is my father's wish.

Maid. Oh, his wish; he arranged for you again. Madam, madam, don't, don't!

Madame Chen. My father did this for my sake, for my happiness. Mr. Yang and I have been friends for years.

Maid. Yes, happiness. But there is something more than happiness we have to consider. Madam, your husband loved you.

Madame Chen. I don't understand you.

Maid. Yes, he loved you, your husband did.

Madame Chen. I cannot believe it.

Maid. Yes, he did. Madam, his Lordship would not force you to this marriage if you refused.

Madame Chen. I am sorry. But this does not concern you.

Maid. (*Weeping; losing control.*) I am a maid; what concerns me? Nothing, nothing.

Madame Chen. How dare you? How could you forget yourself and be so rude to me? I am your mistress.

Maid. Mistress, mistress, no more mistress. I am Madam Chen's bride-maid. Shall never be Madam Yang's maid, never, never.

Madame Chen. Master Chen is my husband only in name. I never loved him.

Maid. But Madam, once you are wedded to him you can never marry again. Master Chen is your wedded husband.

Madame Chen. The ceremony was not complete.

Maid. No, it was not complete.

Madame Chen. It is not a wedding, then. I am Madam Chen, at most, only in name. It is only in name.

Maid. In name. (*Weeping.*) If you knew how he died for you, you wouldn't say "in name."

Madame Chen. Died for me? How is that? (*Standing up and grasping the* MAID'S *hand.*)

Maid. Don't ask me; I won't tell.

Madame Chen. You must.

Maid. I won't. I promised his Lordship I would not.

Madame Chen. You must -- if you are still faithful -- to your master.

Maid. Don't ask me, Madam, you can remember.

Madame Chen. Remember what?

Maid. He nursed you.

Madame Chen. He nursed me?

Maid. When Doctor ordered everyone away, he stayed and nursed you. Of course, he got the plague.

Madame Chen. He nursed me?

Maid. Madam, you remember; you talked to him yourself. He gave you the medicine; you said "Thank you"; he asked you, "Do you like me now?"; you said "Yes"; he said, "Then it is not in vain."

Madame Chen. (*Looking before her.*) Yes, yes, yes.

Maid. When he himself took ill -- Doctor stood there -- Master Chen held my hand and smiled. "It is worth while, it is worth while." Madam, Madam.

Madame Chen. Yes, I understand how. You are good to me.

Maid. (*After a silence.*) Madam, forgive me.

Madame Chen. For my rudeness. I forgot myself.

Madame Chen. I forgive you. (*Silence.* The MAID *slowly stands up.*)

Maid. Yes, madam.

Madame Chen. Why talk about the wedding? He is my husband. Are you glad to be Madam Chen's maid again?

Maid. Yes, to be your maid. I like you and my master.

Madame Chen. I am your mistress, once and forever. I shall never be Madam Yang.

Maid. (*Running to her.*) Madam! (*Weeping.*)

First Servant. (*Outside.*) Does your Ladyship permit me to come in?

Maid. Who is there?

First Servant. Your humble servant.

Madame Chen. Tell him to come in. (MAID *walks to the door and enters with* SERVANT. *The* SERVANT *salutes.*)

First Servant. Congratulations, congratulations, your Ladyship. Allow your humble servant to congratulate you.

Madame Chen. (*Slightly surprised.*) Why congratulations?

First Servant. Mr. Yang has just arrived. Sir Chen bids me to tell you.

Madam Chen. Mr. Yang?

First Servant. From Mongolia.

Madam Chen. Yes, very kind of my father-in-law. I thank him. (*Half kneeling. This salute is to her father-in-law. The* SERVANT *should stand still and receive it for his master.*)

First Servant. Yes, your Ladyship. And Lord Wang requests you to meet Mr. Yang in ceremonial dress.

Madam Chen. In ceremonial dress?

First Servant. His Lordship said "This is a good day." From now on, everything shall be good, pleasant. He ordered anything of white color be put away, but decorate the house with red -- preparing for a wedding ceremony.

Madam Chen. (*Stands up and speaks boldly.*) Tell his Lordship I shall change my dress. (MAID *is very much surprised.*)

First Servant. Yes, madam. (*Walking to the door.*) Lord Wang and Mr. Yang are coming to this room.

Madam Chen. Come with me and help me change. They are coming.

Maid. (*After a pause.*) Yes, madam. (*Both go out. Outside is heard "Sir, her Ladyship thanks you for your kindness. You may retire."* YANG, CHEN, *and* WANG *enter.*)

Lord Wang. My daughter is dressing; shall be here in a minute. Sit down. Mr. Yang, Mongolia benefited you much?

Mr. Yang. Certainly. But Mongolia is such a big country. Three weeks' experience would not be worthy of your Lordship's attention.

Lord Wang. How far have you gone into that country?

Mr. Yang. Traveling is slow on the camel's back. Only three hundred miles.

Lord Wang. Have you seen such historical places as the Great Wall, the Gate, General Lee's Tablet, the Valley of Concert?

Mr. Yang. Yes, they are more or less in ruins now. But there is a tomb, the natives call it "Green Tomb."

Lord Wang. What about it?

Mr. Yang. It is the only green spot in thousands of miles of desert. She sacrificed her happiness for her country; but only in vain. We know her in the legend of "Guitar."

Lord Wang. (*Understanding.*) This was thousands of years ago. Let's forget the by-gones and think of the living.

Mr. Yang. If only we could forget it! Something lives after death!

Lord Wang. (*Attempting to change the subject.*) My daughter must have tried to dress herself as elaborately as a bride; it takes such a long while.

Sir Chen. Indeed!

Lord Wang. I can assure you, Mr. Yang, she will be exceedingly happy to meet you.

Maid. (*Entering.*) Your Lordship, my mistress will not meet Mr. Yang. (*All are startled.*) Her Ladyship bids me to inform you.

Lord Wang. But she must meet Mr. Yang. It is my order, I, her father.

Maid. Yes, your Lordship. (*Withdraws quietly. LORD WANG paces the floor; suddenly takes big steps. Goes out through the left door.*)

Sir Chen. Poor old man!

Mr. Yang. Only eight weeks, he is no longer the same man. Look at the deep lines on his face!

Sir Chen. Yes, quite weak now. I hope nothing more will happen. It nearly broke our hearts.

Mr. Yang. What has happened since my departure?

Sir Chen. My boy died, my daughter-in-law was very ill -- she only recovered last week. Of course you know all this through Lord Wang's letter.

Mr. Yang. Yes, the letter says they were both victims of the plague.

Sir Chen. It was on the wedding day, a very, very hot day, that the bride was attacked by the plague. She was already weak and the ceremony was too much for her.

Mr. Yang. Yes.

Sir Chen. Then my boy. Of course, my boy was insane. He insisted on nursing her and -- and he must have loved her.

Mr. Yang. Did Lord Wang know all about this?

Sir Chen. Yes, but for the sake of his daughter who was ill till last week, he hid the fact from her.

Mr. Yang. Then what's his reason of calling me back? To torture me?

Sir Chen. Lord Wang was told once by the doctor, she and you were once in love. For her future happiness and for yours, he proposed to marry her to you. He came and consulted me. And of course as I never objected to anything he did, I consented.

Mr. Yang. But how could it be possible for Lord Wang to forget the most sacred tradition? A woman once wedded can never marry again.

Sir Chen. The ceremony was interrupted. Lord Wang and I do not consider it a marriage.

Mr. Yang. (*Revolted.*) What did Madam Chen say about it?

Sir Chen. She hesitated; but since a daughter's duty is to obey her father, she consented.

Mr. Yang. Hm, everything duty and tradition. It's absolute nonsense.

Sir Chen. Since you consented to this match by coming here -- the old man (*Pointing to himself.*) gives best wishes.

Mr. Yang. (*Softly.*) Sir Chen, I would not say I consented. No, no. (LORD WANG *enters, pacing the floor and grumbling.*)

Mr. Yang. Will you speak out, my Lord?

Lord Wang. She won't listen to me any more. She refuses to see you.

Mr. Yang. I sympathize with her. (LORD WANG *looks at* MR. YANG *severely.*)

Mr. Yang. Please don't misunderstand me. I mean -- er -- if I were in her place.

Sir Chen. What makes her so change her mind?

Lord Wang. She seemed to know the true state of things. The maid, the maid. (MAID *enters.*) Did you tell her, I forbid you; I forbid you.

Maid. Your Lordship, Madam Chen is coming. (*All are startled.* MADAM CHEN *appears, in heavy mourning dress -- white. Salutes.*)

Sir Chen. Ah, in full mourning dress!

Lord Wang. (*Indignantly, sadly.*) What do you mean by coming here in full mourning?

Madam Chen. Father, father, you have always meant well. It is for my happiness that you arrange this second marriage for me.

Lord Wang. Yes, my dear child, I regret my first doing.

Madam Chen. When I promised you the first marriage, I prepared for a suffering life. But I am quite satisfied, quite happy now as it is. (*Pauses.*) And father-in-law, you are so kind to me. (*Pauses again.*) And Mr. Yang, how do you do? I am sorry for you. Our marriage is out of the question. Remember me as your friend -- as your sister; but for that sacred love, the love between man and wife, (*To* LORD WANG.) father, allow me to reserve it for my husband. He loved me and died. Good-bye, Mr. Yang. (*She controls herself well during the speech, but breaks down at the end. The* MAID *helps her; and they both walk to the left door.*)

Mr. Yang. (*Following her several steps.*) Madam Chen, remember me as your friend, I shall always be at your service. (LORD WANG *sinks into a chair,* SIR CHEN *helps him.* MR. YANG *turns back and walks towards LORD WANG as the curtain falls.*)

1922 -- Clare Kummer -- *Chinese Love*

The author of this play, although nearly completely forgotten today, was a successful Broadway playwright between the world wars. Her plays, all light comedies, consistently enjoyed long runs and good reviews, and only a misunderstanding on the part of the awarding committee prevented her from winning the first Pulitzer Prize in drama.

This is her only play which deals with the Chinese. It combines the then-current image of the Chinese as noble and self-sacrificing with the far earlier image of China as a land of magic and fantasy which was a strong element in *Kim-ka!* Therefore, it is not too much of an exaggeration to say that in the seventy years since that earlier play was presented, the image of the Chinese had come full circle.

Chinese Love

PERSONS OF THE PLAY

WING SO, *A Chinese Pirate*
CHAN FAH, *His Wife*
MING TOO, *Their Son*
AH MEE, *A Dear Lady Friend*
MO YEN, *Emissary of the Law and Custodian of the Tea House*
HING HI, *A Mandarin*

SCENE: *Garden of* MO YEN'S *Tea House.*
TIME: *A summer afternoon.*
DISCOVERED: MO YEN *and* AH MEE. MO YEN *studying from a parchment the pronunciamento relating to* WING SO'S *execution. He is not aware at first of the presence of* AH MEE.

Mo Yen. (Reading and memorizing.) "Hi-yah! Hi-yah! On the high seas for many years, Wing So captured and sunk many ships. To foreign countries he went, and all he did was against the mighty Chinese law which says that no man must do the things that Wing So has done. So according to the most noble wishes --"

Ah Mee. *(Interrupting him politely.)* Sir, if you have quite finished --

Mo Yen. "--of the highly honorable Mandarin, acting for the Imperial Emperor of China, this day is led to execution, Wing So. Hi-yah!"

Ah Mee. Sir -- thanks, please. *(Bowing.)*

Mo Yen. If that is all, I will begin again. *(Turning back to the parchment.*)

Ah Mee. No -- it is not all. Tell me -- we have not made a mistake? It is by this way they will pass?

Mo Yen. This way and no other. You will have a fine view of the road from the tea-house windows. And you cannot mistake Wing So. He is a tall man and carries himself like a prince. But then, a pirate can pick and choose his clothes.

Ah Mee. (*With dignity.*) I am not afraid of mistaking Wing So for any other man.

Mo Yen. No?

Ah Mee. No, I know him very well -- I am the most dear friend of Chan Fah, his wife -- she sits yonder in the tea-house, waiting for him to pass. Also Ming Too, their son.

Mo Yen. Ah -- so that is Chan Fah -- she waits for him to pass. Women are strange. What does she want with him?

Ah Mee. To say goodbye. He has taught her to kiss goodbye in the English manner. Also Ming Too, their son.

Mo Yen. Hah -- that is very interesting. You know it was Chan Fah, his wife, who gave him up to the authorities -- but for her he might not be going to part with his head this fine sunny afternoon.

Ah Mee. I know nothing of what you say. Therefore, I cannot listen to you. You say she gave him up?

Mo Yen. For many thousand yen -- there was a price on his head. He is, as perhaps you know, a particularly skillful pirate.

Ah Mee. Wing So does everything well.

Mo Yen. Yes. He is wanted by the English authorities for smuggling opium -- that is very serious -- so we put a large price on his head. The vast sum was paid to his wife, then she gave him over to the authorities -- she will not want for anything.

Ah Mee. I am the dear friend of Chan Fah and I do not understand what you are saying -- therefore, I do not believe it. She is a most beautiful character -- most devoted to her husband. Also Ming Too, their son.

Mo Yen. If so, then I am glad my wife is not devoted to me -- though not being a pirate, I might perhaps escape with my life. . .

Ah Mee. She is coming -- be very respectful, please -- remembering she will soon be a widow.

Mo Yen. That is certainly her fault; not mine.

Chan Fah. (*Approaching. She is beautifully dressed, wearing many jewels.* MING TOO *is with her.*) Why do you discourse so long, Ah Mee, with the honorable stranger?

Mo Yen. Mo Yen is my name, Emissary of the law and custodian of the Tea House.

Chan Fah. I am pleased to make your acquaintance. I am Chan Fah, wife of Wing So, perfect gentleman and highly reputable pirate.

Mo Yen. I know.

Chan Fah. I am most desirous of having speech with my husband, if there is no objection. (*Giving him gold.*)

Mo Yen. If your husband has no objections, I have not.

Chan Fah. Thank you. Perhaps we may be left alone for a little while together? I have a paper saying it can be permitted.

Mo Yen. (*Taking the paper.*) I see. It shall be as you wish. You give your word that Wing So will not kill himself, thus cheating the authorities.

Chan Fah. My word of honor. Wing So does not believe in killing himself unless it is quite agreeable to everybody.

Mo Yen. And you will not kill him? You have, I see, a very pretty little dagger there -- (*Observing jade handle of tiny dagger which* CHAN FAH *has concealed in her dress.*)

Chan Fah. Wing So's heart is much too deep to be reached by that tiny thing.

Mo Yen. Very good, then -- I will see that you are left together.

Chan Fah. We might even have tea -- (*Giving him another piece of gold.*)

Mo Yen. (*Doubtfully.*) In the Tea House?

Chan Fah. No, here -- where we will be quite alone.

Mo Yen. I will see.

Chan Fah. (*Giving him another piece of gold.*) I am sure that you will see correctly, Honorable Mo Yen. Are there many being executed to-day?

Mo Yen. Only your husband. There will be no procession to speak of, only the executioner and the Mandarin, Hing Hi, who is obliged to be present in accordance with the law.

Chan Fah. Perhaps the highly honorable Mandarin, Hing Hi, will take tea in the tea house?

Mo Yen. If it is served him for nothing, I am quite sure he will.

Chan Fah. See that it is served him for nothing. (*Giving him another piece of gold. Music for the entrance of* WING SO.)

Ah Mee. They are coming.

Mo Yen. I join the procession here. I will divert the Mandarin this way. (*Calling the pronunciamento, exit* MO YEN *R.U.E.*) Hi-yah! Hi-yah! On the high seas for many years, Wing So captured and sunk many ships. To foreign countries he went, and all he did was against the mighty Chinese law which says that no man must do the things that Wing So has done. So according to the most noble wishes of the highly honorable Mandarin, acting for the Imperial Emperor of China, this day is led to execution, Wing So. Hi-yah!

Chan Fah. Conduct yourself with great dignity, Ah Mee. And you, my son -- (MING TOO.) -- make yourself as tall as possible so as to more resemble your most glorious, noble father.

Enter MO YEN, WING SO, *and* HING HI *R.U.E.* CHAN FAH *kneels before her husband. He pats her head tenderly.*

Wing So. Chan Fah! If anything could add to my pleasure this bright, beautiful day, it is to see you here!

Chan Fah. (*Bowing with dignity and concealing her emotion.*) Wing So, honorable husband!

Wing So. And you, Ah Mee.

Ah Mee. Also Ming Too, your son!

Wing So. Also Ming Too! You stand very straight, my son -- see that you continue to do so -- and take the most extraordinary care of your honorable, precious mother . . . I would say more -- if you could understand me.

Chan Fah. I am sure he understands you, Wing So.

Wing So. Yes?

Chan Fah. Yes. When my honorable father went to his ancestors I was of the same age as Ming Too. And I have always remembered every word he said to me -- reminded, of course, occasionally by my honorable mother.

Wing So. That makes me very happy, Chan Fah. Shall I perhaps say a few words more to him -- that his honorable mother may remind him of in the days to come?

Chan Fah. No, it is not necessary. I am quite capable of remembering what you said, Wing So.

Wing So. Without my saying it? Very well, choose what I have said wisely.

Chan Fah. Ah Mee, say goodbye to my honorable husband, and take little Ming Too for almond cakes to the tea house.

Ah Mee. (*Kneeling before* WING SO.) Farewell, and may your ancestors greet you with the most gracious, affectionate remarks, dear Wing So. I am dear friend to you and your honorable wife and so shall remain.

Wing So. Most respectful thanks, Ah Mee, to you and your honorable family. Ming Too, your father -- (*Laying his hand on the baby's head.*)

Chan Fah. He understands perfectly, Wing So -- if he does not, I will tell him. (AH MEE *goes up into tea house with* MING TOO.)

Mo Yen. (*Approaching.*) The most honorable Mandarin, Hing Hi, would like to speak with the wife of Wing So. He may approach?

Wing So. Certainly -- if you do not object, my adored Chan Fah. You will find he is a most agreeable gentleman -- it was with great difficulty that I persuaded him to let me walk on ahead as is the custom -- and have beautiful thoughts of you and our son.

Chan Fah. Certainly then, if you wish it, Wing So, but do not encourage him to talk very long -- for I wish to be alone with my honorable husband as soon as possible, as long as possible. (HING HI *approaches.*)

Hing Hi. Good morning, beautiful Chan Fah -- I wished to say a few words with you, if it would not be too disagreeable.

Chan Fah. Most pleasant, on the contrary -- since my honorable husband speaks for me -- to encounter charming, gracious Mandarin, Hing Hi.

Hing Hi. (*Bowing.*) I am glad to hear that you are to be left in great happiness and comfort, Chan Fah -- and I wish to state, as an old man who is wise as he is ugly, that you did quite right in giving your husband up to the authorities.

Chan Fah. Wing So I shall always obey.

Hing Hi. Oh, so you obeyed Wing So?

Wing So. Since she has told you, yes -- it was I ordered her to give me up.

Hing Hi. Well, but was that known to the authorities? Is it, in other words, legal?

Wing So. It is to be hoped so, honorable, gracious Hing Hi. Since I am about to lose my head, it is better for Chen Fah to have the 40,000 yen than some poor fellow who would not know what to do with it. Besides, no one knows but yourself -- and you will have forgotten by to-morrow, honorable gentleman that you are, the words Chan Fah has said.

Hing Hi. (*Thoughtfully.*) Yes, it is better for your wife to have the money than some poor wretch like Mo Yen.

Mo Yen. Thanks. Please.

Hing Hi. (*Looking at* CHAN FAH.) Now she is rich -- yes -- that is very good.

Wing So. For some time, as you know, Hing Hi, I was a most successful pirate -- but of late all that has changed -- a pirate's wife must not live in poverty. Who will say that is right?

Hing Hi. Very hard for a beautiful wife like Chan Fah.

Wing So. Very. Since Chan Fah did not marry me for gold and jewels, surely it was only to be expected that she should want these things. I could not give them to her -- those she had, she was obliged to part with. Who will say that was right?

Hing Hi. But now she has them.

WIng So. Yes. And she will keep them. Six boys who have been with me on the high seas will see that she keeps them.

Hing Hi. Six boys?

Wing So. Six. Whereabouts not known to the authorities. It might be as well, noble Hing Hi, if you warn anyone going to my house with an idea of my being away -- these boys are very rough!

Hing Hi. (*Duly impressed.*) Very rough? I see. I will remember that. You do not wish your wife to marry again?

Wing So. I am sorry, Chan Fah -- if you should wish to marry again --

Chan Fah. (*Coming down.*) I shall never wish to do so, honorable husband -- do not speak of such a disaster.

Wing So. The idea, I confess, is not pleasant to me.

Chan Fah. I am your faithful, devoted wife -- you are away, on a journey; that is all.

Hing Hi. Very laudable, I should say -- very, yes, indeed.

Chan Fah. Then since we agree so perfectly, let us speak no more of the matter.

Hing Hi. Quite right. I am having tea served in the tea house. You wish to say good-bye to your honorable husband. I will drink six cups of tea, so do not hurry.

Chan Fah. Most honorable, pleasant Hing Hi, all that my

husband said of you is true. (HING HI *goes into tea house*.)

Wing So. Ah, yes -- he would have made a most excellent pirate -- if he had not consorted with low rascals and become a politician. (*Looking at her*.) Now that we are alone together, my little flower, I can permit myself to tell you that you are very beautiful this morning.

Chan Fah. (*Looking at him adoringly*.) And you are like the sun, my heavenly adored one, and most perfect husband.

Wing So. I have tried to be a good husband to you, Chan Fah, but to be a good husband, one must be a good pirate -- that I have not been of late. It gives me great pleasure to see you dressed properly.

Chan Fah. These jewels I bought according to your instructions. Also, I permitted myself to purchase this. (*Showing him the dagger*.)

Wing So. That was very thoughtful of you, my darling. But I cannot use it. It would not do at all, under the circumstances -- I have given my word.

Chan Fah. It is not for you, my adored one, but for me. With your permission I would like to follow you immediately to the halls of our ancestors.

Wing So. No, Chan Fah. I forbid it. Do you not think of Ming Too, our son? Is it not enough that his father should be taken?

Chan Fah. More than enough, honorable, darling husband.

Wing So. Do you not love little Ming Too, who so closely resembles his father?

Chan Fah. Yes. But it makes me sad to look upon him and think that I shall never have another son -- or even a daughter.

Wing So. It is sad -- we should have been married a year sooner -- but then I had not met you. (AH MEE *serves the tea, placing a screen back of* CHAN FAH *and* WING SO. *After this she exits.* WING SO *is surprised and pleased*.) Why, my darling -- tea?

Chan Fah. Yes, honorable husband. I thought it would be pleasant -- if your engagements will permit. (*They kneel to have their tea*.) Do you remember the day we met, Wing So?

Wing So. Before I looked upon you, Chan Fah -- my heart said, "She is here!" (*Song*.)

(CHAN FAH *sings*.)

"GOLDEN LOVE"

Under the slanting Chinese sun

I first met you -- my dear beloved one!
And though you bowed with great solemnity,
Deep in your eyes, I saw that you did smile on me!

Refrain:

Love -- beautiful, golden love!
Shone in your eyes that day --
"Love me," I heard you say,
Not with your lips, but with your
Eyes! Beautiful, golden eyes!
Even before I knew,
My eyes replied, "I do!"

Before the slanting sun had set,
I knew I never could forget,
The way you spoke my name -- and Oh,
I knew, if asked, across the world I'd go!

Refrain

The music of the procession begins. WING SO *looks toward the tea house. They rise.*

Mo Yen. He is taking his sixth cup.

Wing So. I believe I must go. I shall take a very ceremonious leave of you, my dear, in a moment. (*Takes* CHAN FAH *in his arms.*)

Chan Fah. Oh!

Wing So. Do not weep, my beloved. It is nothing. It is a blessed release from all my troubles -- only not having any troubles, I cannot help wishing someone else could be released instead of me.

Chan Fah. That is a very splendid idea, Wing So. I understand the executioner is a most unhappy man -- he is sick and he has a very cross wife -- could you not suggest that he take your place?

Wing So. (*Smiling.*) I could suggest it, yes.

Chan Fah. Could you, with your beautiful hands, chop off his head neatly?

Wing So. I'm sure I could and with all the pleasure in the world. But I fear it cannot be arranged. He is a bad man, too, and not ready to confront his ancestors.

Chan Fah. But you, my darling?

Wing So. I have always been a loving husband and most considerate pirate. (AH MEE *enters from tea house, taking screen.*) I have nothing to fear. (*Enter* MO YEN, HING HI, *and the* EXECUTIONER.)

Mo Yen. It is time; if the honorable wife wishes to walk along beside you, Wing So, I can arrange it.

Wing So. On no account whatever. The honorable wife will walk in precisely the opposite direction. I will say good-bye to you here, Chan Fah. It has been a most pleasurable occasion and your society has been highly appreciated.

Chan Fah. (*Bowing.*) Also to me it has been pleasant, honorable husband.

Hing Hi. Good-bye, Chan Fah -- six cups of tea, I drank -- very good they were, too.

Chan Fah. I thank you with all my heart, noble, gracious Mandarin Hing Hi. (*The procession starts.* MO YEN *follows, leaving* CHAN FAH *alone.* MO YEN *calls the pronunciamento offstage.* AH MEE *and* MING TOO *approach from the tea house.*)

Ah Mee. Mo Yen is a very wicked man, also a liar.

Chan Fah. A wicked man and a liar can do a kind thing, Ah Mee.

Ah Mee. If he is paid for it.

Chan Fah. Yes, and I can well afford to pay him.

Ah Mee. (*Anxiously.*) Those jewels, Chan Fah -- and this gold which you seem so careless with -- have you perhaps suddenly come into a fortune? Or did your honorable husband bring you back these things from his last trip on the high seas?

Chan Fah. What did Mo Yen tell you, Ah Mee? That I sold my adored honorable husband to the authorities for money? It is true. There was no way to hide him or let him make his escape -- so he bade me give him up. I had to obey him. Now I am rich and little Ming Too can be well raised. But me -- I do not think I can live.

Ah Mee. Oh, yes, Chan Fah -- you can live -- I see now all quite clearly. And you did right. You will have some comfort and pleasure still -- and you can wear as many jewels as you wish. You have always loved jewels, Chan Fah.

Chan Fah. Who will see them?

Ah Mee. And you have Ming Too, you must think of him.

Chan Fah. Yes. He loves you very much. Take him home, Ah Mee, and leave me a little while to myself.

Ah Mee. I do not like to leave you, Chan Fah.

Chan Fah. No, but that you must do. I want to sit quietly and remember the things said to me by my honorable husband. I want to say them over like a lesson, Ah Mee, in order that I may never, never forget them.

Ah Mee. You are sure, dear friend, that you wish me to leave you? Also Ming Too, your son?

Chan Fah. Yes, I am quite sure.

Ah Mee. Then I will go. Come soon, Chan Fah! (AH MEE *departs with* MING TOO.)

JEWEL SONG

(CHAN FAH *sings.*)

Yes, this is the gold --
These are the jewels of fashion so splendid.
When stories are told
"Here," they will say, "Chan Fah's story was ended!
This silken brocade,
Wrapping her round with its perfume enthralling,
This dagger of jade,
Was in her hand when she heard his voice calling!"

See how they sparkle, glistening, shining --
Emerald and ruby in gold enshrined,
Glowing in tender, passionate splendor
Sunlight and moonlight and stars combined!
Beautiful pearls -- chain of tears divine!
In dreams I wore them -- and I adore them,
Beautiful jewels, and mine -- all mine!

During song, stage becomes very dim. A spotlight on CHAN FAH. *At end of song,* WING SO *enters L.U. from behind tea house and stands unseen behind tree. At the end* CHAN FAH *takes out the dagger from her dress. She puts her head in her hands, weeping a moment, then looks up as if listening.*

Chan Fah. "Come soon, Chan Fah!" -- that is what you are saying to me, dear honorable husband. Yes, yes, I will come! (*She raises the dagger above her breast.*)

Wing So. (*His voice.*) Chan Fah -- I am saying nothing of the kind.

Chan Fah. Oh, honorable darling, it is your voice -- where are you?

Wing So. (*Appearing below tree in a golden light.*) I am here beside you -- I think you can see me, if you try a little.

Chan Fah. (*Rubbing her eyes.*) Where? Where? Oh, there! Oh, honorable darling one, forgive me.

Wing So. You interrupted me at a most inopportune moment. Chan Fah, I was just being introduced to my great-grandfather, whom I had never met -- in the celestial rice fields when I happened to hear you speak my name.

Chan Fah. In the celestial rice fields, my darling? Then -- then -- you have been there.

Wing So. Certainly. The execution was most successful. One clean stroke and I was looking on with the rest at the absurd affair. The, as I say, I went to the rice fields in the most glorious sunshine -- but I must not tell you about it. It might make you discontented.

Chan Fah. (*Anxiously.*) Do you still love me?

Wing So. I still love you -- but you must live your life out, Chan Fah, you must not even play with your little dagger. When you die I will come and escort you to the celestial rice fields. I hope to find you in great comfort. I do not wish my honorable wife to be lying in a dusty road -- buy yourself a beautiful bed, Chan Fah -- and promise me that you will do your best to die in it.

Chan Fah. I promise -- I promise, dear, darling, honorable husband. Could you kiss me -- or is that forbidden? (*He kisses her. Enter* AH MEE *and* MING TOO.)

Ah Mee. I was frightened after I had left you, Chan Fah -- forgive me -- I felt that I must come back.

Chan Fah. (*Happily.*) Do you not see who is there?

Ah Mee. What do you mean, Chan Fah?

Chan Fah. Can you not see him? (WING SO *takes the dagger from* CHAN FAH, *replacing it in her dress.*)

Ah Mee. I see nothing, Chan Fah -- except that a very strange thing happened just then.

Chan Fah. Oh! Just then?

Ah Mee. I was looking at your little dagger -- and it was replaced in your dress -- and you did not lift your hand.

Wing So. There, we cannot do the slightest thing without its being noticed!

Chan Fah. Oh, I think you must be mistaken, Ah Mee -- surely nothing so strange as that could happen. (*She laughs.*)

Ah Mee. Do you feel quite well, Chan Fah?

Chan Fah. Quite. I never expected to feel so well again -- I have been remembering, as I said, all the things told me by my honorable husband.

Wing So. See that you do remember them, Chan Fah. (MING TOO *goes to* WING SO *and endeavors to grasp him round the knees. He falls down.*)

Ming Too. Honorable parent!

Chan Fah. There, the baby can see --

Wing So. I'm sorry I can't pick him up. It is forbidden -- children would never fall if we could catch them. And it is good for them to fall.

Ah Mee. (*Anxiously.*) Will you not come home, dear Chan Fah?

Wing So. Pray do, my darling -- and allow me to return to my great grandfather. (WING SO *embraces* CHAN FAH.)

Ah Mee. You kiss the air, Chan Fah!

Chan Fah. It is very sweet.

Ah Mee. Will you not come, Chan Fah?

Chan Fah. Proceed, Ah Mee, I will follow you. (*Exit* AH MEE *and* MING TOO. *To* WING SO.) Could you not perhaps accompany me to the gate of our house?

Wing So. Darling, you are keeping me out of heaven. However, I will, and then you will let me go?

Chan Fah. Yes. But let us walk very slowly.

Wing So. (*Tenderly.*) Chan Fah -- sometimes, if you wish, think of me at this sunset hour and I will come to you. Where we part, there we shall meet again.

Chan Fah. Oh, then could you not come just inside the gate, my dearest beloved?

Wing So. Into the garden? Yes -- but do not ask me to go further, my darling --

Chan Fah. No. You are too radiant to be quite safe in our small house. (*She sings. And at the end of song they go off together.*)

In our garden gay with flow'rs,
I'll await the sunset hours --
Close my eyes and dream, dear,
Till I hear you call.

Love, beautiful, golden love,
Deep in your eyes will shine,
Looking down into mine,
Again my own will answer,
Love, beautiful, golden love,
It was our dream, and so
Into the dream we go --
The dream of beautiful, golden love!

Curtain.

DAVE WILLIAMS, a second-generation Cornellian, now lives in Taichung, in the Republic of China on Taiwan. He is Associate Professor of English and Theatre at Providence University, where he pursues his research and artistic interests. Currently, he is engaged in a full-length critical study of the plays presented in this anthology. He is married to the former Xu Xiaoxia, and the proud father of two children, Linus Clark Minhao Williams and Vivian Celeste Jianyun Williams.